Rescuing Haya

rescuing HAYA

confessions
of an
eighth
generation
Israeli
emigrant

SHELLY SPILKA

STATE UNIVERSITY OF NEW YORK PRESS

Published by
STATE UNIVERSITY OF NEW YORK PRESS
ALBANY

© 2001 State University of New York

For information, address State University of New York Press,
90 State Street, Suite 700, Albany, NY 12207

Production and book design, Laurie Searl
Marketing, Fran Keneston

Library of Congress Cataloging-in-Publication Data

Spilka, Shelly.
    Rescuing Haya : confessions of an eighth generation Israeli emigrant /
Shelly Spilka.
        p.   cm.
    Includes index.
    ISBN 0-7914-4869-X (alk. paper)—ISBN 0-7914-4870-3 (pbk. : alk.
paper)
        1. Spilka, Shelly.   2. Israelis—United States—Biography.
3. Sabras—United States—Biography.   4. Jews—United States—
Biography.   5. Israel—Biography.   6. United States—Biography.
    I. Title.

CT1919.P38 S757 2000
973.04'924'0092—dc21
[B]   00-038768

10   9   8   7   6   5   4   3   2   1

To my husbands,

KENNETH REGENBAUM
1939–1978

and

MARK SPILKA

CONTENTS

ACKNOWLEDGMENTS

Gratitude is first due to members of my family:

To my late grandmother, Esther Kazarnovsky, for her fearlessness;

To my late grandfather, Asher Kazarnovsky, for his laughter;

To my mother, Dina Sirotinsky, for bringing me into the world and for giving me—in herself—a feisty and colorful character to write about and at times to emulate;

To my late stepfather, Reuven Sirotinsky, for healing my wounds;

To my father, Zorah Shapira, for endowing me with a Jewish imagination and an American citizenship;

To the late Chaim, for the excitement, the fanfare, and the genuine warmth he brought into our lives;

To my aunts—Bracha, Zipporah, Nomi, and Ruth—for their humor, song, and protection;

To my uncle Avram Kazarnovsky (Kidon), for showing me the high road;

To my uncle Itzhak Kazarnovsky, for showing me the road to light-heartedness;

To my cousin, Meir Greenberg, for challenging me to think through my reasons for leaving Israel;

To my cousin, Michal, and her husband, Uzi Gafter, for their steadfast support during Mark's illness;

To my late husband, Kenneth Regenbaum, for your love and all that you taught me about gutsy high-mindedness;

To our children, Shir and Livi Regenbaum, for bearing with my imperfect motherhood, loving me anyway, and believing in my book;

To Elie Nahari, for all his help, and for taking such good care of Kenneth's grave.

To my stepdaughter, Rachel Spilka, for setting an example of courage and grace under pressure;

To my stepson, Aaron Spilka, for the vital help when his father became ill;

To my stepdaughter, Jane Eckelmann, for her affection and enthusiasm;

To our stepdaughters Betsy Farnum and Polly Fraga, for their comfort in troubled times and for the medical advice;

To my husband, Mark Spilka, for the sweet daily encouragements that prodded the words of this book into being and for the honest, loving counsel that has always called me to be my best self.

Gratitude is next owed to friends and colleagues:

To Norman and Deborah Fedder, for the priceless opportunity to come to the United States;

To Bonnie Nelson, for the brilliant mentoring and the friendship;

To Kay Bascom, for the friendship, for offering illuminating comments on the early drafts, and for laughing in the right places;

To Peter Casagrande, for the friendship and for the generous recognition of my merits;

To Jane Garrett, for the riotous humor that dissuaded me from becoming a bartender whenever rejections from colleges piled too high;

To Kirk Allison, for the prayers and for the excellent (and, ah, so painful) editorial comments;

To Dr. Anthony Caprio, President of Western New England College, and his wife, Dr. Dana Carter, for their staunch support of my writing;

To Burton Porter, for affirming the value of my manuscript when publishers' rejections accumulated;

To Charles Fish, for the instructive comments and for the much appreciated cheering;

To Emmett Barcalow, for the spirited advocacy;

To Richard Haber, for the delightful conversations, the astute writing suggestions, and the sterling friendship that has sustained me through many a dark hour;

To Rosemary O'Donoghue, for arranging the successful Table Talk Reading at WNEC;

To Philip Gourevitch, my mentor in the Writers' Workshop at Wesleyan University, for the heartening response to my nascent story;

To Sandra Gilbert, for the enthusiastic reading of my (then too long) manuscript and for the invaluable suggestions on how to condense it;

To Amos Oz, for listening to Haya and giving me the courage to write about her;

To Edwin Honig, for the engaging presence and for shoring up my writing efforts;

To Toni Warren, for the uplifting optimism and the wise remarks;

To Carol Cook, for the perceptive reading and for caring.

Finally, my hearty appreciation to the editors of SUNY Press:

To Jane Bunker, for the warm and discerning reception of my manuscript and for the thoughtful assurances;

To Laurie Searl, for the enjoyable hours of working together and for the rich, helpful observations.

ISRAEL

I am an Israeli, eighth generation sabra, an offspring of families who lived in the land long before it was called "Israel." My grandmother was born in Safed, my mother in Hebron, and I in Jerusalem. My birth name is Haya. My native language is Hebrew. I have a bachelor's degree in both Hebrew literature and English literature. But at the age of twenty-three, I turned my back on my native Hebrew to pursue English studies in England. Before leaving Israel, I changed my name to Shelly. I completed my master's degree in England and returned to Israel to obtain my doctorate in English at Bar-Ilan University. In 1980, I emigrated to America. Now I am a tenured professor of English at Western New England College in Massachusetts. I am proud to be an American, and yet I live in conflict, in division.

After nineteen years in America, I cannot get Israel out of my mind. I am in love with it, yearning for it, angry with it. It appears in my dreams, sweet or threatening, earthly or metaphysical, the land of heady orange blossoms and whispering pine trees, the land of my childhood terrors. Where is my home? Can one have two homes? Two languages? Can one enter two promised lands? Entering one is hard enough. Entering two is an impossibility, a paradox, hubris itself. My world is rent. My philosophy—eclectic. My being—a journey, a diversity, a longing. How can I find meaning in my checkered patterns? Perhaps only by telling my story.

ROOTS

I come from families of Jewish leaders, thinkers, and artists. In my family tree one can find the philosopher Ahad Ha'am and the musicians Hefzibah and Yehudi Menuhin, as well as lesser known rabbis, judges, doctors, and lawyers. Many of my forebears were active on behalf of Jewry and dedicated to Eretz Israel. Among them were Jews who perished in pogroms, in Palestine or in Europe. There were those who lived in the Diaspora, and there were those, perhaps most, who lived in Palestine—in Hebron, Jerusalem, and Safed.

On my mother's side, I am a descendant of Rabbi Shneor Zalman of Lyady (1745–1813), the founder of the Habad Hasidic movement, whose granddaughter, Menucha Rachel Slonim, emigrated to Israel from Poland and settled in Safed. She came to die in the Holy Land, but her vitality kept her this side of the grave a good number of years; she worked energetically for a yeshiva in Safed and dedicated her life to her family and to mitzvoth. According to legend, people came from far and wide to seek her blessing, and she would put her hands on their heads and effect healing.

On my father's side, I am first generation sabra. Although my father, who came to Palestine from Belorussia, cannot boast of ancestors who struck roots in the land, as my mother can, he does boast of a brother who participated in the creation of the state of Israel. My uncle, Moshe Chaim Shapira, who later became the first interior minister of Israel (from 1949 to 1952 and from 1959 to 1970), was passionately committed to the ingathering of Jews from the Diaspora. In 1938, when union between Germany and Austria took place, he organized a rescue mission of Viennese Jews. During the War of Independence he was responsible for the mass immigration of Jews to Israel. His actions were inspired by a vision of a Jewish homeland where Jews would live in harmony with each other. He was known as a peacemaker who could appease warring factions in the government and in the country.

Thus, on both sides, my family is decidedly Jewish, often bears the marks of Jewish history, and amply exemplifies Jewish achievement and grace. Most members of my family have also been loyal Israelis and Zionists. Some were more devoted to religion, and some to the land of Israel—but they knew

---

Eretz Israel   The land of Israel

mitzvoth   Good deeds

where they belonged. They had a strong and clear sense of commitment, which was as natural in their lives as the sap is to the tree.

How is it conceivable that I would choose to live in many worlds and fully commit myself to none? How is it possible that I would reject my forebears' commitment to Israel and to the Jewish community and, instead, choose America and Western culture? Why didn't I stay in one place? Whence this restlessness, this wanderlust?

BROKEN VESSELS

Since many of my ancestors were Hasidim, I like to describe my parents' divorce in Kabbalistic terms as "the breaking of the vessels." According to Scholem, as divine light was poured into the vessels during Creation, it "was too strong to be held" by some of them, and so "one after another they broke, the pieces scattering and falling." This shattering of the vessels brought evil to the world. The only way to restore the broken vessels is through the process of *tikkun*, the repairing and the healing, the making whole of that which is rent. Most of my life, I have been dedicated to the *tikkun* of my broken pieces. Maybe this is my way of being Jewish, of seeking God, of learning and forgiving.

My parents must have married for love. Blind, passionate love. Otherwise they wouldn't have leapt over the abyss separating the ultra-Orthodox way of life from the secular. My father was (and still is) a devout Orthodox Jew. Unlike his brother, Moshe Chaim Shapira, my father had no political ambitions and few Zionist affiliations. His being found its most eloquent expression in religion. My mother came from a so-called traditional home. My grandmother kept a kosher kitchen and fasted on Yom Kippur even when her health was failing. Yet my mother felt little attraction for the rigors of religion. She longed for the freedom and the beauty of Western culture—concerts, theaters, fashion. She learned to hate the *shtetl* life in the *Me'ah She'arim* section in Jerusalem, where she and my father lived. So why did she marry him? She didn't know he was *that* religious (she says) and she was taken in by his knowledge and charm. Why did he marry her? She was very beautiful, and she lied to him (he says) about her religious devotion. He too was taken in.

---

shtetl   Closely-knit Jewish communities in small towns of east Europe

Furthermore, both of them remind me, a miracle occurred that seemed to indicate that it was a marriage made in heaven. A few days before the wedding, my mother visited a dentist who lost a needle in her mouth, and before he could retrieve it, she swallowed it. My father's community was in an uproar. What did it mean? they asked each other in horror. Was it a sign from the *sitra ahra,* the demonic domain? Shouldn't the wedding be canceled? Meanwhile, the needle continued its meandering in my mother's intestines. My father's community consulted the learned leader, Chazon Ish, who predicted that the needle, with God's help, would leave my mother's body naturally. And so it was. One or two days before the wedding, the needle came out from the opposite opening through which it came in, causing no damage to my mother's intestines, or to her soul. The *Me'ah She'arim* neighborhood burst in jubilation. People danced in the streets, carrying my father on their shoulders. Who could have thought that after such a stunning divine signal, my parents' marriage would end in divorce?

Yet my mother's happiness was short-lived. At times I look at her pictures from that period—a beautiful woman, with blue eyes, short blond curls, soft, sensuous lips, dressed in black, from her black woolen socks to her black head-covering—and imagine her chagrin. How she must have hated covering her wrists and ankles. How she must have grumbled under the burden of religious rituals. Once, she told me, my father caught her making grape juice for me on the Sabbath and commanded her angrily to stop "working." She retorted that she was only feeding me, but she stopped squashing the grapes and resented my father and "his" religion. Thus, the worship that gave my father joy galled my mother; the faith that uplifted him oppressed her. Dylan Thomas's images best capture my parents' paradoxical existence. "The force that drives the water through the rocks" drove my father's "red blood." But that same force turned my mother's blood "to wax."

My father's community was dismayed when my parents sought divorce. In the ultra-Orthodox society of the 1940s, divorce was altogether rare. But who would have dared to contemplate the rending of a marriage made in heaven? How could Dina and Zorah Shapira be separated? Yet my parents could no longer live together. They argued constantly. They resented each other silently. They grew bitter, impatient. Their love, which for a spell bridged over the deepest division in the Israeli nation, could no longer hold. When they realized, after five years of marriage, that their compromises were in tatters and could no longer cover the nakedness of their estrangement, they agreed to separate. I was five years old.

My mother in her religious period, with a head covering, and me at two years old. Tel Aviv beach

THE ORPHANAGE

The storm raged over my head, but the adults were too preoccupied to pay attention to the feelings of a five-year-old. As soon as the divorce was in effect, my mother started working as a nurse on night-shifts in Hadassah Hospital in Tel Aviv. Longings for her, she says, brought my father to the hospital one night; for the last time, he pleaded with her to return to him. But she could not return to the ultra-Orthodox community. Although the divorce brought fear and shame to her life, she could not countenance the imprisonment of her marriage.

It was then that I was sent to the religious orphanage *Beit Ha'yeled* in Pardes-Hannah. Who sent me? I don't know. My mother says that my father forced her to send me to a religious institution. My father says that he didn't even know I was in the orphanage until much later. How long was I there? My father says a year. My mother says six months. Why didn't I stay with my father? He says that his rabbi had forbidden him to live alone with his daughter. Why didn't I stay with my mother? She says that she couldn't keep me because she worked nights. Where was the family? My uncle Abraham (pronounced Avram) and my aunts Ruth and Naomi (Nomi) were too young to take care of me. But my aunts Bracha and Zipporah were of age. Where were they? I was never told. After my stay in the orphanage, I lived with my grandmother in Tiberias for a few months. Why didn't she take me out of the orphanage before? I do not know. Mystery surrounds this, the most crucial event in my life, the event that plunged me into darkness, ripped apart my innocence, and rendered part of my being a waif and a wanderer.

For years I tried to find out information on the orphanage in Pardes-Hannah. I questioned every relative, my mother's sisters in particular. But the more I asked, the less I knew. My aunts, even my favorite, Aunt Ruth, always checked with my mother first, and she had a number of versions and an even greater number of instructions for them. I sensed their caution and mistrusted their stories. In time, details became blurred and nobody could remember what actually happened, when, and how. Finally, I gave up the attempt to discover the exact truth in this Rashomon-like maze and settled for my own version of my history.

It begins with a girl named Haya who was brought to an orphanage in Pardes-Hannah. I remember a squeaky gate, dusty palm and eucalyptus trees, red sands. I am running to the squeaky gate, always, to see if *Imma* is coming. No. Not today. Perhaps tomorrow. I turn away from the gate and climb the steps slowly. The teacher Techiya scowls at me from the top of the stairs,

On my mother's arm by Lake Kinneret. Tiberias

"Haya," she says, shaking her finger at me, "the sun has already set and look how dirty you are. What is this? Where were you? And Haya, don't think I haven't seen you putting your bread in Shoshana's plate. You don't eat, and your mother accuses us of starving you! Now go wash quickly and don't forget to say the *Shema* prayer before you go to bed." My father calls me Haya'le. She calls me Haya. A wild animal. Me. Tomorrow *Imma* will come.

Night is crouching over Pardes-Hannah. The girls in the room are sleeping, but I cannot sleep. Strange smells. At the end of the room one girl is coughing. Is she sick? Perhaps if I prayed *Shema,* I would be sleeping already. *Abba* wants me to pray, but *Imma* warned me not even to think of praying. *Abba* loves God, but *Imma* hates God. What am I to do? Whom do I believe? *Imma,* because *Abba* hasn't come to see me yet. The last time I saw him, he caressed my cheek with his warm, silky hand, bent down to kiss me with his scratchy beard, and said, "You won't forget to pray, Haya'le, what?" and then he was gone. My father. Always laughing. Always humming tunes. Always going away.

The night is breathing heavily. When I close my eyes tight, I see scary shapes. When I open them, I see a room like a hospital. By the streetlamp,

With my mother in the orphanage at Pardes-Hannah. I am five.

the shadow of the eucalyptus tree is swaying back and forth, like my father when he is praying. Br..r..r... Shoshana has been asleep for a long time. Today, during recess, she stuck her tongue out at me because I said that the cracks in the tree trunk we saw lying in the forest remind me of a laughing fox. She says foxes never enter tree trunks. She says foxes never laugh. She says I am a very stupid girl. Perhaps I should try to pray again. Only I don't remember the words. What will happen if I don't pray? Will my breathing stop during the night? I am yawning and yawning. Perhaps all the air will fizzle out of me, as from a balloon, and in the morning they will find me dead! *Imma!*

Imma is not here, I told you, not here. She'll come tomorrow. Those shapes are running around like wild animals. I am sure I saw a laughing fox, no matter what Shoshana says. Perhaps he is waiting for me outside, under the eucalyptus tree. Must think about something else. I already know how to read eleven letters, *Imma*. I love the letters, especially on the big cards the teachers show us. And I imagine, *Imma,* what I would do if a big א came to visit me. I would climb on her like a tree. Then I would swing on ב and slide on ג. ד is boring, but ה is like a beautiful gate, not a bit like the squeaky gate of the orphanage. ח is even more than a gate, perhaps a door to a house, but I don't like her because she reminds me of Haya. ט is a funny letter, and י is small, like me, but כ is almost like an automobile, and if I just add wheels, she'll take me far, far away from here.

There. The night is quiet. Perhaps tomorrow I'll meet new letters. Perhaps tomorrow you'll come, *Imma*. If I pray silently, you won't hear me. "Hear, O Israel . . . the Lord is our God . . . the Lord is One."

DENIAL

To be born in Tel Aviv in 1940 and turn eight about four weeks before the Declaration of Israel's Independence was to grow up in the shadow of monumental history, to be dwarfed by a narrative stretching between catastrophe and redemption. It could dry up an early appreciation for anything personal, for private language, private space, private time, even private life.

—Yaron Ezrahi, *Rubber Bullets: Power and Conscience in Modern Israel*

Within a year of her divorce, my mother married my stepfather, Reuven, a veterinary doctor and a secular immigrant from Latvia. My father remarried an ultra-Orthodox woman and emigrated to America, where, one by one, ten children were born to them. Meanwhile, in Israel, my new family moved to Yavne'el, a small *moshav* near Tiberias, and my life turned into a fairy tale. I was mothered and stepfathered; I was fussed over, cared for, pampered, and spoiled. I had friends, a dog, fields of wheat around my house, gnarly fig trees

---

moshav   Israeli cooperative village

to climb on, long hair to be braided each morning, a clean face and colorful dresses. I was a child like all other children. I had my own room, toys, and books. My stepfather had a car, a rarity then. I still remember it—a Nash with a running board. When he took me in his car to school, on a rainy day, I felt special. If the sun came out later, I'd walk home slowly. The earth smelled sweetly, and the fields were carpeted with wild flowers. Reaching our front door, I'd open it quietly and listen for my mother's whereabouts. I wanted to surprise her. If she was in the kitchen, mopping the floor, or talking on the phone, I would tiptoe quickly to my room, take my books and notebooks out of my bag, sit down by my desk, and do my homework for the following day. Then I'd steal behind her and cry out, *"Imma,* I already finished all my homework!" She'd pretend to be immensely surprised; we'd laugh together and sit down to eat. Life was good then. I knew that I was saved.

But the orphan was forgotten. Pardes-Hannah and the orphanage became forbidden subjects. Even years later any mention of that period was banned. A year of my life had disappeared in a conspiracy of silence. A piece of my life was wiped out—as if it had happened to somebody else. Whenever I mentioned the orphanage, I'd come up fast against my mother's wall of denial. "It was no orphanage," she would say impatiently. "It was just a school where children stayed during the day and sometimes at night. Children whose parents worked long hours, for example. The teachers were very nice. Took good care of you. I visited you every week, don't you remember? You were a happy child! Here look at this picture from Pardes-Hannah." She'd rummage in a drawer, pick up a picture of the two of us sitting on a stone ledge and shove it in my face. "You see?" she'd yell, "you are smiling! How can you say now that you were miserable? You had a very happy childhood. Your stepfather and I gave you the best. What are you blaming me for, I'd like to know? Are you doing it on purpose?" With these words, the door to my past slammed shut.

Fearing my mother's anger, I stopped asking her questions about Pardes-Hannah, and I also silenced the orphan I learned to hate. She is Haya, a wild animal, I said to myself, and I would have nothing to do with her. She does not exist. The past is dead and gone. A neutral historical fact, nothing more. It does not belong to me; it cannot claim me. How could I say to the orphan, I know you, I pity you, I will help you to get out of the orphanage, when my parents ignored her existence? How could I reach out to her when my family preferred to forget her? But she was a stubborn orphan who, for years, troubled my life. At night, especially when the coyotes were howling on the hills overlooking Yavne'el, she would appear in nightmares. During the day she disturbed my

In the orphanage at Pardes-Hannah, with my mother. I am five.

From left: Grandfather, me, my mother, Aunt Bracha, Grandmother Esther, Reuven, and Moshe, Bracha's husband. In a café on Lake Kinneret, circa 1947.

concentration. She started up fights between my parents and me and sowed discord between me and my friends. She cried, complained, and exploded in anger. She was moody and unpredictable; she almost drove me insane. She wanted recognition, but how could I give it to her? How could I do it in a society where denial of feelings is a way of life?

In his book *The Israelis,* Amos Elon points out that in Israel "one does not talk of feelings, one rarely admits that they exist." The tendency "to shy away from feeling, as from some vast unreconnoitered enemy territory too dangerous for loquacious traveling, is a basic trait in the character of the new generation of Israelis [after the Six Day War of 1967]." Why are Israelis so hostile to introspection while Diaspora Jews have usually been skillful at it? In Israel feelings are often shunned and repressed. Do the Israelis associate introspection with weakness? Do they fear that feelings would paralyze their ability to respond to physical threats to their existence? Do they disregard personal and intimate feelings because they are inferior to the concerns of the group or the community? According to Yaron Ezrahi, the Zionist narrative, which "focused so intently on the monumental implications of our ancient tribe's return to its land," is not concerned "with cultivating the solitary self, the lyrical personal voice of the individual." Israelis regard that personal voice a luxury or an irrelevance. And yet, as the poet Rachel admitted, "only of myself" she knew how to tell. Drawing courage from her singular example, I will set out on my own journey to find the orphan I left long ago in Pardes-Hannah.

TIVON

Now the Lord God had planted a garden in the east, in Eden . . . and the Lord God made all kinds of trees grow out of the ground. . . .

—Genesis 2, 8

In 1951, when I was ten, we moved from Yavne'el to Tivon, an attractive summer resort 15 miles east of Haifa, and lived there for eight years. In many ways, Tivon (of nature) was to me a place of healing, the garden of my youth. However, as I later learned, in my garden, as in the ancient one, there was a seductive serpent. My mending world fractured again and suffered a deep division.

Sprawling on gentle hills overlooking Sha'ar Ha'amakim and Zebulun Valley, Tivon was an earthly paradise. Each of its streets was named after a flower or a tree. My family lived on *Ha'rakaphot* (Cyclamen Street); my best friend, Liora, lived on *Ha'shoshanim* (Rose Street); and out of my window I could gaze at winding *Alonim* (Oak Street), the street that, climbing one hill and then another, led to the house of my admired English teacher, Moses. The houses on my street and on Liora's street were surrounded by well-tended gardens. My mother was a skilled gardener, working indefatigably to dig, weed, and plant the small plots of land in front and at the back of our house. Eager irises, tulips, snapdragons, roses, pimpernels, as well as fruit trees, responded to her devoted fingers; striking long roots in thin soil, growing among rocks, they perfumed the summer air. She was rightly proud of her garden. "Isn't it like a picture? A work of art?" she would ask. Indeed, it was.

In Tivon, my stepfather's loving devotion to me also bore fruit. During my Yavne'el years, hounded by nightmares, I'd often wake up from my sleep screaming. My stepfather, Reuven, always rushed to my bed to comfort me. I'd tell him, sobbing, that there was a dark figure in the window, but he, caressing my hand, reassured me that there was no one there. Once I said that I saw my mother in the window. Reuven laughed, "How could that be, Haya'le? Your mother is sleeping in her bed." Slowly, over several years, Reuven dispelled my nightly fears. I remember the morning after a night of uninterrupted sleep. A shaft of light was streaming in from the window, and in it were reflected the branches of the pear tree, swaying in the wind. I gazed at the dance of the luminous shapes on the floor, and thought, how sweet life is.

Tivon was peaceful. My mother was quick-tempered and moody, but nonetheless present, knitting, cooking, fixing my dresses, cleaning my face, covering my schoolbooks. My stepfather made breakfast, took me to school, helped me with math, listened to my problems, and sometimes took me to the kibbutzim to show me what the dirty work in the cowshed was like. I still remember the kibbutzniks in Yagur greeting him eagerly when he got out of his car, explaining to him, on the way to the cowshed, the symptoms of the ailing animal. Wearing dark, round sunglasses and heavy black boots, his bald head shimmering in the sun, Reuven nodded quietly. When he examined the cow, the kibbutzniks stood around him in reverent silence. He opened up his black medicine bag, took out a huge syringe, the sight of which always made me shudder slightly, filled it with white liquid from his sulfa bottle, and inserted it with quick confidence somewhere in the cow's broad back. The animal that appeared to be dying when he got there, rose quickly to its feet. The kibbutzniks thanked him profusely, as if he'd performed a miracle, but he, shy of praise, brushed them off. "It's not necessary," he said with a small ironic smile. "What did I do? Nothing, really." I was so proud of him!

Tivon was also where I met my best friend, Liora. When I first arrived, I was slow to make friends. On many occasions, I became the class scapegoat. Once, after school, the kids pushed me to the ground and danced around me, calling me names ("Wild animal! Wild animal!"). I was too afraid to fight back. When they dispersed, I got up and walked home whimpering. Nobody in class talked to me, except for one chubby girl with expressive brown eyes. Liora, like me, was the butt of her classmates' jokes. We two exiles became fast friends. We discovered that we liked the same things: reading poetry and listening to music, taking long walks in Tivon's pine forests, picking daffodils in the spring, and admiring the handsome and noble face of Zvi Harel, a cellist in the Philharmonic Orchestra.

I loved visiting Liora's home. Her parents, Mr. and Mrs. Cohen, originally from Bulgaria, were friendly to us and respectful of each other. Mrs. Cohen never yelled at Liora, as my mother yelled at me, yet instilled in her a cheerful sense of discipline. A year or two after our friendship had begun, however, tragedy struck. Liora's father died of a heart attack. The happy house was now submerged in gloom. Reluctantly I went to visit my friend in her gloomy house. We ate dinner in silence, and then Mrs. Cohen lit up one table lamp, which marked a solitary circle of light and plunged the rest of the room in darkness. She started reading while Liora and I whispered in the corner, perusing the play of shadows across the ceiling. I never saw Mrs. Cohen cry, but nothing could convey more poignantly the full sway of her mourning than her silence. I squirmed under the weight of that silence and wanted to leave Liora and the house. But I stayed with my friend and watched how, in the weeks and the months to come, her mother slowly conquered her grief by moving into a spacious, two-story house and starting a bustling and successful summer pension. Eventually life, movement, and laughter filled the new house.

I loved dinnertime when the pension was at its busiest hour. Liora and I would sometimes serve lemonade to the guests, but mostly we just ran around the carpet of green grass that lapped the edges of the porch where dinner was

My mother in her garden. Tivon, circa 1952

served, laughing and giggling about this or that attractive male guest, knocking down a chair or two, rushing out again to the green grass, hopping to the edge of the oak woods, peering into its gloom, and backing away from the falling night to the brightly lit kitchen, now empty of guests, where Mrs. Cohen would tell us stories about her young days in Bulgaria.

My friendship with Liora lasted through the high school years, the years of army service, and the first two years at the university. Then we separated, but when I returned from England, I rushed to see her. She was slim, married, a mother to a child, living in a small apartment in Tel Aviv. She was distant and cold, as if we had never spent those delicious summers together at the pension, never shared secrets about the cello player Harel, never run together, laughing, fearful, to the edge of the dark woods. And yet I often think of the pleasure of her friendship and remember her brave mother who taught me that even the deepest loss can be transmuted through work, laughter, and love.

RITES OF PASSAGE

When I was eleven or twelve, I came home from school one day distraught. I looked for my mother, who was out in the backyard digging around a plum tree. I dropped my backpack and rushed to her. Her sharp blue eyes stared at me, "What happened to you?" she asked, instantly reading my mood. I sat down on a rock and looked at my hands. "What?" my mother asked. "Did you get a bad grade in math?" Her eyebrows contracted in a frown.

"No," I answered, picking up a twig.

"So what is it?" she stretched up to look at me, leaning on the hoe, her coarse gardening gloves daubed with moist soil.

"I don't know. I can't tell you." I didn't know how to start.

My mother was impatient with suspense. "Why can't you tell me?"

"The nurse," I whispered, digging a little hole in the ground with my twig, "visited school today. She talked to the girls."

My mother smiled. "Did she tell you about how children are born?"

"No," I said, disappointed at the wrong guess.

"Well, what *did* she talk to you about?"

There was no way out. I had to say the word. I whispered, "Menstruation."

"Is that all?" my mother burst out laughing. "Why is your face so tragic? It's not the end of the world, you know."

"Will I be bleeding every month?" I asked in consternation.

My mother laughed again. "Yes, you will be, like all other women, until you are fifty, or so."

"But why?"

"Why, why. You always ask why. That's the way it is. You'll get used to it," she laughed.

My mother's ringing laughter stayed with me, compounding the mystery. Was that an initiation laugh, inviting me to the secrets of womanhood? Or was she laughing at my bewilderment? Was that the way Sarah laughed when the angels came to tell Abraham that she, at ninety, will bear a son? Was that the way Rachel, sitting on the "household gods" (Genesis 31:19) she had stolen, inwardly laughed at her father when he came to look for them and told him she could not get up because she had her "period"? Was that the way all women laughed when they had their monthly bleedings? Should I, too, laugh?

Somehow, though, I could not laugh. I was worried. What if I started bleeding when I was at school? What if I got up from the chair one day and there it was, a pool of blood, my dress stained with blood, and all the kids laughing and pointing at me? What if the bleeding, once started, never stopped? I could go on bleeding for the rest of my life. What then? When I confessed these fears to my mother, she laughed and laughed. But I could not stop worrying and waited in dread for the onslaught of the "curse."

How grateful I was when it came, with remarkable thoughtfulness, in the hush of the night, dropping a single stain of blood on my panties. Now nobody would know my secret. Nobody would be able to make fun of my womanhood. And yet, I knew that I was a woman, and I was ashamed.

Menstruation opened up in me the floodgates of appetite. I was always rail thin. When I came out of the orphanage, an angry and glum child, I refused to eat. For years, mealtime was a torment to my family and me. I used to stare at the food for a long hour without touching it. When my mother forced me to take a bite, I'd hold the food in my mouth, and my right cheek would swell up. When she tapped my cheek, my left cheek would swell up. Even when Aunt Ruth came for a visit and sang my favorite songs, I'd still hold the food in my mouth and push it from one cheek to the other. As a special favor to her, though, I'd swallow one bite. In those days, food was the enemy. I hated eating and remained thin. In my wildest dreams, I could not imagine myself fat, but fat I did become when I started menstruating. After all those years of fasting, I was suddenly hungry. As I began to devour bread and cookies, my mother had to reverse her exhortations: instead of urging me to eat, she had to keep me out of the kitchen. I would nevertheless sneak a box of cookies to my room and finish it before the day was done. Once Aunt Nomi caught me in the act and cried out to my mother, "Dina, Dina, your daughter Haya has a whole box of cookies in her room!" My mother came running and snatched the cookies out of my hand. "Your fat belly does not need cookies! Why don't you look at yourself in the mirror?" she yelled. I looked. I was no longer the thin girl I used to be. I was menstruating. I was a woman and ashamed.

Although I valiantly fought my enormous appetite, I grew fatter and rounder. My mother was so fed up with my stubborn weight that she took me to a famous gynecologist in Jerusalem. She did not explain to me why she was taking me to a gynecologist for a weight problem, what kind of a doctor he was, and how he would examine me. I remember a small wiry man in a white frock; I remember his grim expression as he asked my mother questions; I remember him taking me to a white examination room; I remember his cold blue eyes looking at me through glinting glasses as he ordered me to climb on a flat surface that looked like a hospital bed; I remember him ordering me to undress and pushing my legs apart as he turned on the light; I remember the sudden incomprehensible metallic pain between my legs and the whirling questions in my mind. Why is he there? What is he doing there? Who gave him permission? What does it have to do with my weight? I remember being dressed again, feeling betrayed, walking out to meet my mother who pretended that nothing had happened, who had nothing to say to me but this, "He prescribed these pills to you. Take them for six months, and you'll lose weight." Those pills were amphetamines. I lost weight, but I was a woman and ashamed.

How could I like being a woman? From the very beginning it meant appetite and trouble. Appetite not only for food but also for sex. At thirteen I started masturbating and had some pleasure until my mother caught me. Usually I would retire to the bathroom for this, my most secret, activity. But that afternoon, for some reason, I was leisurely lolling on my mother's bed, imagining erotic scenes. I was so aroused that I pulled over myself the red silky coverlet and reached inside my pants for a release. At that very moment my mother walked into the room. She guessed what I was doing under the coverlet. She did not laugh as she did whenever I talked about menstruation. She looked stonily at me, as if she wished to strike me dead. I froze with terror.

"May I ask," she started, "why you need a cover on such a hot day?"

"I just like the silky touch of the cover," I mumbled, feeling in every fiber of my body the stupidity of my response.

"Silky shmilky. Don't tell me stories. I know what you are doing. Don't you ever do THAT again," she said and walked out of the room. Both of us knew well what THAT meant.

I was a woman and ashamed.

THE SERPENT IN THE GARDEN

Now the serpent was more crafty than any of the wild animals the Lord God has made.

—Genesis 3, 1

In the midst of that awakening—of appetites and hormones—my mother took me on a trip to Turkey. My stepfather's sister, Rachel, and her husband, Reuven, moved to Istanbul for three years, where Reuven served as a diplomat in the Israeli consulate. My mother decided to visit them for two months and brought me along. Her Reuven stayed at home, tending to his cows. That was my first trip abroad; I was young and enchanted by everything I saw. To me, the city was awash with wonder, not only for its beauty but also because it was NOT Israel. Like most Israelis, who feel caged in a small country surrounded by enemy territory, I was eager to visit any place that could be marked as "abroad."

On many mornings, my cousins Arik and Doron and I would set out early to explore the city. Arik was the leader of our small pack. He knew everything and had a charming and easy laugh that often spilled into giggles. Doron, his younger brother, was the serious student who trailed, brooding, behind us. We would start our expeditions in the plush shopping street, Para, and veer off from there through alleys to the other parts of the city. We crossed, back and forth, the Ataturk and Galata Bridges, toured the Grand Bazaar, stopped at the Hagia Sophia Church, and once even ventured over the Bosporus Bridge to the Asiatic Uskudar area. When we lost our way we spotted the Bosporus in the distance and regained our bearing. We were bold. We jumped on and off trams, conversed with strangers (Arik and Doron knew Turkish; I was learning), sat down at cafés by the Straits and ordered tea samovars. In the evenings we'd return home for dinner, ravenously hungry. The concierge, who lived with his family on the ground floor, would open the gates, and we'd rush into the kitchen, skipping and giggling.

I always hoped that the concierge's son, Ikhsun, would open the gates for us. He never did, but I knew where I could see him. Every morning at six he would exercise with his wooden bottle-shaped weights on the porch below us. I'd get dressed quickly and walk gingerly out to the veranda to catch a glimpse of him. I would lean slightly over the railing and there he would be. Aware of my presence, he would stop exercising and gaze at me until there was nothing for me to do but plunge into his green eyes and drown there. We never talked, we never touched, but in my secret heart I was an Israeli Juliet to his Turkish Romeo.

On the weekends, my family would visit the Beukada resort island, a few miles north of the straits in the Black Sea. As we got off the boat, a carriage and horses would be waiting to take us down a steep, winding road shaded with pine trees to a pristine beach covered with soft white sand. The water was smooth and supple. Only Lake Kinneret had such a silky touch, but Beukada was more exotic because it was "abroad." We used to spend a few hours on the island, and in the evening we'd catch a boat back to Istanbul.

On one of those occasions, I saw a sight that became imprinted in my memory. We were sailing back to Istanbul on a late, crowded boat. The Bosporus Straits were darkening. As we pulled into the dock, the air was hot and humid, and all around us people were shoving and pushing. Vendors were noisily advertising their merchandise, and cabbies were offering rides. Several shabbily dressed people were sitting on the ground, along the wall, talking and smoking. Were they workers, I wondered, or beggars? My mother charged ahead. I was following her through the crowd when I stopped dead in my tracks, as if hit by a sudden force. One of the men sitting on the ground had his zipper open. He was holding his erect penis in his hand, rubbing it back and forth, right there in public, for all the world to see. Incredulous, I looked again and then ran to catch up with the family, my heart pounding. I didn't tell anyone of this incident, but its repugnant impression stayed with me for months.

It was in Istanbul, the city of innocent and insidious charm, that my mother met Chaim, a married Israeli who resembled a redheaded Anthony Quinn. It was also in Istanbul that she embarked on a love affair with him that lasted seventeen years, until Reuven's death in 1972 of a massive heart attack. Chaim outlived Reuven by two years; he died in 1974 in a violent car accident.

In Istanbul, I knew nothing of my mother's affair with Chaim. They met at a party in the Israeli Consulate. It was, Chaim told me later, love at first sight. It was also an undying love, shot through with complications, counterfeits, and strange commitments and betrayals. It was the most passionate affair in my mother's life, but it was the most virulent relationship in my life, dividing my loyalties, confounding my moral bearings, making me an accomplice in an intricate web of duplicities.

I first learned that my mother and Chaim were lovers when we returned to Israel. One morning Chaim came to our house for coffee and cake. I was in my room, dancing to Mendelson's violin concerto. For some reason, I came out of my room and there were Chaim and my mother, kissing. I never saw my mother kiss Reuven on the lips, but there she was, kissing Chaim. What was he doing in our house, in the morning, kissing my mother when Reuven was at work? Chaim immediately occupied himself with a piece of cheese-cake. I was incensed. I jumped up and down. "What are you doing?" I asked breathlessly, as if the couch were on fire. "Eating a good piece of cheesecake," Chaim said with the captivating, whimsical smile I became so familiar with in future years. "I don't mean THAT," I countered. "Why were you kissing?" *(Why were you naked in the garden?)* Chaim burst out in his husky, cigarette-hoarse laughter that led to a fit of coughing. My mother, having overcome her brief embarrassment, sat up tall and stern. "Who told you we were kissing?" she asked sharply.

Although I could already feel the flutterings of anxiety in my belly, I was still undaunted. "I saw you," I said. *(I saw you eating from the tree.)*

"Saw me, saw me," my mother mimicked my speech. "So what? What are you going to do about it?"

"I am going to tell Reuven," I blurted, barely resisting the urge to run away.

"You are, eh?" my mother got up, her arms on her waist. I felt dizzy. "I'll tell you what. If you tell *him,* I'm going to punish you until you forget your name!"

"I hate my name anyway," I whispered.

"What did you say?" my mother scowled.

There was nothing more to lose. I let it all out. "I hate my name," I screamed, "and I hate you," I added with convulsive sobbing as I ran to seek refuge with my friend Liora.

"I DWELL[ED] IN POSSIBILITY"

I gave in. For a day or two, I was determined to tell Reuven what I saw. Many times the name Chaim was on my lips, but I held back. Many times I thought I'd die if I didn't talk, but my heart was beating so wildly that I could not utter a word. Many times I hated myself for being such a coward, but one look from my mother was sufficient to wipe out any brave schemes. I could not risk her disapproval. I remained silent.

And what if I had told him? What did I expect Reuven to do? Secretly I wanted him to throw Chaim out of the house, or like a noble medieval knight, to challenge him to a duel. I wanted him to denounce Chaim publicly, to expose his shame to all and sundry. I wanted him to assert himself, to be a strong husband and father, to restore wholeness to my family, but I knew that this was a Quixotic dream. Reuven habitually avoided confrontations. Even if he knew, he would never have challenged Chaim; he would have called him a windmill and gone back to his cowshed.

And this is indeed what happened. *I* didn't tell; my mother did. At first Chaim came to visit when Reuven was out. But later he came to visit when Reuven was in. The two men, instead of being enemies, became friends; they even conducted animated conversations over a cup of coffee. Several times a year Chaim took my mother to Europe; they left the country separately and returned separately but met in Paris or Rome for glorious adventures. In Europe they presented themselves everywhere as a married couple. On those occasions, Reuven would take my mother to the airport and on the way ask her, like a worried Jewish mother, detailed questions where she'd meet Chaim, and how long they'd stay in which country. When she returned, Reuven came to meet her at the airport, kissed her on the cheek, and inquired how the trip was, and how Chaim was. Then life would return to normal. My mother would again play wife to Reuven, until the next trip.

The outside world knew nothing (we thought) of this arrangement. They saw Chaim come and go, but did they know that he was my mother's lover? She always described him as "a family friend," and what greater support could she have for that definition than the *actual presence* of Reuven at home when Chaim came to visit? My mother used to stage Chaim's arrival carefully. For example, when we lived in Haifa, our house (called the "villa") was situated on the crest of Mount Carmel, overlooking the Bahai temple, the city, and the bay. One would approach the house by going *down* fifty-one winding steps. Although the house was large and fashionable, it was actually a condominium. Three other families, two under us and one alongside us, shared the building, and each one had a luxurious apartment, opening up to the stunning view of sea and mountain. Each of those families also had a good view of the fifty-one winding stairs on the other side, and no one could come into the building, or leave it, without being observed by its dwellers. It was almost like a fashion

Reuven

show. One had to dress up to go down the stairs of our house. My mother's kitchen sink just happened to be under the window facing the stairs. She often washed the dishes, of course, and so just *happened* to see Mrs. Bonner going out for an afternoon tea in her new dress ("Wonder where she got those shoes," my mother would mumble at the window), just *happened* to see Mr. Shellkis leaving with a suitcase for a business trip to Holland, and just *happened* to see the boyfriend of the Richters's teenage daughter coming for a visit when the parents were out. My mother knew that just as she kept vigil, so did all the other neighbors. If Chaim were to enter our house, special precautions had to be taken. And so Reuven was at hand. He would come out of the house, walk to the foot of the stairs, and wait for Chaim by the rosebush. All the neighbors could see him. Occasionally, he even shook Chaim's hand. The best of friends. Who could be suspicious of such a fine relationship?

My mother's cover-up was elaborate. When she flew to Europe, Reuven and I used to invent a tapestry of events to explain her absences: she went to help her sisters, to assist her mother, to save her father, to heal herself in a quiet pension in Jerusalem; we practically gave her a new identity. In the meantime, she traversed across Europe with her lover and sent us cards and pictures to cheer us up. There she was, gazing out of a cable car on the breathtaking sweep of mountains in Switzerland; leaning on the railing of a boat crossing the Seine; looking up the Eiffel Tower; peering over Michelangelo's *David;* strolling across an avenue in Stockholm; bending down in London's Trafalgar Square to feed the pigeons.

This last picture held my attention. The photographer captured my mother in a lovely pose. Her thick blond hair richly contrasted with her flow-ing black dress. As she was bending down, the hem of her dress was slightly lifted to expose her shapely knee. Her hand was stretched out to the birds that circled around it. Her face wore a bemused Mona Lisa smile that I had never seen before. The photographer who snatched this exquisite moment from the jaws of oblivion must have been in love with my mother. That photographer was Chaim. Could Reuven bring out that dance of passion and grace in my mother? Would she have given it to him?

All right, all right, I'd say to myself, they want to be lovers, let them be lovers. Fine with me. Perhaps Reuven and my mother could no longer be lovers. The more I thought about it, the truer it seemed. I did not believe the rumors that Reuven had a fling with a kibbutz woman, but I knew that he didn't make love to my mother. Of that I was sure. After all, their bedroom door was always open. Always. So there. Besides, Reuven used to joke about his failure with "that sex thing." "So what," he'd say, laughing. "I failed? I failed. What can one do?" Yes, at least with my mother he failed. Would he have gone to a therapist? Not in a hundred years. According to Reuven, only insane people went to therapists, and he was not insane. No, just a man with a little failure, so what? "The main thing is your health," Reuven would say. "One *shmekel* more, one *shmekel* less. . . . What does it matter?"

What then was a woman to do, I'd ask myself. What then? Get herself to a nunnery? Not my mother. Well, why couldn't she divorce Reuven and marry Chaim? Even Chaim mentioned it once. No. My mother wouldn't think of it. Was it loyalty and affection for Reuven that kept her married to him? Was it her fear that if she married Chaim, he would be unfaithful to her? Or was it simply her yen for the clandestine adventure?

Fine. Let her enjoy it. What did I care? I was a grown girl, a woman almost. But the problem was that I, too, was beginning to enjoy it—the excitement, the secrecy, the split between heart and crotch. And whom could I imagine as the kind of man I'd marry? Certainly not someone like my Orthodox father, whose religion I feared. Who then? the kind, affectionate Reuven, whom I sometimes pitied but no longer respected, and who was often the easy target of my temper tantrums? Who? The rakish Chaim? The usurper, my mother's lover? Was he the kind of man I'd choose for a husband? Better him, I thought, than kind Reuven. Kindness is weak. Kindness is boring. Kindness has no *shmekel.*

GADNA

He who heeds discipline shows the way to life. . . .

—Proverbs 10:17

In *The Israelis,* Elon denounces the "senseless tests of endurance under excruciatingly difficult conditions of climate and terrain" that the paramilitary youth organization Gadna imposes on Israeli teenagers "in the name of a spartan ideal of physical fitness." According to Elon, this "emulation of military practices," which reflects the country's "cult of toughness," has resulted, almost every summer, in fatal accidents.

I am grateful that I didn't know any of this prior to spending two compulsory weeks in a Gadna camp near Hadera. Had I believed that my life was in danger, I would have remained a coward for life. Instead, I threw myself into the excruciating training to prove that I had courage, that I would not always be the laughing stock of class bullies, that I would not always cower in fear before my mother's anger. As I endured heat, sand, thirst, and exhaustion, I was really fighting past humiliations that burned in my memory.

When I first saw the camp, my heart sank. It was impeccably clean; in its center the Israeli flag was bravely flying and, encirling it, red oleander flowers were doing their level best to look cheerful. However, all around us stretched deserts of vast eternity—sand dunes, and more sand dunes, in all directions as far as the eye could see. We were assigned to wooden shacks that preserved the heat and turned our living quarters into the furnace of hell. There was no escape from the heat, except in the shower, but, with so many kids, the shower was always occupied and the water tepid. Our khaki shirts, clean and fresh in early morning, were drenched in sweat within an hour. Our khaki *tembel* hats, supposed to offer protection from the sun, seemed instead to be conductors of heat and burned like torches on our heads. There was no shade anywhere. I tearfully complained about the stench of sweat to my class-mate Carmela, but she, who managed to appear dry somehow, told me not to feel so sorry for myself.

When training began, I understood the power of God's blessing to Abra-ham that his descendants will be as numerous as the sand on the seashore (Genesis 22:17). In our camp, there was sand everywhere: in my mouth, eyes, hair, bra, panties, socks, and shoes; there was sand in my food, in my water-bottle, under my nails; I chewed, drank, slept with sand. And how could I keep the sand out of my gun, as was required, when everything I touched had sand in it? But the gun *had* to be spiffy clean, and as our sergeant looked down its long barrel, one eye squinting, he ABSOLUTELY did not want to see even ONE grain of sand trapped in that barrel. No romantic Blake he, to see a world in a grain of sand. Yet in spite of my diligent efforts, I always had at least one grain of sand and could never please my sergeant. "Did you check this gun?" he asked me once. "Yes, of course," I answered feebly. "And you didn't see any grains of sand in it?" I was on the verge of tears. "No, I thought I cleaned them all out." He handed me the gun. "Would you mind looking again?" I lifted the gun with trembling hands and looked and sure enough, there were three grains lodged in its metallic spirals. Why were they still there after all my hard work? "Clean it again!" the sergeant bawled at me. "NOW!" Carmela, next to me, always had an *absolutely* clean gun and the sergeant was always pleased. How does she manage it? I thought, as once more I renewed my losing battle with the sand.

The long marches through the sand dunes in full military gear were the most grueling exercises. One day I began to trail behind the group as it was climbing up a hill. I can't do it, I thought, plopping onto the sand with all my gear. My head was pounding and my breath roaring, sweat was streaming down my face, and red and green stains were dancing before my eyes. Enough! I don't care if my gun eats a barrelful of sand; I must rest. I wiped my brow, took a forbidden sip of water, and caught my breath. Now I understand, I thought, why the Israelites complained to Moses about the desert. Would I have made it to the Promised Land? When I got up, my group was gone. I was utterly alone. All around me were sands, some straggling bushes, and the great silence. I panicked. More quickly than I ever thought I could, I was running up the hill, following my peers' footsteps. As soon as I reached the top of the hill, I could see them in the distance, sitting in a circle around the sergeant. My fear of being lost was soon replaced by the fear of being found out by the group. And then they came, with every step I took, like physical blows, the sneering looks, the jeering catcalls, the mocking titters. "There she is, fat Haya, the turtle," somebody said, "she finally made it," and the group laughed glee-fully. The sergeant looked at me with a snickering expression.

And then it happened. In the enveloping, indifferent silence, NO! exploded in my mind. NO! echoed through every cell, every nerve. I won't take it anymore. I will fight! After that day, I gave them little opportunity to mock me. Although the marches over the dunes were difficult, I gritted my teeth and kept pace with my peers. Never again did I trail the group. I even managed to keep my gun clean. However, the crucial test of my resolve was still ahead.

The last Gadna exercise, taking place one day before the graduation cere-mony, was the *jump*. To this day, I feel a knot in my stomach when I talk about it. We were brought to a wooden structure that looked like a military sentry post, approximately two stories high, with a ladder on the side. We were to jump from that post onto a large canvas tarp with handles held by the group. One by one, the kids were to climb up the post and when the sergeant gave the order to jump, the group, all together, would stretch the canvas until it was *absolutely* taut, and the jumper would land safely on it.

When I saw the post, the canvas, and the giggling kids holding it, I was sick with terror. No, I thought, forgetting my earlier determination, I am not jumping. I can't, I won't, there must be a way out. I knew, though, that there wouldn't be a way out. If I had learned one thing at the Gadna camp, this was it: there was no way out. I had to do what I was ordered to do, what everybody else did. With anxiety bordering on panic, I watched the other kids climb up the ladder to their jump and prayed that I'd be forgotten. But there was no reprieve. After the last of them jumped, one of the leaders spotted me. "You haven't jumped yet. Go up, Haya." I walked to the post as one walks to the gallows. I climbed the ladder slowly, on each rung saying farewell to my world. As I rose higher and higher, my head was spinning. From the ground the post looked high enough, but from the top it looked impossibly, unbelievably high. It was inconceivable that I would be ordered to jump from such a high place, without a parachute, onto a tarp propped only by kids who liked to make fun of me! At the top, my sergeant leaned against the railing, his arms folded on his chest. "Are you ready, Haya?" he grinned. I asked for a moment. He was patient. I looked around me. From high up, the view was breathtaking: the soft sand dunes rolled gracefully all the way to the Haifa-Tel Aviv Road, which was busy with traffic. (Save me! I wanted to shout to the passing cars.) Still farther out, a sliver of the blue sea gleamed in the afternoon sun.

"Come on, Haya," I could hear my sergeant's voice. "Time to jump."

I stood on the edge and looked down. In the words of Emily Dickinson, the space around me "began to toll." The kids' faces were slowly spinning. The ground was moving up. The canvas was getting smaller and smaller. "I can't jump," I said to the sergeant, feeling that I was about to throw up.

"That's the only way down from here," he sneered.

"I can't."

"You must. There is no other way down. Unless you have wings," he grimaced.

"Please," I pleaded. "Let me go down the ladder."

"No, you must jump. Are you ready? On your mark, get set, JUMP!" On the ground, the kids stretched the canvas hard. But nothing happened. No body of mine fell into it.

"Listen, Haya," the sergeant became serious. "This is the army. I am giving you an ORDER. Do not disobey my order! On your mark, get set, JUMP!" The kids stretched and stretched, but nothing happened. No flights of angels came to rescue me. I was still up there. The sergeant was losing his patience. "If you don't jump. . . ." he fumed but did not finish his sentence. "On your mark, get set, JUMP!"

And then I was flying through the air, sea and sky turning, ground gyrating. THUD! I hit the canvas. The kids clapped, the leaders smiled, everybody shouted, Haya made it! Only *I* knew that I didn't make it. The sergeant pushed me. I looked at my finger: there was a splinter in it from the railing I'd been holding when I was *pushed*. Forgetting my fears, I became furious. How *dare* he push me? I paced the ground, seething. After a short while, the sergeant announced an optional round of jumps for volunteers. I did not wait. I rushed up the ladder, thinking, I'll show him. When I got to the top, the sergeant saw me and his mouth dropped open. How sweet it was to witness his surprise. "Are you sure you want to jump?" he asked. "Yes," I answered, my heart pounding. I approached the edge—ON YOUR MARK, GET SET, JUMPPPPP. . . . Off I went, laughing, waving my arms, smacking the canvas with a cry, "I made it!"

During the graduation ceremony, when I heard the camp leader call my name, I was dumbfounded. Me? Turtle Haya? Fat Haya? Singled out for praise? Me, the wild animal, commended for willpower and perseverance? And in public, too, for all the kids to hear? Me? The star of the camp? Me? The only one to stand out among stronger and faster kids? Wait till I tell *Imma* and Reuven! I was floating high, higher than the wooden shacks, higher than the jumping post.

The words of our camp leader were seared into my memory. To me, they were more important than coming in first at a running race, or getting the highest grade in math. They attested to my character, didn't they? They affirmed, in public no less, that I could persevere and endure hardships. How sweet they were. It took me a little longer to realize that having the courage to jump didn't necessarily mean that I would have the courage to face my mother, or my aunts, or bullies in class. Yet the bright memory of the jump from a high and lonely post to a shaky canvas inspired me to acts of courage and became, in a sense, emblematic of a life strewn with risky leaps to an uncertain future.

ROOKIES

It was on the very first morning of army service two years later, following my graduation from high school, that I discovered the important difference between the Gadna and the army. It was a cool, crisp morning when my mother and Reuven took me to the bus station in downtown Haifa, which was bustling with excited and scared eighteen-year-old girls who, like me, were waiting for the special bus that would transfer us to the army base for female recruits near Tel Aviv for five weeks of intensive military training. My parents said good-bye and left. I was alone. After awhile, I noticed Carmela, the classmate who shared the Gadna experience with me.

"Shalom, Carmela," I said, relieved to find somebody I knew in that noisy crowd.

"Shalom, Haya," she answered, her thin lips stretching into a penciled smile.

"Are you scared?" I asked.

"Not at all," she said archly. "What is there to be scared of? Are *you* scared?"

"No, of course not," I said, looking around nervously for the bus.

"We've been through this before," Carmela said, her large brown eyes, dotted with green-gold specks, looking directly at me. "Don't you remember our Gadna camp?"

"Of course I remember, but it's not the same."

"The training is the same."

"How do you know?"

"I know," she said. "But actually you are right," she added after a moment's thought. "There is one difference."

I am a rookie in the army. 1959

"There is? What is it?"

"In the army," she grinned, "they don't give distinctions for willpower and perseverance. In the army, they give distinctions only for *real* achievements."

I was taken aback. How could Carmela remember the words of our camp leader from two years before? And why did she sound displeased? Perhaps she was right. Who *would* pay attention to stupid "perseverance" in the army? Why should they?

Indeed, the drill sergeants were not interested in struggles; they were interested in results. I knew that I was too slow and ungainly to give them those results. They were strong women. One of them was a Yemenite with short curly hair, olive skin, and lovely doe eyes. The other was a blond with clear blue eyes, her hair always gathered in a tight bun. They could do anything: run four miles with full military gear, climb trees and ropes, parachute, conduct drills in the scorching sun, crawl in the sand on knees and elbows, holding their guns in their hands, and then take us out at 3:00 A.M. for a nightly stroll. How could I hope to earn the respect of these powerful women?

Indeed, I was not successful. Being awakened at 5:30 A.M. was difficult enough, but having to be ready in three minutes *sharp* for an early morning jog was excruciating. Not to mention the drills after breakfast. I was not made for marching back and forth, left, right, right, left, in straight lines, up and down the square. Somehow, I always managed to make the straight line crooked by marching in front or behind. My fingers forgot to clench themselves into a fist, my beret refused to stay at the right angle, and my hair constantly rebelled against the commandment Thou Shalt Not Wear Thy Hair Below the Collar Line. How could I ever impress these amazons?

It was one of our early morning forced marches that illustrated my inaptitude for army life. It was 3:00 A.M. Suddenly all the lights were turned on. Awakened from a sound sleep, I thought that I must have committed a terrible crime and was now to be executed. By the time I came to my senses, I was supposed to be fully dressed and out in the square with my kit bag and gun. I arrived breathless; my group was already on the march and I quickly found my place in the line. The other rookies marched comfortably at a brisk pace, but I was small and had to jog to keep up with the rest. The night was dark and silent. The cypresses stood by the wayside like tall guards. In the sky, a star or two flickered faintly. We could hear our leader's muffled "left, right, left, right" as if coming from a great distance. In the daytime we used to sing marching songs, but now we were told to be quiet as thieves to "surprise the enemy." My mind, though, was roaring, and my heart was pounding. No, Carmela, this is ten times more difficult than the Gadna. The darkness was alive with moving shapes. I was walking and running, running and stalling. Then I heard the blond sergeant's voice next to me, "Faster, Haya, faster!" I can't, I thought in panic. Would she penalize me with kitchen or latrine duty? I shuddered and tried to hasten my pace. Fortunately, the rookie behind me noticed my distress and came to my rescue. She held her gun horizontally against my kit bag and propped me whenever my energy flagged. I was grateful. Had this happened in broad daylight, I would have been red with shame. Yet, under the cover of darkness, the anonymous recruit gave me a chance to complete, with some dignity, a task I was unequal to. Was a gun ever put to better use?

After a few weeks on the base, all I wanted was to survive and move on, to be out of that camp, away from military training. I was not interested in army life; I was interested in the life of the mind. I wanted to read and learn. I wanted to become a student.

PAPA CHAIM

How could I become a student when I still had almost two years of regular army service ahead of me? Being stationed in Tel Aviv would have been a good start, yet my chances were slim. Everybody wanted to be in Tel Aviv. It was more likely that I would be stationed, instead, in some godforsaken outpost in the Negev or the Galilee. I dreaded such a fate. My mother, too, was adamantly opposed to my spending two years so far away from home. Immediately, she called Chaim, who was then a major general in the Army Headquarters in Tel Aviv. He made some phone calls. A day later, I learned that I was to become a typist in the office of the head of the intelligence forces in Tel Aviv.

Was it right to accept such an unfair advantage over the other recruits, perhaps over the very same recruit who helped me finish the grueling night march? Was it beneficial to be whisked away, Cinderella-like, from the nastier hardships of army life? Was it wise to receive a momentous favor from Chaim and thus tacitly condone his adulterous affair with my mother? From my current mature, independent, Americanized perspective, the answer to all three questions is no. But the coddled and timid eighteen-year-old Haya could not do anything else.

In Israel of those days, and even today, nepotism was common. Everybody talked about "contacts," looked for them, and bragged about having gotten them. Jews helped one another. Hadn't it always been that way in the Diaspora? Why then not in Israel too? Unfair advantage? Who heard of it? *Protektzia* (nepotism) was a way of life. Ironically, it was lack of *protektzia* that forced me, twenty years later, to leave Israel and seek a career in the United States, where I learned about merit and fair hiring practices. But when I was a green eighteen, *protektzia* was as natural as breathing. I didn't hesitate; I took it when it was offered and said thank you.

By that time, I had already acquiesced in the strange and open triangle that Chaim, my mother, and Reuven were pretending was perfectly normal. How could my early objections to it persist? Not only Reuven, but also my mother's sisters knew about Chaim and accepted him as a "special" member of the family. Whenever he went with my mother to visit them, there was a flurry of activity. The table would be set with drinks and delicacies, conversation would flow, and the house would be ringing with laughter. There was never such excitement when Reuven came to visit. Chaim was the favorite guest, the golden boy, the *roué* who set hearts aflutter. Chaim would ever-so-subtly flirt with this sister or that, tell a juicy joke with innuendos, touch this arm, hug that shoulder, laugh affably with shrewd blue eyes narrowing to slits, praise the food, flatter the hostess, listen to her complaints, wink, bid warm adieu, take my mother by the arm and disappear in a cloud of smoke. It was a fabulous show. Chaim was cock of the walk, and they all loved him. And so did I.

How many fathers can a young woman have and still keep her wits about her? I had one father in America. I was taught to forget him. I had forgotten him, but not quite. Once a year, he would come to visit, and I would see him for an hour. The conversations we had were perfunctory, but something remained—a pang of regret, a longing, a fragment of a dream. To me, he evoked the Torah, learning, and prayer. He was the one who was whole, jolly, otherworldly. The rabbinical student. The teacher. Myself as a Jew. His daughter. But I couldn't claim him as my father. Even if we weren't separated by oceans, he was distant, always asking me the same embarrassing questions about keeping kosher and fasting on *Yom Kippur*. What could I say? In those days, I did not even know what to call him. Both my mother, and Rivka, his second wife, each for her own reasons, discouraged me from calling him *Abba*. So what should I have called him, Zorah? Who was Zorah to me? A part-time *Abba*?

At home, in Haifa, I had Reuven. Kind and caring, he tried to be my full-time *Abba*, but how could I call him *Abba* when he allowed my mother to have an affair with another man? At times I pitied him, but often I was so angry at him I wanted to shake him and yell, "Wake up, Ruvke. Where is your pride? How can you walk the two of them to the door, then stretch on the hammock in the front porch, read the newspaper, and fall asleep?" So I sat next to him, reading my book, thinking those angry thoughts—snakes biting their own tails—and saying nothing. I was grateful for Reuven; at times I even loved him. But how could I be proud of the man my mother discarded?

Chaim was altogether different. Quick-witted and glib, he was not simply an officer in the army, but a spy, he told me, who risked his life in Arab lands, a patriot, a powerful man, with an irresistible aura of mystery. Most significantly, he was the one who succeeded where my two other fathers failed—in holding onto my mother. Him I respected. Wasn't I entitled to *his* fatherhood? During those two years of military service, I adopted him as a father.

Although I was stationed in Tel Aviv, my typing job was tedious. Some of the documents were marked Top Secret, which made me feel important, but most of them were dull. For eight hours each day, I typed mechanically, unable, in spite of my best efforts, to find interest in the detailed descriptions of the movements of armed forces along the borders. To escape the boredom, I frequented the Mann Auditorium for concerts.

In Israel, almost everybody loves classical music. One of my bosses at the office, Motke, used to walk in every morning humming Bach's piano concerto. Other Israelis could whistle whole concertos by heart. If by chance, some respectable Israelis did not naturally love classical music, they *pretended* to love it. My mother loved it more than anybody else I knew. When I was growing up in Yavne'el and Tivon, the radio would always be turned to the classical music station. As she was dusting the furniture, or mopping the floors, my mother would hum Brahms's violin concerto, or a Mozart symphony. When an opera was being played, she would bravely accompany the singers through their arias. Reuven loved her singing, but I, who could sing no better than Aesop's infamous raven, envied her strong and melodious voice. And yet I also admired it and was moved by the expression of tenderness and delight that suffused her face when she sang. Music could erase my mother's habitual scowl and transport her to a place of pure pleasure. It was to this place that I too escaped from my humdrum army reality.

Concerts and books, however, could not shield me from the persistent harassment of my boss, Hedva, the head secretary of the office, a young, pretty but harsh woman, whose chief delight seemed to be in tormenting me. Each morning I came to work with sickening flutterings of anxiety. For two years I suffered from bouts of diarrhea. Whenever I heard Hedva's shrill voice blaming me for losing document X, or making errors on document Y, I rushed to the bathroom. When I came back, she scolded me for disappearing when she needed me most. I didn't fully appreciate the importance of the office I was working in, she claimed, I was not serious enough. This was not just any plain, ordinary office. No, this was the office of the head of the intelligence forces. Did I know what that meant? This office was the brain, the central nervous system of the whole army! Important people worked in it, *very* important people came to visit it, and I didn't care! No, I didn't care; I was dreaming all day, reading books.

Day in, day out, Hedva harangued me about my glaring flaws. Every night I cried in my room, yet I was too timid to fight back. I was convinced that if Hedva learned about my anger, she'd transfer me to an outpost in the desert. One day, though, I blew up in the most bizarre manner. Hedva, waiting for very important guests, ordered me to fill a pot of water for tea. I did and then continued reading my book, a biography of Bach. She was rushing around, popping her head into my room. "Is it boiling yet?" She threw her arms in the air. "Why isn't the kettle boiling, Haya?" Her long, bloodred, manicured fingernails tapped my desk impatiently. And then it was my anger, rather than the water, that boiled over. "Why don't you try to sit on it?" I said, heatedly, "perhaps it will boil faster." How can I describe Hedva's fury? I was grateful that she did not exile me to the Negev outpost.

It was Chaim who saved me from Hedva's wrath. He talked to her with humor and confident charm. For a long while, things got better at the office, until the harassment renewed, and Chaim would step into the breach again. At times, he'd take me to lunch in a nice restaurant along the beach, and it was only then that I felt relief from the anxiety of the office.

When I was hospitalized after a strange accident, Chaim was again close by. One evening, I finished my work late and hurried to a concert. Impatiently, I pushed hard on the glass door in the office, but the door's wooden frame was stuck and scraped against the floor. With my left hand I broke the glass, and cut myself in the temple, close to my right eye. I didn't feel any pain and was surprised to see so much blood gushing out of the wound. By "seeing" I am referring to my left eye, since my right swelled up and closed shut. An officer from the office rushed me to Tel-Hashomer Hospital.

After the brief procedure, I was wheeled to a room, stitched up and bandaged, and left there for the night. It was then that I felt the full brunt of the accident. Alone in the dark, my fears and regrets erupted in a torrent of tears gushing out of my left eye. What a good concert I missed. What will happen to my right eye? Who will tell my parents? Suddenly I heard quick footsteps in the corridor. I knew that quick step. I lifted my eye and saw the slim, medium height redhead with a thick mustache—Chaim! How happy I was to see him! He had already talked to the surgeon and found out that my right eye was in no danger. "Tell you what," he smiled engagingly. "You probably just wanted to get *out* of that office and never see Hedva again, isn't it true?" I nodded and smiled. "Trust me. You'll be just fine, Haya'le," he said. "And when you come out, you can say that you were wounded in the line of duty," he laughed. I laughed too. We talked for a long while. Early in the morning, my mother and Reuven came. I was glad to see them, but my heart was already given to Papa Chaim, who was the first to arrive, in the night, when I was most lonely and scared.

Chaim's nocturnal visit still glows in my memory. How easy it was to love him. But this love was stolen. The time he gave me, he took away from his daughter; the time he gave my mother, he took away from his wife. He always bragged that he had enough time and energy for all of us, yet of the wrong-doing he preferred not to think. To *that* none of us paid much attention. My mother's favorite expression of rebuke (especially about my weight) used to be the one with the ostrich hiding its head in the sand, but she never saw the relevance of the adage to herself. Throughout the long years of her affair with Chaim, she was the mother ostrich and I became the daughter ostrich. Both of us were trespassers, thieves.

I remember only one incident when we were forced to take our heads out of the sand by an anguished letter that Chaim's wife had written him. Holding the letter in his trembling hand, Chaim sat down and read it aloud. His eyes looked large and dim through his reading glasses. The woman's pain, as she pleaded with Chaim to return home, penetrated our denials. I was stung. In one fell swoop, Chaim's wife was no longer the "witch" my mother used to call her but a suffering human being. Unlike Reuven, who accepted the affair with benign cheerfulness, this woman, for many years, helplessly raged against it.

My mother listened to the letter with an air of cold disdain. When Chaim finished, she said, "Why have you read me this letter? What has it got to do with me? What do you want me to do?"

Chaim shook his head. "I just want you to understand what she is going through."

"Are you blaming me for what *she* is going through?"

"No, no," Chaim said, "I blame myself, too."

"Go ahead and blame yourself, but what does this have to do with me?" she blurted, her eyes flashing blue fire. "Suppose I understand. So? What do you want me to do? Leave you?"

"I think that Chaim is right," I said, sanctimoniously.

"You keep your nose out of it," my mother shot back, her lips pulled down in disdain.

"But don't you realize what your affair is doing to her?" I insisted, glad to pay her back for all that ostrich talk.

"What do you want me to do?" my mother addressed Chaim again. "Do you want to say good-bye? Fine. Go and don't come back. Go, go. If you love her so much, go back to her." She gazed at the blue bay.

"No, Dina," Chaim lit a cigarette. "You know very well that I don't want to do that; I can't do that."

"So why are you reading such letters to me?" She got up to go to the kitchen. In an instant, I saw that her eyes were glistening with tears.

There was no way out of it. The one betrayal enmeshed us in a web of betrayals. We were all dragged into it. There was no escape from it. One gratified appetite brought on another and another, until we found ourselves in a maze where we could no longer tell right from wrong.

One night Chaim gave me a ride from Tel Aviv to Haifa. When we arrived home, it was dark. Chaim turned the ignition off and lit a cigarette, a sign, I knew, that he wanted to talk.

"So what do you think is going on between your mother and me?" He looked at me from the corner of his eye, as he was puffing up whorls of smoke.

"I don't know," I said. "You are the friend of the family."

He chuckled. "That's what you think?" I didn't really. "Friend, shmend," he said after awhile, "I get a kick out of your mother." I looked at his fleshy lips in the light of the streetlamp. "I want to tell you something," he bent forward slightly and winked at me. "She is great *in* bed and *out* of bed," he laughed. "And you want to know something else?" he roared in laughter. A drop of saliva, luminous in the pale light, was hanging by a thin thread from his lower lip. "All the Kazarnovsky sisters are great. Are they hot women! I haven't tried them, but I know . . . the way they look at me . . . ha-ha-ha, ha-ha-ha. . . . But your mother is the best," he laughed and sucked the saliva drop back into his mouth.

It might have been on that night, or some other similar night, that I began to fear him. If he had an appetite for my aunts, wouldn't he want to seduce me, too? And when will it happen? I quickly dismissed the thought. It couldn't be true. He was Papa Chaim, and I was his special daughter, wasn't I? My mother and her sisters were one thing, but I was another. Surely he knew that, surely he knew the difference between *me* and *them*. So why is he telling me all those things, a small voice asked. He just trusts me; I am his confidante.

Ten years later, on a shimmering, hot day, Chaim gave me a ride to Bar-Ilan University, where I had just begun my studies for my doctorate. He turned off the ignition and lit a cigarette. "You know," he said, "we two could be great together." I looked at him suspiciously. "What do you mean?" I held my breath. He smiled, "Oh, you know. . . ." He flicked the cigarette's ash outside the window and winked whimsically. "I have often been thinking about it. . . . Often, I tell you. And why not?" he laughed hoarsely. "Why not do it? We could have fun! Who is stopping us?" His glance swept across campus as if searching for the person who'd stop us. "Who can say 'no' to us? Your mother won't know, I promise you." For a moment, the world around me whirled. I stared outside at people going in and out of buildings, talking and laughing. I envied their innocent, nonchalant busyness, which had been mine also, until a few minutes earlier. Where was lovable Papa Chaim? Dizzy and shaking, I grabbed my stuff, whispered a breathless "no," got out of the car into the bright sunshine, and slammed the door behind me. Unperturbed, Chaim turned on the ignition, waved his familiar good-bye, and, laughing heartily, glided away. I had said no to Chaim, but I did not forget my seducer. For years, I chased men who, in one way or another, reminded me of him.

"READING MAKETH A FULL [WO]MAN"

After my two years of army service, I finally reached the place I longed to be in: the Hebrew University of Jerusalem. I became what I always craved to be, a student. Without hesitation, I chose to major in Hebrew literature and in English literature. I did not consider the practical uses of a degree in literature; I never thought about what I could *do* with it. I chose literature because I loved it, because it had been my sanctuary. Although I had three fathers and a mother, I was still, in a sense, an orphan looking for a spiritual home that I could not find in Chaim's adventurous life, in Reuven's placid world, in my father's religion, or in my mother's hedonism. It was to literature that I escaped; it was in literature that I found a sense of moral clarity and direction I could not find anywhere else; it was through literature that I discovered, to extrapolate Wordsworth, "the joy / Of elevated thoughts."

My escape into literature started at an early age. When the War of Independence broke out in 1948, my mother and I moved from Yavne'el to Haifa for a few months, to avoid anticipated massive Arab attacks on the area. Reuven stayed in Yavne'el with his gun and was determined to shoot down any Arab planes that happened to whiz by. In Haifa, my mother and I lived in a small rented room on Arlosoroff Street. I was already then an eager reader and found refuge from the commotion of war in *Robinson Crusoe,* which I read in Hebrew. I turned a corner in our room into a Crusoe island, where nobody was allowed to enter, and conducted lively conversations with Sheshet (Friday's name in Hebrew), asking him questions about the war and about the whereabouts of my mother on the evenings when she would go out. If my mother hadn't yet returned when the sirens began to wail, I'd stay in my bed instead of going down to the shelter and talk my fears over with my imaginary friends. In the morning, my mother chastised me for staying away from the shelter, but I thought that if she could stay away from it, so could I. Once our old landlady forced me to go down with her to the shelter, but I popped out again to look at the bombs falling. That time I got a real talking to from one of the civilian guards stationed in our street, and I consented to go down, still wondering about all those grown-ups who were scared of a little siren. After all, I was the brave Crusoe; I made a life for myself on an island all on my own. What bombs could get *me?*

Two or three months later, we returned to Yavne'el, and life became quieter, but I was still yearning for my island. Once, when my mother was out, I closed the bathroom door and filled up the tub and then the bathroom itself with water, attempting to create an ocean on which I could sail to my island, forgetting, of course, that the water would escape under the door to the living room, meander around the table and the chairs, soak the expensive Persian carpet, splash the couch, and flow unimpeded in all directions. I was amazed that even after an hour the bathroom still did not become an ocean, not even a lake, not even a tiny pool. Instead, the house was flooded, and if my mother hadn't returned on time, we might have needed an ark. Little did I know then that, like Crusoe, I too would one day sail the seas in search of a new life. But at that time, the tidal wave of bathwater I had unleashed on the house put an end to my literary adventures.

It didn't put an end to my reading, however. I read all the literature I could get my hands on. When I was a teenager in Tivon, I fell in love with the tempestuous poetry of Zalman Shneour. I was particularly fond of his "Pragim" (Poppies). There was fire in this poem. The poppies in the field were "blazing" and their flames "shimmered in clear crystal air"; they "burst from the earth" like "cries of desire." How often did one come across "cries of desire" in Hebrew poetry? I was secretly enchanted by Shneour's passion. "I was purified in the crucible," he said. Wasn't I too put through the crucible? I could trust a man who exclaimed that the sun "burned" on his head. I knew that *he,* unlike my "real" fathers, would understand me.

In those days, I was also fond of Bialik's lyrical poetry, particularly his *"Zohar"* (Radiance) and *"Ha-Berekhah"* (The Pool). Like young Bialik's heart in *"Ha-Berekhah,"* my heart, too, knew "how to long and yearn and wonder" and was "Seeking a hiding place for its prayers." As I was wandering through Tivon's sparse forests, I was thinking about the majesty of Bialik's East European childhood forest, "When the sun wash[ed] [its] locks. . . . / And pour[ed] a sea of radiance over his curls." At night, if I happened to look out of one of the windows in the second story of Liora's pension at the valley and the reflection of the moon in Sha'ar Ha'amakim's fishing ponds, I would contemplate Bialik's quiet moonlight filtering through the branches of the wood, "embroidering" wonders "in silver and blue." In my adolescent dreaminess, I fancied myself the "bewitched" princess in Bialik's forest, awaiting "in secret" for "the prince, her lover and redeemer," to come and set her free.

As soon as I mastered sufficient knowledge of English, at sixteen, I started reading Keats, Shelley, and Wordsworth. I am not sure how much of their poetry I understood then, but I was fascinated by English. Soon I started reading more English than Hebrew. I gathered new English words as one would shells on the seashore, feeling their texture, examining their colors, trying them out in different combinations, tasting their salty flavor on my tongue, and listening through their hollows to the eternal hum of the sea. Every new word was a gate, a way to a garden or a castle where people who truly appreciated me were waiting patiently for my arrival.

But why was I so attracted to English? At sixteen, I hoped perhaps that English would help me reach my father in America, but mostly I needed to protect my innermost thoughts from my mother. I was sure that if I wrote a journal or a poem in Hebrew she would read it and find out my secrets. English was safe. She may have learned a few English expressions during the British Mandate, but she did not know the language, and she could not read it. I continued to read in both languages, but English became, in Bialik's words, the hiding place for my heart's prayers.

In time, English became more than a hiding place; it turned into my academy for self-expression. During the army service, I realized that all the

English I knew was in my head and that I had little experience speaking it. I therefore joined a group that practiced English conversation once a week, with Dr. Schechter, a distinguished British gentleman with keen eyes and a beard that reminded me of Freud. Each week, I looked forward with excitement to my English conversation in Schechter's house on Frug Street. As I walked in, I loved the musty odor of books that filled up the shelves in the room, the big table around which our small group gathered, the comfortable, worn-down chairs, the fierce dark eyes of our teacher, and particularly the melodious English that came out of his mouth, which so vividly contrasted with the guttural Hebrew I had been hearing and speaking the rest of the week. The clipped British accent sounded to me so refined that it became almost a musical event, a miniconcert at the Frug Auditorium.

When I came across new words, I looked them up in the huge dictionary on the table and greedily hoarded them for future use. I was given numerous opportunities to practice my knowledge in the form of storytelling, which became our staple assignment. I must have told a number of stories, but I remember one—the description of the bloody riots of the Turks against the Greeks, which I witnessed during my visit to Istanbul. I had never recounted this event in Hebrew before. I wondered why. Was it because in Hebrew I couldn't find the words for personal pain and fear? Or was it because I couldn't find an audience? Now the story of the hundreds of Turks marching through our street, under our windows—some of them chanting, some shaking their fists, and some holding knives between their teeth—poured out of me in a torrent of descriptive words, not in my own native language, but in English. When I finished the story, the room was quiet. Gradually our group began to discuss the event. I drew a deep breath, and as I sat back in my chair, answering their questions, I recognized, for the first time, the cathartic power of expressed feelings.

Although I took a number of evening classes in Tel Aviv, Schechter's was by far the most important one. Through English, I was discovering myself; through its words I was able to narrate my inner experiences. It was a revolution whose far-reaching consequences I didn't recognize until years later, when I decided to study English for my graduate degree, and perhaps even much later than that when I emigrated to America. But when I served in the army, I intuitively knew that Schechter's class was my lifeline. Once our army camp scheduled a speaker for the night of Schechter's class. Every soldier was ordered to attend. It did not take me long to decide where to go. Although usually an obedient soldier, this time I defied orders, escaped the curfew, and showed up at Schechter's class as usual. I was caught and put for two weeks under house arrest. I quickly saw my folly—instead of missing one of Schechter's classes, I was now forced to miss two! And yet, I did not regret my decision. It must have been one of those moments when my soul, as Emily Dickinson would put it, decided to select her own society.

When I arrived at the Hebrew University, I was confident in my knowledge of English, yet I quickly discovered that I was wrong. I hadn't realized how long it took to master a foreign language. During my first two years, I was more successful in Hebrew than in English. My Hebrew grades soared; my English grades limped. Hebrew was smooth and accessible; English was difficult and intimidating. I could easily grasp Hebrew medieval poetry, but Chaucer towered over me like a slippery mountain I could never hope to climb. Even the literature of the Enlightenment *(Haskalah),* considered by many to exemplify the most stilted and ornate Hebrew style, did not faze me. But Shakespeare did. I loved him more than any of the Hebrew writers, but I only dimly understood his language and his world. I was a blindfolded Ruth who could barely discern what she was gleaning.

Yet I persisted. In the third year, I was reading the Brontes, D. H. Lawrence, and Joyce, and I understood them, I thought. My grades improved; I even got an A— on a paper I submitted to Professor Nevo on Milton's *Paradise Lost.* When I graduated, my Hebrew scores were higher, but I was also proud of my English achievements. In both subjects I had high enough grades to pursue graduate studies. But which subject would it be, Hebrew or English? It could no longer be both; I had to choose one.

"TWO ROADS DIVERGED IN A WOOD"

Although I had been contemplating it for months, I avoided this momentous decision until the very end of my studies for the bachelor's degree. I had just completed my last oral final in Hebrew Literature with Professor Halkin (then head of the department), which took place in Meiser Hall. I was the last student. A few minutes later, Halkin emerged from the room and shook my hand, congratulating me on my fine exam. Then he asked me, still smiling warmly, if I would like to continue my studies for the master's in Hebrew literature.

What went through my mind as I was finally facing the most important choice of my life? I remember a medley of intense feelings that I shall attempt to recapture in words. I was immensely flattered. The head of the department himself was inviting me, personally, to enter the halls of Hebrew literature! I was one of the elect! How exhilarating! Of course I must accept such an honorific invitation! How could I refuse it? In a flash, I surveyed my three years at the department. I stared at the empty classroom where Professor Shaked used to conduct his seminars, and I could still hear the echoes of the riveting discussions between him and the then fledgling writer, Amos Oz. That's how exciting Hebrew Literature could be, I thought. Then I gazed at the library upstairs where I spent hours writing research papers on Mapu, Achad Ha'am, Aloni, and Brenner, and my enthusiasm flagged. I remembered the long hours of boredom and desolation. What did Mapu's *Ahavat Zion* have to do with my life? How did Brenner's stories, which I admired, relate to my personal struggles? Where, in the Hebrew literature I then knew, could I find introspection, attentiveness to the individual's emotional life? Indeed, it was Bialik's lyricism that opened up my heart to poetry, and Zalman Shneour's passion that stirred my blood. But at the Hebrew University I learned that such personal poetry was rare. Even Bialik, who, like me, was a "child left to himself," cast his intimate anguish in the national crucible, found his soul in his grandfather's "small prayer shawl," and hewed his art, his "songs of life," from the "dead letters" of his tattered *Gemara*. No, everywhere I turned, in fiction as in poetry, private struggles were dwarfed by Jewish history, Jewish destiny, and the Jewish state. Personal relationships played themselves out, if at all, against the gigantic backdrop of the creation of the state of Israel; that's where the real battles were taking place. But where was Haya, who couldn't wrap herself up in a prayer shawl, who read but little Gemara, who was a small girl who dreamed of Robinson Crusoe when the Independence War raged around her, who never fought for her country (and barely survived a forced march in the training camp), who could never glorify its name in "tales of valor," as the poet Rachel longed to do, where could *she* find her place in the halls of Hebrew literature? And where in those halls was the orphan from Pardes-Hannah? Or the teenager from Tivon who had a good friend, Liora, an overbearing mother, and three wandering fathers? Where, in Hebrew literature, was the orphan, the girl, the woman who was me? No, I summed up despondently, in Hebrew literature, I, Haya Shapira, do not exist. I turned to Professor Halkin with guilty, downcast eyes.

Gemara   The Talmud, the anthology of Jewish law and lore

"No," I said timidly, "I would like to continue my studies in English literature."

Halkin's cheeks reddened. "English?" he exclaimed, a deep frown darkening his face. "What is English to you? What do you know of its history and culture? English is not yours!" He stared at me with a pained look, as if I were a daughter who had just betrayed him, and started marching toward the stairs. Suddenly he stopped, turned on his heels, and shook a bony, angry finger at me. "Your place is here! In Hebrew literature. You cannot escape Jewish history!" His words reverberated in Meiser's still air as they reverberate in my soul to this day.

I was cast out, forever, from Halkin's Eden. And yet, I did not want to go back. I was guilty but defiant. I felt that Hebrew literature was a heavy burden, that it was distant, that it did not include me. I felt that English literature was lively and intimate, and that, although foreign in some ways, was in others warm and inviting. Wasn't James Joyce an exile like me? Wasn't his Stephen Dedalus, who refused to be trapped in the nets of "nationality, language, religion" that his country flung at him, my mentor? Wasn't he, who also defied his mother, and who left Ireland to "encounter for the millionth time the reality of experience," my soul mate?

It was then that I decided to travel to England for a few years to study Joyce. I did not intend to leave my country for good, as Joyce had done. In those days, such a thought never entered my mind. Although I chose English literature, Israel was still my home. But I wanted to leave it for a while, to leave my mother, too, to find myself, and to make my own way in the world.

chapter two

ENGLAND

"I WOULD TO GOD MY NAME
WERE NOT SO TERRIBLE"

Before I left for England, I changed my name from Haya to Shelly. I wanted a new identity. I wanted to make a clean break from a world where I was lonely, passive, invisible. I wanted to wipe out the shame of the orphan and start anew. Haya was unruly, helpless, mute; Shelly, I decided, would be articulate, strong, independent.

Yet how could I explain my action to my mother, to Reuven, to Chaim, to all my relatives and friends, who would have to call me Shelly from now on? Would they be embarrassed or resentful? What would I do if they refused to call me Shelly? What would I say when they asked me to explain? Should I say, I have to get away from all of you, from Israel, from the Hebrew language, to find myself? No, they wouldn't understand. They would grill me with questions I could not answer. They would think that I chose my new name because it sounded British. Pretender, they would whisper behind my back. I envisioned their anger, their contempt, their indifference. In reality, though, nothing of the kind happened.

I told my mother first. After lengthy introductions and much throat-clearing, I spewed it out. "I want to change my name."

My mother looked at me with bemused interest. "Oh? To what?"

"Shelly," I whispered, like a criminal admitting her crime.

"That's wonderful!" she exclaimed. "What a beautiful name! Shelly. Ah, what a ring to it!"

I could not believe my ears. "You don't care?" I asked timidly. "But you gave me my name. . . ."

"Me?" her blue eyes grew round in surprise. "What are *you* talking about? Me? I hated the name, hated it. It was *he,* your dear father, who gave you this name. I pleaded with him to give you another name, Yael, but, NO, he *had* to call you Haya after his grandmother."

"You never told me that you hated my name," I said with relief.

"Of course not. What could I do after *he* gave you this awful name? I just had to accept it and live with it. But now that *you* want to change it, I think it's high time!"

"But what will everybody else say? They will make fun of me, or refuse to call me Shelly."

"Leave it to me," my mother said, archly raising her eyebrows. "After *I* talk to them, they will all call you Shelly. It's none of their business, anyway. And what's the big deal? Lots of people in this country change their names. Here, Eva, my friend, and Uzi, they used to be Heimlich, remember? And now they are Hod, and everybody calls them Hod."

"But it's not the same thing," I said, anxiously. "You are talking about last names; I am talking about my first name."

"So? There is no difference. It's your name and you're entitled to do with it whatever you wish. Go tomorrow to the Ministry of the Interior and change your name."

And so I became Shelly with my mother's approval and support. How did it happen? I made my first step toward independence, and there she was, my best ally, coercing the entire family to call me Shelly from that day on or else! Like a battleship, she stood in their gates. "Blot out the name Haya from the face of the earth," she commanded them. "My daughter is no longer Haya but Shelly. (How would *you* like to be called an animal?)"

It worked. I changed my name and all pretended that nothing of note had occurred. As if I were given the name Shelly at birth. Reuven approved of my new name. Chaim admired it. Only my father in America refused to recognize it, but he was far away. Even my few friends acquiesced, as if they knew about my mother's determination. Once, though, I was climbing the steps of the library at the Hebrew University, on my way back to the reading room, when somebody from behind called, "Haya, Haya." Without looking back, without finding out who the caller was, I ran with all my might, opened the heavy door to the reading room, and collapsed breathlessly at my desk.

That was a narrow escape, I thought. I wanted a new beginning, but what kind of a beginning was it, based on deception? How was I better than Chaim and my mother? Was I not pretending to be someone else? Was I not running away from myself, burying my head in the sand?

But Haya was at my neck, throttling me. I remembered how even Moshe, one of my army friends, used to make fun of my name in his letters, calling me "the beast in the beauty," or "the most kosher animal." And if a friend could not resist those puns, what would my enemies do to my name? No, I had to get rid of it. And after all, I was not the first to have changed my name, I reflected. The biblical Abram changed his name to Abraham. His wife, Sarai, changed her name to Sarah. His grandson, Jacob, changed his name to Israel after wrestling with the angel. Yes, those are worthy precedents, I reassured myself. Perhaps my change of name was not a subterfuge but a summons. Perhaps I was called upon to wrestle for my new name, knowing that only through this wrestling I could become my own person—Shelly—a word which, in Hebrew, among other things, means "mine."

"WHAT'S IN A NAME?"

Although I did regard my name as a passport, or a password, to English culture, I saw to it that it had a Hebrew meaning as well. My Israeli roommate in Jerusalem had a sister named Shelly. There, I argued with invisible detractors, Shelly may be a rare name, but it *is* a Hebrew name! Yet in my mind, one live Shelly could not justify the choice of the name. Where does it come from? I went to the Bible. Second Samuel 3, 27 says: "And when Abner was returned to Hebron, Joab took him aside in the gate to speak with him quietly, and smote him there under the fifth rib, that he died, for the blood of Asahel his brother." The word *quietly* is *sheli* in Hebrew, which also means peace. And yet here I encountered a difficulty. I knew that *sheli* was an ambiguous word that meant also secrecy, or deception. Joab beguiled Abner, took him to the gate as if he were his trusty friend, and then killed him. This is a revenge story, I warned myself, full of violence and treachery. How could I be part of it while I was looking for peace? Still, I desired this name and no other. Thus started a moral split whose intensity stunned me. I longed for openness, but I was harboring a dark secret. I wanted Shelly to be an honest woman, and yet she was already cunning. I instilled in Shelly my passion for wholeness, and yet she was irrevocably divided.

However, I liked my new name and was pleased that it was both a Hebrew and an English name, and that in English it was a poet's name. Being uneasy about this vanity, though, I dropped the second *e* from Shelley's name. Yet underneath this disguise, I had worked out an elaborate analogy with the creator of "Ode to the West Wind." How I identified with the youth who pined for the energy and the daring of the wild west wind! How like him I craved to share the "impulse" of her strength and to pant "beneath [her] power." How I, too, longed for the "mighty harmonies" of this "Spirit fierce" that could quicken my "dead [Hebrew] thoughts" to "a new [English] birth." And wasn't I, like Shelley, languishing in "my sore need," bleeding "upon the thorns of life"? I was so taken with the poet's panting, striving, and bleeding that I still ponder my good sense at choosing to study Joyce. It was Joyce's discipline and irony that I really needed.

LONDON

In January 1965, my mother and I arrived to conquer London but were instantly defeated by the grim and icy English winter. Punishing winds waited at corners to pounce on us, turn our umbrellas inside out, and cut through our inadequate clothing to our vulnerable skins. How could I have guessed this by reading Shakespeare? I rushed to Selfridges with my mother to buy fur coats and fur hats. After that things improved, but still the cheering sun, my Mediterranean companion, was nowhere to be seen. Day after day, it stayed behind a thick and impenetrable cover of clouds. Why, I rebuked myself, did I think only about Joyce, Shelley, Lawrence, and God knows who else, when I decided to come to England, but never bothered to find out what the weather was like?

The English, too, appeared to be pale and cold. I asked myself, as I observed the formal and closed faces of the natives, how could one (especially one with an accent), ever strike up a conversation with them? Do they ever lose their tempers, or are they always so polite? Will they ever talk to me? I worried. Sadly, I remembered the easy vitality of the Israelis. What am I doing here? I asked myself pointedly. Couldn't I study Joyce in Jerusalem? Pacing the chilled and foggy streets of London, I reflected bitterly on the rashness of my decision to come to England.

And yet I was there. I couldn't go back to Israel empty-handed. I was no longer Haya but Shelly, and I had a mission to accomplish. I therefore mustered my courage and applied for the following fall's graduate program in English at London University. London University did not recognize my Israeli bachelor's degree, so I applied to one of the provincial universities. I chose Sheffield because William Empson, whose books I had read, was the chair of the English Department there. To my surprise, I was accepted. Empson was interested in my ability to read Hebrew and hoped that I would consent to write a master's thesis on the Hebraic influence on Milton. I accepted his offer but did not confess to him my interest in Joyce. Next fall was far-off, I reasoned, time enough to think of what I'd say to Empson when I saw him.

Buoyed by my achievement, I turned next to search for work for the few remaining months before my studies were scheduled to begin. I got a job at the Israeli Embassy as secretary to the defense attaché and rented a room with an Israeli family. With each passing month, the reality of my mission to study for my master's degree loomed larger on my horizon. I dreaded moving to Sheffield. I was already used to London, and once I discovered its theaters, concerts, and museums, I became quite fond of it. Why did I need to uproot myself to a desolate Midlands town, where I knew no one? How could I possibly write something valuable about Joyce in the land of mist and snow?

The more I dreaded Sheffield, the rosier my job at the embassy appeared to be. What was wrong with being a secretary? After all, I was not just a typist, as I was in the army. Now I was in charge of the office, occupying a position parallel to Hedva's. Wasn't this progress? Furthermore, my boss, the defense attaché, trusted me, and sometimes even asked me to translate his Hebrew letters into English. Wasn't this an intellectual challenge? Best of all, I felt like I was in Israel and in England, enjoying the advantages of both countries. Why did I need to think about James Joyce? For the first time, I was earning good money. True, I blew much of it away on expensive clothes and expensive haircuts at Vidal Sassoon's, but I could learn to be more careful. Wasn't this what independence was all about? If I moved to Sheffield, my parents would have to pay my keep because, as a foreigner, I was not allowed to work in Britain, except on Israeli territory, which is what the embassy was: a small and lively Israeli island in the midst of an ocean of tight-lipped Britishers. Of course, I did remember that I left Israel because I needed a new identity, a new life. But there it was. I had it. Was a master's degree that important?

At times the English winter, with its ceaseless rains and its sudden gusts of wind that took one's breath away, shook my complacency. If I didn't intend to study at Sheffield, what was I doing in England? Why was I working at the embassy? Wasn't that a stupefying, dead-end job? What force propelled me every morning to wrap myself up in my fur coat and climb the top deck of the red double-decker bus that meandered for half an hour to the Israeli Embassy?

The parks were frozen and the trees were bare. Driving rain rattled the bus windows. In the streets, grey huddled figures were running to and fro, seeking shelter from the storm. How could I get used to the English winter, which was holding me by the collar like an old and severe taskmaster, growling, "What are YOU doing here?"

What indeed?

Well, I replied, I am the defense attaché's secretary. Without me, he could not keep his office going for a day. Really? the wind howled. No, I got off the bus, my head lowered against the torrential rain, I am not just any secretary— swish, the bus rolled off, splashing my coat—what I do is important . . . the wind snatched my words. I hopped into the embassy. My job *is* important, isn't it? I looked at the weeping windows. My job is interesting, I took off my dripping coat. My job is meaningful, I sat at my desk and peered into an unfinished letter to a British official. So why think of Joyce? Didn't Halkin already say that I didn't belong, that English was not mine? Outside, the wind and the rain, locked in a fierce embrace, were whistling and dancing like demons.

As the storm subsided, my doubts vanished. I walked through the wet streets at the end of the day, and I rejoiced once more in my safe and genial existence. I climbed the double-decker and traveled back to my room. My Israeli landlady, a good-natured and obese woman, whose chief pleasure in life was preparing sumptuous meals for her slim husband, asked me about my day in the office. I told her about my success in translating a letter for my boss.

"Nu," she said, "you do have a bachelor's degree in English after all; why should a little letter be a problem?" As she laughed heartily, her eyes began to water.

"No, not a problem," I said, miffed.

"You are a bright lady," she added, still laughing.

"Yes, but when I came, I was told that my English was bookish. I worked to simplify it, and today my boss was pleased with my down-to-earth translation."

"That's very good, Shelly'nka, some people work to make their language more sophisticated, some work to make it less. . . . Each to his own," she laughed. When she saw the hurt expression on my face, she relented, "Would you like to join us in the TV room? 'Candid Camera' is on."

"No, thank you," I said, dispirited. "I'd rather read."

I entered my large room. The big, comfortable bed was inviting. I showered, undressed, put on my pajamas, and stretched out on the bed. I turned on the lamp and picked up a book of poems by Dylan Thomas. She won't laugh at me, I thought. I'll show her that I can still read "sophisticated language." In five minutes I was fast asleep. Next I heard my landlady knocking on the door, waking me up for work.

During that year, I met Dr. Sadov, a gynecologist from Hadassah Hospital in Jerusalem, who was sent to England to study family planning. I liked him at once. He was a tall man, with jolly blue eyes that often lit up in wonder, and a dimpled smile. Since his family stayed in Jerusalem, and he was alone in London, he asked me to accompany him to concerts and the theater. I readily agreed, and we soon became regular companions. I expected Sadov to flirt with me, but he did not. Warm and honorable, he became my friend, the father I'd been seeking all along.

One evening, after a theater production at the Old Vic, Sadov and I decided to dine at a nearby restaurant. At some point, Sadov asked me about my plans.

"Oh," I said, "I don't know. I don't have any specific plans."

Sadov looked at me quizzically. "Didn't you tell me some time ago that you wanted to write a master's thesis on Joyce?"

"Yes, I did," I smiled awkwardly. "But that was then."

"Then?" Sadov asked, a whimsical expression on his face. "When was then? Ten years ago? It must have been only three months. When did you have a chance to change your mind?"

Outside a light snow had begun to fall. "Oh, I don't know," I blurted in growing discomfort.

"You don't know?" Sadov's blue eyes gazed at me in astonishment. "You make such an important decision, and you don't even know you made it?" I was silent. "Didn't you tell me," Sadov spoke again, "that you were accepted for the master's program at . . . where was it?"

"Sheffield."

"Yes, at Sheffield University?" His blue stare searched my face.

"Yes," I said feebly, slowly sipping my cooling coffee. "I was accepted. But I can't go there."

"You can't?" Sadov's mustache quivered. "Why can't you?"

"Because I have a job at the embassy. How can I leave it?"

"Let me understand this," Sadov took a deep breath and sat straight and towering in his chair. "You are giving up a master's degree, an opportunity to develop your mind for a *secretary's* job at the embassy?"

My eyes sought refuge in the falling flakes outside, but Sadov was unrelenting. "Some people are made for secretarial jobs. I understand that. But *you?* You want to sit forever at the desk, answering phones? May I ask why?"

Like silent messengers, tears were gathering at the back of my throat. "I know the job already," I mumbled, "and they won't be too pleased if I leave them."

"Come on," Sadov smiled. "You don't *really* believe that, do you? They'd find a replacement for you in one day."

I squashed my cigarette stub and tried to swallow the lump in my throat. "I like my job."

"What do you like about it?"

"I am earning money, am I not?"

"And you'd be doing the same thing, year in year out, for how many years? And what will you do with the money you earn, buy a house in Chelsea? No, the money will never be enough for *that,*" he laughed.

"Perhaps I'll find somebody to marry. . . ." I muttered.

Sadov's face lit up in a wondrous smile. "So you are going to wait around, like Cinderella, for Prince Charming to rescue you from the mind-numbing labors at the embassy?"

"I am no Cinderella," I flared up.

"I was hoping you'd say that," Sadov chuckled. "Of course. You can't wait around for things to happen. You have a good mind, Shelly," his tone mellowed. "Go and study. Get your degree. Do something worthwhile with your life."

The lump in my throat dissolved into tears. "I can't do it," I mumbled.

"You can't do what?" Sadov asked kindly.

"I can't get my master's degree because I am not good enough."

"So many people get their master's degree, and *you* can't do it?"

"It's so difficult. A strange place. I don't even know where to start. And it's not my native language, either."

"It may be difficult," Sadov agreed. "But so what? Would you rather hide in an embassy corner where your military bosses would give you silly orders all day?"

I raised my eyes and looked at him. Nobody had presented me with a worthier challenge in a sweeter manner. My anger and sorrow melted away. When we left the restaurant, it had stopped snowing; the night air was cold and bracing. As we were walking to the Underground, I gazed at a piece of clear sky dotted with stars. Everything around me looked new, as if I were seeing it for the first time. Everything snapped into focus, as if I had been awakened from a deep sleep. I was filled with energy, with a great longing to read and study again, to find myself, to live up to the possibilities of my new name.

In the following weeks, I decided to move to Sheffield. One day in April, I announced my resignation to my boss and put an end to months of indecision. I felt lighthearted; I was revving to go. Once I made up my mind, my fears vanished. Spring was in the air. The rains let up, and although drizzles were common, the sun sometimes came out of the blanket of clouds and shone the whole day. Ducks and swans returned to the ponds, flowers bloomed, and the trees were sprouting fresh leaves. "In the spring," I used to say to Sadov, "no city is as lovely as London, except for Jerusalem." "Of course, Jerusalem," he rejoined. We continued our outings, yet our meetings were touched by sadness. While the world was renewing its vigor, our friendship, we knew, was coming to an end. A few months later Sadov would be back in Jerusalem, and I would travel to Sheffield, to start studying for my master's degree.

SHEFFIELD

The car was making its way up the steep hill flanked by houses on the right and a basalt stone hedge on the left. Groaning, the car labored to mount the stubborn hill that was rising higher as it turned onto Redcar Road. From the top, the view was spellbinding: a wide vista of sky opened up and underneath it the city displayed its red-roof houses, church steeples, tall trees, a pond or two, and meandering streets and alleys. In the far distance, the rolling moors melted into the horizon.

Sheffield. There my uncle Avram and his wife Sharona brought me and my suitcases on a cool Sunday afternoon in the fall of 1965. My uncle, ten years my mother's junior, was then an officer in the Israeli Air Force, stationed for a year in a small place called Dunstable, near London. I was glad that he was able to accompany me to the place that I still dreaded—Sheffield.

The house where I had rented a room by phone from London was the third or the fourth on the right of Redcar Road. It was a typical two-story English stone house with a pointed roof and front bay windows, surrounded by bushes and a low stone fence with a wooden gate. We knocked on the door. When it opened with a creak, I gaped. The woman who greeted us must have come out of a Dickens novel: she was old, perhaps in her eighties, stooped but firm on her feet, her blue eyes peering at us angrily through a pair of fragile glasses that rested crookedly on her beaked nose. Her snow-white hair stood on edge around her face. "Yes?" she asked in a hoarse voice. We identified ourselves. I was fervently hoping that we had made a mistake, but, no, it was the right house. This ancient woman with the flying white hair was indeed my new landlady. She showed us the way to my room. It was a spacious and meticulously clean room with a fireplace and antique English furniture, overlooking a lovely garden at the back of the house. "It's a nice place," my uncle said. The landlady asked us if we needed anything else. We said no, and she disappeared, but it seemed that her white hair, like the Cheshire cat's smile, was still floating in the room. "It's a nice place." Avram repeated his initial impression. Sharona agreed. "It's really a clean place, you know." Avram brought the suitcases in. "So," he turned to me, "What do you think?"

I was so miserable I could barely talk. "Did you see her? She looks like a witch."

Avram laughed. "She's not a witch. Just old. She'll be all right. After awhile, she'll probably cook chicken soup for you."

"There isn't even a shower here," I grumbled, as I was examining the bathroom.

"Look, *meida'le,* this is not home. You know it, and I know it. But don't forget, you wanted it. Besides," Avram lit a cigarette, "You don't have to stay in this room. In a few months you can move to another room somewhere else. What is the problem, eh?"

"I hate it here."

"Do you remember," Avram smiled, "what I used to tell you when you were young and didn't want to do something you had to do? *Ein breirah,* I used to say. There is no choice. You must face reality and make the best of it. But listen, Shelly, my dear, we have to head back. Okay? You have my phone number. Call me tomorrow from the university. Tell me how it's going." He winked at me, and then they were gone.

Only in nightmares did I ever revisit a night like my first one in Sheffield. There I was, alone in a strange Yorkshire town, without a phone, without a car, without a soul I knew except for that old lady with the flying white hair. The neighboring room was also occupied by a student; I knocked on the door but no one answered. I didn't know what the town looked like, or where the university was. I walked out to the front of the house, but no one was even walking a dog. Where was everybody? Was this a ghost town? Was my landlady, whom I saw peeping out of the window, the only inhabitant? Did anybody live up or down the street? Did Empson really exist, or did I dream him up? Night fell. The darkness deepened. Silence. I returned to my room, unpacked, put *Dubliners* and *A Portrait of the Artist as a Young Man* on the bookshelf, ate the dinner Sharona prepared for me, and sat down in the brown leather armchair.

Would somebody please talk to me? Say one word? Say I exist? Let me just hear a human voice. Is this what a solitary cell feels like? Why am I here? Why didn't I stay in London? Or in Israel? What am I looking for? Why can't I find my place? How did I ever contrive to live under one roof with an old, white-haired English lady, who would probably slit my throat with a sharp knife as soon as I closed my eyes? Did I come to this remote Midlands town to find my death? I could see the caption in the newspapers: "A young Israeli woman, who traveled to Sheffield apparently to study James Joyce, was brutally murdered last night. Details about the murderer are still unknown." Yeah, I know who she is. Let me tell you. My ancient landlady, that's who. Thank God for electricity. I won't turn off the light all night, no matter what *she* says. No use looking at books, I can't read anyway. If I just had a TV, or a radio, at least. Who's there? A rasping sound outside. I jumped up from my chair, my heart galloping. That's it, I thought in panic, this is my end. *Imma,* HELP!

The front door opened. My neighbor, Jane, a young redhead, a doctoral student in biology, had just returned. To me, she looked like an angel. I rushed to introduce myself. We talked excitedly in the hall, until a white head emerged from the opposite room saying, "Shhhhh!" We retreated into Jane's room and talked for an hour. When I returned to my room, I turned off the light and went to sleep.

"I WILL NOT SERVE. . . ."

Next morning I set out early to discover the university and Professor Empson, who was still only a voice on the phone to me. As I was walking down the steep hill, everything looked new. This is the real England, I mused, as I was leaving behind the handsome houses on my street, going down another street that exhibited big, grey apartment houses. Yes, this is England, I reflected, passing two women with rollers in their hair who were cheerfully chatting at the entrance to one of the houses. How strange, I thought as I was listening to the musical lilt of their Yorkshire accent. How am I ever going to understand this language? No Israel, no embassy, no Hebrew. No one to help. Alone. Among strangers who speak a funny language. With a landlady who gives me the chills. Silence, exile, and cunning, indeed. Yes, Joyce was brave. He wanted to create an image of beauty, to forge the consciousness of his race, but what do *I* want? What is *my* mission here? Adding another master's thesis to the stacks that are now being written on him? And what is it that I want to say about him? Do I have an original idea, a *thesis?* What will I tell Empson? Shall I say, like Stephen Dedalus, I am an exile, trying to learn from him how to be brave, how to fly by the nets? Passing by the tennis courts near the university, I slowed down. Empson will laugh at me and ask me to do something useful like explore the Hebraic influence on Milton.

The English department was located on the third or fourth floor of a modern building next to the library. I stopped in the hall to take an elevator, but there was none. Instead there was a paternoster, which consisted of moving platforms without doors, onto which one simply . . . jumped. I looked at this moving thing in dread. What if I miss a step, will my head be decapitated? Although people laughed and said that there was nothing to fear, I froze. I looked for the stairs and noticed that I was the only one using them.

When I reached the English department, I saw a man with glasses, a notepad, and a funny beard that had its roots under the chin, dragging his feet quickly across the hall. *This* must be Empson, I thought. In a minute, he shuffled back to the office, absorbed in his notepad. I introduced myself to the secretary, who took me to the professor's spacious office. Empson was reading. The secretary and I stood in reverent silence. Finally he lifted his eyes and said, "Yes?"

"Professor Empson," the secretary said, "this young lady is Shelly Shapira from Israel."

"Oh, yes, yes," Empson said, getting up from his chair to shake my hand. The secretary left the room. "Have a seat, please," he added. I sat on the edge of the chair. "You have some digs already?"

"Some what?"

"A place to stay, a room, or a flat, yes?" He glanced at me briefly above the rim of his glasses.

"Oh, yes, thank you."

He was looking for something on his desk and finally picked up a file and leafed through it. "You said that you can read Hebrew, didn't you?"

I knew it! "Of course, I can read Hebrew, Professor Empson. Hebrew is my native language." Tell him about Joyce, I urged myself.

"Excellent, excellent," the professor said and smiled at me for the first time. "Milton was influenced by the Hebrew, you know that," he looked at me, "and you are the best person to write a thesis on the subject. Have you read Werblowsky's book?"

"No," I whispered.

"That's a good place to start, Miss Shapira. It's Miss, isn't it?" I nodded. "You can find the article in the library. Good day." He got up, grabbed his notepad, mumbled something, and vanished.

That's just wonderful, I fumed to myself, as I clutched my Joyce books and walked out of the office. I see a professor and I melt. When will I learn? I walked to the stairs, changed my mind, and before I had time to think, jumped on the paternoster. On the ground floor, I jumped off it and felt a momentary elation. But I still couldn't say no to Empson. In fact, I walked straight to the library and read the book he assigned me. When I finished it, my mind felt numb. Yes, Milton was influenced by the Hebraic tradition, but what more could I say about it? Why should I want to say more about it? Because, I heard my practical voice, you can please both Empson and Halkin, your English and Hebrew masters. You'd kill six birds with one stone. Look at the professional benefits here and at home. Besides, if you work on something that belongs to you, you won't feel so isolated.

No, I retorted. Have I come here to study Hebrew? Didn't Joyce say, "I will not serve that in which I no longer believe, whether it call itself my home, my fatherland, or my church"? It is *him* I must study; *him* I must follow. What can I learn from Milton?

But one doesn't always do exactly what one wants. Sometimes one has to plan, to calculate, to use *cunning*. Isn't this Joyce's own word?

Yes, I countered, but he used his cunning to escape his home and his language, not to be trapped in them. He used it to create art. He took off in "an ecstasy of flight. . . ."

But you haven't come here to create art.

What does it matter? My research is as urgent and personal.

All right. You want to take off, take off. But since you don't have your Dedalus's wings, make sure you don't miss the canvas. . . .

A day or two later, I made an appointment with Professor Empson, steeling myself against fear. He received me in his office and was, again, reading. I sat firmly in the chair and waited. "Have you read the book?" he said without lifting his eyes. "Yes," I said. "So what do you think?" he now looked at me.

"I must admit to you, Professor Empson, that I am not interested in the subject."

"Oh?" Empson raised his eyebrows.

"When I came to England," I steadied my hands, "I did not want to get involved with Hebrew. I came here to get away from Hebrew." Now he'll throw me out of the program, I thought, for having misled him.

"Hmm, is that so?" Empson was stroking his beard. "I hadn't thought of that. For many years, I was looking for a scholar who could read both Hebrew and English, and who could write English as well as you do. Such a study could be quite a feather in your cap. But you don't wear a cap," he chuckled.

Hearing his compliment, I wanted to take everything back, but it was too late.

"And what is it that you want to work on?" Empson asked.

"James Joyce."

"Really?" he intoned. "Interesting. Interesting. What subject in Joyce do you propose to work on?"

"I am not sure. Something to do with his escape from the nets, or the moral history of his country, or himself. . . ." I was getting entangled.

"Fine," Empson said. "Do what you want to do. We have a bright professor here in the department, Mr. Roper, who is interested in modern literature, and he, I am sure, would be glad to be your mentor. I'll write him a note. Have a good day, Miss Shapira."

In one fell swoop, I was banished from Empson's kingdom. I chose Sheffield because of Empson. I admired his *Seven Types of Ambiguity,* and I even knew some of his poems by heart. "It is the pain, it is the pain endures." Now I had lost him. But at least I could start my work on Joyce, I consoled myself.

Roper was an attentive mentor. He taught me how to organize my ideas, balance my sentences, and sharpen my arguments. In many subtle and kind ways he challenged my thinking and urged me to improve my writing. Most importantly, he understood my need to work on Joyce and believed that I was equal to the task.

Roper became my best academic ally. After I turned down his topic, Empson hardly spoke to me. The only time we engaged in a conversation occurred during the oral defense of my master's thesis. Empson, the internal examiner, and Roper, my mentor, were supposed to help me defend my thesis against the criticism of the external examiner. Ironically however, the external examiner liked my thesis well enough, but it was Empson who attacked it. As I was struggling with his astute scrutiny, I had to admit that I got my just deserts.

FENCING WITH JOHN

Jane, my neighbor in the old woman's house, introduced me to John, her biology professor, and his wife Sophie, a painter. John was a bearded, jolly, robust man; Sophie was a beautiful, tall woman with soft brown eyes and short blond hair. We three became fast friends. We went out to restaurants, concerts, painting exhibitions, and fencing sessions. Sophie and John, both accomplished fencers, tried to teach me how to parry and thrust, but in my fencing suit I felt no more adroit than Sancho Panza in medieval armor, and after awhile I gave it up. Still I enjoyed watching my friends' spirited games.

In some ways, Sophie reminded me of my mother. Both women had a proud, Nordic beauty and both were lovers of art. The walls in our Haifa villa were covered with paintings by Israeli artists. Sophie's walls were similarly covered with paintings—her own. When I came to her house, I felt instantly at home, buoyed by swirling oranges, blues, purples, and mauves. Yet it was not merely the paintings that drew me to Sophie, but the longing I detected in them for warm climates and love. Like me, Sophie was an orphan who had been raised by her grandmother. We were both wanderers at heart, wistful, dissatisfied, attracted to the distant and the mysterious. That was our deepest bond.

Sophie and I became good friends. We walked for hours on the moors; we cooked meals in Sophie's spacious country kitchen; we shared stories; we discussed books and Sophie's art; and we marveled, with deep sighs, at the cocky assurance of John, who thought he knew everything and needed, we knew, to be taught a lesson in humility. We therefore united our intellectual and artistic forces to render chinks in his armor.

Once Sophie and John came to visit my room on Redcar Road, which was by then fully equipped with a radio, a stereo set, and numerous new records. When they knocked on the door, a head of flying white hair looked out of one of the rooms. My landlady hadn't yet offered me chicken soup, but she no longer seemed malevolent. I motioned to her that the guests were mine. With the coffee and the cookies, I put on my favorite music, Jacque Loussier's *Play Bach*. Since I had presented myself as a lover of classical music, I now had to withstand John's jocular taunts directed at my deviation from the straight and the narrow.

"This is jazz," John said laughing, "not classical music, and certainly not Bach!"

"No," I protested, "these are Bach's tunes!"

"Yes," John looked at me gleefully. "But listen to what Loussier *does* with them. He is giving them modern rhythms that Bach knew nothing about; he is using them for his own *improvisations*. Bach was interested in formal structures, not in improvisations."

"Why are rhythms important? This is Bach's music. The rest is mere interpretation. Gould does one thing, Loussier another."

John was rubbing his beard, thinking of a different way to explain my mistake to me. Sophie rejoined our conversation. "Shelly knows this field better than you do, John," she pouted at him, "she's working on her master's degree in English."

"I know that," John smiled at her, "but what does this have to do with *Play Bach?*"

"Oh?" Sophie lunged her blade, "you are a scientist. What do you know about art? We, artists, are sensitive to all kinds of artistic expressions."

"But Shelly is not an artist," John parried. "She is writing a thesis on an artist, and he wasn't even a musician."

"Yes," Sophie responded with a running attack, "but she knows much more than *you* do about music and the arts, in general, wouldn't you agree? What do you do all day? Sit in your laboratory. Have you read *books* about Bach, as she has? Have you gone to *hundreds* of Bach concerts as she has? Wouldn't you agree that she is much more of an *expert* in these things than you are?"

With a mischievous glint in his eye, John prepared to close in on Sophie. "With all due respect to Shelly's knowledge, Sophie, Loussier is not playing classical Bach here, but jazz Bach. It is still beautiful, of course. It is an art form, yes, but it is not the same as classical music. It says so on the sleeve. Read this explanation." He waved the sleeve triumphantly. We stared at it glumly. I knew that it would be gallant at that point to concede, but in my deep-rooted Israeli stubbornness I wouldn't give in an inch. John finally laughed off the argument, and we all went out to dinner, but Sophie and I continued to look for opportunities to prove the mighty John wrong.

HAM AND JEWISH HISTORY

Soon Sophie's home became my hiding place from my Jewish and Israeli identity. I was attracted to Christian symbols and art. On many occasions, I traveled with Sophie to remote antique stores in search of Russian icons. I remember her ecstasy whenever she found one in some small shop. As I observed her caressing a dusty and placid gold leaf Madonna, I was strangely stirred. How did this formal, religious icon inspire her? Her own paintings were so different—Dionysian I'd call them. I gazed at the icon again and felt repulsed. Why was *I* fascinated by this forbidden image? Yet when Sophie hung it on the wall, my eyes were riveted to it.

Sophie's best dish was ham and pineapple. I could not pretend, of course, that I ate only kosher food, but I had never eaten ham. Ham was the big *no,* the great sin that would forever separate me from my father, who never mentioned the word, and could not even hint at it, without a shudder and a quickly muttered *tfu, tfu.* One night, Sophie had prepared chicken for me, but I was drawn to the juicy ham and decided to eat it even if I were condemned to perdition. I traveled on the Sabbath and usually forgot to fast on Yom Kippur. Why couldn't I eat ham? So I sat and ate the delectable ham with Sophie and John, feeling that it was to them, rather than to my father's shadow, that I truly belonged.

When the 1967 war broke out, I turned my back not only on my father but on my country.

The sleepy Sheffield community was rudely awakened by the war. Hour by hour, the radios and the TVs in the student union blasted news about the war. Fierce debates between pro-Arab and pro-Israeli students erupted. Every morning a Syrian student I knew taunted me with Syria's radio news about a resounding Israeli defeat. People asked me about the outcome of the war as if I had a direct link with the Israeli chief of staff. I was suddenly at the center of attention, not as Shelly who left Israel to study the Irish exile, Joyce, but as an expert on Israeli affairs. The attention flattered but embarrassed me; I realized that after two years in exile, I knew no more about my country than those Britishers did. But I nevertheless expressed the confidence that Israel would win the war. I know the Israeli character, I said. When we have no choice, we fight; not even a united Arab front could defeat us. Shortly afterward the Israeli triumph became clear even to my Syrian acquaintance, and I was regarded as a miniprophet, a bona fide Israeli.

At the start of the war, I heard reports about thousands of volunteers from America, England, and other places, who hopped on planes and landed in Tel Aviv to help the Israelis. I was torn by guilt. Jews who were not even Israelis traveled to my country in droves, and I was here, hiding in Sheffield. Wasn't it my duty to go back home? I took my tormented questioning to Sophie and John, but they did not know what to say. John was inclined to advise me to go back home, but Sophie thought that that would be silly and wasteful. My state of indecision became acute. Finally I called my mother. *She,* I thought, would be able to put an end to my agitation. When I told her that I worried about the country, she laughed. "What can *you* do about it? Don't worry, we'll be just fine without you."

"But so many volunteers are coming to Israel, and it is not even their country. Shouldn't I go back to help?"

My mother laughed again. "How can *you* help? You are a woman. Can you drive a tank? Can you shoot down an enemy plane? Who needs you here?

If you were at least a nurse, or a doctor as I always wanted you to be, I'd understand. Then you could help the wounded, but you are an English student. Will you go to the front to give them lectures on Joyce? Ha, ha, ha."

I laughed too. That was funny. I told Sophie and John that my mother said all I can do to help Israel is give lectures to soldiers on Joyce. They laughed. "Oh, good, good," Sophie said as I put the phone down, "now you'll be staying with us, and we'll protect you."

Relieved by my mother's breezy dismissal of my quandary, I stayed with my friends. Later, an afterthought crossed my mind that if my country were destroyed, I wouldn't be without a home in the world. I shamefully dismissed the thought. How could I think of saving my own skin? Where was my loyalty to my people? What kind of an Israeli was I? Perhaps not much of one, I reflected guiltily. If all Israelis were like me, there wouldn't be an Israel. But didn't I want to escape Israeli nationalism? Didn't I want to find ways in which Shelly could express herself and control her own life?

"COULDN'T [S]HE FLY A BIT HIGHER THAN THAT, EH?"

In the fall before the 1967 war, I moved to a room on Crookes Moore Road. Situated on the second story of a dingy, faded red house, my room was undeniably ugly. Covered with a repellent wallpaper and furnished in a helter-skelter way with an old dresser with peeling paint, a small closet with creaking doors, a narrow, hard bed under the window, and a small hot plate and some chipped dishes in the "kitchen" corner, the room looked like the impoverished, orphaned brother of my previous abode on Redcar Road. "Oh, no, Shelly," Sophie exclaimed. "Don't take this room! It looks so depressing!" I agreed, but I was attracted to one promising piece of furniture: a huge and sturdy desk on which I could pile my typewriter and all my books and notes, and there would still be space enough on it for a dancer to execute a pirouette. I was also pleased with the large windows, which let in abundant light even when the sky was grey, and with the jolly landlady, who lived downstairs with her husband and five or six children and who minded her own business.

After cleaning the room and putting my clothes, books, and miscellaneous paraphernalia in place, I looked at it again. Yes, it was my own room now, but it needed something personal, one thing of beauty. I remembered Sophie's painting depicting shimmering blue flowers in a blue vase. That's it, I said to myself, I must have this painting now. I bought it, hung it on the wall above my desk, and whenever I got up, or sat down to work, I was spurred on by its radiance.

My thesis on Joyce was progressing rather well. I had to revise the *Dubliners* chapter twice, but my chapter on the *Portrait* elicited Roper's modest praise. "This is worthwhile disagreeing with," he said. Spanning some 120 pages, the thesis was my chief pride, the testimony to Shelly's worth. All I had to do was write a chapter on *Ulysses*. But here I ran into an unexpected difficulty. I just did not understand the book. To me, *Ulysses* was a foreign world, complex, abstract, symbolic, a bewildering ocean. Instead of being "father" and "artificer," Joyce became a stranger—aloof and inaccessible. How could I write a brilliant essay on *Ulysses* when I couldn't understand it? And if I couldn't write a chapter on *Ulysses,* how could I get my degree? And without a degree, how could I go back home?

Looking for a quick solution, I turned to the critics. They explained Joyce's world to me; they interpreted *Ulysses* for me. Particularly impressive was S. L. Goldberg's book on Joyce, *The Classical Temper,* which defined moral responsibility, self-knowledge, and compassion as the pivotal elements in Joyce's humanistic vision. The book taught me much about ethical behavior, but it spelled disaster for the chapter I was trying to write. I could not escape Goldberg's interpretation. My writing was becoming a quilt of quotes from his book. Like Stephen Dedalus in the "Proteus" episode, I felt that I was a "pretender," but I was unable to change my course. The more I wrote, the farther away I drifted from my own honest voice which, as Joyce knew, had to be won over piecemeal and pressed out "slowly and humbly."

"ALL YOU NEED IS LOVE"

It was at that time, in the spring of 1967, that I fell in love with a handsome gentile, Derek, a premed student. If I were unconsciously looking for an escape from my Joycean difficulties, I could not have found a more attractive one.

The rooms in the house on Crookes Moore Road were let mainly to students; there were two or three on my floor, and two on the third floor. We shared the one bathroom on the second floor, which sometimes meant subjecting our bladders and bowels to a spartan discipline. To avoid the morning rush, I usually took my bath at night, when everybody was asleep. On one particular night, however, the bathroom was occupied. I waited. Half an hour passed and it was still occupied. I went back to my room, made myself a cup of coffee, and read a book. Twenty minutes passed. I looked again. Still occupied. I heard the happy splashing of water. Yawning, I went back to my book. Fifteen minutes. Still busy. My anger was stirring. True, not many people used the bathroom at night, and even I sometimes lingered in the tub, but *so* long? I peeped again. Still occupied. I stepped out of my room and knocked three times on the bathroom door. Then I scuttled back to my room and waited. Nothing happened. I ventured out again, rehearsing angry retorts in my mind, and once more knocked on the door. But before my fist descended on it the second time, it opened. There stood Derek in a bathrobe, tall, slim, with light brown hair and thick eyebrows, staring at me apologetically. My anger dissolved. I smiled at him, hoping he did not see my scowl and lifted fist. "Forgive me," he said in a deep, resonant voice, which contrasted with his delicate features. "I should not have stayed so long." Clutching the soap and towel in my hand, I said that it was perfectly all right, nothing at all, I was not in any hurry, of course. Then we introduced ourselves to each other, and he smiled. What a smile—like ripples in a sunlit lake.

I was smitten.

The following morning I got up earlier than usual, in eager anticipation. I *had* to see him again. Did he really exist, or was he an apparition? I looked outside my window. Heavy footsteps were clamoring down the stairs. The door opened, and there he was, elegantly dressed in a tie and blue shirt, his suede jacket flung on his arm in captivating abandon. Yes, he existed, and what's more, he was even more handsome than he appeared the night before in his bathrobe. He entered a red car and drove away. What is it? I asked myself. Am I falling in love, after two brief glances at the person? Am I out of my mind? Do I even know who he is? He probably does not even remember me. This is sheer madness, Shelly, I chided myself, go to work.

But I couldn't read one page of *Ulysses* the whole day. I went out for a walk, sat in the library for an hour—to no avail. I had to see him again. Finally I returned to my room and waited for the red car to arrive. When it did, Derek emerged from it and approached the door; my blood was racing. I opened the door to my room and pretended to be walking to the bathroom. We met, and as he lifted his eyes, I knew that he remembered our chance nocturnal meeting.

I invited him to my room. We talked till three in the morning, excitedly, as if there would never be time enough to tell all, to unlock the doors of the lonely heart, to share, with trembling delight, the multitudes of secret stories.

Before he left, he kissed me. Waves of joy swept my body. Yes. This was love; I was sure. He was the one I had been waiting for. He must be the first to. . . . Yes. Why not? The time had come to jump. . . . But, I cautioned myself, Derek was not Jewish. Didn't Reuven warn me that a goy could not be trusted? "Love, shmove," he used to say. "No matter how much he loves you, one day he will call you 'a dirty Jew,' and what will you do then?" How could I tell Reuven that I was madly in love with a goy? Impossible. Forget him, Shelly.

For a few days I managed to avoid Derek. But instead of reading *Ulysses,* I read *Lady Chatterley's Lover.* I carried the book with me everywhere. Lawrence was the first to tell me what I always wanted to believe, in spite of my family proclivities, that sex and tenderness were not necessarily divided but could dwell together in the minds and bodies of lovers, and that love was "more lovely than anything ever could be." I was moved by the moment when Mellors watches Connie holding a newborn chick in her hands, and he is fired up, not only by desire, not only by gentleness, but by a fine fusion of the two feelings, as "compassion flamed in his bowels for her." Ah, I thought, this is beautiful. Would I, like Connie, also experience ecstasy, I wondered, those "new strange thrills rippling" inside me?

What, on earth, are you thinking about? I put an abrupt end to my fantasies. Even suppose Derek and I become lovers, what then? I mused as I walked to the corner grocery. Would I consent to make Sheffield my home? I looked around me at the grime-covered houses. Is this where I want to live? I shuddered. No, I want to go back to Israel. And how could I marry a goy? Ham is one thing, but marriage is another. If I marry a goy, I warned myself, I'd be crossing the soul's Rubicon.

By the time I entered the store, I was distressed and confused. I bought milk, rolls, cookies, and chocolate bars. I felt the onslaught of depression and stocked up, as I used to do in those days, on sweets. Then I walked slowly back to my room. The red car was parked outside, but I was too despondent to notice. I put my hand on the knob, and there he was, standing right in front of me, smiling. "Can I help you?" he asked, reaching for my grocery bags. "Thank you," I said, surprised. "Would you like to come in?"

When I remembered the mess my room was in, with things strewn about, the bed unmade, and *Lady Chatterley's Lover* lying open in a prominent place on my desk, I regretted my hasty invitation, but it was too late. He was already in the room, in his full slender height, looking at me with searching brown eyes. I laid my groceries down, and with them the heavy weight that just a moment before so oppressed my spirit. Forgetting Israel and Jewish history, I turned to him. He gathered me in his arms. I drew close and stroked his hair and neck. The thrill of that touch was overpowering. Muttering "Shelly, my Shelly," Derek bent down and gently kissed my face and lips while unbuttoning his shirt. I put my flushed face against his chest. His long and lithe fingers groped for my breasts. We stretched out on the bed, seeking each other's nakedness. Thus, after twenty-five years on this earth, without asking my mother's permission, my stepfather's approval, or my father's blessing, without waiting for the wedding bells, or the termination of my thesis, or my return home, I, Shelly Shapira, born Haya, finally sacrificed my long-preserved virginity to the gentile Derek, in a swoon of loving desire.

Afterward, I was slowly coming back, speechless and dumbfounded. I am still me, I thought. Wasn't I supposed to have crossed the great divide to womanhood? Didn't everybody at home talk about *this* as the decisive moment in a woman's life, the watershed of her femininity, the instance of her fall from or rise (depending on circumstances) to power and glory? Where was it? I was still the same me, except for a strange pain between my legs. The blood on the sheet made Derek curiously proud, but I didn't even know if it was my wounded hymen that was bleeding, or my period that arrived shortly afterward. Besides, where were the rippling thrills, the "flapping overlapping of soft flames" that Lawrence's Connie so rapturously experienced? I felt cheated.

But Derek stayed with me till the break of dawn, caressing, coaxing, rubbing the sting out of my disappointment. He reassured me that it was not my fault, that such things happened often. Was it on that night, or was it on the next day, when he rushed to the store and bought me flowers, or perhaps on the next weekend, when he took me in his red car to visit a water reservoir that I fell in love with him? I do not remember. But it was not long before I wrapped my life around him.

At times we set out with Sophie and John on short trips to the rural environs of Sheffield, traveling on winding mossy roads, passing through wooded glens, and dining in picturesque country pubs. I was enchanted by the pastoral landscape. I used to think, I really love it here. I love Derek, I love my friends, I love the English countryside, what more do I need? Why not stop my wanderings and pitch my tent right here, in remote, misty Sheffield? All I wanted was to be near Derek. So what if he was a British gentile? Didn't Ruth the Moabite also marry a foreigner, Boaz of Judah? Of course, to Jews Ruth was the "woman of valor" because she married one of *us,* a Jew from Bethlehem, but to her, to *her,* he was a foreigner. And yet she didn't hesitate to leave her "mother's home." She followed Naomi to Judah, married Boaz, and according to the Midrash, converted to Judaism. Why then should I waver? Was Ruth "right" and I "wrong" just because I was moving in the opposite direction, from Jerusalem to Moab-Albion? Who was there to tell me which direction was the right one? Why couldn't I create my own destiny as Ruth created hers? Did she ask anybody's permission?

And yet, when I went home for a short visit, in July or August after the 1967 war, my confidence petered out. When my mother heard that I had a boyfriend ("Finally, at last, I have a normal daughter!") she was jubilant. She already saw me as a bride and started planning the wedding and her visits to England. Reuven was more circumspect. He wanted to know if Derek was Jewish. I wavered. How could I possibly tell them that he was not?

"Well," I muttered, looking sideways, "he is not exactly Jewish, but he is not *not* Jewish either."

"What are you saying?" Reuven asked. "I don't understand you. How could he be both Jewish and non-Jewish?"

"Derek is one-eighth Jewish," I lied. "He told me. His great-grandmother was Jewish, and he himself really likes and respects Jews."

"I am glad to hear that, but how do you know he respects Jews?"

"Oh," I hesitated, "I don't know. I know he respects me, and he even asked me to teach him Hebrew. He already knows how to write Shelly in Hebrew. Here, look at what he wrote on the back of this picture: Shelly *sheli* in Hebrew."

Reuven stared at Derek's love note. "Come, Dina," he said to my mother. "Look at this," he laughed. "The guy must be serious, eh?"

My mother looked and remarked on how handsome Derek was. My visiting grandmother, who used to watch the weekly wrestling match on TV to see "two goyim beating each other up," now looked at the picture and said, "*Feh,* Haya'le. He is not Jewish. Don't marry an uncircumcised goy."

"But he *is* circumcised, *savta,*" I blurted.

Reuven looked at me and roared in laughter. "How do you know that?" Soon everybody was laughing while I was blushing crimson red.

In a moment, Reuven's expression became more serious. "England! How can I come to England? How will I talk to my grandson when I don't know a word of English? I'd rather you married somebody who is eight-eighth Jewish. Why do you need this headache? Why can't you marry an Israeli?"

"I don't like Israeli men," I answered glumly. "I can't talk to them. They don't understand me."

"Have you tried them all?" Reuven chuckled. "How do you know they don't understand you? Just don't mention Joyce to them. You don't have to show every man how much you know."

It was my mother who now came to my rescue, urging me to go on with my plans. "What does it matter if he is Jewish or not Jewish, Israeli or English? Really, Reuven, stop this nonsense. Don't listen to him, Shelly. If Derek loves you and you love him, get married. All you need is love."

LOVE'S LABOR'S LOST

Derek never talked about our future. The uncertainty of our relationship was trying, especially to an impatient Israeli like me, who, in spite of her Joycean defiance of the "nets," still held dear her country's belief that a woman who approached the twenty-sixth year of her life still languishing in her unmarried state had good cause to be ashamed of herself. I did everything in my power to secure his love. During my visit in Israel, I fasted and lost weight. When he picked me up at the railway station in Sheffield, he was impressed with my slim shape. He loved it, but he was still silent about his intentions.

I told my worry to Sophie, but she did not see any cause for concern. "Oh, Shelly," she reassured me, "he will marry you in the end." Which end? I wondered. It would probably be *my* end before he ever proposes. At times Derek looked so deep and long into my eyes that I held my breath, waiting for the magic words, but then I had to breathe again, and all Derek said was something about a piece of lint on my sweater. The more I wanted his proposal, the better it eluded me.

Good times were still abundant. I liked going on Friday nights to the student union bar for a drink with Derek and his friends. Derek, who started me off on a number of things, also taught me to drink. At first he offered me beer, but I disliked its bitter taste. Then he tried spiked cider. The sweet taste of the drink deceived me; I gulped it down before I realized that the room was spinning and that I was giggling silly. From that night on, I was eager for the weekly draught of Derek's vintage.

Yet there were tensions. Sober or intoxicated, I could not climax. No matter what Derek did, and he was probably as inventive as any Lawrencian lover, I still did not experience Connie's "pure deepening whirlpools of sensation." Disappointed with Lawrence's false promises, I put *Lady Chatterley's Lover* aside. It was all Lawrence's fault, anyway, I thought. He made it sound so easy, but it was not, not for me. Mellors blamed the women for their failure to climax, as if they held back on purpose. But I did not hold back on purpose. I just couldn't, and the more I strained, the farther I strayed from Lawrence's luminous ocean. When I read Freud later, I began to understand the probable Oedipal source of my difficulties. But if the Oedipal problem existed in me, it was far more entangled than the "normal" one. I had not one, but three fathers. My fault line between love and eros was fractured tenfold, its broken-ness permeating all subterranean layers of the psyche.

Through years of work, I have narrowed the rift between the body and the spirit. But when I met Derek, I had just become aware of the existence of this rift and learned that I could not escape it. I carried it within me, and it was only within me that I could mend it. But how? My self-knowledge was scanty. Therapy was unavailable to me. Joyce, who launched my defiance of mother and country, could not help me with *this*. And except for Lawrence, who broke my heart with longing for an unattainable harmony, I did not know any writer who understood my predicament. Thus my poorly navigated raft was moving inexorably toward the falls whose thunderous clap I could hear from a great distance.

Derek was determined to wrest from my body the gratifying cry of ecstasy. Yet time and again he failed, and his frustration grew. On several occasions, especially after drinking, he became quite angry. Was I denying him on purpose? he wanted to know. Why was I shutting him out? Why couldn't I be sensual like other women?

What could I say? He was right. I failed in love as I failed in everything else. What then was I good for? Yes, other women were sensual, but I was frigid; they were free, but I was imprisoned by three fathers and a mother who stared at me forbiddingly whenever I ventured to taste of love's pleasures. No, no, they were saying. You can't have that, shaking their heads, stop, stop. What could I do? I moaned in misery.

We were drifting apart. Sometimes, we could not stop talking about the "O" word, as if all other forms of loving disappeared from the world. My guilt settled like soot on my tongue, in my bowels, under my heart. I was penitent but could not make amends. Even though Derek was still affectionate and sometimes passionate, I was losing hope in our future.

THE GIFT

We were mostly unhappy lovers. What then kept us together for a few more months? Why did Derek invite me home for Christmas? I am not sure. Time blurs feelings and reasons, as well as sequence of events. I do remember, however, that we had one important thing in common. Derek was anchored in his community and family, and yet in one corner of his being, for a period of time, he was, like me, an exile.

At that time Derek was preparing for the chemistry exam that he had to pass to pursue his medical studies. He had three tries; if he failed in all of them he could never practice medicine in England. To Derek, who wanted to do nothing else in his life but be a doctor, this verdict was akin to a death sentence. He had already failed in two exams, and that winter he was preparing for the third and final exam. During that period, he and I were soul mates. We were both facing a "do or die" tests. His chemistry exam and my *Ulysses* chapter became larger than themselves, mysterious challenges pitted against the spirit.

When Christmas came we were still traveling together, encouraging each other. Derek's invitation to meet his parents might have been a friendly gesture to a fellow fugitive, but in me the proverbial hope sprang back to life. Could it be that in spite of the withdrawals and the silences, he still loved me? What if his parents didn't like Jews? I worried. What if they urged Derek to marry a nice Christian girl rather than an Israeli with an accent? I could not tolerate the thought of another woman. I wanted Derek's parents to like *me*. I decided to bring them a special gift, a gift that would cover up my flaws.

For hours I searched the stores downtown, but everything seemed gaudy and corny. I soon grew tired of the hunt and went back to my room. I sat down heavily on the chair and looked at the scattered Joyce books on my desk and at Sophie's bright flowers on the wall. There! flashed through my mind. The painting! Yes. Why not give Derek's mother something I held dear? Let her know how much I loved her son. For a moment I hesitated. How could I give away this painting that had been my delight on many a dreary evening and a sweet reminder of my friendship with Sophie? But my rash urgings pointed out that I had some of Sophie's other paintings, that I could always buy more, and that, who knows, perhaps one day even this painting would return to me. I wrapped it up and took it with me, not revealing my secret gift even to Derek.

This was not my first Christmas. I had celebrated it before with Sophie and John. Yet this particular Christmas was different. Although I liked the cheerful festivities, I was tormented by doubts. Derek's parents were courteous but distant; I tried my best to belong to the family, but I remained the outsider. The house was warm and festive, yet the Christmas tree, the carols, and the church distressed me. I remembered the story about Mira, from Tivon, the sister of one of my mother's friends, who married an Englishman, converted to Christianity, and moved to England. Her parents responded with a swift and summary punishment: they made a tear in their clothing and sat *shiva* after her, as if she were dead. If I married Derek, and celebrated Christmas every year, would my father sit *shiva* after me? Would I still be able to go back home, or would I, like Ruth, cross over to the other side without ever returning to my native land?

Before the visit was over, however, I knew that I would never have to face this decision with Derek. He was remote and chill. He did not even look at me when I gave his mother the painting. She was delighted with it and hung it on the wall in a prominent place, but he turned away, as if ashamed of my sacrifice. As I gazed at the bright flowers that were no longer mine, I felt an inconsolable sense of loss.

"'TIS BETTER TO HAVE LOVED AND LOST. . . ."

The dreaded day of the chemistry exam had finally arrived. I waited for Derek in the student union cafeteria, where I had waited for him after the second chemistry exam. I vividly remembered his pale, panic-stricken face as he walked in, having failed that exam. Now I feared his return from the decisive test. What if he didn't return at all? I could see his red car smashed against a tree. Didn't he say that he would not survive a failure, I thought darkly?

The hours passed slowly. The cafeteria was filling with students who came for dinner. I nursed my fourth cup of coffee. And what if he passes? I wondered. Would he still want me? He would become an accomplished gentleman, a British doctor, while I would still be the wandering Jew. What would keep us together then?

I finally saw him enter the cafeteria, tall, elegant, and radiant. He passed, I knew. He quickly made his way toward my table, smiling triumphantly at me. "I passed the exam," he said and sank into a chair with a broad, happy grin.

"Congratulations," I said quietly. I couldn't be cheerful.

"What is it?" Derek scrutinized my face. "Why don't you smile? Aren't you glad I passed?"

"Of course I am glad," I said with a strained smile, feeling the ground slipping under my feet. I was not glad. I did not share his accomplishment. I feared it. I envied it.

"Damn it, you are not!" Derek raised his voice. "You think I can't read your expression? You look as if somebody dear to you had just died!"

Cowering under his explosive anger, I would have given anything to erase that moment, to revise my face, to replay my response to his victory. But it was too late. Derek got up and pushed his chair back noisily. "What kind of a girlfriend are you? Why can't you be happy in my success?" He turned away and walked alone to the bar, where his friends were awaiting him to celebrate his victory. I followed him, stunned. I sat down next to him and ordered a cider. He was describing the exam to his friends. Emboldened by the alcohol, I turned to him. "Why did you leave me?"

"I can't talk to you tonight," he said, still addressing his friends.

"What is it?" I cried, trying to suppress a wave of panic.

He looked at me with a mixture of contempt and pity. "Go home, Shelly," he said, "I'll talk to you tomorrow."

"No, no," I pleaded. "You must talk to me now, please. What have I done to offend you?"

"Don't you know?" he snickered and turned back to his friends. I emptied my glass and put on my coat; tipsy and swaying on my feet, I set out on my long walk home.

For several days and nights, I did not see Derek. But one afternoon, I looked out of the window and saw his red car approaching. He got out, holding in his hands a huge bouquet of yellow flowers. He carried the flowers upstairs, knocked on my door, and put them in my hands. His eyes were red and chafed. He talked about our great love, which he said he would always remember. After an hour, he got up and left. I threw myself on the floor and sobbed like one who would never see the sun again.

"SEABEDABBLED, FALLEN, WELTERING"

I think of the following months with fear and trembling, for I was courting disaster.

Shortly after the breakup with Derek, I submitted to Roper my chapter on *Ulysses,* which, I knew, was poor. Indeed, within a day or two, Roper called me into his office and kindly explained to me that the chapter was derivative and incoherent.

"Do you think I should drop Joyce?" I asked him.

"Oh, no," he smiled. "Don't give up. I'm confident you can find a way to improve the chapter."

"But how?" I asked. I couldn't think of a single way.

"Well," Roper rubbed his chin slowly, "perhaps you can approach Joyce from a different direction. For example, would you consider writing a chapter on the development of his stream-of-consciousness technique?"

This new direction seemed a setback. What I really wanted to do was explore the moral growth of Joyce's characters. I wanted to learn from Joyce how to achieve such growth. Furthermore I wanted to say something important about Joyce's characters, who, like me, were exiles. But what was that important something I had to say? I didn't know. Now I had to admit my defeat. I agreed to shift my focus, as Roper suggested, to Joyce's technique.

Sheffield, however, was haunted with the presence of Derek. The student union, the streets, and the house on Crookes Moore Road were potent reminders of my loss. Although Derek moved out of the house, I still saw him in the student union, in the company of a pretty, long-haired, English woman. My days were dissipated in listless brooding. I had to leave Sheffield. Since I had already fulfilled the university's residence requirements, I decided to continue my work as a reader in London.

THE BRITISH MUSEUM READING ROOM

The bustle of the big city, the theaters and the museums, the stately dignity of the British Museum uplifted my spirit. In the Reading Room I befriended two readers, one from Israel and one from Egypt. Daniel, my Israeli companion, was a Hebrew Literature professor from Tel Aviv who came to London with his wife Nitza, a doctor, for a sabbatical. Atypical among Israelis in his sensitivity to emotional life, Daniel was the one who introduced me to Freud and to psychoanalysis. Although it was mainly in America that I profited from therapy, the revelation that some of my tangled conflicts and tormenting desires could be explained, and perhaps even resolved, was to me as vital as hope.

The Egyptian scholar I befriended had olive skin, black shining hair, and a throaty laugh that reminded me of Chaim's. He was the one who introduced me to Dostoevsky. *The Brothers Karamazov,* he used to say, was the greatest novel ever written. When I came to the Reading Room, instead of calling my name, or saying "good morning," he greeted me with the resounding roar, K-A-Rrrr-A-M-A-Zzzz-O-V, flailing his arms for dramatic effect. We would then go down to the Museum cafeteria and over a cup of coffee discuss the outrageous passions of the Russian brothers.

With the help of my intellectual companions, I became a hungry reader of a variety of writers, none of whom included Joyce. I browsed in bookstores and carried a book with me wherever I went. In the Underground, in the British Museum, and in the parks, I read Cassirer, William James, Laing, Hesse, Freud, Dostoevsky, and others. My readings expanded in various directions, but my work on Joyce stalled. I wasn't interested in Roper's new topic, and I made little progress. Every morning I'd wake up with a fresh resolve to work on my chapter, and every afternoon I'd find myself miles away from it. Occasionally, I did manage to return to *Ulysses* and write down some notes, but I could not muster the discipline for the long haul. Gradually I neglected my work and gave myself over to my far-flung explorations.

One of those explorations had little to do with books. One night I saw a dance performance of the Martha Graham company and was so stirred by that strange and pithy art that I signed up for a beginners' class at the new Martha Graham dance school, situated then in a narrow alley off Oxford Street.

When I was ten or eleven, my mother sent me to a ballet class because, she said, "a lady should learn how to walk and move gracefully." I fell in love with the dance. Although never a good dancer, I felt that I could express my feelings through movement. For a few years I became absorbed in dancing and once I even got the main role in a dance performance at school. It mattered little to me that I was the Sleeping Beauty and therefore "slept" on the stage through most of the dance, while the other dancers skipped and hopped around me. When I was finally "awakened," I was proud to show them all how well I could execute my *petit-pas*.

Later, I put on weight and quit dancing. But now in London, I was fit to return to the dance world. During class, I learned that the intricate patterns of the Martha Graham dance were rooted in three basic movements—contractions, spirals, and leaps. Through them, desire, disappointment, hatred, and joy were sculpted into strong shapes that moved across space in syncopated rhythms. "Listen to your spine," one of the teachers said, as we were laboring to turn our heads backward in a spiral motion. How imaginative, I thought. What longing, what grace does this motion hold! "Stretch," another teacher explained "until your fingers touch the stars. Now contract, no, no, do not fall to the floor in a heap; *contract* to the floor, holding your body together. . . ." I collapsed many times, but on rare occasions I held on, centered, and descended to the floor, controlled, as if I were, at one and the same time, rising from it. Through disciplined preparations, I learned, the body could express bold passion and transcend it into art.

At the Martha Graham school, I discovered my point of balance. Yet outside the studio, alas, I easily lost it. Neither my body nor my feelings could be harnessed to a sustaining discipline.

THE SECOND CIRCLE

I learned that those who undergo this torment
are damned because they sinned within the flesh,
subjecting reason to the rule of lust.
. . . .
I fainted, as if I had met my death.
And then I fell as a dead body falls.

—Dante, *Inferno*, Canto V

On some of my darkest days during that period, it seemed to me that I was very close to fulfilling the requirements for the seven deadly sins. I could check most of them off.

Pride. Yes. Didn't I plan to write the most brilliant work on Joyce? Didn't I believe I could do it? And look at me now.

Envy. Of course. The familiar companion that drove a wedge between Derek and me.

Greed. What else would you call letting my parents foot my bills while I went to dance classes?

Gluttony. Let's see. Three Kit-Kat wrappers in my pocket.

Anger. Not recently, but known to blow up, like my mother.

Sloth. How long has it been since I worked steadily on *Ulysses?*

What is missing? Lust!

On some nights, I'd look for relief from my oppressive loneliness in an African dance club, near the old Covent Garden. Like my mother, who was virtuous at home but sinful in secret European places, I too wandered off from the respectable British Museum and the Martha Graham studio to a clandestine place, where I sought rapture and oblivion.

One night at the club, I met Assai, a Nigerian student who was completing his bachelor's degree at London University. Although not handsome, he was a good dancer, of medium height, and slender build. His broad, bony face and his ready laugh were riveting. That night I did not return to my room in Tufnell Park; instead I went with Assai to his room near the British

Museum. Effortlessly, we rode together to ecstasy. There it was, the exquisite shudder Lawrence was talking about. Like a hungry beggar falling upon a table loaded with sumptuous food, I held onto Assai's lithe body until the break of dawn, when I finally stretched out on the lustful bed and, drunk with pleasure, fell asleep.

This time, I thought, I had really fallen in love. I began to imagine living out my life in Nigeria, yet when people in the street measured us with critical glances, I remembered where I came from. In those days, I didn't even know what I thought of miscegenation, but I knew that the sun would have to stand still in the sky, as it did for Joshua, before my three fathers and mother would accept my association with, let alone marriage to, an African. Even my friend Daniel, I knew, would try to dissuade me from pursuing this relationship, and therefore, to avoid him, I stopped reading at the British Museum. In fact, I stopped reading altogether. I was dancing, drinking, lusting. I was absent from my life.

My isolation, though, was oppressive. I wanted to tell other people about Assai, but whom could I tell? I needed to talk to a friend. Yes, a close friend, like Sophie, who would not condemn me for loving an African. I dropped everything and took the train back to Sheffield. From the window, I gazed at the rolling green hills of the countryside. Fog and ceaseless drizzle blurred the outlines of the landscape, but here and there, a farm, a grazing cow, or dark green hedgerows could be discerned. When I arrived at Sheffield, I took a cab to Sophie's house, and as it was making its way through the town's winding streets and shady groves enclosed by stone-fences, I felt a surge of calm joy, as if the train that had been riding in my head for weeks had come to a standstill.

How delighted Sophie and I were to see each other again. How peaceful it was to sit again in the large house I had left a few months before. While Sophie was preparing a meal for us, I was looking at her new paintings. As we sat down to eat, I could no longer wait and told her that I was in love with an African student from Nigeria. She gazed at me. "Are you going to end up in Nigeria, Shelly?" she asked sardonically.

"I don't know," I said. "I don't have any idea what I am going to do. If I marry him, my parents would disown me."

"Are you sure you want to marry him?"

"I'm not sure of anything," I said. "I only know," I was smiling in spite of myself, "that I have never had such a good time!"

"That's what you said about Derek, remember?" Sophie quipped.

For a moment, I was silenced by the painful memory. Then I said, "It's different this time."

"How is it different?" Sophie laughed. I looked around me, but John was out. We were alone. I told her. "That sounds wonderful," Sophie chuckled. "Tell me more." I told her more. She looked at me and sighed. "London is a groovy place. I wish Sheffield could be more like London." In those days, I thought myself an expert in relationships. Of course, I had read some of Freud and knew everything and understood everything, and what I understood then was that Sophie was unhappy with John, as my mother had been unhappy with Reuven. I therefore offered Sophie my mother's solution.

"Why don't you come with me to London for a week, Sophie?" I said. "I miss you in London, and I want you to meet Assai."

"But where would I be?" Sophie was laughing. "Where would I stay? What would I do when you two go out?"

"Well," I said, "Assai has friends. We can all go out."

Sophie came to London with me. For a week, she had an affair with one of Assai's African friends. When we went out to a restaurant, or to the African club, I was no longer the odd one out, the only white woman with a black man. I had company: my best friend, Sophie, whom I persuaded to come down to London with me to celebrate the female's orgasmic liberation, regardless of the fact that she had a husband in Sheffield, who was, purportedly, my friend also. Sophie did not come to London against her will, but would she have come without me, her erudite, trusted friend? Before she returned to Sheffield, Sophie asked me if she should tell John about the affair. Thinking of Reuven, I said with confidence, "Yes, of course, you must tell your husband." But John was no Reuven. When Sophie told him about the affair, the two fought for months afterward. Whenever I visited Sheffield, John declined to meet me, and I couldn't understand why.

I had become an instigator, and I didn't know it. Nothing mattered but pleasure. By introducing Sophie to pleasure, I was acting for her own good, wasn't I? And if she did not mind the adultery, should I have minded it? Was any of this my reponsibility? I did not think so. Blinded by lust for Assai, I pulled my friend with me to the edge of the pit.

Twenty-three years later, in the winter of 1991, during a visit to London to meet my mother, I planned to travel to Sheffield, to ask for Sophie and John's forgiveness. After calling Sheffield University, I found out that Sophie and John had separated five years earlier, that John had left the university, and that Sophie was living in a small town outside Sheffield under her maiden name, which I had never known. I was relieved to learn that it was not I, apparently, who directly caused the breakup, but I still felt responsible for it nevertheless. I called several places to find John's new address and phone number, but nobody knew his where-abouts. And so a curtain of silence fell between me and the friends I betrayed.

When Sophie returned to Sheffield, I felt wistful. I missed her, I missed my friends in the British Museum, and I even longed for my work on *Ulysses*. I was beginning to grow tired of the cycle of drinking and dancing, but I did not know how to break it. Although I knew that I would never follow Assai to Nigeria, my desire for him was kindled to a fine and persistent flame. I craved him; all he had to do was touch my lips, or put his hand on my thigh, and I would surrender to him.

Then one day—how it happened I cannot remember—or was it night, perhaps a friend told me, or somebody else, or something I saw, or heard, and did not believe, but then knew was true, saw, one day, or evening, in his dorm room, on the south side of the British Museum, coming back from somewhere, I myself saw Assai shooting heroin up his vein, saw his arm, a sieve (how could it be I never saw it before), saw the syringe, his soft smile, heard his chuckle, "you are early," clicking his tongue, "but you are here, so have a seat." Was the sun setting, or had night come: I was standing there speechless, time contracted like a womb in an agonized birth, what will he do to me flashed through my mind, but still I couldn't move, looking at his bony face, looking at the arms that held me, hearing him laughing softly, "You won't tell, will you?"

"No! No! Noooo!" I was already running out, across the street, through the park, NO, NO, not that, not that, take me back, passing by the fountain, how could I have known, NO, leaping up the stairs of the British Museum, breathlessly running, through the swinging doors, books, here, where are you, Daniel, sobbing, please, take me back, where am I coming from, I saw evil, I saw a fire burning, I saw Shelly dead.

"HOMING, UPSTREAM, SILENTLY MOVING, A SILENT SHIP"

How does one begin to repair one's soul? Perhaps by admitting, as David had done, that one is "poor and needy" and "cannot see" (Psalm 40). I sought out the company of Daniel and his wife Nitza, whose friendship and simple accep-tance of my chaotic life were a balm to my spirit. With their encouragement,

I attempted, once more, to rewrite my chapter on *Ulysses* and thus turn the tide of destruction away.

I worked on *Ulysses* eight hours a day. I no longer wanted to write a brilliant thesis on the moral development of Joyce's characters; I just wanted to survive, to find the way back to my world. Instead of soaring with "bright wings," I tried to say what I could say with clarity. Like Stephen, who discovers that he must be "a learner" before he can be an artificer, I subjected myself to the plodding labor on Joyce, knowing that only through it could I repair my broken life.

In three months I finished my new chapter. I knew that it was not outstanding, yet I sent it to Roper with a sense of accomplishment. Those were my best efforts. I took the turn. I was rowing on the other side of darkness. In a few days, Roper sent the chapter back to me with these two words on it, "Wonderfully improved."

THE VISIT

A few months after the Assai episode, my mother, in some mysterious way, sensed that I was in trouble. She came to London, talked amiably to my sour-faced landlady, rented a room on a street up the road, in a house owned by a jolly old Englishman, and settled down to supervise my comings and goings. She didn't care how long it took, she said, she had to see the bound copies of my thesis before she returned to Israel. She and Reuven talked long and hard about it, called in the family for consultation, and even discussed the matter with Chaim, and all agreed that that's what she had to do. There was no other way. I apparently thought that money grew on trees. I left Israel for two years, and there I was, into my fourth year already, and no end in sight. Where *was* the thesis? Where *was* the degree? What did I do all day? Play games? How long did I expect them to support me in London? Did I think that it was easy for them to keep me in England, writing a master's thesis that was never coming to an end? She and Reuven could no longer tolerate such irresponsible behavior. She would stay here in England until she saw what was what, and that's all there was to it.

What could I say? She was right. It was she who paid for my interminable Joyce, for Sheffield, for London, and for the stormy affair she knew nothing about. And what did I have to show for it? Yet my anger flared up. *Now* that I survived both Assai and *Ulysses* she was giving me this lecture? For a moment,

I was sorely tempted to shock her a little and tell her about Assai and the wild parties in the African dance club, but I held my tongue. Things were bad enough. In resignation, I let her spew out her complaints and agreed to go out with her on a shopping trip in town, to buy some new clothes because the dress I was wearing was just too awful! How could I show my face in the British Museum, she wanted to know, with such tasteless, ill-fitting clothes?

A few days later, after my mother had settled down in her room, and made arrangements for evening TV viewing with the old man (who became so fond of her company in his living room that he was disconsolate when she left), we went shopping. On the way to the Underground, my mother, as usual, was walking ahead in her determined pace, and I trailed behind.

"You take this route every morning?" my mother asked, breathing more heavily as she was climbing the hill.

"Yes," I said. "It's all right, except when it rains hard and the wind is blowing."

"And you travel to the British Museum every day?"

"Almost every day," I said. A trap, I thought.

"But in the five days since I've come, you haven't been there once." We entered the station. I bought a paper, and my mother was examining the Underground map. We descended to the platform. I was hoping she had forgotten the subject of our conversation.

The train arrived. We walked in and sat down. "The Underground is nicer than the French Metro," my mother said, remembering her European experiences. "You haven't done a stroke of work in five days," she casually added.

"I am doing all right," I muttered, feeling a grumbling activity in my bowels.

"How many pages do you still have to revise?"

"I don't count them, *Imma,*" I lied.

"So how can I tell how much you still have to do?"

"So don't tell," I snapped.

"Really! Don't tell, don't tell," she mimicked me. "That's the thanks I get from you."

"I can do it! Why don't you trust me? I have already written my chapter on *Ulysses.* I just need a little time." I was looking at the passengers in the car, envying each one of them, even those who looked down and out, because they didn't have to go through *this.*

"*Ulysses,* Shmulysses. What do I care? I want to see the bound copies. Where are they? Perhaps you can't do it, Shelly. We have to consider this possibility seriously. Perhaps you just don't have what it takes to write a master's thesis!" The train screeched to a halt. Four more stops. I was now feeling acute discomfort. "I have to go to the bathroom," I said to my mother.

"Really?" she said, concerned. "Can you make it?"

"I don't know," I said, feeling the pressure increase with every motion of the train. Another stop. Sure I can make it. I breathed deeply. Three more stops. We traveled in silence. My mother's mood softened. I gulped air, but the train threw me about, frustrating my efforts to hold the air in. I grabbed hold of the steel bar and squeezed it.

"Nu," my mother sounded solicitous, "what do you think we should do?"

"Get out at the next stop," I said hurriedly, biting my lips. Victoria Station. I jumped out of the train. She jumped after me. Hundreds of stairs. I was climbing, running, pushing my way through throngs of people. Finally I arrived at the bathroom a second before the explosion. My mother was waiting for me outside. "But how does such a thing happen to you, Shelly? You probably had too much coffee this morning."

For the sixth day, I did not do a stroke of work on Joyce.

On several occasions, I ran away from my mother. I stayed in the Reading Room until the late closing hour, took long trips on the double-decker bus, munching Kit-Kat bars on the way, or wandered to the Royal Festival Hall for a concert. Once I stayed out the whole night at Daniel and Nitza's apartment. In the morning I let Nitza call my mother to tell her that I was safe. When Nitza's hand started to tremble, I knew the reason for it. Nitza received the brunt of my mother's anger that was directed at me, that I should have been brave enough to take. But I couldn't. Fortunately, Daniel and Nitza remained staunch advocates in my struggle with my mother. With their support, I was able to find a way to exist with her and to complete the final revisions of my thesis.

"A WHISPER OF TRUTH"

When I reread my 214 page thesis today, the subtext jumps at me: here is an early section I discussed with Derek, here I was struggling with Goldberg's influence, here are the gaps in my thinking that must have occurred when I changed my topic, and this hurried part was written when I was recovering from the affair with Assai. The thesis has many good sections, but, no, I must admit, it does not hold together. And yet, at the time, what an achievement it was! What did Empson, who shrewdly picked up every weakness in my essay during the oral defense, know of the excruciating growth my imperfect composition attested to? What did he know of the lonely night of the soul my printed pages traversed with me? Nothing, nor should he have known. He had the right to test me. However, I felt proud that I finished my thesis and was awarded the master's degree four months after my mother joined me in London.

For years I could not forgive my mother for meddling in my affairs and coming to London to "help" me finish my thesis. And yet now I must express an additional truth. I've always paid attention to what people said, but to my mother words were unimportant, if not entirely irrelevant. Who needed words? To my mother, as to many Israelis, insulting words or loving words were equally insubstantial. Words were, at best, mere signposts; the road itself was paved with actions.

I must now try to imagine my mother from a different point of view, as I replay the past in a silent movie version, screening out her wounding words. She came to England because she knew that something was wrong and yet did not know what or how to ask. She came without prior knowledge of English, inexperienced in the harshness of the English winter. She rented a tiny room and coaxed her landlord to let her watch TV every night, not only for the diversion but to learn English faster. She was controlling, interfering. But every morning, she went to the store and bought coffee and fresh scones for her daughter. She stayed in England four months, without Reuven and without Chaim, passing the time somehow, anyhow, waiting for me to finish my thesis on Joyce.

I didn't ask for such a sacrifice. I didn't want it. I didn't want its burden, its bravado. And yet now I can see something else, too. My mother came for me. She did not come for Shelly, who was busy with Joyce's "signatures"; she came for Haya. It was Haya who needed somebody to watch for her outside the squeaking gate of the orphanage, somebody to wait for her four months while she was raging and throwing tantrums and getting lost. Somebody to worry about her all night when the darkness swallowed her up. And somebody to remind her of her boundaries and insist that she respect them. "Finish your task, Haya. Bind your words."

Haya needed her mother.

chapter three

REUVEN

ABOARD SHIP

E ven before I reached the port of Haifa and spotted our villa on top of the Carmel mountain, I was excited to be returning home. My mother flew back from England, but I chose the slow land-and-sea route; crossing France and Italy by train and sailing from Naples, I was pleased by the opportunity to rest and reflect on the ship's deck. Gazing at the luminous Mediterranean, I noted with satisfaction how different this sea was from "the dull green mass of liquid" that Stephen was looking at from his "tower" in Dublin! Yet as soon as I mentioned Stephen, I felt a sharp stab.

Four years in England—gone. Disappeared, as if by a sleight of hand. Gone is the British Museum Reading Room. And the coffee shop across the street, where I had cappuccinos and piping hot scones. Gone is the Old Vic. The Martha Graham school. The Underground. Sheffield. Crookes Moore Road. Sophie's house. And Sophie . . . gone forever.

I stared at the fragments of white lace floating on the silent waves. How could one live four years in a place, develop habits, learn customs, make friends, get used to shops, streets, smells, food, language, and then one day, all at once—be banished from it? It's like death, I brooded. Now, I looked at my watch, they are probably coming in from the drizzle for their afternoon tea. Then the news on the telly in an impeccable British accent. Then the theater, or the concert. And then, the red double-decker back home through the fog.

I wish I were still there, I admitted, but here I am, going home. And why, I sat straight in my deck chair, why am I going back to Israel? *Imma* will be giving me orders again, and advice, and money, and rides, and food, and clothes and . . . there I'll be. Invisible, dependent Haya, scared of her mother. I stood up. Even my struggles will no longer be mine. I paced the deck. How can I fight her? I asked, scrutinizing the vast expanse of the azure sea, which offered no answer. And what would happen to Shelly and her English? It was all right to be Shelly in England, but in Israel they know that all I am is Haya. And who, in fact, is Shelly? What has she done with her life?

I walked across the ship to the shadier side of the deck and sat down again to continue reading Dostoevsky's *The Idiot*. But the sun was too bright, and I couldn't concentrate on the words. What have I gained then? Four years in England, and what have I got to show for it? A mediocre master's degree, a failed love affair, a failed friendship, a few wild adventures I don't care to remember, and an expanse of loneliness! What can I brag about when I arrive home tomorrow? My knowledge of English? Who needs English in Israel? Soft breezes wrinkled the smooth surface of the sea. But without English I cannot live, I repeated to an imaginary opponent. Without English, Shelly does not exist. Without English, I added for emphasis, my mother would swallow me up whole. . . .

The evening was settling in, blurring the borders between sky and sea. The dim horizon was streaked with reds and purples, and in the tall sky one or two stars were lit. Why am I so upset? I thought more calmly now. After all, I do miss them, Reuven and Chaim, Ruth, and Avram. The ship was moving forward at a good clip, swishing through the glossy water surface. Anyway, I could not stay in England, without money and without a work permit. But Shelly exists, I reflected. Hers are the struggles in England, the mistakes, the achievements. Hers and mine. And Shelly will exist, I resolved. I will continue my studies for the doctorate in English. There, I thought, I do know who I am. I shall not get lost.

THE HOMECOMING

Gradually, as if rising from a dream, Mount Carmel was etched against the sky in soft curves whose flow was interrupted only by the tall and ungainly building of Haifa University. I leaned against the railing, impatiently waiting for the ship to moor in the harbor. Next to me, people were chatting excitedly, pointing to the exquisite gardens surrounding the Bahai Temple. Slipping between boats of various sizes, the ship approached the dock at a snail's pace. Above us, the city displayed its loveliness, but my eyes were busy searching for my family down on the quay. Shouts and instructions in Hebrew buzzed around us.

So much life! My language! How I love its energy, its crunchiness, even its harshness! At that moment, I saw Reuven, dressed in his festive white shirt and grey pants, his thick-rimmed glasses glinting in the sun. He was looking for me, pulling on his mustache, as was his habit when he was anxious. "Reuven! Reuven!" I shouted, but my cry was lost in the tumult. Next to Reuven stood my mother and Ruth. In a moment, I heard Ruth calling me, "Haya'le, Haya'le!" and pointing my mother in my direction. My mother waved to me and then said something to Ruth, who, realizing her error, put her hand on her mouth. Then I heard her calling again, "Shelly, I mean, Shelly." I waved with both hands, "Here I am!"

Two days later, the preparations for the homecoming celebration were in full swing. From morning till night, my mother toiled to brush, clean, dust, and shine the floors, the furniture, the walls, every corner in the house. She forbade me to help her. No, she said, I was the honored guest and guests were not allowed to work! So I slept late, read, and watched my mother cook and bake her delicacies: gefilte fish that melted in the mouth, stuffed peppers done to perfection, burekas of amazing cultural diversity from east and west, cream puffs that were made simply of air, and strudels bursting with the goodness of the land, nuts, sesame seeds, and honey. "Eat, eat," my mother would say. "There is enough for you and for everybody, enough for an army." I ate, and with every bite I was thinking how happy I was to be in my mother's house, luxuriating in comfort, surrounded by paintings, happy to watch Reuven coming down the winding steps from his work in the kibbutzim, with melons on his shoulders and the smell of the cowshed odors on his work clothes, happy to gaze, in the evening, at the last glimmers of the setting sun on the ocean that two days before brought me here from wintry England, happy, happy to sit on the porch and read into the night, lifting my eyes occasionally to watch the ships coming slowly into the port, flashing their blue and red lights across the silent, dark waters.

For a few days my soul was hovering over Israeli reality like a sea gull blissfully gliding over the deep. But I knew that soon I would have to dive and spar with salt, foam, and crashing waves.

"I HAVEN'T SUNG YOUR PRAISE, MY COUNTRY"

Finally the day for the party arrived. One by one they came, uncles, aunts, cousins, and friends. My mother was running around like a "chicken with her head cut off," as she was saying, and Reuven was running after her, taking her orders, making sure the guests had chairs to sit on and food to eat. All kissed and hugged me, glad to welcome home the lost sheep.

Avram and Sharona came first. "Isn't it good to be here again?" my uncle gave me a bone-crushing hug. "Tell me the truth, isn't England cold and dreary? I couldn't stand it," he raised his eyebrows. "One year in Dunstable, I'd had it up to here," he lifted his hand above his head. "But I am glad," he added with a dimpled smile, "that I was there for you, that you had a place to go on the holidays, or when you needed money. . . ." he laughed, and I laughed with him. "Especially after the Oxford episode," his ringing laughter reached my mother's ears.

"What Oxford episode?" she asked, a tray of burekas precariously balanced in her hands.

"It does not matter, *Imma*," I said, blushing at the memory.

"No, I want to know," my mother said and put the tray down on the green marble table.

"Tell her," my uncle nudged me. "What was so terrible about it? Nothing to be ashamed of, in my opinion. She never told you, Dina, how I picked her up from Oxford and brought her back to Dunstable? 'Avram,' she called me on the phone, crying, 'I can't stay here one more minute. You must pick me up, right now!' That's what she said," he chuckled, "so what could I do? I am her uncle, am I not? I drove two hours to bring her home."

Reuven, too, showed interest in the Oxford episode, which soon became the focus of attention. People were staring at me, waiting for my story. Yet seeing my reluctance, Avram relented. "Never mind," he said, "she does not have to tell you. It's personal." Leaning against the fireplace, Chaim was smoking and drinking. He approached my mother. "I think I know what the Oxford episode is about."

"So tell me now," my mother insisted. He took her aside. I craned my neck to listen but, at that moment, my Aunt Bracha, a school principal, and her husband Moshe framed themselves in the open door, bearing a gift.

"Shalom, shalom to the prodigal daughter," Bracha looked archly at me. "Aren't you glad," she said with a knowing smile, "to be back in *our* country?"

I nodded. She handed me her gift, which was a large book on Jerusalem. "Thank you so much," I mumbled embarrassed, looking from the corner of my eye at Chaim recounting the Oxford episode to my mother while gesturing with his hands in an animated manner.

"I thought that this would just be the book for you," Bracha smiled. "To keep you here with us." She bent over, picked up a cream puff and ate the whole thing, her eyes widening in pleasure. "Ahh, this is sooo good," she sighed, "I must tell your mother. Dina, Dina," she called my mother, who was still talking to Chaim, "the puffs are simply *magnificent!*" Then she turned to me again. "And how does it feel to have a master's degree? From a British university, no less?"

"Good, good," I said, thinking, what does she expect me to say?

"But what do you intend to do with it?" her eyes narrowed.

"I don't know," I cleared my throat, "I hope, perhaps, to continue my studies for a doctorate." In the corner, I could hear Chaim roaring in laughter.

"Really?" Bracha took a deep breath and scrutinized me for a few seconds. I swallowed hard. "That's commendable," she finally said. "Admirable. Really. But tell me. . . ." she held my chin in her hand. "What about a husband, Shelly? A doctorate is fine. Very fine." She raised her eyebrows while still clutching my chin. "But you are already twenty-nine, you know." She sighed. "Time doesn't stand still. My daughter Michal," she released my chin, "is already married to Uzi, a doctor as you know, and she is younger than you are."

"Perhaps I don't want to get married," I said resentfully.

"What do you mean?" she gasped. "Don't ever say that in public. You don't *really* want to be an old maid, do you?"

"No. I am waiting for love."

"But how long can one wait for love?" Bracha looked at me intently. "And what if you don't meet Prince Charming?" she smiled. "What then? Meeting the right man doesn't *necessarily* happen. And you know how it is," she chuckled, "the older we get. . . ." Reuven interrupted her with a tray of finger sandwiches. "Dina would like to speak to you in the kitchen," he said to her, and then she was gone.

I stood there stunned, like a student who had flunked a test. It is none of her business, I thought angrily. In England nobody cared whether I was married or not. Here, the whole country cares. And where was my presence of mind? I chided myself. Why didn't I say something to shut her up?

To my relief, at that moment, Aunt Ruth and her husband Chezi, from moshav Tel Adashim, walked in. Ruth hugged me. "So good to see you," she intoned. "I said to Chezi," she continued, "that you'll certainly return to Israel! What is England to you? And you can always read Joyce here, can't you?"

"That's true," I smiled with pleasure at my aunt's round face and jolly green eyes. "But did you really think, Ruth, that I would stay in England?"

"It's your mother, *meida'le,* who was afraid of that! Me? I never doubted that you'd come back. Right, Chezi?"

Aunt Ruth, circa 1951

Chezi's thin lips stretched in a smile.

"Don't you remember, Haya'le. . . . Oops," she put her hand on her mouth. "Shelly, forgive me. Don't you remember how you loved to visit us in Tel Adashim? Since you were a little girl. And how you used to cry when I sang *Dudu* to you? Remember?" she burst out laughing. "You couldn't let go of Dudu. You asked me who he was, why he died in the war, why his body was dripping as they carried him back, why the cypress tree lowered its head, and then your eyes filled with tears, as if you were carrying the sadness of the world. . . ." she laughed and hugged me. "Anybody who can cry over *Dudu* loves this country! Period!" She lifted her finger like a stern but sweet-natured teacher.

"Enough, Ruth," Chezi said, "she hasn't been here even one week and you are already making a kibbutznik out of her?"

Ruth laughed. "No, no, not a kibbutznik, that's for sure. I know her. She will go to the university, right?"

"What are you going to study?" Chezi asked.

"I will get my doctorate in English."

"Not Hebrew? English?" Chezi laughed.

"Why not?" Ruth protested. "Of course English. She always liked English, Chezi."

My Aunt Nomi joined the conversation. "I noticed your new hairstyle," she said with a broad, lipsticked smile. "Who did it for you?"

"Vidal Sassoon."

"I heard about him. But let me tell you something, Shelly. In Tel Aviv you must go to Violette. She is a wonderful hairstylist, isn't she, Dina?" Her eyes searched for my mother. "And by the way, I *do* like your dress!" she smacked her lips.

Through the open French windows, one could see the evening descending on the mountain and the ocean. Streetlights were turned on, and the city became a mythical night queen

Aunt Nomi in the Air Force, circa 1951

trailing a starry gown. Inside our large living room, spirits ran high: mouths were chewing, laughing, and smoking. The conversation was loud and animated. I talked to Dr. Zilber, one of Reuven's colleagues, and his wife Yael, who live in Tivon to this day, about the history lessons Zilber used to give me when he was doing his residency with Reuven, twelve years earlier. Still an avid reader of history, Zilber jokingly reproached me for deserting real history for imaginary fiction. "It's all fantasy," he said, his blue eyes twinkling behind his clear glasses. "What can you learn from literature? I told you," he lifted his pointed nose, "history is the only truth. Why waste time on literature?"

"It is not a waste of time," I remonstrated. "Literature also reveals the truth, in a different way."

"Ach," he said with a dismissing gesture, "Literature is *bubbe meises.*" He turned briefly toward his wife, as if looking for support, but she smiled enigmatically. "Literature is made up of air, like the clothes of that king in Hans Christian Anderson's story. You know that story?" I nodded. "Cheap imitation," he stabbed a long, thin, finger in the air. "That's all. Only history is *real,*" he continued with renewed ardor. "For example, if I wanted to find out something about our War of Independence, would I read history or literature? I ask you. And what do you think we are doing here, in this country?" he grinned. "We are making history! Did you know that?"

"Yes, I agree," I mumbled, "but I don't know if I. . . ."

"Of course you," he lifted his sculpted eyebrows. "Why not you?"

"Enough, Shimon," Yael spoke, wrapping her arm around her husband's. "Leave her alone. Besides, we must go home." Shimon's mouth remained open, as if he wanted to say something else, but his wife's firmness prevailed. "All right," he said, "let's go home. Remember our history," he repeated to me, as he moved toward the door.

Finally, the guests broke ranks and began to depart. Some looked weary, some yawned on their way out, but they all smiled and complimented my mother on her food. Chaim was also leaving. "What did you tell *Imma?*" I asked him.

"Oh, nothing much," he laughed, his eyes narrowing to slits. "Just about my nephew Uri, you know."

"Why did you tell her?"

"Don't you worry, Shelly'nka," he smiled whimsically. "It's all in the family."

"INSUBSTANTIAL PAGEANT"

"The house looks like a battlefield," my mother sighed, as she scrutinized the strewn napkins, piles of empty dishes, and crumbs of cake on the floor. "But," she insisted, "I am going to clean it all up now, because I don't want to get up to this mess in the morning!" She assigned me the task of drying the dishes. Reuven piled up dishes around the sink. "You know," he said, "the gefilte fish were really excellent!"

---

bubbe meises   Grandma's stories, old wives' tales

"And the plum pie?" my mother inquired. "What was wrong with the plum pie? Wasn't it delicious?"

"Yes, of course," Reuven said, "I was just saying. . . ."

My mother eyed me. "Look, Shelly," she said, "these glasses are not dry. I can see the water drops from here."

"They are too dry," I insisted.

"What's this?" my mother stood still, her hands covered with suds, "I throw such a party for you, spend days working to prepare it, feed hundreds of guests, and you argue with me about a drop of water?"

"Shhhh," Reuven shushed her. "The neighbors will hear you, Dina."

"Let them hear," my mother said, giving a tired glance at the numerous dead soldiers around her—dirty silver forks that had lost their sheen, empty coffee cups with cigarette butts swimming in their dregs, abandoned pieces of plum pie, and a cream puff floating in a champagne glass. "Who has the energy for this?" she sighed, gazing out the window at the fifty-one stairs that were plunged in cool darkness. "I'll help you, Dina'le," Reuven crooned. "Just don't yell, okay?"

She resumed her dishwashing and I picked up my towel. For a while, we worked in silence. Then my mother remembered. "How come you never told me about the end of that affair you had with Chaim's nephew, Uri, in Oxford?"

"It was not an affair," I said. "Nothing happened between us." The huge yellow bowl I was drying almost slipped from my fingers.

"Be careful!" my mother chided. Then I remembered. A sunny day in Oxford. Second floor of the record shop. Listening in a glass booth to Bach's cello suites. The maple tree in the square with glistening red leaves. Ah, the brightness of that morning.

"So what happened between you two?" My mother peered into the night. "You liked him, didn't you? Isn't he the only Israeli you ever liked? The intellectual?"

"Yes," I nodded. "He came to visit me at the embassy, bearing regards from his uncle Chaim."

"Yes, so what happened?" she inquired. "After all, he was smart and was in Oxford to do what? Be careful with this crystal plate. It's precious, you know."

I held the plate with both hands. "His master's in philosophy."

"How long did you go out with him?" She was scrubbing a stubborn pot.

"Not very long," I reflected. "We went out a few times, but nothing happened," I added quickly. "Once we were late for the Underground, so we

walked all the way from Oxford Street to my room, can you imagine? About
five miles, or more. We got there at four in the morning, and then he walked
back to his place," I laughed. Stopped in Hyde Park to rest. Horizons ringed
with yellowish-orange light. Walking a step or two ahead of me, he hummed
the Beatles, "Help! I need somebody's help" all the way home.

"What?" my mother gasped. "Walked all the way from Oxford Street?
Were you out of your minds? Why didn't you take a cab?"

"You wouldn't believe it," I said, putting a delicate glass on the counter.
"Both of us ran out of money." Reuven laughed heartily.

"So what happened?" my mother wanted to know. "What went wrong?
How did you get to Oxford, the town?"

"He invited me. We drove his car on a week's trip to Scotland, and then
we came back to Oxford."

"You don't say," my mother intoned, "so he did like you a little, didn't he?
He must have!"

"Dina, where do I put this plate?" Reuven asked, holding up to her view
a delicate china.

"*Oi vei,*" she called out, as if he had already broken it. "Leave it on the
table. I'll take care of it." She turned to me. "So if he invited you, why did
it end?"

"You should have grabbed him," Reuven spoke abruptly, "and whisked
him to the *huppah*. I've always wanted you to marry an Israeli. What was the
problem?"

"Let her speak," my mother hushed him. "So what was the problem?" she
asked.

"I don't know," I cleared my throat. "He tried, I think, but he did not like
me, I suppose, as I liked him." Oxford. A shaft of sunlight under the door.
Two shadows pacing across it. Two voices, talking.

"I don't understand what you mean," my mother put her hands on her
waist. "What do you mean he didn't like you? Did he know that you liked
him?"

"Yes, I think so."

"Then what happened?"

"When we came back from Scotland. . . ."

"Yes, yes," she nodded eagerly.

---

huppah   Wedding canopy

"He became cold and silent."

"So what if he was a little silent?" she insisted. "How do you know that he didn't like you? Some men are naturally silent. For me, this is not a sign at all."

"Would you wait a minute?" I said, testily, "I knew! We were staying at a bed and breakfast. My room was one floor above his."

"You mean, you didn't even sleep with him?" Reuven cried out. "Now I understand everything!"

"Let me speak. The morning we came back, I got up. . . ."

"Yes?" my mother asked. She had finished the dishes and was untying her apron. "Yes?" she repeated. "You got up and? . . ."

"I came down the stairs to his room," I swallowed hard. The bright shaft of light on the landing. My hand lifted to knock.

"Nu? Nu?" Reuven bent his bald head forward, his ear cupped in his hand.

"Then I heard Uri say to his friend, 'How can I tell her?' "

"Tell her what?" my mother asked.

"That's what the friend wanted to know," I answered. "And Uri said that 'we can't go on. I just don't love her.' "

"And then?" my mother asked.

"Then, I ran to the nearest phone, called Avram, and asked him to pick me up."

"And then?" Reuven asked.

"Then I walked back to Uri's room and told him that I was leaving in an hour or two because I heard what he said."

"So what did he say to that?"

"He was sweet," I sighed. "He offered to stay another night. 'There is no rush,' he reassured me, but I left. I walked into a record store and listened to Bach until Avram came."

We were now sitting around the table, drinking tea. My mother was holding a lump of sugar between her teeth. "I wonder why," she ruminated.

"Why what?" I asked.

"Why he liked you and then didn't like you," she sipped the tea and sucked the sugar. "What was wrong with you? Were you too fat? Are you sure you showed him you liked him? Because sometimes, Shelly, you have such a sullen expression on your face that no wonder you are still unmarried!"

"What do you mean," I replied angrily. "I had no sullen expression on my face! I liked him! I admired his mind! He was the only Israeli man I *ever* dated who respected my ideas! With *him* I didn't have to pretend I was dumb. On the contrary, *he* was interested in my thoughts, he drew me out. We used to talk about *important* things."

"So?" my mother asked. "If it was so good, why was it so bad?"

"Because I never knew what he *felt,*" I asserted. "He never spoke about feelings. I was always in the dark. . . ."

"The one way to find that out is in bed," Reuven quipped.

"Why must the bed come first?" I protested, remembering the remote inn somewhere in northern Scotland, which had only one room left for the night, the broad brown bed where I sat, anxious, saying no, wanting him to talk first. Then the troubled sleep under the strip of light from the streetlamp that illumined two huddled figures, lying back to back, clutching the opposite edges of the bed.

"A woman who is almost thirty should not be so principled when she meets a man!" Reuven retorted.

"What are you talking about?" I jumped. "This happened a few years ago when I was only twenty-four. Before Derek even. Today. . . ."

"So why, Dina," asked Reuven, "are we talking about him now?"

"Because," Dina stood up, "she is still unmarried, obviously, and so is *he,* Chaim told me. He is a professor at Tel Aviv University and also an editor of the literary supplement of . . . I forget the name."

"I see," Reuven rested his chin on the palm of his hand.

"He is still unmarried?" I asked in surprise.

"Yes, yes," my mother put the tea glasses in the sink, "he is still unmarried! Now what do you say to that? The only available Israeli man, who is also smart enough and enlightened enough for *you,* is still . . . available. Who knows? Perhaps now he would like you. After all, now you are more mature and thinner too. I would even say more experienced. . . ."

Then I was dreaming. I saw Uri's soft brown eyes, his broad intelligent forehead. I remembered how he threw rocks into Loch Ness, as he was explaining Sartre to me, and how he carried my red raincoat through the main street of Edinburgh. Why did I refuse him then? But now, everything is different. Can you imagine what Aunt Bracha would say, I chuckled to myself, if I married *him?*

"It's late," Reuven interrupted my musings. "Let's all go to bed. Tomorrow is another day."

"Just a minute," my mother said. "Do you have any plans for next week, Shelly?"

"Applying to the Hebrew University for the doctorate program." The thought of the doctorate brought on the distant drumroll of my fears, like an enemy detachment approaching the edge of my consciousness.

"So you could," my mother was thinking out loud, "just drop in on him, at the newspaper, and say that you have come back, you know. I am sure he'd be glad to see you."

"No, I can't do *that*. I must have a reason to see him."

"Why must you have a reason?" my mother protested. "You are just coming to see him. After all, he is a friend of yours, isn't he? I never feel that I need reasons to see my friends!"

"You know what?" an idea crossed my mind. "I can offer to write dance reviews for his literary supplement! Yeah!" I executed a caper in the air. Reuven smiled and put his hand on his bald head. "That's a *very good idea,*" he said. "What do you think, Dina?"

"Interesting, interesting," she nodded. "And you can wear your new dress, you know the one with the tawny-black stripes, the 'tiger' dress, that I bought you on Bond Street, remember?"

"Yes, yes," I exclaimed, flushed with excitement. "But really, I am qualified to do that, am I not?" I looked at both of them for approval. "After all, I studied three years at the Martha Graham school, and I am sure I can review a dance performance better than any dancer, and better than any reviewers who have never danced! But which newspaper does he work at?" I asked.

"I'll find out from Chaim," my mother stifled a yawn. "Now that we have plans, let's go to sleep."

She and Reuven went to bed, but I could not sleep. I sat on one of the straw armchairs on the veranda, folded my legs, smoked a cigarette, and gazed at a ship leaving the harbor. And so the pale pink dawn, rising over the ocean and the city, must have found me at four or five in the morning, giddy with visions of a powerful future.

"BUT LOVE HE LAUGH'D TO SCORN"

In broad daylight, the plan we hatched the night before seemed silly. Why would he want to see me? He probably has a dance reviewer anyway. No, I thought sensibly, I was not going to chase him. Instead, I applied for the doctoral program at the Hebrew University of Jerusalem.

While waiting for the reply, I became bored and restless. There was no one to *really* talk to. How long could I read, watch TV, or stare at the blue sea? I needed friends. . . . So why not try Uri? Perhaps he does need a dance reviewer. . . . Why not dare? Perhaps we could be friends again. Our misunderstandings might be swept away. . . . And who is to say? Perhaps even love, which in London and Oxford eluded us, could now blossom. . . . One Sunday morning, I put on my best dress, with the tawny-black stripes, collected a few papers and documents, threw in my Dostoevsky, and took the first train to Tel Aviv to visit Uri Mor in his office at the *Kulmus Literary Supplement.*

Ha'masger Street in South Tel Aviv, where the office of *Kulmus* used to be, has no literary pretensions whatsoever. On the contrary, it is prosaic and humdrum, lined up, as its name (The Locksmith) indicates, with locksmith and metal workshops, iron forges, and garages. The senses of the unsuspecting visitor, arriving on Ha'masger Street from the tidier parts of town, would be assaulted by the shrill sounds of forging hammers, the thick odors of car oil, pressed metal, and broken tires, and the prickly sight of blue and red sparks flying out of blacksmiths' caverns. It was only ten in the morning when I arrived at Ha'masger Street, but the asphalt was already burning and the tar was oozing in spots along the road. By the time I reached the grey and dilapidated building of *Kulmus,* I was perspiring. My dress looked disheveled. Damp wisps of hair were plastered to my forehead, and a thin, sour odor of sweat under my armpits was now mixed with my perfume. What a way to meet a man I was working so hard to impress, I thought in exasperation. As I reached the glass door of the building, I caught my reflection in the glass. Why am I so anxious?

I climbed to the second-floor office of the literary supplement, a large room with grey, bare walls. Uri was sitting behind a desk piled with papers, talking on the phone and passing his hand back and forth over his unruly hair. When he saw me, he raised his eyebrows, and motioned me to sit down. I sat on the edge of the chair. From time to time, Uri eyed me curiously but did not stop talking. "But I must have it *this* Thursday," he bellowed into the phone. This is a mistake, my rumbling stomach warned, a mistake! With a tissue, I wiped the sweat from my lip. Uri put his hand on the phone receiver and whispered, "When did you come back?" but before I could answer, he was talking into the phone again. Perhaps, I thought, I could sneak to the bathroom, but at that moment, Uri finally put the receiver down and got up from his chair to shake my hand.

"How are you?" he asked warmly.

"Fine," I smiled faintly.

"When did you come back? What brings you here?" I summarized the years after our separation in Oxford in short breathless sentences.

"Would you like to go out for some coffee?" Uri asked. I nodded. "Relax, Shelly, relax," he added on the way out, and I wanted to bury myself twenty feet underground. I am behaving like a teenager, I fumed. When we reached the first floor, Uri stopped to show me the printing press and introduced me to his printer, on whom, he said smiling, his whole world depends every Friday, when the supplement comes out. Uri still has the same kind smile, I thought, trying to breathe deeply when nobody was looking.

In the car, I told Uri of my interest in Joyce. "Oh, really?" he muttered, "that's good." We passed by the smithy shops and slowed down in the heavy traffic. Where, I fretted, is my best self? Why can't I put it forward? For a while we traveled in silence. Then Uri asked me about my plans and was pleased to find out that I was going for my doctorate. "Of the three women I knew in London," he flashed a charming smile, "you were the most intelligent. Tami," he recalled, "was the most beautiful, and Tova the best cook," he chuckled, "but you definitely were the most intelligent." I didn't know what to say. Was that a compliment?

It was only in the café that I dared to ask him if he needed a dance reviewer for his supplement. I described my experience at the Martha Graham school. Uri lit a cigarette and inhaled the smoke thoughtfully. He was interested. "Can you review different dance styles?" "Yes," I said, "I think so." "Okay," he remarked, "let's go back to the office; I'll give you a form to sign." Did that mean that he wanted me to write for him? I thought excitedly, following him out of the café.

On the way back, I was feeling more at ease and talked about England, but Uri seemed preoccupied. At the office, he gave me the form to fill out as one of his colleagues walked in. The two exchanged a few words and laughed. Uri instructed me to leave the form on his desk, and then walked out with his friend.

Alone in Uri's office, I tried to sort out my feelings. Flushed with excitement at the opportunity to review dance performances, I nonetheless felt disappointed. Why can't I speak in my own name, here, in my own country? I traveled to England, to learn, to grow, to get rid of Haya. Now I have come back, and Haya is right here, embarrassing me with her adolescent tremors! As I was filling out the form, my distress was thickening. All I need is for Uri to find out that what I really am is a wild animal. A growling tiger . . . with a growling stomach. . . . The smiling face of the printer showed in the door.

"Can I help you with anything? Are you waiting for Uri?" he asked, puzzled. "Didn't I see you here before with him?" he stared at me. I nodded. "So where is the rascal? Has he left you alone here?" he looked around. "No, no, I am fine," I said quickly. "He had to go; I'm just filling out a form." The printer nodded. "I see. If you need anything, just holler." He waved and disappeared in the quiet corridor.

It had been an hour since I finished the form, and I was still sitting there, glued to the chair. Did Uri want me to wait for him? I wondered. He did not say good-bye; how am I to know? I took my book out of my briefcase. Perhaps if I wait for him, he'll invite me for dinner, and we can talk more about dance. Perhaps I can even offer him to write an essay on Joyce . . . just to talk to him . . . to show him that I'm better than what he must have thought. Another hour passed. The workers of the newspaper went out for lunch. The building was now enveloped in silence, except for the distant hum of the printing presses.

Finally, I heard voices coming up the stairs. It was *his* voice, the voice I heard in Oxford outside his door. He was jovially talking to his friend about his classes in Tel Aviv University. "I do love teaching, definitely, but you know what," I overheard him as he was reaching the top of the stairs, "I often fight the compulsion, ha-ha, to unzip my fly, take my thing out in the middle of class, and piss on them all. . . ." Both Uri and his friend roared in laughter. Then they exchanged a few more words, which I could not hear, and parted. Uri stepped into his office. We gazed at each other. Everything that I did not say, everything that I labored to hide, everything that my trembling lips and rumbling stomach betrayed stood there between us, in the crossing of our gaze. Then I heard his laugh, cool, curious, contemptuous. "You are still here? *Still* here?" I was dumbstruck. How could he laugh like that? I thought, as I was furtively picking up my things. My face was hot as I mumbled apologies for the misunderstanding and moved quickly toward the door. Out, out of here, I ordered myself and slowed down only when I was outside, in the soft light of the afternoon sun. Suddenly I was utterly exhausted, and the small hill between the building and the bus station rose before me like a mountain. When I arrived late that evening to the villa, I imagined myself a wounded soldier returning from the battlefield. My mother pooh-poohed my defeat. "So what?" she said, "who needs him? There will be others! And why should you sit here gloomy as if it were *Tisha B'Av*? Was he a husband? Was he a lover? No. So what is there to cry about?"

Tisha B'av A day of fasting to commemorate the destruction of the First and Second Temples

"He laughed at me again," I explained, feeling a knot in my stomach, "and I gave him the opportunity for it. As if I had no pride at all."

"So what?" she said, fingering the soil in the plant pot next to her chair. "Dry. I must water it." Still talking, she walked to the kitchen and brought a bottle of water. "Pride shmide. You can't be so sensitive," she turned to me. "If you want to live and work in this country, you need a thicker skin."

"Like a rhinoceros?" I asked sourly.

"Not that thick. Don't exaggerate, but you have to know that not everything is the end of the world."

Reuven, who was slowly rocking in the hammock, remarked quietly, "At least he wants you to write those reviews. That's a good beginning."

"I am not sure he wants them now," I replied. "Or that I want to write them."

"But of course you want to write them," my mother's eyes blazed. "I really don't understand you! Why should you throw away an opportunity like that to write, to meet people, to become famous? Gradually people will know about you! You'll have a name, an influence, power! And all this you are throwing away because he laughed?"

I was too dispirited to argue. Reuven yawned. "Come, Dina," he said, "let's go to sleep. Tomorrow is also a day."

My mother picked up the used cups of coffee and, on her way in, reminded me again not to be stupid.

Alone, I folded my legs on the straw chair and abandoned myself to remorse. How could I make such a fool of myself? I agonized. How could I set myself up for such a fall?

GETTING STARTED

A few days later, I decided to rescue my job. I called Uri and asked him if I could review a Bat-Sheva dance performance. For the next two or three years, I became a regular dance reviewer for the *Kulmus*. In addition, I expanded my writing to book reviews, and then to long literary essays in Hebrew on Joyce and Dickens. But as I was refining my Hebrew writing, I received a disappointing response from the Hebrew University, advising me to do my master's thesis over again. After consulting with my friend Daniel, I applied to Bar-Ilan, the only other university that in 1969 granted doctorates in English. I was accepted with the provision that my course load be doubled to compensate for the lack of course work in the British system. Although Bar-Ilan was a religious university, I found out, from observing other women, that I would not have to change my attire, or keep kosher. And so, in January of 1970, I started my work toward my doctorate with Professor Fisch's course on William Blake.

Shortly before I started my studies, I moved to a small rented apartment on Remez Street in Tel Aviv. On my desk, Hebrew and English typewriters sat amicably side by side. For two or three years, I wrote and read in both languages. It was a period of great learning and excitement; whatever I lacked in one language, I found in the other. I devoured several scholarly books on Blake before the course even began, and every Friday I read all the literary supplements in the Hebrew newspapers. On some Friday afternoons, I would drink coffee in Café *Kasit* on Dizengoff Street, which used to be the haunt of the Israeli literati. When I had my fill of Hebrew, and Israel, I'd chat in English with my American or British colleagues. Sometimes we talked Hebrish—a haphazard combination of English and Hebrew—which was the most satisfying, informal arrangement for the wandering souls among us who longed to speak in both languages at once, like reckless drivers who insist on driving in two lanes simultaneously. I did not know then that one day I'd have to choose again between the languages.

In the early days of my doctoral program, my dance reviews did not compete with my English papers. In fact, in those reviews, I was able to speak in my own voice. Dance was my territory. I was free to make my own judgments. I talked about rhythms, temporal or spatial tensions, symbolic meanings, and dramatic uses of props. I compared performances. I watched rehearsals. I searched for the honest expression of feeling, the dedicated ensemble work, the movement of the spirit that transcended the body. I labored on each review as if it were a poem, seeking the precise words that would do justice to the art I admired.

Yet my social life among Israeli dancers and intellectuals was one of terrible isolation. The lonelier I felt in Israeli society, the more decidedly I gravitated toward the friendly English-American island at Bar Ilan University.

S—FOR SINGLE

When, sometime in the early 1980s, I read Lesley Hazleton's book *Israeli Women: The Reality Behind the Myths,* I felt, to appropriate Emily Dickinson's description of her response to poetry, "as if the top of my head were taken off."

Hazleton's definition of marriage in Israel as the "national panacea," and her conclusion that "it is the rare Israeli woman who dares to buck the marriage system for a life of her own" gave me a shock of recognition, as if the entire chapter were a blueprint of my own experience. But in the early 1970s, Hazleton's book had not even been written. I had no guidance and little understanding—except for intuitive flashes—of Israeli reality. Outwardly, I rebelled against the unmitigated pressure to marry. But inwardly I wanted to marry and often accepted the blame for my wretched condition. When my grocer saw me scowling and said, "all you need is a husband," I'd argue with him. "When I find the right man, I will marry," I'd say, or "I am a person in my own right," but deep down I did not believe it. I thought that I was wearing an invisible letter *S,* for Single (and for Shelly), that everybody could see it, that most women pitied or feared it, that some men, like Uri, ran away from it, and that married men ran toward it, hoping for an easy conquest. And it was all my fault. I was too choosy, too lustful, too needy; I was too intellectual, my head in the clouds; I did not know how to please a man—didn't they all tell me that? I rejected the best offers and chased the good-for-nothings. Who could understand me, who could sympathize? What could I say to the grocers and the aunts, the mothers and the stepfathers? Yes, I wanted to get married. I was as obsessed with it as they were. But I refused to compromise on love. That's where I held the line. And yet, I asked, what would I do with this loneliness until I found the man I could love? ("If ever," Aunt Bracha would say.) "Have an affair," Aunt Nomi would wink at me. "Why not?" she'd roll her eyes. "You are a ripe woman. You want to dry up like a prune?"

It was in this dried-up-prune mood that I met Noam, one of the star Israeli dancers, in his room backstage, after one of his performances. I introduced myself to him as the dance reviewer for *Kulmus.* "So you are Shelly," he looked at me through his mirror, as he was taking off his makeup. I was glad that my earlier review of his performance was complimentary, except for a passing comment on some sloppiness in his dancing. "So you are Shelly," he repeated, laughing. He turned around, one eye still marked with fierce black lines, and shook my hand. "I have been wanting to talk to you," he said, turning toward the mirror. "I enjoyed your review of my dance," he remarked without a smile. "A good review. Well written. But you know," he took off the rest of the makeup and covered his face with white cream. "You are wrong about something. You are simply wrong. Never mind," he was rubbing his face, "I can teach you." "What am I wrong about?" I asked. "Sit, sit," he said, noticing that I was still standing. "You said that some of my movements were sloppy." I was silent. "That's all right. Quite all right. But I would like to know which movements," his green eyes were gazing at the mirror again. "I don't know," I muttered, "I can't really remember." He finished wiping off his makeup and stood up. He was wearing a simple pair of jeans and a black shirt. "Do you have a moment?" he asked. A catch in my throat. "Yes," I said. "Then come with me," he said, "to the studio. I'll show you what I mean."

The night draped the city like poured silk. Intoxicated by the fragrance of jasmine mixed with salty sea breezes and flattered by the proximity of the great dancer, I forgot my role as a critic. I could not believe that the famous Noam would give me a private demonstration of his dance! After all, who was I? How could my puny review, in a minor newspaper, detract one iota from the beauty and the ecstacy of his dance? Why should he spend so much time and energy on *me?* And yet, that's what he was going to do, I reflected, as we traveled in his car to the studio. The whole way he talked about the dance, his hands flying about, his handsome face intense and serious. As if he needed to persuade me. As if he were a beginner fighting for recognition. And all this, I thought, for my benefit?

The studio, which I had visited so many times before in the daytime, was completely dark except for a shaft of light from a streetlamp that gave the mirrors and the costumes hanging about a sinister and droll look. Noam turned on a desk lamp that threw a strong circle of light in the center of the studio. Then he looked intently at a point in space, took off his shirt, and began to dance. In the Martha Graham style, he contracted in such a decisive movement that he seemed to take in all the air in the room. Even the mirrors seemed to contract with him. Then he relaxed, exhaled, and stood on one leg, perfectly still, like a flamingo. A minute, two minutes passed. He was still balanced, gathered, on one leg. Then his arms lifted slowly, like arched wings poised for flight, casting huge shadows on the ceiling. Suddenly he slithered like a snake, bounded like a leopard, flowed like water. He jumped and turned and swirled around himself like a corkscrew. And then landed, unwound, and threw himself to the floor, straight as an arrow, catching his weight with his hands in the last available second. Finally he sat up, his eyes closed, rested, like a Buddha.

I was awestruck. Never had I seen anything like that before. It was a stirring, stalwart performance. I admired it and longed to possess the dancer, touch the body that could create such beauty. Gradually Noam came around, as if waking up from a trance, and spoke quietly to me. "You see," he said, "my movements are disciplined. There is no sloppiness in them." I nodded in agreement, but like a survivor in the ocean holding onto a plank of wood, I refused to go back on my written judgment. He wiped his face and his back with a towel, staring at me the while with unsmiling eyes. Then, he stretched out his arms to me. My heart was racing. I wanted him. He was married, I knew, but I still wanted to touch that glory. He laid me down on a dancing mat and made love to me without a caress or an affectionate word—in silence. He did not even hold me. He was quick and serious and impersonal, as if he were performing a duty.

Later he thought he heard somebody coming and instructed me to get dressed quickly. In silence, he drove me to my apartment, mumbled something about being tired, said shalom and left. I ran up the stairs, skipping two at a time, buoyed by pleasure. But the sight of the empty apartment, the piled books, the unmade bed oppressed my spirit. What am I so happy about? I asked myself. He had his will of me, and now he is gone. So why do I still feel good, as if I've accomplished something wonderful?

It was only when, a few days, or weeks, later, another married dancer, from the same company, grabbed me in his car that I finally understood: not only that had I become what I feared, an "available single woman," but worse, I was deemed a hungry female critic whose good opinion could be bought with a brief moment of pleasure. For how could I write a negative word on dancers who honored me with their glorious bodies?

And then there were others: a writer who used me to defend his book in the newspapers, another writer who invited me home to show me pictures of erotic sculptures in Indian temples and whisper in my ear that what he wrote in his books—that women love humiliation—was true, and finally a poet—the kinkiest of them all—who wanted me to watch him masturbating. And I did.

At night, I was haunted by a recurrent nightmare. A figure in white opened the door and was slowly approaching me with malicious intent. I wanted to scream, but my voice died in my throat. I wanted to run, but my legs turned to water. I lay there, whimpering, waiting for the end. Then I'd wake up, moaning, drenched in sweat. Often when I closed my eyes, the dream would instantly return.

"Daniel," I called my friend one morning. "I can't sleep, can't read, can't write. I can't stand myself. I do things I am ashamed of, and yet I can't stop. Help!" Daniel invited me for coffee on Dizengoff Street. After awhile, he said, "Do you remember that in London I talked to you about Freud and therapy? Well, a few years ago, I went to a therapist." I watched him intently. In those days, in Israel, such a confession was tantamount to an admission of madness, or a subvertive political activity. "Yes," he repeated, "there is absolutely nothing wrong with it. On the contrary, anybody who takes himself seriously must undergo analysis. Remember Socrates? 'The unexamined life is not worth living.'"

"Yes, but why does therapy have such a bad reputation here? My parents would giggle for a week if they knew I was considering analysis."

"Because," he said, "people are afraid of their feelings. They say that only the insane need therapists," he laughed with abandon, his straight black hair falling playfully on his forehead. "But it's not true. Most of us need therapy, simply to understand what we are doing, and why we are doing it. My therapist helped me a lot. Her name is Rina Silver. You want her phone number?"

"Yes," I said.

"MORE PRECIOUS THAN RUBIES"

Mrs. Silver, who did not have a doctorate, or a medical degree, but a master's degree in psychology, received her patients in her penthouse on a small side street, not far from Dizengoff Street. When I knocked on the door, a slim tall woman in her fifties, with large forbidding glasses, opened it and asked me in. The house was filled with sunlight coming in from a large window in the ceiling. Plants graced the floor, paintings hung on the walls, and a sizable library of records stood in the living room. The apartment looked spacious and refined, inhabited by people who liked music, art, and, judging by the elegant dining table, festive dinners. Mrs. Silver showed me the way to her therapy room, which was awash with sunlight. On the left, a floor-to-ceiling bookshelf held various books in psychology, most notably Freud's writings. In front of me, behind Mrs. Silver's chair, hung a large portrait of Freud. As if painted by Rembrandt, the piercing eyes of the father of psychoanalysis followed me wherever I stood or sat in that room. "So how can I help you?" Mrs. Silver said. She took out her knitting-needles, as was her habit, and started to knit and to listen.

I was grateful that somebody was there, ready to hear me. So much was oppressing my mind that words came tumbling out over each other. I told her about my nightmares and about my uncontrollable tremors. "Why is it that when I meet intellectual men, my stomach makes such rude noises I have to use all my energy to calm it down?" In spite of my embarrassment, I was surprised by the rush of relief that followed my confession. I was no longer alone with "It." "It" could be looked at, examined. Mrs. Silver smiled and said simply, "It sounds like an anxiety attack. It can be cured."

Encouraged by the normalcy of my affliction, and by the promise of healing, I threw myself with unflinching devotion into the work of psychoanalysis. In the weeks that followed I learned that by tracing the sources of my fears, I could better control my behavior. The new insights that surfaced almost every week were charged with excitement. I was gaining the self-knowledge that was the beginning of change. After a few weeks, I was better able to control my jitters. I identified the authority figures whose stares turned me to jelly and negotiated my way out of my anxious space. I persuaded, reasoned, and pleaded with my "unconscious" not to betray me. On several occasions, I raised my hand in class and spoke. I heard a timid voice, but it was my voice.

With Mrs. Silver's help I also overcame some of my sexual submissiveness. When I mustered the courage to tell her about the poet who pleasured himself in my presence, I was hoping that she'd find a way to tell me that it was "all right," that it was somehow understandable and acceptable. For a while she was silent; her knitting-needles went clickety-click, clickety-click. Then she asked me, "Why did you let him?"

I was dumbstruck. "It didn't occur to me to stop him," I said, shamefaced.

"Why not?" she asked. "Why did you tolerate such behavior?" Clickety-click.

"I don't know," I answered, chagrined.

"He's a terrible man," Mrs. Silver said, "messed up, don't you see?"

"But he is a successful poet. . . ." I said weakly.

"So what?" she said. "Famous poets can't be crazy? I know quite a few of them," she chuckled, "believe me. You don't need to give in to men who humiliate you, even if they are poets."

The session was painful, but, riding home on the bus, I felt clear and lighthearted. I can say no, I thought, as if I had just discovered a new word. And if the whole country thinks me a miserable spinster, a dried-up prune, or a pathetic dance critic, I can still say no. And the more I say no to dirty-minded men, the sooner I'll meet the man I love. Like pulling out the weeds that smother a rose garden. A labor for love.

The struggle, though, was difficult. My resolve often weakened. And yet, each time I slipped, I had to account for it to Mrs. Silver; I could no longer escape responsibility for my actions. Gradually, my efforts bore fruit. At the time, I knew a young student from Tel Aviv University, Yoram, whom I had let stay over in my apartment three nights a week, against my feelings. "Why?"

Mrs. Silver asked. "Because I don't want to be alone," I said. "Isn't it better to be alone than with him?" she retorted. She was right, I thought. That night I asked Yoram to collect his things and leave my place. Before he left, he smiled reluctantly. "No woman has ever done this to me before. You know what you want. I respect that." I repeated his words quietly to myself. Those words, I thought, are more precious than rubies.

A MUDDIED SPRING

At first therapy clarified and healed. For a while, it flowed vigorously, but after a few months, it became sluggish, like a muddied spring. Was it I who turned indolent, or resistant (a new meaning I learned in therapy)? Or was it Mrs. Silver who could no longer offer me what I needed? I didn't know. I noticed changes in her conduct. At times, she talked about herself for the whole hour. At the end of the hour, I would leave disappointed, but I still handed her the money. After all, I'd rationalize, she had already helped me a great deal, and besides, wasn't it my good friend Daniel who recommended her? Could he be wrong?

More troubling than the wasteful hours was Mrs. Silver's adherence to Freud. At the beginning, I did not sense his presence. Later, however, when Mrs. Silver invited me to lie on the couch, her therapy became absolutely Freudian. If I quaked in fear of a professor, it could be only one thing—penis envy. "Think about it," she would say. "What does he have that you don't? What is it that he has that you want?"

"I don't know," I'd say, groping, "success, status. . . ."

"Perhaps. But think about it," she'd say. "Isn't there something else, too? Deeper, more fundamental?"

"What could that be?"

"Well," she'd laugh, "his majesty, the penis, of course. That's what Freud called penis envy. Look at this, for example," she drew from her desk a drawing that must have been waiting there specifically for this moment. "This is a sketch one of my patients, a five-year-old girl, made of herself. And look," she said gleefully, "what she drew here—a penis, instead of her own genitals! Wasn't Freud right?" she smacked her lips. "You may think that you envy something else, but what you really envy is the penis," she asserted.

Never having felt penis envy before, I asked cautiously if all women felt it.

"Of course all women do," she smiled, "even when they don't know it. But what do they need the penis for? They just *think* they do, and that's the cause of their misery."

I believed her and worked hard to please her. Whenever I was overcome by panic, particularly in the proximity of my male professors, I chastised myself for my aggressive designs on their genitals. But although I searched every corner of my psyche, I could find no such designs. On the contrary, instead of feeling guilty like a dangerous criminal, I often felt that it was I who was in danger. Wasn't it I whose success in my doctorate depended on my professors' judgment?

The penis envy was important, but nothing, in Mrs. Silver's world, was more important than the Oedipus complex. According to her, all daughters were their mothers' sexual rivals. My guilt and my deep-seated fear of my mother, Mrs. Silver affirmed, stemmed exclusively from early erotic rivalry. Indeed, I could see the truth in her observation, but I got hopelessly muddled by the Freudian strategies she used to drill it into me. Instead of giving me insights into my choices of and conduct with men, as she had done early in the therapy, she now instructed me to recall my erotic fantasies about my father before my parents' divorce. I was at a loss. Lying on the couch, I tried hard to evoke my primal guilt from the tender age of three, to remember the incriminating scenes, to imagine the erotic feelings for my father; I cried, I cringed, I broke into cold sweat—all in vain. My stubborn unconscious refused to spew out the Freudian evidence. All I could remember was the sadness I felt when my father left me, but Mrs. Silver ignored this event as well as the orphanage period that followed it.

Similarly irrelevant, in Mrs. Silver's view, were my complaints about my mother's overbearing conduct. Whenever I mentioned it, Mrs. Silver would be silent. The only sound came from her knitting-needles. "My mother always puts me down," I'd say. Clickety-click. "I am afraid of her," I'd admit. Clickety-click, clickety-click. "She always takes over," I'd flare up. Clickety-click-click-click. "You are the guilty one," Mrs. Silver would finally say, "but you don't see it. It is this important truth that you are resisting. You are blaming your mother, but you should take a good look at yourself. Relinquish your desire for your father." Click, click.

"But I have no such desires," I'd plead, as I was getting up from the couch, "and that's not what our fights are about."

"Yes, they are," she'd smile, "but they are unconscious, of course. And your unconscious, as we have seen, is not very cooperative."

"But why is it," I persisted, "that I am so dependent on my mother, that I give in to her so often? What does this have to do with Oedipus? How can I overcome it?" I asked in anguish.

Mrs. Silver's brown eyes, enlarged by her glasses, looked severely at me. "Never," she said, putting her needles down. "You are too old for that. Can't you see? When I was seventeen, I left home and earned my own money, but you've been dependent on your mother for—what are you twenty-nine, or thirty years old? You can't change now. It's too late."

Is it true? I asked myself riding the bus back to my apartment. No, I resolved, Mrs. Silver cannot be right. From that day, my trust in her was shaken. Only once—in an important event to be narrated later—did Mrs. Silver rise to her full stature to oppose my mother. And for that one time—as well as for the times she taught me to say no to exploitive men—I remember her with gratitude.

A HOST OF GOLDEN DAISIES

In my second year at Bar-Ilan, I was assigned two sections of Introduction to Romantic Poetry. This was my first teaching assignment. In my first week of classes, I saw with absolute clarity the method behind some of my maddest choices: my impractical devotion to literature, my journey to England, my submission to the rigors of the master's and doctoral programs. As soon as I walked into class, put my books down, and looked at the students, I knew that I had made the right choice. What better way to spend my life than to share with these students the wisdom and eloquence of English literature? What could be more right than to point out the vitality of the human spirit that moved in the stirring words of a poem or a story? This is my hallowed ground, I thought. Here I stand. In future years I found that teaching could also be a rough and unyielding ground, but I never lost faith in it as the most worthy ground. Its challenges made it the ground for my growth.

I worked hard to prepare for each class. I read books on the Romantic period, no longer for myself and my papers, but for the students. Knowledge took on a tangible, dramatic dimension; it became a dialogue, a responsibility. My life was no longer aimless but had a form and a purpose, I explained to my Israeli colleague, Dorit, a tall, good-looking brunette, on our way to the cafeteria one day. "Your purpose in life is teaching?" Dorit asked, shaking her long hair. "I never felt that way," she added, "I *have* a purpose, but it is certainly not teaching." It was a warm spring evening; the orchards around Bar-Ilan gave off a strong fragrance of orange blossoms.

"What is it then? English?" I guessed.

"English?" Dorit laughed. "My mother is English. I spoke English from birth, all my life, along with Hebrew. Isn't somebody in your family English or American?"

"No," I said, looking at the round red sun setting behind the orchards.

"That's interesting," Dorit smiled. "So how did you learn English?"

"On my own," I said hesitantly. "At the Hebrew University, and then in England. But tell me," I added quickly, to deflect attention from my inferior origins, "what is your purpose, if it isn't teaching or English?"

"Funny you should ask," Dorit chuckled, her shapely green eyes illumined by the sun's orange light. "Living here, in Israel, is already a purpose. The problems of this country are much more important than our teaching or our English, don't you think?" I silently contemplated my double defeat. Not only was Dorit's English superior to mine, but so were her Israeli loyalties. And yet my excitement about teaching soon returned, as strong and buoyant, I thought, as any Zionist conviction.

The semester flew by. The last day of classes arrived. I came to Bar-Ilan in high spirits. I went to the library for a few minutes, to go over my notes for my last lecture. When class time came, I was ready. I picked up my books and my notes and walked downstairs to give my last session for the year.

Afterward, especially in times when I despaired of my ability to reach students, I'd replay in my mind the moment I walked into class on that last day of my first year of teaching. There on my battered desk stood a huge bouquet of yellow daisies. In a plastic water jug, forty or fifty of them were quietly gleaming. I approached them slowly. Don't jump to conclusions, I warned myself, these are probably not for you. "Has somebody forgotten these flowers here?" I asked my class. The students burst out laughing. "They're for you," someone said, "read the note." I dropped my heavy books to the floor. With trembling fingers, I opened up the note. "To Miss Shapira," it said, "Thank you for a great year. With appreciation. Your Romantic Poetry class of 1972."

I cannot recall how I managed to finish that class period. Afterward, I rushed upstairs, the flowers clutched in my hands. "Who are these flowers for?" somebody asked. "Give me one flower, you have so many," somebody else hollered. At the top of the stairs, I saw Aaron Streiter, one of the popular professors in the department. "Look," I said breathlessly, "look what my

students gave me." He stared at the flowers. Then he said, "If I were the head
of the department, I'd promote you. Right away." Alas, he was not.

For the next two weeks the daisies lit up my apartment. I kept them until
all of them, to the last, withered. My mother said, "How long do you intend
to keep dead flowers in your vase?" How could I explain to her what wealth
this host of wilting daisies had brought to me?

1972

Nineteen seventy-two was a year of profound changes. My initiation as a
teacher was one of the crucial turns. Another was meeting Mark Spilka. When
Mark came to teach at the Hebrew University for a semester, in the spring of
1972, he was already a "big gun"—the chair of the English department at
Brown University, a famous scholar, the author of *Dickens and Kafka,* as well
as ground-breaking, seminal books on D. H. Lawrence, and the editor of the
prestigious journal *Novel: A Forum on Fiction.* Anticipating his visit at our
modest Bar-Ilan English department, many of us experienced what the Lil-
liputians must have felt when Gulliver called on them. I, at least, thought the
only thing to do in the presence of that giant was to squeeze myself into a corner, be quiet as a mouse, and avoid any questions that might expose my igno-
rance. Two or three days before he came, the name Spilka was on everybody's
lips. His talk was to be the big event of the year. We were all prepared to be
humbled by it or, looking on the bright side, inspired to return to our various
neglected research projects.

When Mark Spilka finally arrived, he materialized as a distinguished-
looking Jewish gentleman with a Dutch-cut beard that emphasized his resem-
blance to Hemingway. Neither Gulliver nor a hotshot professor, Mark was an
unassuming, soft-spoken man with a kind smile, so soft-spoken, in fact, that
when he gave the lecture in his inaudible voice, never lifting his eyes from the
paper, I was disappointed. I could barely make out what he was saying. Instead
of fireworks, I got mumbles. He probably did not care for us at all, I thought.
Only later did I learn that even the famous Spilka had to struggle with anxiety
about public performances.

I cannot recall what occasion threw us together in a car with colleagues,
traveling to some place in Tel Aviv. But I vividly remember this picture: we are
all spilling out of the car, stretching our legs, talking. I was walking up front
but, realizing that I was moving too fast, I turned around and saw his eyes for

the first time, the eyes that during his lecture were hidden behind the heavy double curtain of reading glasses and eyelids. What striking eyes, I thought surprised, soft brown, probing, guileless, inescapable, opening to depths—who would have imagined? I looked aside, but I had to look again. Those eyes were still staring at me *(at me?)* with an if-you-don't-speak-to-me-very-soon-I-will-surely-die expression. I was flattered.

The next picture I remember is the two of us riding together in a car, at night. Was it the same night? Perhaps. Smiling shyly, Mark asked me if I would like to go out to dinner with him. "Are you married?" I asked him. "No," he said, "divorced." "Yes," I said, "I would be delighted."

I was thrilled to be seen with the famous professor from America. I paraded him among my friends and colleagues, as if he added to my natural height. I was no longer unimportant in the world; I was enhanced and made vivid by *him,* my companion. It was true that I did not quite comprehend his erudite references and—as a solemn Israeli—did not grasp his American self-deprecating humor, but I knew enough to laugh in the right places and to fool others. Yet I could not fool myself when I was alone with Mark in his breezy Jerusalem apartment on Benjamin of Tudela Street, watching him sitting on the porch, storming his typewriter, cranking out page after page of evident brilliance on the controversy between Henry James and Walter Besant. It was then, when I sat behind him shooting envious stares at his back, that I most keenly felt my inadequacy. He had a vigorous mind and a creative, independent life of his own, but I didn't even know which author or topic I wanted to write my dissertation on. I admired Mark, but how could I love him? Yet I did my best to "catch" him.

When we traveled to Haifa, where Mark gave his talk on James and Besant, I brought him home and introduced him to my parents. Mark felt that it was much too early for introductions of this sort and withdrew into his shell. Oblivious to his feelings, I set out to test his attitude toward my mother. The man I married, I knew, would have to be my advocate, my ally against her. The first five minutes of the visit manifested that Mark had no intentions of fighting my mother. He was a graceful, polite visitor, unaware of the boiling cauldron that set my mother and me apart.

When I found out that Mark did not intend to marry me, I cut off the relationship with a finality that both pained him and aroused his admiration. As he wrote to me in his last letter, "You knew what you wanted." Right! I nodded proudly. Yet my sense of triumph soon vanished as I wistfully pondered the abrupt end of our two months of pleasant courting. What went wrong? I asked. Did my envy have anything to do with it? No, it was all Mark's fault, I reassured myself in my brazen Israeli defensiveness; he didn't appreciate me. I labored to erase his memory, yet somehow it continued to glow amid shadows of vague regret.

"BECAUSE I COULD NOT STOP FOR DEATH—"

The year 1972 also brought the meeting with Kenneth Regenbaum. However, in between these two meetings, with Mark and with Kenneth, Reuven died.

On the 17th of June, 1972, at noon, I called my mother, but Reuven answered. "What are you doing at home?" I asked, "no sick cows today?" "Today *I* am a bit sick," Reuven chortled. "Nothing to worry about," he reassured me, "just a headache and some nausea. Tomorrow I'll go back to work."

I put the receiver down with misgivings. Reuven never stayed home for a headache. He never missed a day of work, except once, I remembered with unease, eleven years ago, when he had had a heart attack. But it couldn't be his heart again. Why should it be? I turned back to my books. But I could not read. I jumped to my feet and paced the room. Finally, I called him again. "Are you sure you are all right?" The sound of his voice calmed me. "Don't you worry, Shelly," he said, "I'm fine. Just fine. I am already feeling better. Besides, you know the saying, 'the coward dies many times, but the brave man dies only once?'" I shuddered. "What do you mean?" I asked. "Nothing," he said, impatiently, "there is no point in fretting, is there? What will be will be. Go about your business, and don't spend so much time thinking about me."

But the sense of dread did not leave me. Two hours later I boarded the train to Haifa. When we passed Haderah, I felt inexplicably lighthearted. Looking at the stretch of sand dunes and squatting bushes I thought, I am just imagining things. The train sped along the coastline, sometimes so close to the blue ocean that one could clearly see its sand floor and its *kurkar,* sharp, fossilized sand reefs, lying in their shadows, a silent menace to the unwary swimmers. So much beauty, I sighed, sipping the coffee I ordered from the tiny cafeteria. So much brightness. Who can think of death on a day like this? I am probably worried for nothing. Always worried. I stretched my arms on the comfortable seat, yawned, and picked up my newspaper again.

At the Haifa station I took a bus to Carmel. As it was slowly climbing up the mountain, I looked with interest at the city I once lived in. We passed by the gardens of the Bahai Temple, where the bus began the longest and steepest leg of its climb. I remembered the many times Reuven drove up this road in his Mercedes, which was much faster than the creeping bus and always smelled of medicine and cow dung. Suddenly the sense of dread, like a silent wave, stole up on me again. With difficulty I calmed myself by remembering Reuven's reassuring words. When I got home and found Reuven's Mercedes parked in its place, under the large pine tree, I felt even more at ease. But when I saw the kitchen window closed shut, I descended the fifty-one stairs with knocking knees.

Aunt Bracha opened the door. "We've been trying to call you all afternoon," she said, sighing. "Reuven had an infarct, a massive heart attack, and he is now in the emergency room of Rambam Hospital." Then, anticipating my question, she added, "Dina is there also, and Ruth."

I clutched the nearest kitchen chair and sat down. "When did it happen?" I whispered.

"This afternoon," Bracha said, putting up a pot of coffee for us.

"But I talked to him at noon," I remonstrated. "He said he was nauseous but all right. When did this. . . ." I choked on the word.

"At one o'clock," Bracha replied quietly, "there was a change for the worse. He complained about pressure in the chest and breathing difficulty. Dina immediately took him to the hospital, and then called me to come here, to wait for you. I stopped at the hospital to see your mother. You know how she is when she is scared? Her eyes are two blue pools, have you ever seen them like that?" I nodded. "She is so beautiful then," Bracha smiled. "And in a minute she is mobilized into action, like a powerhouse. You may not believe it, but she was already telling the nurses what to do. . . ." she laughed softly, shaking the ash off her cigarette. "Later I came up here and tried to get you on the phone, but you were already on your way here!" We drank our coffee in silence. "He may still pull through," Bracha sighed. "Come," she stood up and put her cup in the sink. "I'll take you to the hospital."

The Cardiac Intensive Care Unit at Rambam was located in a circular, one-story building, separated from the rest of the hospital and surrounded by oleander bushes. Housing only six or seven beds, complete with state-of-the-art machines and monitors, it provided a comfortable and efficient setting for the critically ill. When Bracha and I arrived there, my mother and Ruth came out through the white swinging doors. My mother's eyes were two blue pools, and the corners of her mouth were pulled down with worry. "What took you so long?" she complained, but before we could answer she added, "He is a bit better now, but his situation is serious," she wiped her forehead with her embroidered kerchief. "It was a massive attack, Dina," Ruth said soothingly. "But you know," she smiled, "the doctor said that there is still hope." "Well," my mother said, "there is nothing more for us to do here." "Can I see him?" I asked quickly. My mother looked distracted at my dress, "No, he is sleeping now," she said. "Why didn't you wear the orange dress?" Ruth frowned, "Come on, Dina, what does a dress matter now?" My mother sighed, "You are right, Ruth. All is lost anyway. Let's go home."

Having to go to work the following day, Bracha began her journey back to Tiberias, but Ruth stayed with us that night. When we got to our darkened house, my mother said, "I am so glad you are staying, Ruth; I could not face this night alone."

The night air was hot and humid, but I could not stop shivering. My mother was going in and out of rooms, turning on the lights. "What are you looking for, Dina?" Ruth asked.

"What I am looking for," my mother took off her rings, "I'll never find again. So strange not to hear his voice in this house. 'Dina'le, you want something to eat?' What an empty house this is going to be now. . . ." she sighed.

Ruth looked at her pleadingly. "Go to sleep, Dina. You need your rest. You have to be there early tomorrow."

"Yes," my mother nodded, gazing into space. "I'd better take a Valium."

"Ruth," I said after my mother turned in, "What if he dies?" I clutched her hand.

"I know, I know," she muttered softly. "It will be terrible, especially for your mother. What will she do, I wonder, without him. He has given her everything, served her from morning till night, been loyal to her in spite of everything." In spite of Chaim, I reflected. "And who is she after all?" Ruth continued. "She often said to me, 'I didn't even finish high school, I came from the slums of Tiberias, I lived in abject poverty, and got up at four o'clock every morning to dress and feed my sisters and brothers, and look at my husband— a veterinary doctor! Haven't I come up in the world?'" Ruth sighed deeply and looked around. "And this house he gave her? You know how hard he worked for it? Your mother has very expensive tastes, you know," she laughed quietly. "But how he loves her," she added sadly.

"Yes," I nodded, "he loves her very much. Perhaps too much," I ventured.

"He loves you, too!" Ruth, aware of my drift, quickly changed the subject. "How he loves you!" Her green eyes lit up. "It was he who insisted that you be taken out of the orphanage. It was he who took you to your private math lessons and brought you a dog and four rabbits, remember? And when you were in London, it was he who worried more than anybody else about you and urged Dina to go there, to be with you. He used to ask me, 'Do you think that Shelly will finish her master's degree, Ruth?' And when you did, he was the happiest man in Israel," a smile spread on her round, kind face.

"But he has always been afraid of her," I blurted in sudden anger, "always took her side, always gave in to her, never protected me."

Ruth's eyes squinted as if she were out in the sun. "Do you know what you are talking about?" she looked at me askance. "Nobody cared for you as much as he did. He's always tried to protect you, from her, too."

"I don't feel protected," I cried out. Then, sensing the surge of a new wave of dread, I mumbled guiltily, "Forget it."

"And as for your mother," Ruth added, "we all know that she can't control her temper. But she loves you, *meidá'le,*"she hugged me, "deep down Dina has a heart of gold. I am her sister; I should know."

The following morning, I accompanied my mother to see Reuven. Wired up to beeping machines, he looked pale and gaunt, as if he had lost fifty pounds in one night. Our conversation was brief and stiff, and I remember wanting it to end. Reuven talked mainly to my mother, and when he asked me about Bar-Ilan, I gave him dry, one-word answers. More than anything else I wanted to be outside the white swinging doors again, near the oleander bushes, in the sun. Beyond that, I wanted to be back in my classroom, cheerfully teaching, released from the clutches of mourning and death.

On the third day, Reuven's condition deteriorated further, and the doctors prepared us for the worst. My mother ordered me to stay out of Reuven's room, but moved by regret or curiosity, I walked around the building and looked into his room through the window. I saw him in profile, lying still, breathing regularly in and out, his eyes closed, his glasses on the bureau by his bed. Suddenly, he raised himself on his elbow, turned his head toward the window, and looked directly at me. His green eyes were round, startled, and strange-looking without his glasses. What was in his eyes? A rebuke? A plea? I didn't know. For a few seconds, I gazed at him stunned. Then I looked aside at the bluish sheen of the sea. For a moment, I was ashamed. He saw me running away from him. I missed the last opportunity to tell him. . . . Tell him what? I didn't know. Anyway, I calmed myself, he couldn't have seen me without his glasses. He probably wasn't even looking at me, didn't even know I was there; at most he saw a shadow passing by his window.

The next morning, June 21, 1972, there was an emergency alarm. Six or seven doctors marched into Reuven's room. They tried hard to stop his dying, but they couldn't. An hour later, one of the doctors called us in. *"Oi,"* my mother said, "I am fainting." My uncle Avram tried to hold her, but she refused his help. We walked in slowly. By the nurse's station, the doctor described to us how they tried in vain to save Reuven. "Sorry," said the doctor with a sad smile, as if lamenting the way of all flesh. At that moment, and I have no idea how or when it happened, or how it could have happened, at that moment, when my eyes lingered on the doctor's sad smile, and on the nurse who came out of Reuven's room, exactly at that second, by my side, there was suddenly a hollow space where my mother had stood. I looked around for her. There she was, stretched out on the floor, motionless and rigid as if herself had undergone rigor mortis. "Dina!" Avram cried out and jumped to her side, pale with fear. But the doctor bent down and felt her pulse. "She will be all right," he said, "just a shock." Then he helped her to get up. With alacrity, my mother sprang back to life.

Hundreds of people came to the funeral, causing a major traffic jam in Haifa that day. Somebody counted five hundred cars, snaking their way down from the mountain to the seashore cemetery. Friends, relatives, kibbutzniks, and all the veterinary doctors in Israel came to the funeral. Dr. Shapira, a tall, burly vet with a deep voice, hugged my mother and said, with moist eyes, "Reuven was a wonderful man! A wonderful man! May you be comforted." Dr. Zilber and his wife Yael approached us sobbing. "I can't imagine life without Dr. Sirotinsky," Dr. Zilber bawled, holding his glasses in one hand and wiping his eyes with the other. "Such a dear man," he wept, "such an excellent mentor." Reuven's sister, Rachel, threw her arms around my mother and cried, "Oh, Dina, how much we have lost, how much we have lost." My mother, supported by Avram on her right and Ruth on her left, nodded and moaned, "Yes, Rachel, yes, whatever shall we do now?" The cemetery air was vibrating with groans, sobs, and cries of dismay, as the procession of mourners drew close to the grave. When the prayer *El Male Rachamim* (God of mercy) was sung, and the plea for a proper rest for the departed went up to the blue sky, there was not one dry eye, as my mother used to say later, in the crowd.

There were two dry eyes, though. Mine. During the slow march to the grave, through the burial and the searing prayers, I could not cry.

1950 snow. On the hills of Tiberias, overlooking Lake Kinneret. Reuven, Imma, and I.

I should have cried, but I couldn't. Even later I couldn't. And later still, in October and November, when my teaching plummeted, I should have known why, but I didn't. On the 21 of June, 1972, I buried my grief for Reuven in his grave. I didn't even light a *Yahrzeit* candle on the anniversary of his death; all I wanted was to forget.

If you are still there, Reuven, this is for you. It is hard to talk. You never had faith in such "talks." "What is there to talk about?" you'd say. I can see you raising your hand to silence me. "Let bygones be bygones," you are protesting. But I must talk to you, Ruvke. Let's sit, as we used to, on the straw chairs on the veranda.

In truth, I am scared, but I am not going to run away this time. Here I am, looking at your pictures. In one of them, you are sitting at a meeting of vets where all are listening gravely to a speaker. You stand out in your bald head and white shirt; your finger rests on your mouth, as if ordering yourself to be quiet. In another picture, you are sitting on the armchair in the living room, your head resting on your tanned arm. You are smiling slightly, and there is a whimsical look in your eyes, one that would be there now, if you were here. But it is this picture that cuts me to the quick. The three of us— you, *Imma,* and I—are standing in a field of snow overlooking Lake Kinneret. That was one of the two times it snowed in Israel. Of course, the snow melted after a few hours, but in the picture the ground is visibly white, and the clouds overhead are thick and dark. I am nine years old. I have my boots on and a cheerful smile on my face—I must be terribly excited by the snow. *Imma,* wearing a fur coat and a scarf, is resting her hands on my shoulders and leaning lightly on your shoulder, while you are embracing her firmly with your right arm. How mysterious is this picture! We seem to be such a happy family: *Imma* so loving, I so confident, with my arms folded on my chest, and you so strong. There we are, together, in our Beulah land, Reuven, before Chaim came.

I see you raising your finger to your mouth with a hushing gesture. You don't want me to talk about him, I know. But I must, because this is where my pain begins. He charmed *Imma* away from you, and he charmed me too. He became my powerful Papa Chaim. So many times, Reuven, I preferred his glitzy fatherhood to your homespun one! And you didn't care. That's the thing, you see. All you wanted was to love us; you never asked us to love you in return. Never mentioned it, never required it. That's why you had the reputation of a saint, because no matter how badly I treated you, you never protested. You never demanded respect from me. And without respecting you, how could I respect myself? So I held your love cheap.

Now I can see you smiling faintly, the left side of your mouth lifted slightly. Your bittersweet grin. I know what you are thinking. You are probably asking why I am vexing you, an unhappy ghost, sitting here at my behest. But bear with me, Ruvke. You see, I was so angry with you that I could not grieve. You became my punching bag. The more I punched your memory, the less it hurt. When *Imma* spoke mournfully of you, I blamed her for hypocrisy. How could she sing your praises after having enjoyed the affair with Chaim all those years? In my mind, loving your memory became entangled with dirt and deception. I, of course, was blameless. I didn't have to say how wonderful you were; I didn't have to grieve for you; I didn't have to take stock of my own flaws. I, naturally, was above all that.

I see a soft glint in your eye, dear Reuven. Oh, how sorry I am for loving you so poorly. Please forgive me. You are shaking your head, but I know the truth. I am looking at another picture of you, taken at a party. You are elegantly dressed in a dark jacket, white shirt, and a tie. You are standing alone, as was your habit, staring at the guests, sucking on a candy, your hands folded behind your back, and on your face—a jolly, peaceful expression. The picture takes my breath away—how I've missed you, Ruvke, standing there sweet and serene at the backstage of my life, always ready to catch me when I fall. I must tell you now, Reuven, what I couldn't when I looked at you through the hospital window. I can see you raising your hand again to silence me; you never wanted to hear your praise, I know, but this time you'll have to bear it. I have always loved you, Ruvke. You were my best—most beloved—father.

chapter four

KENNETH

LIFE AFTER DEATH

After Reuven's death, a pall of depression darkened my life. At the time, I was engaged in two writing projects, one in Hebrew and one in English, and I did poorly in both. The projects were long overdue, yet I could not write. For hours I'd sit in front of my typewriters and stare at the wall, or I'd write a page, yank it out, and throw it into the wastepaper basket.

During that summer, I didn't go out to Dizengoff cafés, I avoided the streets and the parks, I shunned Bar-Ilan. If I went out at all, it would have been to the home of my friends, Dvorah and David, who for years held an open house on Friday nights in their tiny apartment in Ramat-Gan. Dvorah, a South African, was my colleague at Bar-Ilan and a friend. Her husband David, an Israeli, taught philosophy at Bar-Ilan. Although they were moderately religious and politically conservative, I quickly struck up a friendship with them and found sufficient common ground in literature and music, to which the three of us were enthusiastically devoted. In David's huge record collection, he kept two, three, and sometimes five versions of the same work. One Friday night we'd listen to a Bach cantata with Karl Richter, another night to the same cantata with Fritz Werner or Eugen Jochum—discussing the differences with the kind of passionate interest that most Israelis reserved only for politics. Whenever David put a record on, he ordered all of us, a group of ten to fifteen people, to be absolutely quiet. His indignant "sh . . . sh . . . sh. . . ." could be heard throughout the concert, directed at those whisperers who dared defy the music. But not many of us did. Music was the magic yarn that bound us—the diverse Friday night visitors—together. Had we met anywhere else, we might not have exchanged one word. But on Friday nights, at Dvorah and David's, we were held by a spell. When the music ended, David would slowly open his eyes and ask, with a rapt smile, "Isn't it beautiful, eh? What do you say, Mindi?" he would address his old friend. And so the conversation would kick in again, loud and jolly, and sail through the lit porch into the darkness.

Yet when Friday night was over, my distress would return. At Dvorah's I had great ideas, but as soon as I approached my typewriter, they flew away. At Dvorah's I seemed to be focused and replenished, but at home I was scattered and empty. My life had become a vast blank. I continued to see Mrs. Silver, but the thought that this vast blank was somehow connected to Reuven's death never occurred to her.

During that summer, I read George Eliot's *Middlemarch* for the first time. Rather than Reuven's death, or my mother's grief, it was this book that brought me, sobbing, to my knees. Although I detected my own apathy and self-centeredness in Rosamond, I longed to identify with Dorothea's generous nature. I was humbled by her "active" goodness, awed by her ability, as Eliot describes it, to "change the lights for us." I was moved by her brave advocacy of Lydgate, when everybody else condemned him, an advocacy that made him feel for "the first time in his life" the "exquisite sense of leaning entirely on a generous sympathy, without any check of proud reserve." Ah, I sighed, I wish *I* had such an advocate, or that I were such a one! When I reached the climactic scene between Dorothea and Rosamond, where Dorothea overcomes her own jealousy and does what she thinks is right by Rosamond, and where Rosamond, too, rises above her selfish impetuousness and reassures Dorothea that Ladislaw had been loyal to her, the scene where "pride was broken down between" the two women, I abandoned myself to tears. When will I be able to find in myself such generosity? When will my own sullen pride be broken? When will love come to my life?

THE ENGLISH DEPARTMENT SOCIAL

"Have you heard of Dr. Regenbaum?" Gloria, the English department librarian asked me one bright autumn day, at the beginning of the new 1972 to 1973 academic year.

"No," I said with little interest.

"He is the new theater professor, you know, and everybody has been talking about what a great teacher he is," her eyes shone.

"Oh?" I asked. My classes at that time were rather glum, and I was in no mood to listen to the successes of the new "star." Wasn't it enough that everybody was raving about Streiter? Now they would rave about Regenbaum, too? And what would happen to Shapira then? She would have no students left!

"You really ought to visit his classes," Gloria added as she was pushing a cart of books. "People say he is using psychology to make students act."

"Psychology?" I was quick to criticize. "What does he know of psychology?"

"I have no idea," Gloria shrugged. "I only know that the students love him," she chuckled.

I left the library determined not to visit Dr. Regenbaum's classes. I had enough of my own to contend with. Besides, I clearly had no time for that. The semester was in full swing; I had to write papers, grade papers—how could I fit him in? No. If I met him, fine, but I was not going out of my way. A month passed. I didn't see the new "star," and I forgot my conversation with Gloria. It was at the English department social, on November 21, that I met Kenneth Regenbaum for the first time.

Later he told me that he looked closely at my name tag to see if it was "Miss" or "Mrs. Shapira" ("Ms." did not then exist in Israel). I already knew, from department gossip, that although he was only thirty-two, he was a widower. But on the night of the social, I did not particularly care about that piece of information. At first glance, I already saw enough in Kenneth Regenbaum to know that *I* was not going to marry him. No way! His hair was honey blond shading into dark brown (the color of our daughter's hair), his eyes were brown and fiery, his mouth curved in a good-natured, jolly smile. His voice was strong and assured, and I heard him, before I even fully saw him, telling a story to his interlocuter with accelerating pleasure as if, for a moment, he were a kid running down a green hill with his kite, ahead of the pack, his hair flying in the wind, his eyes shining, his feet sliding to the end of his story with a splat, his voice bursting into a resounding laughter.

Then I looked at the rest of his body. His legs were firmly planted on the ground, like a man who knew what he wanted, but his right arm was withered and bent out of shape. What had happened to it? I was repelled. No, I could not marry such a man, I decided (although no such proposal was presented to me), a man with such an obvious handicap.

He had arrived from the United States a month before, he told me, and was learning Hebrew at the Ulpan. He had a doctorate in theater and was indeed fortunate to have found this position at Bar-Ilan on such short notice. He also told me that his young wife of five years, Suzanne, had died of medical negligence a year before. "She had diabetes," his eyes widened, "and she had to undergo minor surgery in a country hospital near Pittsburgh, where we used to live. The operation was successful," he smiled sardonically, "but they forgot to give her glucose and she slipped into a coma from which she never awakened." He took a deep breath. "Then," he perked up, "I decided that it was time to carry out my intention to make *alia* to Israel. So here I am," he laughed.

At the end of the evening, I decided that I liked Kenneth. But I certainly did not love him.

"LIKE A MIGHTY FLAME"

And now good-morrow to our waking souls
Which watch not one another out of fear;
For love all love of other sights controls,
And makes one little room, an everywhere.

—John Donne, "The Good Morrow"

One day I was in a foul mood and sought Kenneth out. I asked him boldly if he would take me out to dinner. He would be glad to, he said, if I could wait for him until he finished his evening class at eight o'clock. Of course, I'd be welcome to attend. Then he asked to be excused—he had to "psyche up" for class. I remember being somewhat miffed by his response. It was friendly enough, I admitted, but I expected him to be flattered by my invitation, and he wasn't. As I waited in the hall for class to begin, my dejection was gathering steam. Perhaps I should have gone home, I thought, but the prospect of a lonely forty-minute bus ride in the dark, during which I'd have little to do but mull over my bad afternoon class, was not appealing. So I paced the hall and waited.

Finally, the class began. With a quick and confident step Kenneth walked in and tossed his heavy bag on the desk. He greeted the students with a con-

---

alia Immigration to Israel; ascent to the higher purposes of the Zionist vision spiratorial smile, as if to say, "wait till you see what a great pleasure ride we are going to have tonight!" I observed the students, and even before Kenneth began his lecture, I knew what Gloria was raving about. On their faces there was an expression of pleasant expectation, an eagerness to hear him.

The subject of Kenneth's class that evening was the method school of acting. In response to a question about the ability of mere students to act, Kenneth told the class a juicy story about Marlon Brando's first experience in acting on the Broadway stage, an experience described by Harold Clurman in his book *On Directing*, which, in Kenneth's rendition, leapt to life. Even Brando, Kenneth pointed out with jubilant emphasis, was not a "born" actor. In fact, Kenneth looked at us with a mischievous glint in his eye—were it not for Clurman, the director of the Broadway cast that had rebelled against Brando's inaudible mumblings and wanted him out of the show, were it not for Clurman who took Brando after rehearsal into the large empty auditorium and forced him to YELL his lines as he climbed a rope dangling from the ceiling as Clurman walked to the last row and boomed "louder, I still can't hear you" to the enraged Brando, were it not for that shrewd director who intuited the powerful expressiveness in the fumbling young actor, whose potential nobody but he could see—were it not for his conviction that acting was not a mysterious, ready "talent" but rather *hard work,* Kenneth drew to a breathless close—there would not have been a Brando today for all of us to admire!

"In fact," Kenneth continued, "how do we ever know who the 'born' actor is, or what he or she looks like? If you saw me in the street," he chuckled, "would you have believed I am an actor, that I was admitted into the selective Strasberg's Actors Studio in New York?" Some of the students smiled. "Look at this arm," Kenneth pointed to his right withered arm. I shrank in my seat as if I'd been splashed with cold water. He was openly talking about what I was afraid to look at. "At the beginning of the semester, I told you about the polio that almost killed me and left this strange-looking arm, which underwent twelve rehabilitative surgeries, as a souvenir," he smiled winningly. "My father didn't want me to study theater, but theater was my passion. He did not believe I could act, and although he did not mention my arm, both of us knew what was on his mind. But I wanted to be an actor and a director, and that's what I have become. And so," he laughed softly, "each one of you can act, too, if you work at it."

I relaxed in my chair. During the energetic class discussion that followed, my depression flew, like a startled bat, out of the window into the night where it belonged. I looked with wonder at the brave, spirited man with the warped arm and, like his students, was ready to listen to him for hours. Unawares, I was already in love with Kenneth Regenbaum, but I knew it only in the restaurant on Ben-Yehudah Street where we ate our dinner and talked, over black coffee and green olives, until four in the morning, oblivious to the subtle pleas of the waiter—the yawns, the shuffling of feet, the clearing of the throat—who wanted desperately to go home but was reluctant to interrupt what even he felt to be the kindling of a mighty flame.

Soon we were inseparable. Our colleagues and friends greeted us with delight. Professors Roston and Fisch were as pleased as if they were directly responsible for the match. Everybody approved. One sunny day we walked with colleagues to the cafeteria, above the parking lot where Chaim once propositioned me. As we drank coffee and shared a bagel, I sensed my crammed inner spaces expanding and filling with light. I looked around at our friends, at the university, and at the orchards surrrounding it and contemplated my good fortune. This is my place, I thought, my community, where all that is rent in me can become whole. My native country, family, and language are all here, and so are my Anglo-American friends, my studies, my teaching. Most importantly, this kind and brave American Jew is here, whose love for me is sweeter than anything I had ever known. What more could I ask for?

There was one thing. When I made love to Kenneth for the first time, I recoiled when he took off his shirt. The polio had damaged not only his arm. Part of his shoulder and back appeared hollowed out. "Ugly" flashed through my mind. For a brief moment, I wanted a man with normal limbs. Kenneth seemed to read my mind. "Take your time," he said, smiling. "I've lived with this most of my life," he put his heavy left arm on his thin shoulder, "but others are sometimes shocked when they see it at first. We don't need to rush. We can talk about it." Ashamed, I denied my discomfort. We made love, but I was miles away, unable to feel anything.

Our love life improved. Since I loved Kenneth, I learned to love his wounds and his scars. But my ambivalence remained, hidden and unresolved. How could one love another so much, I agonized, and still be so divided? For our growth, we needed help and time, but we had neither. Instead, we got a good dose of my mother's fury, which only exacerbated our difficulty.

A FATEFUL MEETING

When I met Kenneth, my mother was working as a private nurse for an elderly man in Dgania, near Tiberias. Although far away from Tel Aviv, she guessed that I had "a serious boyfriend," in her words. She just *knew* that something good had happened to me. Yes, I admitted guiltily, I had a boyfriend, but I did not mention his polio. She wanted to meet him. I said, why not? We arranged a dinner date, and she came, in her car, to pick us up.

When she came upstairs, Kenneth, as was his habit, offered to shake her right hand with his right hand. My mother touched the polio-ravaged arm and quickly took her hand away. Kenneth gave her a brief history of his polio and his near miraculous recovery from it. My mother nodded coolly. Without smiling, she said, *"Nu,* let's go."

We ate that night at my favorite fish restaurant in Jaffa, on the edge of the ocean. In the car Kenneth chatted happily with my mother. She was polite to him, but knowing her well enough, I was queasy with the premonition of what was to come. I tried to put it out of my mind. Perhaps, I was thinking as we were passing by the long and splendid stretch of the Tel Aviv coastal promenade, perhaps she too would rejoice in our happiness and forget what is troubling her now. Perhaps, I thought, looking at Kenneth who was talking cheerfully, unaware of her icy stares, perhaps she would now be different, perhaps she would rise above the slums of Tiberias, rise in all her beauty like Aphrodite from the gentle waves of this Mediterranean sea, to bless our union. "Wow," Kenneth exclaimed as he saw the orange ball of the setting sun hanging in the horizon, threading together sky, sea, and sand with orange filaments, suffusing the whole creation with mellow peacefulness. Opposite, we could see the minaret, the markets, and the old stone buildings of Jaffa. As we passed through the main drag, flanked on both sides with counters loaded with huge sesame bagels, sunflower seeds, baklava, and other eastern delicacies, and continued our journey to the other side of the hill, we caught a glimpse of the artists' colony perched on high, gallery atop gallery—old, deserted Arab houses, renovated by Israeli painters and sculptors. Kenneth, who had never been to Jaffa, was beside himself with enthusiasm for the flamboyant mixture of East and West. We arrived at the restaurant and sat down on the porch, overlooking fishing boats gently rocking on the waves, and ordered the fish; Kenneth smacked his lips with pleasure and told my mother that he'd been waiting for this moment to thank her for bringing me into the world. He was so happy that he'd met me, he told her, and he was looking forward to many wonderful years of our shared life.

"You are welcome" my mother replied coldly. My premonition returned. The waiters had begun to bring out the pitas, the olives, the drinks, and finally the huge fish, but I was looking anxiously at the darkening waters and at the twinkling lights of the scattered ships on the sweep of the unknowable ocean. Kenneth dove into his fish, took a big piece on his fork, and started chewing it greedily when suddenly he choked. Coughing, wretching, and wheezing, he finally spat the fish out. "Oh," he laughed, his cheeks flushed and his eyes watering, "you should have warned me about the bones in this fish." When my fright subsided, I remembered how unskilled Americans were at finding their way through bony fish, or at cracking sunflower and pumpkin seeds, popular Israeli snacks. We laughed in relief at the averted crisis. My mother offered Kenneth her expertise in taking bones out of fish and, to his grateful applause, cleaned his fish out. He relaxed and ate heartily, and we retuned home that night in high spirits.

A PERILOUS JOURNEY

In my bones, though, I knew that trouble was brewing. A week or so after our dinner, my mother came to town unannounced and offered to give me a ride to Bar-Ilan. "I want to talk to you about something," she said in a quiet voice, and my blood froze. Although it was winter, the day was warm, and I knew that my mother's car would be hot. But little did I know that the journey, studded with traffic jams, would become an hour of roasting in the spewing and sputtering furnace of my mother's hell.

It was my mother's most passionate tirade ever. "Shelly," she said quietly, as she started the car, "you are about to make the worst mistake in your life." I squinted, knowing that it would be best not to interrupt her now. "Shelly," she repeated with rising pitch, "you are blind. You don't know what you are doing." Approaching the traffic light on Derech Haifa, she adjusted her rearview mirror and looked at me. "Shelly," she said for the third time, "I beg of you." I must have grown pale at this point because my mother was not in the habit of begging for anything. "I beg of you not to marry this man!"

There it was. Didn't I know it from the first? She does not like Kenneth. I sank in my seat, wishing for a minor accident or an unexpected meeting with somebody important—anything to take my mother's attention off her topic. She put on her sunglasses. "I am telling you, Shelly," she raised her voice above the din of the traffic, "do not make this mistake. Do not marry him." She neared the major intersection at the Haifa-Tel Aviv railroad station, where the first traffic jam awaited us. We stood behind unmoving cars; the traffic lights were red, and when they changed to green, two or three cars moved through, and the rest of us waited. And waited. "*Uff,*" my mother complained, "this will take forever." I was secretly pleased by the distraction, but the car was heating up, and both of us were soon sweating. "You know how much I want you to marry, how I have waited for the day of your wed-

ding! You are thirty-one already, an old maid. You know how Reuven wanted
you to marry!" With a tissue, she wiped the beads of sweat off her lip. "He
would have given three years of his life to see you married. But to *him?*" She
looked at me sharply. "To *him?*" she repeated incredulously. "Out of the question!" she sputtered. "Reuven would turn in his grave if he knew. . . ." The
traffic jolted forward, and we finally made it through the light.

In the pit of my stomach a subtle dread stirred. Is she right? Am I making a mistake? My mother's hands were clutching the wheel. "Why shouldn't I
marry him?" I asked in a trembling voice. The traffic was slowing down again.
"WHY?" my mother yelled. "You don't know why?" "No," I answered softly, "I
don't know why." The traffic was inching forward, but the car in front of us
did not move. "What an idiot," my mother bawled and honked. "I'll tell you
why," she shrieked, "because he is a cripple. That's why."

All around us, drivers were losing their patience. Some cars tried to sneak
to the front of the line, and other cars honked furiously at them. The street
soon turned into a cacophony of shrill, angry horns. Drivers shook their fists
out their windows and others cursed juicily. The pandemonium released my
own anger. "How dare you call him a cripple?" I raised my voice.

"How dare I?" my mother turned to me, the vein in her neck swelling.
"Because that's what he is. You may bury your head in the sand as long as you
wish, but that's the truth."

From a neighboring car, the formal, ceremonial voice of the newscaster
could be heard. "That's not the truth," I countered. "He had polio, so what?"

"So what? I'll tell you so what," she puckered her lips. "So you won't be
able to have any children because he will be sterile. Sometimes they are even
impotent."

"What?" I shouted. "Where did you ever hear that?" I turned to face her
fully. "I can tell you for sure that impotent he is *not.*"

"I don't know about impotence," my mother backtracked without losing
ground. "But their sterility is well known," she declaimed with an air of
authority as if she were a medical expert. "Ask whoever you wish. Polio victims
have a very difficult time bringing children to the world."

"What about Itzhak Perlman?" I remembered gratefully. "He has children."

"There are always exceptions," my mother fumed. "Don't compare Kenneth to Perlman."

Why not, I wanted to ask when I recalled Kenneth's description of his
and Suzanne's failure to conceive children. Kenneth said that the difficulty lay
in Suzanne's sickness, but now a new doubt slithered in my mind and silenced
my retort.

Ten minutes later the traffic jerked into motion again. My mother renewed her attack. "Do you think," she said, "that if I wasn't so sure of what I was saying, I would have stood in your way to happiness? Why would I do that?"

"A good question," I mumbled, thinking that perhaps she was right after all. Would she have been so brazen otherwise?

"I want my daughter to be embraced by a man with two arms," I heard her strident voice.

"Why is it so important? He holds me better than any man has ever held me." Better than Reuven and Chaim ever held you, I wanted to add but bit my tongue.

"With one arm?" my mother bawled. "With one arm?" she was pounding the wheel. "I want a whole man for my daughter, you hear?"

"He is a whole man."

"Not to me he isn't. He is all crooked and evil."

"Evil? What are you talking about?"

"Yes, he is a cruel man. I know it in my bones. He will make your life miserable."

We turned right at the Geha intersection and started the last leg of our journey. Traffic here was moving fast. A light breeze from the open window alleviated the heat. She is crazy, I was thinking furiously. He is *not* evil. She is wrong, wrong. Relieved of my doubts, I was now convinced that it was *she* who was evil, not he. Yet as we were approaching Bar-Ilan, I became despondent and did not rightly know how I could face a class in half an hour. We stopped in front of the English building. I took my things, got out, and slammed the door. Then I bent down and said, "You are wrong. I am going to marry him anyway, and what's more, Reuven would have approved." She didn't say a word. While my hand was still on the door, she began to reverse the car, turned around, and disappeared.

Shaking, I climbed the stairs of the English department building. The sense of impending doom clung to me for days. I realized that my mother—whose approval I still needed—had become my enemy.

A MEDIEVAL JOUST

When I told Kenneth about the journey with my mother, he was astonished and furious. "But she was so nice in the restaurant," he said. "She even picked the bones out of my fish! I can't believe it!" His fingers touched his forehead.

"What is the matter with that woman?" he was pacing the room. "How could that woman be your mother?" he wanted to know. "You had to take this kind of stuff from her all those years?" With lips pursed and hands shoved in his pockets, Kenneth stopped pacing and stood in the middle of the room. "I'll tell you what," he said. "That woman insulted me and terrorized you behind my back. I want to see if she'll call me a cripple to my face. Do you think we can arrange a meeting with her?" I nodded, feeling exhilarated that I had finally, after thirty-one years on God's green earth, found an advocate brave enough to confront my indomitable mother. My elation, though, was mixed with terror. My one-armed knight was leading the charge, and I was right behind him, but I knew that this war was my war and that one day I, alone, would have to engage it.

Through the ministrations of go-betweens, my mother finally agreed to meet Kenneth and me for coffee in my apartment, on condition that Chaim and Avram would accompany her. We agreed. It was late afternoon on a bright, cool winter day. We opened the window and fresh breezes flew in, scattering papers, ruffling hair, puffing Kenneth's long-sleeved shirt out until it was hard to tell the good arm from the bad. On the coffee table, I put a white tablecloth, my nicest dishes, and a plate filled with my mother's homemade cookies. We waited for the guests, tense but also festive, hoping that the grotesque quarrel with my mother would be soon forgotten.

When they arrived, my mother sat down on the couch with a martyred expression on her face. Both Chaim and Avram walked around in high spirits. Both liked Kenneth and plunged into a lively conversation with him about his impressions of Israel, his teaching, his meeting with me, and the extent of his Hebrew. They quizzed him on his knowledge of the language and made good-natured fun of his mistakes. Kenneth said that there was one sentence he did know how to say correctly: *Ani ohev Shelly* (I love Shelly). "Bravo, bravo," Chaim exclaimed as he finally sat down near my mother and whispered something in her ear. My mother remained motionless.

I brought the coffee, and we sat around the table. There was a long moment of silence while everybody took the first sip. Kenneth grinned at his audience. "I want to announce," he said solemnly, "that we are getting engaged at the end of the month." Avram cried out "Congratulations!" and shook Kenneth's right hand. Then he got up, came over to my seat, and gave me a hug. *"Yofi, meida'le,"* he said with feeling. Chaim smiled quietly at me, as if waiting to see the development of events. My mother said nothing; her eyes were staring at the tip of her shoe. Kenneth turned to her. "I wonder, Dina," he said pleasantly, "if you could help us with the preparations. I hear from your daughter," he smiled, "that you make great parties, and I thought. . . ."

"You leave me out of it!" my mother exploded. Tense silence fell on the room. Avram stopped chewing his cookie and looked amazed at my mother. "What is this?" he asked, smiling sheepishly. "You heard me," she said hoarsely. "He can get engaged or married to her if he wishes, but he cannot expect any help, or any congratulations, from me."

Kenneth's sunny expression vanished. His body tensed up, his eyes darkened, his right hand trembled slightly, but his left hand rested firmly on his thigh. "May I ask, Dina, why you don't want me to marry your daughter?" he said in a quiet voice.

I looked at my mother. How could I ever have hoped that this meeting would be sane? She got to her feet and glowered at Kenneth with contempt. "I'll tell you why," she hissed. No, I thought, as if the walls of the house were shaking; no, no, she was not, NOT going to say it. God, please stop her, stop her; don't let her, please. "Because," she pelted the words at Kenneth, "you are a CRIPPLE!"

I looked around me. The house was still standing. Couch, books, records, dishes were all in place. Avram and Chaim were studying the carpet design. Kenneth rose to his feet, his hands on his hips. "I was telling Shelly," his voice was trembling, "that I didn't think you'd say it to my face. But you did. At least you are gutsy; I'll give you that. But you know what? Some of us have crippled bodies, and we can't do much about it, but some of us (and this is far worse, believe me) have crippled souls." He snapped his lips shut and glared at her. For a long moment no one said anything; no one even dared breathe. I cast an admiring, grateful glance at Kenneth, but my mother was getting ready for the second round.

"Don't talk to me about souls shmouls. You can't teach me what a cripple is," she spewed, "I see what I see. Maybe in America it's different, but we live in Israel, and I want my daughter to marry a man she can be proud of in *our* society, a man who can father her children." She thrust her chin at him.

"Why don't you ask Shelly if she is proud of me?" Kenneth countered, folding his arms on his chest. "And as for children, I can father children," he said. "We are going to have children, don't you worry."

"How do you know," my mother retorted, "that you can have children? Do you have proof? What *I* know is that polio victims often have a hard time bringing children to the world."

"I have proof," Kenneth said without batting an eyelid. "Suzanne and I were trying to have children and couldn't, so we both took tests. My tests were normal."

It was fitting that at that moment everybody, including my mother, should have laughed and shaken hands. But not she. Not Battleship Sirotinsky. I knew that she would never accept or admit defeat. She stood there, a stone statue, gazing outside the window at the gathering dusk below. Avram took a deep breath and ventured to speak to her. "Dina'le," he pleaded. "What do you need this for? How many daughters do you have, really?"

My mother turned to him as if it were all his fault. "Don't tell me what to do," she snapped. "Keep your nose out of it."

Chaim lit a cigarette and tried to say something funny, but nobody even smiled. Kenneth was undaunted, surveying the scene like one who had withstood many a storm and could not be easily intimidated. My mother turned to me. "And you," she asked, "what about you?"

"What do you mean what about me?" I was startled.

"Do you still plan to marry this man? You haven't changed your mind? After all, I have seen you like a man one day and hate him the next."

"What are you talking about?" I said irritably. "I love him. I am going to marry him."

"Well, in that case," my mother pronounced, "there is nothing more for me to do here. Thank you for the coffee." With an arched movement of her arm, she picked up her jacket and purse and walked straight to the door. Her two bodyguards jumped to their feet. "Hey, Dina," Avram said, winking at me, "aren't you going to wait for us?" My mother stopped and waited without turning her head. Chaim picked up his cigarettes and two cookies, and on the way out whispered in my ear, "Don't you worry, I'll work on her. It will be all right."

Soon after this explosive meeting, the family at large divided into two camps: the pro-Kenneth camp and the pro-Dina camp. To the best of my recollection, no one was actually against Kenneth, or our marriage, but some chose, for political reasons, to support my mother publicly. Still others, like Aunts Ruth and Zipporah, tried to be neutral and support both sides, which was not easy to do.

The most courageous and outspoken in the pro-Kenneth camp was Aunt Nomi. She liked Kenneth and was incensed when she heard of my mother's opposition. "There she goes again," Nomi stewed, and her dark blue eyes, which she inherited from my grandfather, flashed. "What does she have against him?" she asked one day when the two of us were sitting at a café on

Dizengoff Street. "What can I tell you?" she asked as we ordered the coffee. "I am ashamed of my sister," she put sugar in her coffee and lit a cigarette. "Ashamed, ashamed," she repeated. "How dare she interfere? And Kenneth is such a nice guy! Isn't he?" I smiled and nodded. "Such a nice guy! What is the matter with her?" she searched my face for an answer. "I'll tell you what," her hand cupped her mouth conspiratorially, "she is envious!" I looked at her quizzically. Nomi filled her mouth with cake. "She is lonely, and so she does not want you to be happy. Don't I know my sister?" her whole face asked.

"And Chaim?" I ventured.

"Chaim?" Nomi's face contorted with an expression of disgust. "Chaim?" she repeated. "Since Reuven died," she said authoritatively, "there is no Chaim."

"What do you mean?" I asked. "I still see her with him."

With an emphatic motion of her arm, Nomi explained. "Yes, but that's nothing," she said. "It's not what it used to be. They are just 'friends' now, you know. He helps her here and there. Poor man," she added reflectively, "he is still crazy about her, but she can't stand him now. She can't stand Kenneth either. Since Reuven died, Dina can't stand anybody!" She put out her cigarette. "But mind what I say to you," she sat straight in her chair. "I won't let her get away with this nonsense! I'll see to it that she changes her tune about Kenneth!"

I looked at her bemused. There she was, my flighty, giddy, pretty Aunt Nomi, whom nobody took seriously, going to war with the family Goliath! I was grateful, although I didn't think she would make a dent in my mother's attitude toward Kenneth. Yet Nomi was as good as her word. She took my mother to task and rebuked her noisily for her treatment of Kenneth. Did it help? Yes, I think it did. So did Chaim and Avram's backstage deliberations. My guess, though, is that the process of turning my mother around was greatly accelerated by Mrs. Silver's intercession. Family was one thing, but when an "objective" outsider, and a professional woman at that, rose of her own free will to Kenneth's defense, my mother, in spite of herself, was impressed.

Although Mrs. Silver always believed that I, the "Oedipal daughter," was the one to be blamed for my troubles with my mother, when I told her about the new crisis, she changed her position. The attack on Kenneth astonished her, and she decided to invite my mother to her office for a talk. My mother arrived elegantly dressed and excessively polite. As she walked into Mrs. Silver's sunny apartment, she—who never failed to salute refinement—was appreciative, I am certain, of the tasteful furniture and the interesting paintings. Mrs. Silver asked my mother why she had such strong objections to Kenneth who, Mrs. Silver stressed, was an excellent man and would be a wonderful husband.

My mother appeared quiet and subdued. Then Mrs. Silver sprang the pointed question, "What would you have done," she scrutinized my mother's face, "if it were your daughter who was inflicted with polio? After all, the plague raged here as it did in America." My mother thought for a minute while her eyes wandered around the room. Then she said simply, "But my daughter did not contract polio. What's the use in speculating?" Mrs. Silver laughed and said that sometimes speculation can show us the truth. My mother seemed uninterested in this theory, or in the truth, but she did not argue. Her uncharacteristic docility surprised me, but later I realized that, to counteract my reports about her, she must have been hell-bent on making a favorable impression on Mrs. Silver. Indeed, the meeting ended amicably. The two women shook hands, and my mother walked out proudly, a dainty and serene ostrich.

Some time after the interview, my mother let us know, through the family go-betweens, that she was ready to relinquish her objections to our marriage. Kenneth, the buoyant optimist, was delighted, but I was uneasy; I knew my mother's fierce nature and suspected that the battle had just begun. Indeed, she came back with plans for our wedding, but another fight broke out when Kenneth objected to some of her ideas. "What do you know about weddings?" my mother asked. "I have already prepared many of them. I know what I am doing." "Well, Dina," Kenneth said. "I don't doubt that, but, you see, I am willing to learn. This is *our* wedding." Again, the door slammed behind my mother's proud form and once more we were treated to her sullen silences, which threw me, even with Kenneth by my side, into a tizzy of anxiety.

One Sabbath, Kenneth and I were luxuriating late in bed. It must have been eleven. Suddenly we heard a key turning in the lock. The door opened. Kenneth jumped to his feet, "a thief, a thief," he cried. But it was only my mother. Unannounced, she showed up, and since she had the key, she used it. There she stood, in the door, looking directly at the young, scantily dressed lovers in bed (which was in direct visual line with the door), and said, "You are not up yet? It's eleven already. Who sleeps at eleven?" I knew what was coming and crawled under the blanket. Kenneth put on his robe and came out to face my mother. Without a word, he took her to the door and showed her the bell. "You know what this is for?" he asked. Then he pointed at the phone. "You know what this is for?"

She looked at him with haughty indifference. "I don't need bells and phones when I come to visit my daughter."

"Really?" Kenneth asked, breathing hard to control his anger. "May I ask why?"

"Why?" my mother took off her sunglasses, "because this is my daughter, and this is my house, if you have to know. I bought it."

"So? Does this give you the right to barge in here without a warning?"

My mother put down the sack of fruit she brought us. "I don't need to ask anybody's permission to come here."

"Really? Have you ever heard of privacy?"

"Look," my mother said impatiently, "this is not America. This is Israel. In Israel there is no privacy. People always drop in without warning. You don't like it, go back to America!"

"Even here, people knock on the door, or ring the bell," Kenneth's cheeks were flushed.

"I don't need to knock," my mother's voice became strident. "I never knock on my daughter's door."

"Well," Kenneth bellowed, "from now on you will, or you won't come here at all."

Once more my mother slammed the door behind her, and the whole building shook. This time her icy silence lasted a long while, but she finally returned to us, by complicated backroads, and never again used her key to open the door. On the contrary, she took to calling us on the phone at least two days before her planned visit, and she even rang the bell. A short happy reunion was established until the arrival of the next inevitable confrontation.

Thus, in a strangely ritualistic manner, equipped with heavy armor and lances, amid pomp and circumstance, each with his or her cheering section in the audience, the two modern-day Jewish warriors, Kenneth and Dina, would periodically gallop their horses toward each other with deadly intent. Both were determined combatants, and their jousting was neither a game nor a contest but a ferocious, serious, all-out war. The stakes were high, indeed. Kenneth was fighting for the integrity of our marriage; my mother was fighting—for what? How hard it is to say exactly. For control, surely. Control of the house, the furniture, my wardrobe, and my loyalties; control of our plans, our holiday visits, our privacy; and later, control of our children, particularly our son Shir, and the methods of raising them. But there was more in this ancient warfare that she initiated. Was it envy, as Nomi claimed? Was it cruelty? Or was it the recognition that in Kenneth she had met, for the first time, a fearless antagonist whom she was compelled to challenge and subdue? It could have been any of these, or all of them together rolled into a bolt catapulted at us, time and again, with precision and with a mysterious and relentless punch.

"ALL THE WORLD'S A STAGE"

My mother's periodic assaults were stressful, but they did not diminish our happiness. The wintry winds she blew on us did not impede our spring; we were lighthearted and loving, ensconced, as Kenneth put it in one of his poems, in "one ripening place." We took long walks in Tel Aviv streets, frequented the theaters and the movies, visited Dvorah and David on Friday nights, dined in favorite restaurants, and watched the pomegranate sun sink into the sea. We wrote sentimental lovenotes to each other, which we hid in sandwich wrappers, under pillows, in purses, or in books. We even tried to write poems, which were not very good but paid homage to our exuberant feeling that our love was the first and the best in the world, and nothing short of a miracle.

In the spring of 1973 I discovered Kenneth's theater world. Whenever I finished teaching, I'd sneak into the rehearsal auditorium to watch him work. I sat and listened with fascination. "Everything you do on the stage," Kenneth would say, "everything you do in this 'magic space' called 'theater,'" drawing a circle in the air with his strong left arm, "must be justified. What do I mean by that? I mean that there must be a *reason* for everything you do. If you get up to open the door, you must know *why* you are doing it. Are you opening the door for some cool breeze? Or are you opening the door for your mother-in-law who's come to snoop around?" Then he'd ask the students to perform an action and justify it; we in the audience were to guess the motives for the action. Some of the students drew applause from the spectators, but some were incoherent. "No, no," Kenneth would holler, "I don't have a clue why you did what you did. On the stage, you *must* be psychologically active. Even," his eyes would flash, "even if you *don't* do anything on the stage, even if you're just sitting down and saying nothing, even then, and especially then, you must be absorbed in inner activity. Without controlled (controlled, mind you), emotional activity," he'd put the right palm of his hand in his left, "there can be no coherent and *alive* character on the stage. I don't know about you, but when I go to the theater, I expect to see living, breathing, feeling human beings, not automatons who can declaim great lines! Now," he'd take a deep breath, "I want you to think about something that makes you feel deeply. It could be a whiff of perfume, a flower, a picture, a song—anything. Then write it down."

In the hush that fell on the auditorium, he'd come up to my seat, smile, and touch my hand, but his hands, normally warm, were then cold. "All right," he'd address the students. "What have you got?" Inevitably, one or two students would say that they couldn't think of anything. "There is nothing you care about?" Kenneth would ask them softly. Then his voice would rise in indignation. "If you can't feel deeply about anything, you are dead. On and off the stage."

I fell in love with the theater. It was a brave new world of action and feeling, beauty and community. Over time, I watched Kenneth's students develop from self-conscious individuals to confident actors who knew how to bring out the "subtext," and how to relate to their partners. "All for one, and one for all," Kenneth used to say when his burgeoning actors began to fight for bigger roles in the *Inherit the Wind* production the class was preparing for the end of the year. "As Stanislavski said," he pointed out, "'there are no small parts, only small actors.' This is not the star system," he'd chuckle. "What we are doing here is creating an ensemble."

Bar-Ilan University had never had a theater troupe before, and as the date of the production drew close, the excitement grew. The preparations were hectic. The first difficult task was casting. Where, Kenneth wondered, could he find somebody to play the role of the Bible Belt fundamentalist preacher Brady? The best he could hope for was an American Jew from the Bronx. Yet here he had an unusual bit of good luck. A few days after he advertised the auditions, he was approached by a young Baptist from Texas who had come to Israel because God spoke to him in a vision, instructing him to leave everything in America and go to the Holy Land to learn Hebrew. There he was, Matthew, a smiling blue-eyed blond speaking in a Texas drawl, wearing a *yarmulke,* capable of reading the first two chapters of Genesis in Hebrew, and offering himself for the part of Brady, and his young wife, Betsy, as Mrs. Brady. Kenneth was overjoyed. He never dreamed he could have such an authentic Brady who would not even have to use the Magic If to sermonize "here in Hillsboro we are fighting the fight of the Faithful throughout the world!" Matthew *was* one of the faithful; he believed in the story of Creation, and he spoke in a southern accent. He was it! Brady! After an extensive search Kenneth chose a British student, Fred, to play the part of Drummond. Matthew and Fred soon became formidable antagonists. Their dialogue sizzled; when they faced each other in court, during rehearsals, sparks flew.

The last week before the performance was frantic. One actor couldn't remember his entrances, another was late for rehearsals, and still another couldn't find materials for the setting—it was a storm-tossed ship at sea. Only Matthew's cheery disposition seemed to steady it from time to time. Yet even he could not have anticipated, or prevented, the crisis that broke loose during dress rehearsal on the night before the opening. Fred, who, as Drummond, had the largest share of the dialogue, forgot his lines. His mind wiped out all memory of his role. He stood there, pale and bewildered, unable to recall a single sentence. Matthew gave him cue after cue, but Fred looked at him perplexed as if he had just met him for the first time. Somebody gave Fred the script, but he recited the lines without comprehension as if he were reading some esoteric text. The cast gasped. Some members hurled angry remarks at the faltering star. The whole place was in an uproar.

Kenneth then took Fred aside and urged him to work on improvisations. "Imagine," Kenneth told him, "that you are walking away from the courthouse. It is evening, and you are irritated and fed up with the ignorant Hillsboro crowd. You have had it! You decide to go to a bar for a drink. What else could you do in this Bible-preaching, godforsaken town? But where could you find a bar? Then you remember that there is a bar, probably the only one in town, in your hotel. You head over there, you go in, and you throw your tired body into a chair. You order a drink. Then you look around, and whom do you see?" he chuckled. "Brady! Yes, Brady is sitting in a corner, staring at you!" The whole cast laughed. Fred smiled. "That's not a bad idea," he said, his glasses glinting. Then he got up and walked over to Matthew. Indignant at the outrageous hypocrisy, an evangelist in a bar, Fred invented a furious and funny tirade, but, alas, he still could not remember his lines. The hour was late. Kenneth dispersed the cast, with the only reassurance that disastrous dress rehearsals often led to great opening nights. The students left dispirited; some complained to Kenneth about his poor casting decision and bitterly deplored Fred, who, they were sure, was going to sink their ship.

That night, Kenneth kept vigil until early dawn. Although he was composed during the rehearsal, at home his multiple worries broke loose. This was his very first production in a new country, in a new university, and he was clearly heading toward a disaster. Would Fred fail? Would three months of rigorous preparations go up in smoke? He was pacing the room, biting his lips. In his mind's eye, he saw stark visions of cast rebellion, actors running to and fro on the stage in utter confusion, people in the audience screaming and yelling, and then—lights out, darkness, end of theater. "Furthermore," Kenneth was ruminating, "what would my chair think of my efforts? Not only do I have the *chutzpah* to stage, in a religious university, a play that questions religion and makes fun of its literal reading of the Bible, but I don't even know *how* to prevail on my actors to remember their lines!" On and on he grumbled, beside himself with worry. Yet, despair was not in Kenneth's character. Before long, his optimism took charge, and he said to me, smiling, "You'll see, Squash [his term of endearment for me], it will be a great night."

The following evening, the house was packed. Everybody—professors, students, administrators—in the Bar-Ilan community came. Even my mother came. The audience walked in to a stage-in-the-round, featuring a courthouse and a jail, with seats flanked on the right and left. A single spotlight illumined the arena. When all sat down, there was a tense hush. Kenneth finished his last-minute instructions to his actors and then sat next to me, the pen in his hand pressed to his lips. I touched his fingers; they were ice-cold.

The first scene between Rachel and Cates moved at a fast pace; the dialogue was crinkly with tension. Kenneth breathed more easily, but the real test, we knew, would begin when Fred/Drummond stepped on the stage. The courthouse was warming up with the lively Hillsboro crowd, the gleeful Hornbeck, and the voluble Brady, accompanied by his smiling wife. "Yes! Yes!" Kenneth was whispering to me, "they are right on the mark!" Finally, Drummond made his entrance. Kenneth held his breath. Fred walked in slowly, thrust his head back, and shaded his eyes. Yes, Kenneth thought he was in character. But when we saw the ironic grin on his face, as he asked one of the potential jurors, "Ever read anything in a book about Evolution?" we knew that in the last twenty-four hours, by an effort of the will, the imagination, and whatever else, Fred had recaptured the figure of Drummond and made it his own. He had all his lines; crisp and sharp, they whipped Brady. "If they say that the sun stood still, they must've had a notion that the sun moves around the earth. Think that's the way of things? Or don't you believe the earth moves around the sun?" He leaned over Brady's chair and smirked. Each statement, each question was a concise lasso shot that ensnared Brady in an ever-tightening noose. "God tells Brady what is good!" Some in the court snickered. "To be against Brady is to be against God!" Now the audience, too, laughed. Fred had all of us in the palm of his hand, as he continued to chastise Brady. "Must men go to prison because they are at odds with the self-appointed prophet?" The audience applauded. Brady was rapidly sinking into defeat and from all directions eyes watched his fall with glee. Yet when he cried out to his wife, "Mother. They're laughing at me, Mother!" his anguish reached the audience. The conflict between the two antagonists climaxed in a spectacle of suffering that transcended their quarrel and wrapped the theater in reflective silence.

Thunderous applause signaled the success of the evening and launched Kenneth's career as the director of the English theater at Bar-Ilan. His fame

spread, and his cast grew. The following two years he was able to stage two productions a year—one in the winter and one in the spring. For three years he
stirred up the Bar-Ilan community. After awhile, he was invited to Haifa University to speak and later to teach. Like many other professors who could not
make it on the meager academic salary, he held, in addition to his full-time position at Bar-Ilan, a part-time position at Haifa. And this is what later saved him.

After three years, Bar-Ilan fired Kenneth. His productions excited the students, but they annoyed the powers-that-be at Bar-Ilan. "Your plays are too
revealing," one professor told him, "too close to the knuckle." When Kenneth
announced that he was going to stage *Streetcar Named Desire*, tensions
mounted. The religious administration of Bar-Ilan gasped. "What? Williams?"
they cried out, "the sex-crazed playwright? No way!" Kenneth refused to compromise, and so he had to go. Fortunately, Haifa University was eager to have
him and gave him free reign in all his productions.

W H O ' S   A   J E W ?

The summer of 1973 was the happiest in my life. As Kenneth and I were
preparing for our wedding day on June 26, in Tel Aviv, I was conscious of the
fact that I had never experienced so much happiness all at once. It kept coming, truckloads of it, in the morning, in the evening, at work, at play. Surely, I
used to think, it would disappear tomorrow, but, unabashed, it showed up
again the next day, gleaming with promise. This is unbelievable, I'd say to
myself; nobody, least of all I, can be this happy and get away with it. Surely
tomorrow I'll be hit with a brick falling from the sky. But the sky continued
to shimmer benevolently. There will be *some* trouble. When did good things
ever come easy to me? But where is it going to come from? Even my mother
complied with our plans.

We discovered it one simple day in the place we least expected it. We
applied to the Rabbinic Courts for a marriage license. What could be easier
than that? After all, we were both kosher candidates. I was an Israeli, eighth
generation sabra, and Kenneth was an American Jew. Everybody could see
that. We arrived at the Rabbinic Courthouse early in the morning and waited
in line for a long time. Finally we were asked to come in. Three rabbis sat
behind a long elevated desk, open books, and glasses of water in front of them.

The rabbis were sitting with their backs to the bright window; their features were blurred in the shadows, except for one, the youngest, with a sharp

goatee, who sat askew on his chair and from time to time dipped his face in the sunlight. Without greeting us, and without asking us to sit down, they observed us austerely. I suppressed an impulse to run out of the room. At length, the young rabbi spoke. "What is your request from the court?" he addressed Kenneth.

"We want to get married," Kenneth said readily, "and we need a marriage license," he smiled.

"I see," the rabbi intoned, and then bent over and whispered something to his colleagues. "Where are you from?" he asked, not unpleasantly, and rubbed his beard.

"I am from America," Kenneth announced, "from New York. And I had just been here a few months when I met this wonderful Israeli woman, whom I love and wish to marry."

The rabbi gazed at him astonished. "I did not ask you if you loved her. I asked you where you were from."

"Sorry," Kenneth grimaced, "I was just adding that because I am such a happy man these days."

"Do you have your documents?"

"Yes, yes, of course," Kenneth handed the rabbi his passport, his Israeli ID, and Suzanne's death certificate.

The rabbi looked at him sharply. "You were married before?"

"Yes, I was," Kenneth replied. "My wife died, as you can see."

"How old was she?"

"Twenty-eight," Kenneth said, biting his lip.

"Very young," muttered one of the other rabbis, who was older than the first and sported a full white beard.

"What did she die of?" the young rabbi inquired, his eyes narrowing. Kenneth briefly explained. The rabbi nodded sympathetically, wrote something down, and asked, "Was she Jewish?"

For a long moment, Kenneth did not reply. He shifted on his feet and gazed at the rabbis suspiciously. Finally he said, "No, she was not Jewish. She was a Roman Catholic. And I loved her all the same." His lips snapped shut.

The young rabbi took a drink of water from his glass and cleared his throat. "We have already said that the court is not interested in love, my dear man. But my next question is of extreme importance. Are *you* Jewish?"

Kenneth stared at him in disbelief. "What?" he gawked, "you are asking me if I am Jewish? Of course I am Jewish! What else could I be? Why else would I be here, in this country, when I can't even speak Hebrew?"

Kenneth and I on our honeymoon in Lake Lugano. Summer, 1973

The third rabbi laughed. "A good question," he said, nodding, "a good question."

The young rabbi smiled at Kenneth. "How do we know that you are Jewish? Your former wife, may she rest in peace, was not."

Kenneth looked at me as if he didn't know whether to laugh or cry. "But my name is Jewish, my family is Jewish, my upbringing has been Jewish—I can recite all the holidays by heart—even my nose is Jewish! Don't you see?"

Kenneth and I in New York. Summer, 1973

The rabbis laughed heartily. "But where does it say that you are Jewish?" the young rabbi chimed in, "none of these documents attests to that. The Israeli ID says that you are Jewish, but this is merely a record of what you told them. You say that your family is Jewish, but how do I know that? They are in

America. I don't know them. Here people know each other. But America? America is big."

"Let me tell you something," Kenneth spoke excitedly, his left index finger raised in the air, "I know what a *b'rit* is. A *b'rit* is circumcision. How about that? Would anybody who is *not* a Jew know that?"

The rabbi quickly consulted his colleagues. "We appreciate your knowledge," he finally said, "but this is no proof."

Kenneth was pacing the room in growing frustration. "What do you want me to do? How can I prove to you that I am Jewish? Really, Rabbi," he tried the philosophical route, "who would want to be a Jew if he wasn't born a Jew?"

The rabbi smiled benevolently.

"Listen, Rabbi," Kenneth pleaded, "I don't know what else I can do to prove to you that I am who I am. Have you ever read Kafka?" he asked suddenly. The rabbi said that he had heard the name. "Well, this conversation looks more and more like it's coming out of a Kafka novel. What do you want of me?"

"I need proof," the rabbi repeated calmly.

"Okay," Kenneth answered with a flushed face. "I'll give you the ocular proof. I am a Jew, and, like all Jews, I am circumcised. You want to examine me? Go right ahead."

The rabbi burst into a loud laughter. "That is no proof at all. Many goyim circumcise their sons." The other rabbis laughed gleefully. "Let me tell you something," the young rabbi noted finally in a practical tone. "Were you *bar mitzvahed?*"

"Of course," Kenneth said.

"If the rabbi who *bar mitzvahed* you writes to me that you are a Jew, that would be proof."

"Oh, no," Kenneth groaned, "I don't remember him, and I don't even know if he is alive! Besides, it would take months, and we want to get married on the 26th of June."

"Why did you come so late?" asked the rabbi.

"Who could have known that you'd be making such demands?"

The rabbi consulted his colleagues again. "Do you have a relative here who can testify to your Jewishness?" he asked.

"A relative. . . ." Kenneth looked at me, and his eyes glowed. "Sarah, my cousin, is here, in Jerusalem. Yes, I have a relative." He turned to me, "Honey, we are saved!"

"A woman?" the rabbi asked curtly.

"Obviously a woman," Kenneth protested. "I haven't yet met a man with the name Sarah."

"Sorry," blurted the rabbi. "A woman cannot testify in court."

"What?" Kenneth grabbed his head in despair. "Why can't a woman testify?" The rabbi observed him coolly. "This is the law."

"Well, change the law," Kenneth bawled. "After all, my Jewishness is your problem, not mine."

The rabbi pursed his lips irritably and asked Kenneth if his cousin was married. Yes, Kenneth said, she was married to an Israeli. The white-bearded rabbi then motioned to the young rabbi, and the three conferred for a long time. Periodically, they searched in the halakhic sources in front of them, and then continued their whispered debate. Finally, they seemed to have found what they were looking for. They decided that in the interest of the marriage, they would allow Kenneth's cousin to testify.

We left the court exhausted and drenched, as if we'd just escaped an overheated sauna. At one point, Kenneth was tempted to call the whole thing off, but I reminded him that without the approval of the Rabbinic Court there would be no marriage. After a few weeks of deliberations and expeditions to the court, with and without Sarah, we were granted the permission to wed. On June 26, 1973, with the rabbis' blessings, Kenneth and I were married.

SHIR

On January 23, 1976, our son, Shir Reuven Regenbaum, was born. At that time, Kenneth taught at Haifa University, and we lived on Ha'prachim (Flowers Street) on Mount Carmel, in a small apartment facing a wooded mountain slope. We loved the apartment because we furnished it ourselves, valiantly resisting my mother's attempts to tell us how to do it. Mostly we liked Shir's small but bright room and our study, which was actually a closed-in porch, spacious enough to hold our two desks and flooded with sunlight.

On the morning of January 23, I received by mail from my mentor, Professor Fisch, his favorable comments on the first two chapters of my dissertation. After a long quest for a topic, I had accepted his suggestion to explore the biblical motif of the binding of Isaac (the *Akedah*) in the relationships between fathers and sons in the literature of modern writers. At first I feared the topic, but later I became absorbed in the subject, which, although dealing with the tyrannical authority of fathers rather than mothers, resonated with my own experience. When Fisch's encouraging report on my work arrived on the eve of Shir's birth, Kenneth and I were delighted and felt that things in our lives were working together for the good.

At noon, when my labor pangs started, we took a cab to Elisha Hospital, on Mount Carmel. Kenneth, a graduate of the Lamaze class, stayed with me to help birth our child, "a bright beacon for our future," as he described him in his diary. We called our obstetrician, Dr. Kaduri, and braced ourselves for the big event. As my labor contractions got underway, Kenneth was excitedly writing down their frequency: "1:58—surprise contraction. 2:08—first long contraction. 2:14—another contraction, 35 sec." The doctor and the nurse arrived. They settled down to their busy tasks and chatted cheerfully with us. Kenneth was standing by my side, holding my hand. And then the pain came, like a funnel cloud from hell, whirling hot and furious inside me. I emitted a scream in the voice of a wild animal in a primordial forest, yet the baby was not coming down. An hour passed, and then another. I was fully dilated. With the contractions, everything else was gushing out of me—air, fluids, feces—but not Shir. For some reason, Dr. Kaduri refused to take me to the operating room. Later we speculated that perhaps he didn't know how to perform a caesarean. Finally, when the baby's heartbeat became faint, he relented and called another doctor for help. I looked at Kenneth and saw that he was crying. His notes became an agitated scrawl and then stopped altogether. At 5:00, I was wheeled to the operating room. At 5:20 P.M., Shir was born. His father described him as "bright and fierce, stinging with life!" At 7:10 P.M., I was wheeled out, and for two hours, according to Kenneth, I was asking, "When will it be over?" He assured me that all was over and that it went very well!

Within a day, members of the family were swarming around us. My mother, who by then was living in Tel Aviv with Elie, the man she fell in love with after Chaim was killed in a car accident, forgave Kenneth much for bringing a son to the world. She came to visit us often in Haifa, giving us advice on how to take care of Shir. From time to time, to lighten our burden, she'd take him with her to Tel Aviv for a few days. When he was misdiagnosed as having a dislocated hip and put unnecessarily in a cast, she skillfully devised ways to alleviate the chafing on his tender skin, and taught us how to ease his pain. Time and again, we were compelled to rescue our son from his overly-fond grandmother, but we had to admit that her teaching was invaluable. No wonder she became a caretaker of newborn babies and in time made quite a career and a name for herself.

MELANIE

In August 1976, when Shir was six months old, we traveled to New York to visit Kenneth's family and to show Shir to the Regenbaum tribe. I fell in love with the city. I loved its incomprehensible size, its broad streets and tall buildings; I loved its museums and theaters, its quirky rhythms and its noisy, sinister subway; its slate-colored ocean and its outstretched, sandy beaches; its department stores and Chinese restaurants; and more than those the Regenbaum hospitality and the thick woods on the way to suburban Monsey, where Gary, Kenneth's brother, a dentist, and his wife Barbara lived in a fine, two-story house, with their two children, and where we stayed. When had my life felt so good?

Sometime in August, we left Shir with his uncle and aunt and traveled for a week to the American Theater Association Convention in San Francisco. It was my first convention, and every talk, every workshop was exciting. In one of the panels, Kenneth took issue with the panelists and challenged them in such a daring and adroit manner that the audience, to the panelists' chagrin, applauded him. Where does he get this kind of courage? I thought with admiration. After the panel, people came up to talk to him. One of them was Professor Norman Fedder from Kansas State University. The two of them—voluble, jolly, Jewish theater buffs—hit it off instantly and started hatching plans for joint projects, dismissing the fact that Kansas and Israel were separated by stretches of land and two major bodies of water.

When we returned to New York, we were so buoyed by our trip that we did not notice the early warning signs of an approaching storm. We should have seen the change in Barbara and Gary's conduct, whose boisterous, carefree conversations were replaced by a strange, embarrassed tension, but we didn't. We were full of life and future possibilities. What could go wrong for us? Yet when Gary announced that Lew, a plastic surgeon and Gary's friend, had invited us for dinner, the memory of the itching mole Lew removed from Kenneth's back before our visit to San Francisco burst into my consciousness with the force of a rock shattering a window.

At dinner, my fears were confirmed. Lew had found that the mole on Kenneth's back was a malignant melanoma that had already penetrated the fourth level of his skin. Kenneth had to have surgery at once. The prognosis was grim. I quickly downed a glass of wine and ordered another. My fingers went numb; my heart froze. The sense of terrible dread was suffocating. I had known dread before, but not like *this*. This dread was final. I could not escape it, as I did when Reuven died. I could not appease it, or bargain with it. I could not make it disappear. This dread, this Death, would pitch its tent in our hearts. And what would Death look like? Would he be, as in Bergman's *The Seventh Seal,* a tall, imposing figure, with a pale face and piercing intelligent eyes, wrapped in black silk? Would he eat breakfast with us? Would he shower with us? Would he sit on the sunny corner of Kenneth's desk when Kenneth would be gathering his thoughts for the next class? Would he gracefully lean on the railing of Shir's crib as I diapered my son? Would he accompany Kenneth and me to our bedroom and slip soundlessly into bed with us?

That night, Kenneth was agitated but composed. His soul shifted to a higher level of discipline and courage. When we sat around the table, with Gary and Barbara, Kenneth wanted to find out everything about cancer. He wanted to know what could be done, where, when, and how. He wanted to learn about the nature of the disease—its dimensions, behavior, habits, and vulnerabilities. He even gave it a name—Melanie—and later often joked about my fierce rival. He was sizing up the enemy, with absolute and alert concentration, and was determined to fight it to his last breath.

Gary had specialized in oral surgery at the Sloan Kettering Cancer Center and had substantial knowledge on the disease. It was then that we realized that melanoma had run in the family. Kenneth's grandfather had it, and so did Kenneth's father, Will. His had appeared in the eye; he gradually lost his sight, then his eye, before the malignancy reached the brain. Kenneth's was clandestine and lethal. Like a stealthy submarine, it operated secretly in the deeper layers of his skin, and when it burst out to the surface, it had already scattered its deadly shells in his bloodstream.

LIKE MOTHER, LIKE DAUGHTER?

That night, snuggling up to Kenneth, I tried in vain to borrow his calm. When he fell asleep, I was still tossing and turning, staring in the dark at the sleeping body of the man who suddenly seemed to be slipping away from me. I wondered how long he had. I tried to imagine my life without him and jumped out of bed in terror. I stood up, then sat down again. I lit a cigarette and paced the room. I leaned over Shir's crib, dizzy with apprehension. Would he, like me, lose his father? No, no, my mind was racing; it could not be! Never in the world! I won't let Kenneth die! I sat on the bed, looking at the rows of literary classics on the shelves, which Gary never read in spite of his brother's exhortations. What did it matter? Now it was Kenneth who needed the medical books that Gary had read. The darkness knocked about in my head. But how did it all happen so suddenly? I gazed at Kenneth. His breathing was regular; his body restful, his face, barely visible in the dim night light, ruddy with health. How could it be that Death was already nestled in him? I stood up, drenched in cold sweat, struggling to breathe. No, no, it could not be; it won't be! There is still hope! Noiselessly, I opened the door and went out to the kitchen.

When I turned on the light, Gary's huge dog, Shoe, was napping by the sink. She stirred, opened one eye, and looked placidly at me. I took orange juice out of the refrigerator and sat down. I felt my pulse. Normal. I am alive. Shoe is alive. Gary and Barbara are alive. Shir is alive. Kenneth is. . . . How ironic, I addressed an invisible audience, that, during my labor, he was afraid that Shir and I would die. And now, now, he is. . . . But the melanoma had already been boring into his flesh, and we didn't know. During the ten days I spent in the hospital, Kenneth looked after me lovingly, arriving every morning at nine, when the sun had just scattered the morning fog and poured its honeyed warmth through the large French windows to the hospital hall, which overlooked the curved, wooded Mount Carmel slopes. I could hear his strong steps from a distance; he would come in, smiling, wearing his brown leather jacket, smelling sweetly of fresh air, leather, and the bouquet of daffodils that every morning he brought to my bed. My roommate—also recovering from a caesarean—would grumble, "my husband never brings *me* flowers." Holding me with both arms, Kenneth would wait for me to muster the strength to get up from bed. We emerged from the room to the big squares of sunlight in the hall, walking carefully, slowly, like an old, frail couple.

And all this time he was already dying, and I didn't know.

Indeed, I thought, sipping the juice in Gary's kitchen, I enjoyed his care so much that I hardly wanted to get better, really. I complained about the stitches, the backaches, the sore nipples, the difficulty in urinating. What a *kvetch* I was, I shook my head and stared pointedly at Shoe, who yelped, yawned, and fell asleep. What was there to cry about? A happy occasion. But now, *now*. . . . Suddenly I spoke out loud, "that *kvetching* was not the worst, though," I said. Shoe opened her eyes and looked at me in mild surprise. I stood up and gazed outside the window at the black night. The clock struck three. Am I talking to a dog? I listened for sounds of human stirrings in the house, but the silence was undisturbed. The worst, I bit my lip and sat down— I knew what the worst was. In my mind, I lusted after Dr. Kaduri, who, while delivering my son, saw my terrible nakedness. I put my hands on my burning cheeks. When Kenneth went home from the hospital, after we fed Shir, I stretched out on my bed, closed my eyes, and abandoned myself to lustful fantasies about my doctor, who had two strong arms and a smile that so strangely reminded me of Chaim's. How could I have ever wanted him? Mortified by the memory, I rose to my feet again and paced the kitchen floor.

Shoe barked. Wrapped in his robe, Gary came out to the kitchen. "What are you doing here?" he asked. "You know what time it is?" I nodded. "I can't sleep," I said. "I can understand that." Gary attempted a smile. "I haven't been sleeping too well myself. I cannot promise you he'll live," he added, "but we'll do our very best to save him. And who knows? He may yet beat the disease. Don't I know my brother?" he chuckled. "He is a fighter. But you should go to sleep," he urged me, as he turned back to his bedroom after giving Shoe water. "Tomorrow will be a tough day."

I listened to Shoe lustily gulping the water down. Who was I? How could I have longed for *him* after we'd returned from the hospital to our home with our baby? How could I, on the way back from an occasional shopping trip at the Carmel Center, get off the bus three stops early, walk over to *his* street, and pass, two or three times, in front of his house, just to catch a glimpse of him? Once I heard him talk to his wife and then saw his face floating in the kitchen window. By sheer chance, he did not see me. I ran all the way back to the bus stop, thinking that I'd rather die than be spotted by him outside his house. Yet three or four times I was compelled to repeat that silly stalking, my mother's adventurous blood roaring in my ears.

I put the juice glass in the sink. Fully awake, I stared at the backyard. The children's swings, sandbox, and scattered toys were visible in the grey dawn light. I love Kenneth, so how could I have been so taken up by a gaudy fantasy? Could I have so much coveted my mother's adulterous affair that I wanted one myself, pretended that I was entitled to it, wished that I could get away with it? When I told Kenneth about my attraction to Kaduri, he simply said that I'd have to get over it, and I resented him for not being like Reuven, allowing me the forbidden fun. Hot tears of remorse stung my eyes. True, I reflected, sniffling, I did not have an affair with Kaduri, but how close I was to it. How the threat of Death throws a new light on everything! Now the very thought of it disgusts me.

I went back to our room, stood for a moment by Shir's crib, covered him with his blanket, then returned to bed and curled up next to Kenneth, who, like his son, had been sleeping quietly the whole night. "How are you, honey?"

Kenneth muttered in his sleep. I whispered, "I love you. I want to be a good wife to you." Kenneth wrapped his arm around me and said, "Oh, but so you are, so you are, my dearest!" Together we fell into a deep slumber for two hours until Shir's hunger cries woke us up.

"TEACH ME TO FEEL ANOTHER'S WOE"

The operation was scheduled for mid-September, in Nyack Hospital, half an hour from Gary's house. The strategy was to perform radical surgery, to carve out a hefty chunk of Kenneth's back around the mole area, send it to the lab to detect tiny cancer particles, graft skin to patch the wound, and hope that all the lab results would be negative.

Kenneth accepted the plan in good spirit, but I could see that he was scared. How I saw this fear I don't know, for he had not shown it, nor spoken of it, but there it was, in the way his mouth twisted, his brown eyes enlarged, and the whites around them froze. I could not witness his terror; I wanted to reassure and protect him, but how? There was not much I could do except be with him, conscious of the widening, unspeakable divide between the living and the dying.

The surgery took five hours. When Gary emerged from the operating room, he told me cheerfully that the operation was successful but that they encountered problems with the skin graft. "Now, though," he smiled as he took off his mask, "he is fine. All patched up!" he laughed. Shortly, they wheeled Kenneth out. He was groggy and heavily bandaged. Relieved to see him, I kissed his forehead. He smiled at me. "You see, Squash, we came through. What did I tell ya?"

The first news to arrive after surgery was very good. The lab results came back negative, which meant that the melanoma had not yet spread. But two or three days after the operation, the bad news came. The skin graft did not take. Again, Kenneth had to go into surgery, once his wounds were sufficiently healed. Time passed. October arrived. The leaves were beginning to turn. Kenneth underwent his second surgery, and again, the skin graft did not take. A third operation was scheduled. By then, Gary and Lew had already identified the problem. Because Kenneth's right arm was bent at an angle, he slept on his left side, rather than on his belly, and at night turned over on his back, thus wiping out the slow, delicate workings of the graft. We had to devise a method to keep him from turning on his back. I offered to stay nights with him in the hospital.

I packed my stuff and said good-bye to Shir, who was so much in love with his uncle, aunt, and cousins that he wore my absence lightly. Gary drove me to the hospital for the third operation. It must have been mid-October. All along the way, the trees were decked in brilliant reds and yellows, their leaves shimmering and trembling in the wind. I had never seen such trees. The olives, pines, and carobs in Israel—whose leaves never turned—seemed sparse and slight next to these oaks, maples, and aspens. I was strangely uplifted by nature's spectacle.

The third was the shortest of the operations—a mere hour and a half. On the way back to his new room, Kenneth joked about the view from his window—a cemetery—and wondered if it was put there to cheer up the patients. Then he fell into a deep sleep, and I sat by his bed, fully awake, guarding his movements. Once or twice, I caught him just before he rolled over on his bandaged back. When the nurse checked him in the morning for signs of blood—which would have meant the graft failed—and didn't find any, we were delighted. I curled up to rest on a cot and slept, on and off, for five hours.

The second night was more difficult. I was tired. As I was sitting up, my head would nod off to sleep. Suddenly I'd jerk up, having dreamed that Kenneth was lying on his back, his graft bleeding profusely. But, no, he was still lying on his side. The night wore on at a turtle's pace. Keeping awake was a torment. The novelty of my sacrifice was wearing off. Gradually, I became irritable. Looking at Kenneth, I'd sometimes envy the luxury of his sleep. In the morning, the nurse checked Kenneth's back, and found no signs of blood. "My wife was up all night," Kenneth told the nurse proudly. "She takes good care of me." The nurse smiled and promised to bring me a cup of coffee. "One more night, and we'll be in the clear," Kenneth noted with a broad smile. "Now go to sleep," he ordered me. "I am fully awake and promise not to roll on my back, as if this were the beach, or something."

The third night was the most trying. I was so exhausted that at times I could not remember why I was up. Coffee no longer helped. Even love didn't help. All I wanted was to sleep, and only the dread of another operation kept my eyelids open. Angry thoughts crawled about in my mind. What is the purpose of all this work, I asked. He is going to leave me anyway. Alone, with a child. I know it. By morning, I felt numb, and my head was spinning. As usual, the nurse checked Kenneth's back. Again, there were no signs of blood. "Your graft," the nurse said with a happy smile, "seems to have taken!" She turned to me. "You did a great job, Mrs. Regenbaum." We cheered.

Yet in spite of the good news, I felt annoyed. I went over to a corner on the other side of the hospital, where I could drink coffee and smoke. In utter weariness, I looked outside the window at a flamboyant, bright red maple tree. I wanted to touch it. All this vibrant beauty over there, and I am here, buried in the hospital, without an end in sight. Then I heard, very near, an angry voice say, "I wish you were dead! I wish you were dead!" I turned around in horror. There was nobody around. The voice came from within me. "No, God, please," I mumbled, "don't listen to me; pretend I never said that. I don't wish Kenneth dead. I don't! I don't! I have no idea where the voice came from. How could I have thought that? I love him! I don't know what in the world I'd do without him!" For a long hour, I sat there shaken and distraught. Why did I wish such a terrible thing? Why? Did I resent him for being sick and putting me through terrible hardships? Did I pity myself more than I pitied him? I must change that, I thought, gazing at the intricate design of the maple leaf. But how? How? I sighed at the enormity of the task. I did not know the answer, but I hoped that love would find a way.

FAIR-WEATHER FRIENDS

At the beginning of November, just as the leaves were starting to fall, we returned to Israel. Gary, Barbara, and Kenneth's parents saw us to the airport with hugs, kisses, and best wishes. We took off and soared into the black night sky, our hearts weighed down with worry and sadness.

In Lod Airport, my mother and Elie waited for us, waving their hands. When we came out, Elie relieved us of the suitcases and my mother of Shir, whose cranky face she covered with kisses. "You look so good, Kenneth," she smiled, "what's this talk about cancer? You look as healthy as a bull."

Kenneth laughed happily. "I feel great, but I did have a little unpleasant visit from Melanie. I hope she never comes back."

"You mean melanoma?" my mother asked as she was making funny faces to Shir. "Don't you remember your *savta*, Shir? It's me, your *savta*. Yes. Have you forgotten me after four months? I bought you so many toys!"

"Yes, melanoma," Kenneth answered. "And we've got to be very vigilant, so she doesn't come back."

"Of course, she won't come back!" my mother asserted, pressing Shir's cheek close to hers. "You look so well, Kenneth; you are not sick! No way! I know; I used to be a nurse. You'll be perfectly all right."

Once we returned to Haifa, Kenneth threw himself into teaching with renewed rigor. He was filled with ideas and plans for the future. He envisioned productions, conferences, and lectures. His appetite for action was insatiable. If he had to die, he was going to meet his death standing up, "proud for goodness," as he used to say. Nothing, not even death, could change that. He rose cheerfully each morning, played and ate with Shir, picked up his heavy bag, kissed me good-bye, and went forth to conquer the day. Mostly, he didn't think about death at all.

It was, indeed, easy to forget it. Kenneth was healthy. His monthly blood tests were normal, and his physical exams, with a Rumanian doctor on Derech-Hayam Street, were normal too. I continued to work on my dissertation. In the evenings and on the weekends, we'd go out with Shir to playgrounds and parks, pushing his stroller along. At times, Kenneth would hold Shir in his strong left arm and shoot down the slide with him, father and son screaming with pleasure. When we stopped to chat with neighbors, they must have thought that we were a normal family, young, vigorous, and full of a glorious future. We looked, and mostly were, happy. We craved industry, regularity, each other's closeness, and the sweet hours with our "irrepressible rascal," Shir.

In January, Kenneth visited an American gastroenterologist on the Carmel for minor stomachaches. The doctor discovered two enlarged lymph nodes under Kenneth's right arm, which escaped the attention of our Rumanian internist. Melanie had returned. Mistrustful of Haifa doctors and hospitals, we decided to take Kenneth to the best hospital in the country— Hadassah Hospital in Jerusalem. We made an appointment with the chief surgeon, Dr. Durst, left Shir with his willing *savta*, got in touch with Matthew and Betsy (from the *Inherit the Wind* production), who were then living in Jerusalem and who thankfully invited us to stay with them, packed, and set out for our favorite city.

It was a bright blue winter day when we took a *sherut* (shuttle service) to the capital. When we reached the plateau of Me'vaseret Yerushala'im, Kenneth remarked on the beauty of the terraced hills on the outskirts of the city. "They seem so solitary and austere," he smiled at me, "but they are also so majestic; aren't they, those hills?" he smacked his lips with pleasure. Soon we could see Jerusalem itself, pitted like a crown of stones against the blue sky. Two more minutes and we were at the gates of the city. It was almost time for the meeting with the surgeon, and I was anxious. As if reading my mood, Kenneth kissed my cheek. "I'll be in good hands, darling," he reassured me. "Hadassah doctors know what they are doing, not like that Rumanian doctor who can't even identify a swollen node!" He put his fingers to his face in a gesture that said, "Give me a break!" I laughed, and my anxiety inexplicably vanished.

We met Matthew and Betsy, who took us to the hospital, and our cheerful mood soared. After two or three years, we were delighted to see them again and catch up on recent developments. Moreover, humor had always been our deepest bond. Whether we were exchanging juicy tidbits from the work on *Inherit the Wind,* or listening to Matthew and Betsy, the good Baptists, making fun of the Catholic Church or describing the difficulty of the Hebrew language, our conversation was punctuated with explosions of merry laughter. Now, as before, we were amused, and so arrived at the hospital in a mood of fine hilarity. We even walked in the halls as if we were merely visitors, but the stark reality of Kenneth's illness soon stared us in the face, eyeball to eyeball.

Dr. Durst and his assistant, Dr. Freund, invited Kenneth to the examination room. Matthew, Betsy, and I talked quietly in a corner. Half an hour passed. Finally, Dr. Freund walked out and called me to his office. We sat down. "How are you?" he asked warmly. I stared at his friendly brown eyes and thought, surely such a kind person wouldn't give me bad news! Then he said, "Your husband is very ill."

"What do you mean?" I asked weakly.

"What I mean is," Dr. Freund explained, "that when a melanoma metastasizes, as it did in your husband's case, it rarely leaves the person's body until it is done with it."

My throat burned. The doctor's desk, the white office walls, the terraced hills outside the window were spinning around. "But you are going to operate to take out the infected nodes, aren't you?"

"Of course we are—tomorrow morning," Dr. Freund said.

"Doesn't that mean that there is hope?" I swallowed hard.

"We operate to slow down the progress of the disease. And of course, theoretically there is hope. There are such things as spontaneous remissions. But they are rare." He got up, put an encouraging hand on my shoulder, and showed me out of the office. "Your husband is probably waiting for you in the hall." Once more he smiled and then was gone.

I walked out of the office shaken and dazed. I saw Kenneth talking to Matthew and Betsy in the corner, but I could barely order my feet to walk toward him. How could I tell him what I just heard? I knew that he would want to hear the news, no matter how bad it was. But I couldn't tell him. Help!

"Matthew," I said, "could I have a word with you for a minute?"

"What is it?" Matthew asked when we reached the staircase. His gentle blue eyes looked at me with alarm.

I broke down in tears. "The doctor told me terrible things about Kenneth," I cried, not noticing the change in Matthew's expression. "He is dying, Matthew, dying; how am I going to tell him that?"

"What do you want *me* to do?" Matthew asked.

I glanced at him. His face was flushed with anger. I had never seen it this way before. "I don't know," I mumbled. We were silent. "Let's go in," I finally said, wiping my face. I don't remember what I told Kenneth, but I must have softened Dr. Freund's message.

When we went back to Matthew and Betsy's apartment, all of us were gloomy. A big row erupted. Blames and counter-blames flew around. We accused them of running away from Kenneth's illness, and they charged us with making impossible demands on them. We called them cowards, and they called us selfish. We retorted that they were fair-weather friends, and they asserted that we had never been any friends at all. We said that they lacked Christian compassion, and they said that we behaved like self-righteous Old Testament prophets. By the end of the evening, our so-called friendship was in shreds. In the morning, we left the apartment with admonishments never to return.

Kenneth went back to the hospital for his surgery. I stayed at my mother's cousin's house. We managed. But Kenneth was determined never again to reveal his illness to friends, and we thus embarked on a rough and lonely road.

"A RED HERRING"

Dr. Fuchs, the head of the oncology ward at Hadassah Hospital, was dark, handsome, and very tall. To speak with him, from my short vantage point of five feet, I soon learned to crane my neck. Unlike Freund, Fuchs projected a breezy optimism. While we were waiting with him for the elevator, he noticed that I was "pale with fear," in his words. He smiled at me from his serene height and said, "Don't worry, Mrs. Regenbaum; your husband will be all right; he'll be just fine!" I was wondrously uplifted by his statement. What does Dr. Freund know? Dr. Fuchs is the expert, and he says there is hope!

In the oncology ward, Kenneth met his doctors. Among them he was particularly fond of Dr. Shaike Halperin, a young man with flaxen hair, who had a brisk sense of humor and an interest in books and ideas, which Kenneth appreciated; he was the only doctor in the ward who always managed to find veins in Kenneth's arm for the chemotherapy—the doctor who, in spite of his aversion to showing feelings, communicated his caring to Kenneth.

As soon as he was settled in oncology, Kenneth was put through a barrage of tests—blood tests, x-rays, liver scans, brain scans, and more. One by one, the tests came back negative. We cheered each one of them. Finally, there was only one left, a brain scan, which was taken merely for the sake of formality. Kenneth and I thought so little of it that we had already started packing for our trip back to Haifa—via Tel Aviv to pick up Shir— the next day.

In the evening, Dr. Biran approached me in the hall and told me that Kenneth's brain scan had come back "positive," namely, that the melanoma had metastasized to his brain. I looked at Kenneth, who was pleasantly conversing with his neighbor. How could it be that he had only a few weeks to live? And yet how could I doubt the doctor's report? Kenneth motioned to me and I knew that he expected me to tell him what I heard, but I couldn't. Instead, I rushed upstairs to the seventh floor, and looked for Rachel, the American nurse who took care of him in surgery. For the second time already, I reflected, I am chickening out of telling Kenneth the truth.

When he heard the news, Kenneth did not believe it. "How could it be," he asked Rachel "that I have a tumor in my brain without any headaches or dizziness?" he laughed. After Rachel left, we held each other and stared out of the window into the blackness outside. That night we slept fitfully; although Kenneth pooh-poohed the report, he was terrified by it.

In the morning, Dr. Fuchs appeared, cheerful as always. "I heard that they gave you a real scare last night," he said.

"What do you mean?" Kenneth scrutinized the doctor's face.

"What I mean is that the result of the brain scan was a mistake," Dr. Fuchs laughed, "a red herring."

"What?" Kenneth jumped from his bed. "A mistake? Are you serious?" his eyes glowed.

"Very serious," Dr. Fuchs laughed again. "Your brain is just fine; don't worry. Go home today and come back in a week for the beginning of your chemotherapy."

"Yes, sir!" Kenneth cried happily. "Thank you!" Then he picked me up, gave me a resounding kiss, and twirled me around the room.

IN THE EYE OF THE STORM

Dr. Fuchs's words sounded like a providential reprieve. Indeed, for the next thirteen or fourteen months our life was burgeoning with creativity and hope.

Yet, they were not easy months. The chemotherapy regime was grueling. Every two and a half weeks, Kenneth and I traveled from Haifa to Hadassah Hospital for five consecutive days of DTIC injections. Each injection would bring on eight hours of nausea and vomiting of foul-smelling, white foam. Only in the evening would Kenneth be able to eat a light meal. On the fifth day, the nausea would subside, and we would go back to Tel Aviv, stay with my mother and Elie for the night, and then return with Shir to Haifa.

In Jerusalem, we usually stayed at the YMCA. After the injection, we'd hop in a cab and return to our room for the allotted wrenching hours. At night, we'd come out of our room, which would smell strongly of chemotherapy and vomit, and walk slowly to the King David Hotel across the street for an omelette and a cup of tea. The bright lights in the area, the galleries and jewelry shops adjacent to the hotel, the people milling about, and the soft breezes, which sometimes carried a whiff of jasmine, mollified Kenneth's embattled spirit. He'd gaze at the imposing arches of the YMCA and at the stars and sigh gratefully. "Only two more days, Squash," he'd smile.

In spite of the difficulties, the treatment seemed to be working. Month after month went by, and Melanie did not show any signs of coming back. Although we never forgot her, we were able to enjoy our family life and our work. With the exception of the department chair, nobody knew of Kenneth's illness. The students accepted his odd schedule—a week's absence every two or three weeks, and then makeup time in the evenings or on the weekends—in good spirit. And so Kenneth continued teaching full time and mounting productions.

In spite of the terror that was never far away, I also managed to work. In fact, I wrote most of my dissertation during that period. Kenneth urged me to finish my doctorate, for without it, we both knew, I could never get a decent job. I worked fast, in a white heat. The authors I was studying became my personal teachers and mentors. From Faulkner I learned that I'd have to find ways to prevail, to be braver than I was. I'd have to relinquish my neediness, my dependency on Kenneth. Instead of expecting him to solve my problems and to fight my wars, I'd have to learn to make do on my own. Moreover, I'd have to support and sustain him. The princess and the pea part of me trembled in apprehension, but I knew that I could rely on the other part, the tough Gadna youngster, who was ready for the struggle.

While Kenneth was creating theater, and I was writing my dissertation, Shir learned to walk. This new skill released his energies. He ran in the halls and hid in corners; he jumped off chairs and tables, and threw his ball straight at the chandelier; outside he pushed his stroller ahead of him and soon disappeared from view; on the beach, he raced the waves and squealed in delight when they caught up with him; and he drove the toy car his *savta* got him so fast that Kenneth had to run to stop him from rolling down the hill. But Papa Regenbaum didn't mind this roughhousing one bit! With Shir he spent some of his best hours. "My son is my song," he used to quip on the Hebrew meaning of Shir's name.

It was in the midst of that fruitful and relatively calm period that we decided to have another child. It was an impulsive, passionate decision. Surely, we were aware of the dangers ahead, but we brushed them aside. As my desire for this new child was stronger than my terror, sometime in April, I stopped using contraceptives. When we found out I was pregnant, Kenneth and I were beside ourselves with excitement. Life, new life! We cried out. We killed Death! Death is dead! We exulted.

THE CHOICE

For a whole week we were flushed with joy. We told the good news to friends, family, neighbors, and even to the shopkeeper of our favorite deli up the street, where we used to buy the herring and cheeses that Kenneth loved. The woman, whose teased and dyed blond hair surrounded her round face like a halo, congratulated us. "Bravo, bravo," she said with a pronounced German accent. "Children are ze blessing from God. Zey are more important zan husband, wife, anybody, I tell you, especially for us in zis country," she smiled. Kenneth nodded and said, "Yes, children are important, but not more important than a spouse," he emphasized. "Ach, you Americans," the woman laughed. "Vhat is a spouse, I ask you? Here today, gone tomorrow," she was slicing the *challah* for us. "Divorce, other *meshugas*, who knows? But a child is a child forever. Anyvay, good luck," she handed us the goods. "You

---

meshugas Craziness

are young. Maybe you have many more children." Kenneth smiled ruefully. "Two are all we want," he said, as we pushed Shir's stroller into the sunny street.

The choice of life, however, was not easy. A few days later, Kenneth traveled to Jerusalem for the chemotherapy. I was to join him in two days. That night, when we were talking on the phone, I was startled by a thought. "Did you tell your doctors at Hadassah that I'm pregnant?"

"No, I haven't yet," Kenneth said. "Should I tell them?"

"It just occurred to me that since the chemo is everywhere in your blood, it must also be in your semen."

"It must be."

"Could it have affected the fetus?"

"I'll talk to the doctors tomorrow," Kenneth promised.

When I got to Jerusalem the following afternoon, I hailed a cab and rushed to the YMCA. Kenneth came out to meet me, smiling. We walked into the empty guest room. I sat down on the couch, but Kenneth was still standing up.

"Why don't you sit down?" I asked.

"I'm afraid I have bad news," he said.

My heart sank. "Has something showed up in your tests?"

"No, no, I'm fine," he said. "But you see, they don't know much about the effect of the chemo on the fetus."

"What do you mean?" I asked, feeling chilled.

"Well," Kenneth explained, "at first Fuchs, instead of congratulating us, got mad at us for getting pregnant without telling him. Would you believe this?" he gawked.

"What did you tell him?"

"I said, 'what do you mean, Dr. Fuchs? Why shouldn't we get pregnant? Is there any reason for it?'"

"So what did he say?"

"He didn't know what to say to that. Then I asked him if the DTIC might have an adverse effect on the fetus."

"Yes?" I looked at him intently.

"He said, No, he didn't think so, but he didn't know. 'Nobody knows,' he said. 'There is no literature on it, no reports on it,' he added, and at this point," Kenneth explained, "he is becoming frustrated. 'What are you telling me?' I asked him. 'What do you mean there is no literature on it?' I was getting just a little angry, Shelly, because the man, important as he is, seemed to be waffling. 'Well,' he said, 'there is some literature on the effects of the chemo on the mother, when she herself is the patient, but no literature on the mother when the father is the patient.' 'Why didn't you warn us?' I asked him. Fuchs looked at me from his impressive height, you know, and said with an incredulous expression on his face, 'It never even occurred to me, Dr. Regenbaum (he always calls me Dr. Regenbaum, which, from a doctor, is a nice compliment, I suppose) that in your condition you'd want another child! Besides,' he added, 'this is not America. If I told my Israeli patients the truth about their conditions, I wouldn't have any patients!' At that point, dear, I just lost it. 'Is this your policy?' I yelled at him, 'telling lies to patients?' He was really flustered. 'You are sick; don't you understand?' he asked. 'Isn't it rather foolhardy to bring another child into the world?' 'Not at all,' I said, 'we want this child. But would you mind telling me if this child is going to be all right?' Finally, he put his arm around my shoulder and simpered, 'The child would be fine. But you know what? Why don't you let your wife see me? We can easily arrange an abortion, right here in Hadassah, with one of the best doctors. Don't you have enough worries already?' I looked at him in disbelief. 'Why are you saying this?' I must have been shouting at that point. 'Why should we abort the child? Do you know something you are not telling me?' He assured me that he knew nothing more, and that the child would be all right, but he explained that if we are so worried, abortion would be the best solution. I told him that this is my wife's decision, not mine. And that's where we are now, my dear. So—sorry to dump this load on your head."

"What is the worst that can happen to the child, did he tell you?"

Kenneth sighed. "He was never clear on that. At one point he mentioned possible physical mutations, but he quickly added that that happened to mothers who were patients."

"So where do we stand?"

"I don't know," Kenneth answered. "If you want an abortion, dearest, I'd understand. It's your decision, not Fuchs's, or your mother's, or mine. You are the one to tell us what will happen to this child."

I wanted the child, and I knew that Kenneth wanted it, and yet I was tempted by the opportunity that presented itself to me. Here was my chance, my one perfect, moral chance to spare myself and bail out of a difficult future. Who would blame me if I decided to abort the fetus?

I turned to Kenneth and touched his hands. They were ice-cold. "I don't mind seeing Dr. Fuchs," I heard myself saying. "But I will tell him that I don't want his abortion."

"Ah, my dear," Kenneth hugged me, "I am so glad you made this decision," his eyes were luminous, "and I am so proud of *us* because now we three
will be four and we'll not let anything stop our life!"

LIVI

This time we wanted the best obstetrician, and I knew a doctor who exactly fit
that description and who also worked at Hadassah—my friend from England,
Dr. Sadov. We paid him a visit and told him our story. No, he said with the
dimpled smile I remembered well, he did not anticipate that the chemo would
affect the fetus, and yes, he recommended a birth by caesarean. The operation
was scheduled for December 21, 1977. We left Dr. Sadov's office reassured and
in high spirits.

Looking back, I don't rightly know what kind of faith, or impetuous daring, had spurred us on during the months of the pregnancy. Sustaining our
family routines at times exacted daily heroic efforts. Kenneth kept teaching, on
his quirky but reliable schedule; more than before he helped with the shopping
and would not allow me to carry heavy weights; also more than before, he
played with Shir and kept his wild energies from exploding anywhere near my
growing belly; he preserved our family tradition of bringing roses on Friday
night and lighting the candles; and he lovingly urged me to write my dissertation. I often thought of him as a tightrope walker, juggling three or four balls
in his good hand.

In addition to his busy life at home, Kenneth, of course, traveled regularly to Jerusalem. Whenever I could, I traveled with him, trying to synchro-
nize his chemotherapy with my checkups with Dr. Sadov. Shir stayed in Tel
Aviv with his doting grandmother. Humbled by the seriousness of Kenneth's
illness, my mother treated us to sumptuous dinners whenever we returned
from Jerusalem, avoided arguments with Kenneth, and, on the contrary, gave
us energetic and confident moral support. Each time we came, she was ready
with another story she heard or read about a miraculous recovery from cancer,
even from melanoma. Yes, she used to say, we should not lose hope, recoveries
happened, she was sure, and Kenneth looked so healthy, there was no doubt in
her mind that he was the one destined to survive this disease. I did not believe
her, but all the same, I felt comforted. It was on those evenings, when I was sitting on the porch of Elie's house on Frug Street, watching Kenneth and Elie
discussing recent Tel Aviv theater productions, Shir running around with his

new toys, and groups of people milling about on the pavement, that I found refuge from the exhausting work and the pounding anxiety. Although I feared that both the calm and the harmonious interaction with my mother were fleeting, I loved those hopeful evenings when all seemed possible, even a future with Kenneth.

The months stole away. Kenneth's tests still came back negative. I was growing bigger and developed a voracious appetite for oranges. When the child, whom I somehow knew to be a girl, was kicking hard, I'd put Kenneth's hand on my belly, and he'd sigh in pleasure. There she was, his life, his future, his triumph over despair. "But we shouldn't call it a 'she,'" he cautioned me playfully. "What if it's a 'he'?"

Finally the 20th of December arrived. I entered Hadassah Hospital and was put in a room with three or four other pregnant women, who, like me, were scheduled for caesareans. I particularly remember one of them—an intelligent, forty-two year old hunchback, who was determined to have a child, even though she wasn't married. In those days, in Israel, that was a bold step, and I admired her courage. She was cheerful, funny, and talkative; she gave us no rest, but her stories were amusing. She was also a chain-smoker who continued to smoke in the ward. At night, when Sadov made his rounds, she immediately put out her cigarette and opened the window, but she couldn't fool him. He chastised her soundly. Then he looked around the ward and chatted with each one of the patients. "How are you?" he smiled as he approached my bed. I told him that I was fine. "And how is your husband?" he asked. "He is doing all right, I suppose," I hesitated. "It must be hard on you," Sadov said kindly, his youthful blue eyes smiling. "Yes, thank you," I mumbled in the rush of feelings that threatened to break out in tears. "But don't you worry a bit about tomorrow," he added cheerfully, "you'll be fine. We'll take good care of you."

At 8:00 A.M. I was wheeled to the operating theater. Dr. Sadov, in his OR attire, was chatting with the anesthesiologist. "You know," he told him, "I met Shelly in England ten years ago. And I convinced her to continue her studies for her master's degree," he smiled happily, "and now, guess what?" he asked. "Now she is finishing her doctorate! How about that?" At that very moment I lost consciousness. When I woke up, I saw Dr. Sadov bending over me. "Congratulations," he said, "you have a daughter!" "Is she all right?" I quickly asked the question that had been on my mind for seven months. "She is just fine!" he said, "go back to sleep." Which I did, easily, and for a long, long time.

When I awoke, Kenneth was sitting near my bed, reading. "Hi," I motioned to him. "We made it," I laughed, feeling wonderfully relieved and happy. "I saw her," Kenneth could barely wait to tell me. "She is so tiny, but, ah, so beautiful!" His face was radiant. "Our Livi!" At that moment, the nurse wheeled her in. "Here's your tiny incubator baby!" she said, smiling. "Is something wrong with her?" I asked anxiously. "Oh, no," the nurse said, "she is just tiny, and she needs some help, that's all." I held Livi in my arms. Kenneth joined me to gaze at her. She was indeed a tiny slip of a thing, but perfectly shaped, a flower in perfect repose.

"MALARKEY, IT METASTASIZED AGAIN!"

It was after the birth of Livi that all hell broke loose.

I remember the period from January to August 1978 as if I were running breathlessly in a violent storm, one child on each arm, unable to see or hear for the beating rain, trying desperately to hold onto Kenneth. But he was already drifting away from us, carried out by the torrent to Death's dominion.

It all started with an infected sore, the size of a dime, which appeared on Kenneth's left side, a month or two before Livi was born. We showed it to two oncologists at Hadassah who were convinced that it was a minor infection, treatable with heat and antibiotic cream. We treated it daily, but instead of disappearing it grew. We tried to ignore it, to pretend that it was getting smaller, but each night it looked us in the face, redder and angrier. I urged Kenneth to see Dr. Fuchs, and we resolved to do that when the new chemo cycle was due.

It was the third or the fourth day after Livi was born. Together Kenneth and I walked from obstetrics to oncology. After Halperin found a vein in Kenneth's arm, he looked at the "infection" and, while he was still convinced that there was no cause for alarm, he suggested that Fuchs see it. An hour later, Fuchs walked in and asked about the birth. We told him that all went well. "I am so glad to hear the good news," he smiled wryly. Then he wrapped his arm around Kenneth and asked him how he was. "I have this thing here," Kenneth said, "which refuses to go away. We were told that it's an infection so we treated it with heat and cream, but it is still there. Could you look at it?" Fuchs frowned. "Heat?" he asked, "why heat? Take off your shirt," he ordered Kenneth. The "thing" was red-hot and looked like a small firebrand. Fuchs looked at it as if it were a personal enemy and said, furiously, "Malarkey, it metastasized again! We'll start radiation." And then, with two long strides, he disappeared.

"WHAT KIND OF A MOTHER
IS SHE?"

For ten days and nights after we brought her home from the hospital, Livi did not stop howling. She cried before feeding and after feeding, in her crib, and on the tired arms of her father or mother. She often woke Shir up, and he cried too. Then he fell asleep again, but she continued bawling, as if nothing in the world could ever comfort her. We took her to the pediatrician, but he concluded that she just had colic. We returned home and resumed our vigilance. Night after night, Livi's howls pierced our sleep. What in the world does she want? I'd ask, gritting my teeth. Why won't she shut up? Finally, after ten days, we took her to Carmel Hospital. Blood tests revealed immediately the reason for her anguish—high potassium in the blood. No connection to the DTIC, we were told. A minor problem, we were reassured. But it took the doctors three months to find a way to bring the potassium down—by adding salt to Livi's milk. For three months, they refused to release her for fear of heart damage; for three months, we had to devise ways to skip from the Carmel Hospital in Haifa to Hadassah Hospital in Jerusalem and back again, while also taking care of Shir and doing our work—Kenneth in the classroom, and I—on the dissertation. I needed my mother's help, but I did not have it. We were in the midst of another feud, which was signaled by my mother slamming the door behind her. Shir, who was sad to see his grandmother go, joined Livi in heartrending cries. Kenneth and I collapsed on the sofa, hugging each other for comfort, expecting any minute to drown in the pool of tears whose level was steadily rising in our little apartment.

Managing without my mother's help was not easy. Burdened by chores and greedy for each hour I could spend with Kenneth at home, I cut short my visits to Livi at Carmel Hospital. I rushed there in the morning, leaving Shir with the neighbors, or with Kenneth, and then hurried back home for lunch. In the afternoons, I worked on my dissertation, then in its final stages, and prepared dinner. In the evenings, I took a cab back to the hospital and stayed with Livi for an hour or two. When I was at home, I worried about Livi in the hospital; when I was with Livi, I worried about Kenneth at home. The nurses somehow sensed my impatience. Once, coming in through the back door, I overheard a conversation between Debbie, the head pediatric nurse who knew about Kenneth's illness, and one of the nurses, who didn't. "This baby is neglected. She is alone most of the day," the nurse complained to Debbie as she was picking Livi up to feed her. "Her mother comes for an hour in the morning and an hour at night. I have never seen anything like it. What kind of a mother is she?" The nurse's face was hot with indignation. "Perhaps she has her reasons," Debbie muttered. At that moment she caught sight of me and motioned to the nurse to be quiet. As I took Livi from her hands, the nurse gazed at me with a silent reproach and walked away. I was stung.

"You know," Debbie tried to cheer me up, "your mother was here yesterday and managed to make this baby laugh." "She was here?" I asked, surprised. "When did she come?" "Oh," Debbie replied, "she has been coming here three, four times a week. You didn't know that? She's a tremendous help. Terrific with your little Livi. Don't you worry," she smiled, "your daughter will be fine. Go home and take care of your husband."

"I'M SIXTY-FOUR, AND I WANT TO LIVE!"

Shortly afterward, my mother and I reconciled. Livi recovered and in April came back home. The rains had stopped, and a boisterous spring covered the mountain slope outside our window with pink cyclamens and red wild tulips. Every day we took Livi and Shir out to the playground. At times, Kenneth raised Livi in his arms, gingerly, caressing her small porcelain face with his finger, which seemed to cover half of it, and lifting her up to the warm sun and the sky that was forever blue. He'd look at me, and at her, and say, "my two best ladies." Meanwhile Shir, who was not interested in sentimental displays, would try out his hand with the ball. For a short month, the four of us—a family again—were hale and well. In April, too, I finished my dissertation, traveled to Bar-Ilan with three copies of the manuscript, and laid them on Professor Fisch's desk. "My third child," I said, and Fisch laughed. Like everybody else, he, too, did not know that Kenneth was dying.

In April, Will and Helen Regenbaum, Kenneth's parents, came for six weeks. The reunion was heartfelt and eager. Kenneth, who believed his father to be the greatest teacher ever born, the only professor in New York University, he used to say, who managed to make a subject as boring as taxation fascinating not only to accountants but also to humanists, now enjoyed telling his mentor about his teaching experiences. And yet at the end of those talks, Kenneth would be exhausted and pale; at times, beads of sweat would cluster on his forehead, and a brief tremor would twist his lower lip.

Yet neither Will nor Helen paid attention to their son's sickness. They came late in the morning, talked about things they saw, people they met, and the wonderful weather. They played with Shir, ate lunch with us, talked some more, and then returned to their hotel for dinner. Their relaxed manner became the target of my mother's fury. "What are they doing here all day?" she'd complain to us. "They sit around, they talk, they take Shir out for an hour, and that's it! They behave as if there was no emergency here, no sickness! In their world," she fumed, "nothing has changed."

Gradually, a distance opened up between Kenneth and his parents. Our apartment became crowded. The carefree discussions of the first week were replaced by tense arguments on sickness and responsibility. One such sharp exchange brought the father and the son to the brink of war.

"How can you keep your daily calm routine as if nothing was happening to me?" Kenneth asked impatiently.

"What do you want me to do?" Will retorted shrilly.

"Why don't you ask me about my sickness, or my treatment? Why don't you care?"

"If I didn't care, would I be here? No, I'd still be in New York! What do you think I'm doing here?"

"I don't know. You've come here for six weeks, and what are you using them for? Think about it, Dad. There is this big white elephant between us, called Melanie, and you ignore it, as if it weren't there. How can I talk to you around it?"

"I've been trying to distract you. What do you want me to do?" Will's artificial blue eye, replacing the one lost to melanoma, seemed to have acquired a life of its own and stared angrily at Kenneth. "I survived this damned disease. So? What do you want me to do? Die for you? I am sorry, son. I am sixty-four and I want to live!"

Kenneth rose to his feet, pale and shaking with anger. "I don't want you to die for me," he said. "I want you to live for me. Is that too much to ask? How long do you think I have? Dad, I am thirty-nine, and I also want to live!" He stopped, exhausted from the effort. At that moment, as if by tacit agreement, Livi and Shir began to wail. The Regenbaums looked upset and resentful and soon left for their hotel. I went to the children's room and, unable to comfort them, joined their wailing.

When I entered our bedroom, Kenneth was lying in bed, tired and chagrined. "My father," he said, "my own father. Why can't he talk to me? Sure,
melanoma is not a pleasant subject, but where is his courage? Why doesn't he
hold me?"

Two days later, the Regenbaums returned, and things calmed down for
a while.

"AS LONG AS I CAN STAND, I'LL TEACH"

During the period from January to April, 1978, Kenneth's health deteriorated.
His normal ruddy complexion was gone forever, it seemed; he was pale and
tired most of the time. May arrived with scorching heat waves, and the air outside was quivering and steaming. The walk to and from the bus stop became
an exhausting effort for Kenneth; he used to come back weak and perspiring.
I pleaded with him to quit teaching, but he refused. "As long as I can stand on
my own two feet," he said, "I'll go on teaching."

One day he came home earlier than usual. He dropped his heavy bag to
the floor and asked me for a glass of water. His face was white as chalk. "Oh,
my dear," he moaned as he sat down to drink. "I collapsed in the classroom."

"Why?" I asked foolishly.

"I suddenly felt dizzy and weak and had to sit down," he was breathing
heavily. "I wanted to get up but couldn't. Can you imagine that, Squash? I
just couldn't stand up on my feet." His eyes were moist. "I was so ashamed.
My students circled me, gaping. 'Dr. Regenbaum, are you all right?' 'No,' I
finally admitted. 'I am not all right. So sorry. Could you please call a cab?'
They rushed out. Fortunately, there was a cab outside. You know how rare
that is at Haifa University! And so here I am, your useless, unemployed
teacher!"

"No," I protested. "You are not a useless teacher. You are the best, the
bravest teacher I have ever known, and so you will always be!"

We put him in bed and made preparations to bring him to Hadassah the
following week. He asked me to take his place in the classroom for one more
session, to finish the discussion of *King Lear* and to give the students their final
assignment. "No," I refused, "I cannot take your place. I haven't taught a class
in two years. And where would I find the time to study the play?" He looked
at me, as of old, with a sweet reproach. "What do you mean you can't take my
place? Of course you can. Don't give me that!"

I did as he asked. I remember being almost ashamed of the thrill that teaching gave me again. I told myself that I shouldn't be having fun while Kenneth was ailing in bed, but there I was, loving every minute of it! When I came home, I tried to hide my excitement, but Kenneth found it out. We talked and laughed for a long hour, not knowing then that this was to be our last happy evening.

"THE DYING OF THE LIGHT"

Sometime at the end of May we packed for a few weeks in preparation for our journey. We took clothes, books, and toys for the children, who were to stay with their *savta* in Tel Aviv, but we left everything else in place because we intended to come back to it. The cribs in the children's room were clean and ready. The big bed in our bedroom looked restful and inviting. Our two desks in the tiny study were, as always, crowded—loaded with books and notes. The high chair in the kitchen waited for Shir, and for Livi, too. In the living room, our red-and-black checkered couch promised cozy evenings by the TV, and the grey swivel chair, Kenneth's favorite, stood shyly in the corner, ready for its master's spin. Hundreds of books were lined up in the bookshelves along the walls. In between one case and another hung our favorite painting by our friend Chaim Naor, depicting a huge yellow-orange sun setting behind a hill overgrown with bushes and eucalyptus trees and dotted with cheerful, ramshackle houses. We closed the door and hastened to Jerusalem, not knowing that we'd never open it again.

At Hadassah, Kenneth's hospital room was ready for him and the special hospital bed, which could be raised and lowered, offered him real rest. He even gulped with relish the lunch that his mother brought him from the cafeteria. I, too, settled down. In the small closet space, I piled up my things and put our books and radio on the spacious windowsill, the place where a few weeks later, when things got worse, I hid a bottle of sweet Vermouth behind the curtains. There was no tub in the bathroom, but in time I learned to appreciate the strong hot current of the shower that calmed my nerves. I found a folding cot and stretched it under the sink, next to Kenneth's bed.

During the first month, we developed a routine. In the morning, before the doctors' visit, we'd talk and listen to the radio. After lunch and Kenneth's nap, we'd take a walk around the ward and converse with doctors and patients. In the afternoon and the evening, I'd read poems and excerpts from novels to

Kenneth. The nights, however, were restless, eerie; the place was alert with neon lights, ringing phones, and nurses pacing the halls at all hours. Every now and then, a deep sigh, or a stifled sob broke the fragile silence and chased away sleep. Once, at two or three in the morning, a woman at the end of the hall shrieked. The nurses, in a group, ran to her room. I got up shivering, put on my robe, walked to the kitchen, and lit the flame under the kettle. A moment later a man walked in. "Would you like some tea?" I asked him. "Yes, I would," he said and sat down heavily. "Thank you. My name is Ya'acov," he said, as I handed him the cup.

"I'm Shelly."

"You are up too, eh? Who can sleep in this place?" he laughed ruefully. "My wife is here," he explained.

"Is she? . . ." I pointed in the direction of the shrieking woman.

"No, no," he smiled bitterly. "I wish. I wish she screamed and yelled," he said in sudden vehemence. "But she has given up. You know what I mean? Resigned herself to dying," he tapped his spoon against the cup. "I have been telling her to fight, fight! She is only thirty-six, but she—no. She smiles at me, all sweet and loving, and says that it's all right, she is ready. 'Ready for what, Nurit?' I ask her. 'You talk about it as if it were a summer resort,' I say to her. 'Don't give up, Nurit,' I plead with her, 'there is still hope.' But she looks at me with a forgiving smile, as if I were just a spoiled child who needed humoring. She breaks my heart." He looked at me as if he had known me for years. "Why does she want the silence and the dark? Why does she want to be away from us, her husband and her son?" He held his head in his hands.

I listened to him, not knowing what to say. Finally, he shook his head, as if snapping out of a trance. "Sorry," he smiled faintly and sipped his tea. "I just couldn't hold it in any longer."

"It's quite all right," I said lamely.

"And you?" he asked. "What are you doing here?"

"My husband," I muttered.

"A young man, eh?" he said.

"Yes. Thirty-nine."

"What does he have?"

"Melanoma."

"*Oi vey,*" he shook his head. "That's a bad business. But tell him to fight it."

"He does," I said. "He has been fighting it from the beginning. He will never give up."

"Good," Ya'acov said. "Good. That's the way. Well, I'll try to get some sleep, and you too," he smiled wearily. "Thanks for the tea."

When I returned to our room, I was startled to see Kenneth awake, waiting for me in the dark. I told him about Ya'acov and his wife, Nurit. "I will never," Kenneth said, a strange fire flickering in his eye, "never go gentle into that good night." In the hall light, I could see him grinning impishly at me. "You married a passionate man," he said, "who believes in the joy of living even in this damned place." I bent over to kiss him and buried my face in the nape of his neck, seeking out his smell that was now mixed with the pungent odor of medicine. "Fight, Kenny; please fight," I whispered.

One afternoon I came out of Kenneth's room and saw Ya'acov leaning against the wall, bent over, his hand pressed to his stomach. A nurse ran to Nurit's room, followed by a group of doctors. I walked up to Ya'acov and put my hand on his shoulder. He turned to me, his mouth twisted in anguish, his eyes bloodshot. I asked him if he needed help. He said "Thank you. No one can help me now," and walked away.

"You look as if you have just met a ghost," Kenneth said when he saw me. I could not tell him that Nurit had died. Between us, *death* had become an inadmissible word. We believed that by an effort of the will, we could defy it, wipe it out. But it pursued us doggedly, taking the rebellious Kenneth down step by jolting step.

GOODBYES

During the first month, Kenneth's parents came to visit him, for a few hours, every day. At times, they brought food. One day Kenneth's mother gave him spinach, but he wouldn't eat it. "Eat it," she said, "it's good for you. You always liked it." Her tired face stared at him vacantly and her short red hair flamed in defiance.

"Mother," Kenneth said, "thank you, but I don't want spinach. I can't eat it now. I am feeling nauseous from the chemo."

"How can you get better if you don't eat?" she flared up.

"This spinach," Kenneth retorted, his fist coming down on the bed, "won't make me better."

"So I don't know what will make you better," Helen yelled. "How can you ever get better if you don't take care of yourself?"

"I do too take care of myself, Mother," Kenneth said. "I want to eat but I can't."

"You'd rather eat the hospital food." She turned her head impatiently toward the window. Will tried to placate her. "Leave the spinach alone, Helen," he muttered, rubbing his hands. "It doesn't matter now. Let's go down to the cafeteria for coffee." She picked up her pocketbook and left the room. Kenneth shook his head. "I don't know what is happening to these people. They were always such great parents, and now, I don't understand them! Perhaps they are scared."

The next day, the Regenbaums came back refreshed and cheerful. As the date of their return was drawing near, they were buying souvenirs in the old city and showing them to us. At times, I would take advantage of their presence and steal an hour of two of sleep in the interns' comfortable bed. On my return to Kenneth's room, I'd hear the rollicking, infectious laughter of the father and the son, their enduring intimacy. Then, one day, the Regenbaums were gone. They took off in a plane and disappeared into the blue sky.

It was only in the hospital that Kenneth lifted the secrecy gag and allowed people to visit him. One by one, my aunts made the pilgrimage to Hadassah. Professor Fisch also came to visit. We sat down in the waiting room and talked. "It is like an execution; isn't it?" Fisch said in his clipped British accent. "What do you mean?" Kenneth asked. "Well," Fisch rubbed his nose, "one wouldn't mind death so much if one didn't know when it was going to happen," a cramped smile appeared on his lips. "But here, one is just waiting for the end. Like a prisoner waiting for his execution." After Fisch left, Kenneth said, "Here's one man who is not afraid of talking about death." One Sabbath my mother brought the children to the hospital. Shir, dressed in his festive white suit, was running around, touching everything and getting into trouble. Kenneth put his hands on his curly head and said proudly to Dr. Halperin, "This is my son. I can already imagine him *bar mitzvahed*. And this is my beautiful daughter," he pointed to the wrapped bundle on my mother's arms. A few weeks later, when Kenneth's condition deteriorated, his brother Gary came for a forty-eight hour visit, and Kenneth wept in his arms.

Then we were alone, in the dark and ultimate universe.

LEVELING WITH DR. FUCHS

Most of all, Kenneth liked our evening readings. He was fond of Thomas's poems, Singer's *The Family Moskat,* and Wiesel's *Messengers of God.* He was particularly excited by Wiesel's essay on Moses. As soon as I read the sentences, "When Moses learned that his hour had come, he refused to accept it. He wanted to go on living. . . ." Kenneth's face became animated and his eyes kindled with interest. But why was "Moses so attached to life, to the point of opposing God's will?" Wiesel asks. "Why, indeed?" Kenneth chuckled. "Was that his way of protesting heaven's use of death to diminish, stimulate and ultimately crush man?" "Yes, sir," Kenneth nodded. Or did the most inspired prophet want to tell us, through his example, that "to live as a man, as a Jew, means to say yes to life, to fight—even against the Almighty—for every spark, for every breath of life?" "That's it! That's it!" Kenneth sat up in his bed, clapping his hands. "That's good stuff, Squash!" He reached for his teacup on the night table. "Let's take a short break and read another one." He hurried to the bathroom and settled in his bed for another essay.

We chose the essay on Joseph, who, according to Wiesel, was "anything but mediocre, anything but boring." "I think I like this guy," Kenneth remarked. I continued reading. "Some sought him out, while others avoided him, but nobody failed to notice him. Nobody failed to take a stand for or against him." Kenneth had an amused expression on his face. "Go on. Let's hear some more." I read, "He was hated, mistreated and finally sold by his brothers. . . ." Kenneth groaned. "What happened?" I reached for him. "My brother," he wept helplessly, "my own brother. When we were children, I took care of him, taught him things, made him laugh. I wish he were here. Where is he?"

One day, Dr. Fuchs stopped me in the hall. "Could I see you for a moment?" he said. With his long arm, he opened the door to his office and invited me in. He offered me his chair, and he sat on the "patient" chair, his tall figure squashed between the desk and the bookcase, his scraggly feet sprawled before him. "I want to tell you something," he looked at me with blue-purple eyes, "on condition that you won't tell it to your husband." "Please tell me," I pleaded. "I will tell you," he repeated, "if you don't tell your husband." I bit my lips. How could I not tell Kenneth? I failed him twice before. I must be brave now. Dr. Fuchs straightened up in the chair, glanced at his watch, and bent slightly toward me. "Well, what do you say?" he asked patiently. I sat there in an agonizing indecision, my heart pounding.

"No," I heard myself say, "I promised my husband to tell him everything I know about his illness."

"Well then," Fuchs smiled, "in that case, I can't tell you," his long fingers were drumming the desk.

"So be it."

To my surprise, Fuchs was still sitting in his chair. Again he looked at his watch, and then at me. "Your husband is a very sick man," he started.

"Yes," I said, "but it is his life. He is entitled to know."

For a few seconds, Fuchs stared into space. Then he turned to me. "All right," he said. "You can have it your way. Our last scan revealed that the cancer has spread throughout his liver. This is very bad news. Not only is there little hope for his recovery, but the end may come sooner than expected."

A few minutes later, I conveyed the news to Kenneth, who, instead of plunging headlong into bleak despair, congratulated me on standing up to the mighty Fuchs. "I have learned it from you," I said, my spirit strangely uplifted, even in the most dismal moments, by the mettle of the man I married.

Melanie, though, fooled even Dr. Fuchs. One morning, during the doctors' visit, Kenneth and I were both sitting on the bed, absorbed in conversation. Suddenly, we were surrounded with doctors. From his tall height, Dr. Fuchs dropped down to his knees, his eyes level with Kenneth's, and held his hands in both his hands. "How are you, my man?" he asked.

"Thank you, Dr. Fuchs," Kenneth swallowed his tears. "I am fair. Some days are quite bad, but today I am fair. Nothing hurts, actually."

"Good," Fuchs nodded, still holding Kenneth's hands, "good. Hang in there." He got up slowly. "We'll check you now, okay?"

"Sure," Kenneth stretched out on the bed. Fuchs put his hands on Kenneth's stomach and prodded around. Then he turned to Dr. Halperin. "Did you see this?" Halperin shook his head. "The tumor is smaller." Fuchs looked attentively at Halperin. "Give me his file. Yes, you see here," he was showing his colleague, "it is definitely smaller. Feel it. The radiation is working." Halperin shook his head again with an expression of disbelief. Then he felt Kenneth's stomach and nodded, "Yes, I think you are right. It seems to have shrunk. Right here," he was holding his finger. Fuchs smiled broadly and patted Kenneth's shoulder. "Keep it up, my man," he said and winked at him. Then the whole group filed out of the room.

Kenneth's eyes glistened with hope. Even now, twenty-two years after his death, the memory of that look wrings my heart.

THIN ICE

The miraculous remission was short-lived. Kenneth was becoming weaker; his face looked gaunt. He was still a vigorous talker, but he could no longer walk more than two or three steps without support. Every day, I helped him to get up, put on his red robe, and walk around the ward. The bathroom routine was the most taxing. At first, he could manage on his own; I'd come in to flush and wash his hands. Later, though, I'd wipe him and help him to get up. To take a shower, he'd sit on a chair and let the water wash over him. As I would soap his body—his hair, his neck that was becoming quite thin, his good left arm, his withered right arm that seemed twice as helpless now, his sinking belly, his shrunken penis, his thighs covered with the red marks of the skin grafts, and his scarred back—pity shot through me like hot iron. All the while, Kenneth would smile and caress me with his eyes as if I were taking him on a pleasure trip. Then he'd say, "You take such good care of me, Squash."

Gradually the hospital routine wore me down. I ate and slept poorly; on some nights I carried Kenneth to the bathroom several times, and in the mornings I'd get up exhausted. I longed for the sun and the trees, for a breath of fresh air, but I was afraid to leave him alone even for an hour. Instead, I took long, long showers. I became haggard and thin. One night, an intern took me to the staff cafeteria and forced me to eat. He was nice and funny, and I ate and laughed, too. An hour later, though, I was back at my watch, feeling remorse for the innocent stolen pleasure. How could I enjoy myself when Kenneth was dying? And yet my body was in a state of constant revolt. Once I fell asleep so soundly that I did not hear Kenneth calling me. He pressed the button for the nurses, but no nurse came. Alone, he dragged himself out of bed. At 6:00 A.M. I woke up and saw Kenneth's feces on the floor. "I couldn't make it to the bathroom alone," he moaned, "and nobody came. So sorry." I jumped out of my bed, ran up and down the ward, like one demented, and yelled at the nurses, "Why didn't you answer his call? Where were you? How could you let this happen?" One nurse immediately rushed to clean the room, while another said, "We knew that you were there, so we thought that you were taking care of him." I never overslept again. Yet the incident brought me up sharply against the frailty of my overwrought restraints.

A SPIN, A SWING, A DELICIOUS THING

At times, after my nightly glass of wine, I'd feel—who would have imagined it, how was it even thinkable in the cancer ward—the urgings of sexual desire. In the midst of smells of chemo and sighs of despair, there it was, tormenting my body. I couldn't figure out what it was doing in the house of death, why it couldn't stay outside with the rest of the world. I was so incensed by it that I refused to reckon with it. But it, I learned, did its own reckoning.

I longed to be held, caressed, loved. I yearned for my husband, but as I looked at his ailing and wasted body, I knew that he'd never hold me again. Most of the time, I didn't think about it; I just wanted him to live. But every now and then, after taking him to the bathroom and waiting for him to finish, and then bringing him slowly to bed, fluffing his pillows, holding his hands, covering him with the blanket, propping his head for a sip of juice, and looking into his eyes for the old love passion but instead finding gratitude, fear, and exhaustion, I'd walk out of the room, smoldering with rebellion.

One afternoon, when Kenneth was asleep, I ambled to the nurse's station for a cigarette. One of the visitors, a young and handsome man, was celebrating the birthday of his aunt, a patient in the ward. He sliced the birthday cake and offered each of the nurses and the visitors a piece. "Please, take, take," he urged us, "my aunt is too sick to eat, and if you don't eat it, nobody will." Then he opened a bottle of wine and offered each one of the group a small glass. *"Le'chaim,"* he smiled in all directions. *"Le'chaim,"* the relatives and the nurses cheered and clanked their glasses. An irrepressible spirit of ribaldry spread in the ward. Even some of the patients came out for a taste of the birthday cake.

I could not eat, but I drank a glass of wine and chatted with the nurses. In a moment or two, I was quite tipsy. The visiting nephew looked at me with bold, arrogant eyes. "What is a young attractive woman like you doing here in this ward?" he asked, smiling charmingly.

I told him about Kenneth's sickness. The nephew clicked his tongue tsk, tsk, and shook his head. "And what about you?" he asked. "You've been cooped up here for so long, surrounded by smells of vomit and cries of pain. How can you stand it?"

"I love him," I said, thirstily drinking in the stranger's pity. "And he needs me."

"But when was the last time you went outside for a walk?" the stranger persisted. "Look how pale you are. I bet you haven't seen the sun for two months, at least! You are smiling. Yes, I know I am right. You are killing yourself, aren't you? You don't want to die with him, do you? Listen, *moteck,* honey, I have a brand new Jaguar parked outside. Would you like some more wine?"

"No, no," I refused.

"Just a little bit," he protested, pouring wine into my glass, "just a little tiny bit. There, drink it." I took a sip. "Drink some more; don't be shy. You need to enjoy life a little, even when your husband is sick. So, as I was saying, I have this new Jaguar outside. Would you like to come with me for a short spin?"

"No," I insisted, "my husband may need me. I must stay here."

"Really, Shelly," he said with an arch smile, "your husband is sleeping now. He won't miss you for a short—very short—hour. Besides, isn't he in a hospital here? If he needs anything, the nurse will help him. What you need, Shelly, is a short swing, a quick spin; the hills of Jerusalem will sing. Come." I stared at his white teeth and his tanned arms, and my heart was pounding.

When we stepped outside the hospital, night had already fallen. I took a deep breath of fresh air, lifted my head to the breeze, to the shadowy pine trees and the black, star-dotted sky. The stranger walked ahead of me, swaying his hips and executing little dance movements to a tune he was whistling. As I followed him slowly to his bright red Jaguar, my wine wooziness was beginning to wear off. "Isn't this a smashing car?" he said, his eyes twinkling, as he opened the door for me. Who is this guy? I asked myself. The car smelled of leather and Old English after shave lotion. I sat down and thought, what, on earth, am I doing here with *him?* I put a cigarette in my mouth. He pulled it out and bent over to kiss me. "Are you out of your mind?" I yelled, stone-cold sober and revolted by the sight of his wet lips.

"All right, all right," he said, startled. "What's the matter with you? I didn't twist your arm to come here. You needed support, comfort, don't you remember?"

"You call this comfort?" I charged. "My husband is dying, and you want to seduce me? Aren't you ashamed? How could you think, even for a moment, that . . . that. . . ." I opened the door and leaped out of the car, his cry "you wanted me, you wanted me" blasting my ear, into the hospital, up the stairs, two at a time. Perhaps Kenneth called me, and I wasn't there; oh, my God, perhaps he needs me. What if something happened to him? As I clambered up the stairs, visions of catastrophe exploded in my mind, until I arrived, breathless and distraught, at his room.

He was sleeping.

I sat down, catching my breath. Relieved and ashamed, I studied his regular breathing. So glad you are all right, dearest. Tonight, I must tell you, tonight I lost my mind. Or else, how could I have gone downstairs with him? But as soon as I got out to the fresh air, I could see my folly. Oh, my dear, I am so ashamed. For a few moments, he, even he, opened a window to a delicious garden, and I looked at it, looked at it from my prison cell with such longing. Please, Kenneth, forgive me. . . .

HOME, SWEET HOME

About a month before Kenneth died, my mother presented me with an auda-cious plan. She was going to sell our apartment in Haifa, she said, rent an apartment in Ramat-Denia, near Hadassah, move all our furniture and books from Haifa to Jerusalem, and bring Kenneth home for a weekend.

"What?" I gasped. "This will take months."

My mother looked askance at me. "What are you talking about, months? One, at most two weeks. Avram and Itzhak will help. What do you say?"

"All right. But we wanted to return to that house."

"That house, Shelly?" my mother remonstrated. "Are you dreaming? Who is going to return to that house? You, alone? Kenneth is not returning to that house. Don't you see? And why would you want to live alone in the same house? You remember our villa in Haifa? I left it immediately after Reuven died. Listen to me. Move to Jerusalem."

The whole family mobilized to help with the move. In ten days, the deed was done. The contents of our apartment in Haifa—the cribs, the desks, the books, the paintings, the swivel chair—were lifted, as if by a magic carpet, and transplanted into a spacious three-bedroom apartment in Ramat-Denia, an affluent suburb where several Hadassah doctors, as well as lawyers and jour-nalists, resided. "You see?" my mother said gleefully when she came to visit us. "We did it. The apartment is wonderful. A bit expensive, true, but we'll worry about that later. In the meantime, we need to plan Kenneth's weekend at home. What do you say, Kenneth?"

Kenneth nodded and smiled. "That's great, Dina," he said. "I don't know if I can make it, but I would sure like to try."

"We'll give you a real good time. Aren't you tired of hospital food? Wouldn't you like to be home a little? You'll see the children."

Kenneth's eyes filled with tears. "The children," he whispered, "the chil-dren. Won't that be great?"

"After weeks of dragging around in pajamas, it's a pleasure to put my pants and shirt on," Kenneth said as he was trying to get dressed. "I am now a regular cit-izen of the world," he jested. But he was pale and weak and could not dress without help. Afterward, he sat in the chair, exhausted. Seeing him so frail, I had misgivings. "Perhaps we should stay here," I said. He shook his head, "No,

I want to see the house where you'll live. I want to see the children. I'll be careful and take plenty of rest."

"Ready?" my mother's blond curls appeared in the door. Dr. Halperin gave us final instructions about food, rest, and emergencies and wished us a happy weekend. We took Kenneth down in a wheelchair. My mother's car was parked outside the hospital door. Kenneth got up and walked, leaning on me. He was quivering under the strain, but his face, turned to the sky and the sun he hadn't seen in months, was radiant. "We're going home, Squash," he smiled at me, "our own sweet home."

On the way, Kenneth gazed longingly at the terraced hills outside the city. "Jerusalem," he said, "my favorite city. Do you remember our summers here, honey? You did your research in the library, and I read plays. In the evenings we went to the Savion Restaurant for dinner, and then to the theater, remember? I dragged you to all the shows. You whispered in my ear an English translation of the Hebrew, the neighbors got mad and told us to shut up, remember?" A fit of coughing interrupted his reminiscences. "Don't talk so much, Kenneth," my mother said. "Wait till you come home."

Elie opened the door. Shir stood behind him, at a distance. He looked at us suspiciously for a moment, then ran to the living room shouting, *"Imma* and *Abba* are here," and hid behind the couch to see what happened. Kenneth cried out, "Shir, come here, let me hug you," but Shir ran to his room. We put Kenneth on his swivel chair to rest and gave him a glass of juice. In a moment, Shir returned, laughing and holding a ball in his hands. *"Savta* got me this ball," he said and looked at his father. "A nice ball, Shir," Kenneth said, reaching out to pat his son's curls. *"Abba,"* Shir chirped, "let's play outside." Kenneth looked at him sadly. "I am sorry, son, I can't play." Shir pleaded again and Kenneth shook his head. Shir smacked the ball angrily and ran out of the room. "He is my spirited son, all right," Kenneth smiled wanly. My mother came to the living room with Livi in her arms. "You see your daughter, how nice she looks?" she turned to Kenneth. "Here, hold her." Livi did not recognize her father. When Kenneth held her, she gave him a startled look and started crying. "She is so beautiful," Kenneth said as he handed her back to her grandmother.

Soon Kenneth needed a nap. We gathered all the pillows in the house to give him comfortable support, but he couldn't find a restful position. Excited and puzzled, Shir rushed in and out of our bedroom; eager to see his father and troubled by his frailty, he vacillated between laughter and tears. Finally he gave up and took Elie down to play ball with him. My mother offered Kenneth the delicacies he used to love, but he could not eat. I tried to read to him, but he seemed to be mysteriously preoccupied. Groaning in bed, he was mustering his feeble energies to meet the crucial assault of his formidable adversary.

The hours on that Friday passed slowly. I didn't know what to do with myself. Too exhausted and tense to pay heed to the children, too worried to be anywhere else in the house except with Kenneth, I tried to find a corner on our bed to stretch out next to him. Friday night dinner, the crowning glory of Kenneth's visit, turned into a sad occasion. Kenneth tried to join us at the table, but after ten minutes he returned to bed. I could not eat and soon retired. Elie and my mother ate in silence and finished quickly. Night came.

I am convinced that all the red-eyed, long-tailed devils executed their nefarious dance that night. Kenneth was tossing and moaning, tormented by bad dreams. I rushed back and forth to the kitchen to bring him water and juice and tea. Once, with great effort, I stopped him from rolling out of bed. Back in bed, he stretched the whole length and breadth of it. I sat on a chair and tried to doze off, yet he was shouting, as if he were whipped and flogged, and cried for Dr. Halperin. Several times Livi woke up crying. My mother hurried to her bed and on the way asked me how Kenneth was. "He can't sleep," I said. *"Oi vey,"* my mother said. "And you?" "I can't sleep either." At five in the morning I finally dozed off. At six Kenneth woke me up. A long hallway separated the bedroom from the bathroom. Kenneth leaned on my shoulders, and I wrapped my arm around his waist. Huddled together in the narrow space, we kept bumping against the walls like drunks. When we arrived, Kenneth collapsed on the stool. Dizzy with fatigue, I sat on the edge of the tub and waited for him to finish. Out of the narrow window, I saw a strip of grey dawn. The minutes oozed slowly. Kenneth was sitting and sitting on the stool, like a statue. "Are you all right, Kenneth?" I asked. He nodded. Ten minutes passed, and then fifteen. I must sleep, I thought. I looked at him, but he didn't budge. "Don't you want to get up? Aren't you all done?" I asked, irritated. Kenneth was silent, his head hanging down on his chest, but his left index finger, as I later remembered, was lifted, trying to signal something to me. But I was helplessly riding the wave of anger. "WHY DON'T YOU GET UP?" I yelled. My mother hurried to the bathroom. "What is happening?" she asked, her eyes two blue pools. "Why are you yelling at him?" "I don't know," I cried. "I don't know, I am so tired, and he just sits there." My mother approached Kenneth and raised his head. His mouth was twitching uncontrollably under a massive attack of seizure.

"IT'S ALL OVER"

We immediately called the ambulance. Contrite, I apologized to Kenneth for yelling at him. For a while he was too busy with his breathing to answer. Then he looked at me with a small, strained smile and asked, "What are you talking about, dear? When did you yell at me?" I was dumbfounded. "You didn't hear me in the bathroom?" He shook his head. "Thank God," I sighed with relief, but, still tormented by guilt, I resolved to make amends.

The following morning they wheeled Kenneth on his bed to have a brain scan. The test was conducted in a narrow round structure covered with huge screens. Machines beeped, lights flashed on and off, Kenneth was strapped to a chair, and a helmet was put on his head. I was told to sit on the bed near the door, opposite Kenneth, and not to step into the scanning room. The technician was monitoring the scan, and Kenneth was alone on the chair. I sat on the bed and tried to smile at him. His terrified eyes were fixed on my face. Green and black shapes danced on the screens, quivering, merging, changing. It's a normal scan, a normal scan, I kept saying to myself. "Hang in there, dear," I said, "soon, it will be over." But the machines continued to beep, flash, and click. Suddenly Kenneth raised his index finger. I jumped to my feet. "*Gveret*," the technician hollered, "stay out. You can't come in!" But there was Kenneth's face, contorted, twitching, his lips purple, his tongue twisted, and I was already moving forward, murmuring "I am here," reaching under the helmet, putting two cool hands on his cheeks, holding him there until the twitching subsided. "Thank you, love," Kenneth whispered.

Half an hour later, Dr. Halperin returned. He read the results as if he already knew them. He stood between Kenneth and me. Don't look up at him, I ordered myself. Examine your fingernails, much to do here, no, not the brain, not the brain, what would Kenneth do without his thoughts, his talk, his tongue, not true, not the end, can't be, I want to laugh, Dr. Halperin, what are you blubbering about his brain, his scan, a perfectly normal scan, nothing wrong with it, I tell you, I didn't see any tumors, I'll stare at my hands, at the tips of your shoes, never, never raise my eyes to your lie—

"It's all over the brain, Mrs. Regenbaum." His words ripped the silence like gun shots. "And I am standing here between you and him so that he doesn't see your face. He needs hope."

I raised my eyes. "How can I give him hope?"

"I don't know. You must believe in hope. I do too, or else I wouldn't work here. Talk about the brain radiation and spontaneous remissions. Who knows? Miracles are rare, but they have happened."

"CROSSING A FINAL BRIDGE"

But how could I have given Kenneth any kind of hope on that hot day in July which, in my memory, is forever overcast and chill? The words of comfort died in my throat. When he asked me if they found anything, I said yes. "But they are starting radiation tomorrow," I added, "and perhaps . . ." I could not finish the sentence. He knew, and I knew. A pale, raw silence rose between us. What can I say now, I thought. A terrible sob was caught in my throat. And still I could not look at him.

It was Kenneth who spoke. Fighting for breath like an asthmatic, he began to say what he planned to say to me before his death, words which I later wrote down. "Come to me, love," he said. I rose from my chair and sat on his bed. "You know," he coughed, "there is no one who loved me half as much as you have . . ." he stopped for air. "When I say 'love,' I don't mean 'maybe' love . . . I mean crossing a bridge that may be a final bridge . . ." His eyes bulged, and his pale-yellowish skin stretched across his cheek bones. I gave him water. "You will go on and on living your own life. You may even marry again." "No, no," I protested, weeping, "I won't . . ." He put his finger on my mouth. "Shush," he said, "let me speak. I have been doing a lousy job taking care of myself," he choked up, "but I am so glad I have my woman around to depend on her. A wife knows who you are," he looked across the room as if he were pleading with an invisible audience, "a wife knows who you can be, a wife can care about the things that make you happy, even when communication is . . . is . . . una-w-ailable. . . ." His head sank in the pillow, and his eyes gazed at the ceiling. "You are tired, Kenneth," I pleaded with him, "would you like to rest?" He persisted. "In this cold, sometimes cynical world," he was wheezing, "it is important to say that, so that those bastards don't get the better of you." A thin smile appeared on his chapped lips. "Remember, dearest?" he fought for air, "on our honeymoon I said, we'd become a great couple . . . I said, we are going to grow, and we did grow. And that, Squash," his eyes became luminous, "nobody can take away from us." Drained, he closed his eyes and slept until morning, when Dr. Veshler came to take him down for his brain radiation.

IN THE GATES OF DEATH

Do not be far from me
for trouble is near
and there is no one to help.

—Psalm 22:11

The radiation eliminated the seizures but did not slow down the advance of death. Kenneth's health deteriorated so rapidly that each day, it seemed, another organ shut off. His feet became so heavy with edema that he could no longer walk and had to move his bowels in a bedpan. In the mornings, when I washed his back with a sponge, tufts of hair fell off his head. His breathing was labored, and his speech garbled. His flesh became inert and flaccid like dough. When I put my hand on his thigh, my finger sank and left a hole in it. Melanie was having her field day at last in Kenneth's poor body.

Three days before Kenneth's death, my uncle Avram came to the hospital and watched with me till the end. Together we listened to the terrible moan that surged from Kenneth—wow . . . wow . . . ouoo . . . wow—for three days and nights, rhythmic, persistent, mournful. I knew then that I would never hear such pleading, such beseeching again, that I would never again come across such sadness. "Avram, Avram, did you hear that moan?" Avram nodded. "What can we do, *meidal'e;* what can we do?" Wow . . . oooo . . . wow . . . like a lonely wind in the wilderness, like the ebb and flow of the waves . . . don't leave me . . . ooo . . . wow . . . dearest Kenneth . . . oooooo.

Dr. Halperin comes in, his mustache drooping, his face grim, and he puts tubes in Kenneth's orifices, one in his penis, one in his nose, I jump up to stay his hand, no, Dr. Halperin, no, not in his nose, Dr. Halperin, he told me he can't bear a tube in his nose, he has sinus problems as it is, Dr. Halperin grabs my shoulders and looks at me, saying nothing, saying, it does not matter anymore, Mrs. Regenbaum, what he likes or doesn't like, saying even this won't help, just routine, like washing the corpse, respect for the dead, don't you see, don't you understand, no, I don't see at all, wearing the red dress Kenneth loved, with the little flowers, hundreds, like a field of wild flowers, what do you want me to do, Dr. Halperin, you want me to give him up, how can I do the impossible, I don't want to die, he says he says he says,

how can I let him die, how, Dr. Halperin, his eyes are oozing yellowish pus, save me, he says, I am wiping the pus with a wet rag, my wife, he moans, but it comes back, yellowish brown, groaning, don't leave me, dabbing his cracked lips with a swab, propping his pillow, all his hair lost in radiation, his honey hair, my children, he cries, his hot tears funneling through the yellowish pus, I am here, Kenneth love, wiping the pus, I am here, Kenneth, I keep saying, wetting his lips, I am right here, but he moans, wou, wow, ouo, ouo, don't leave me, no, no, all this distance between us, you on the other side already, this is not happening, I never thought the moment would come, Dr. Halperin, after all your work, your sweat, your care, after all the needles, and the chemo, and the blood tests, and the urine tests, and the liver scans, and the brain scans, I did not believe the moment would come up against me, demanding my recognition, breathless, I let the moment pass by me, never penetrated me that moment of his death, his breath, last, I can't cry, I can't scream because that moment passed by me, not through me, and I looked at it, as it came and went, stupefied, wondering, whose moment is this, not mine, not for me, surely, I don't recognize this moment, such a moment, what kind of a moment is it when someone dies, often thought about it, now missed it, why should I claim it, no, not through me, blank inside me, white space, no blood, screaming, rage, night, no, just white and gone and impenetrable . . .

But his eyes cleared up, suddenly, Dr. Halperin. Just before. Big and brown and wonderful. Sucking all his life in. Summing up all his days. The last plea, the final rage, why me, so young, so wasted, so alone, what do you see, Kenny, what do you see?

Mrs. Regenbaum, we've got to cover him with a sheet

What? What are you talking about? Go away

Mrs. Regenbaum, he is gone, please understand . . .

Oh, Kenneth, Kenneth, nails clawing in your flesh in your dough the white sheet the white fire between us forever dividing . . .

THE MOUNT OF OLIVES

The Mount of Olives glares in the sun. There are no trees in the cemetery on the Mount of Olives—the ground is rockhard. Only further down the mountain, on the way to Emek Kidron, there are terraces of olive trees. The steps leading to the graves on the mount twist and wind around the rock. Rows of white graves cast no shadow. I wobble on the rocks; I slip; I stumble. Ya'acov is here, and he grabs my arm when I fall. The mount is swaying; the blue of the sky pierces my eyes. *Imma,* Elie, relatives, friends, students are walking ahead of me, behind the coffin. Kenneth's parents and his brother are not here. In the distance, the cantor sings the prayer for the dead, wistful, tremulous . . . Merciful God . . . *El-male ra-hamim . . . hamze menuha nekhona . . .* grant a proper rest for the soul of my beloved, my lovely departed. "In the hospital you gave me tea," Ya'acov says, "so I thought I'd come to comfort you, too. You see, this is Nurit's grave, right next to your husband's. I have decided to make a little flower-bed around her, add a little cheerfulness here, such a barren place, no trees, no flowers, just white stone. . . ." The cantor's voice is pleading, "In the lofty levels of the holy and the pure ones. . . ." Ya'acov leads me down the stairs. The funeral stops by the assigned grave. *Imma's* sunglasses float before my eyes. "They want to bury him, Shelly," she says, "can you walk a little faster?"

No, Imma, please don't let them! Please, talk to them! I can't see where I am going. How many hands are holding me? This is his body wrapped in the shrouds. How he has shrunk. Imma, how small he is. Why is he so small? His shrunken body falls, falls, falls down into the dark earth. On the white Mount of Olives a scream explodes, bounding, rebounding, echoing in the valleys below.

O, full of mercy, bind his soul in the bond of life. "How fair, how pleasant he was, the chiefest among the thousand" (Song of Songs, 5:10).

chapter five

AMERICA

GRIEF

L ike a wildfire, Kenneth's death, on August 14, 1978, consumed and charred my life. My desires wilted; my hopes burned to ashes. In the evening, after I put the children to sleep, I'd sit on the swivel chair and gaze at the lights of cars going up and down the road. At night I'd toss and moan; in the morning I'd get up to a day aflame with pain. I could find no refuge from my grief, no rest from worries. Where could I get a job? How would my earnings be enough to support the children and myself? Who'd stay with the children when they were sick? And what if I became sick? In between the worries, the despair over Kenneth's death fell on my head like hammer blows. "There does not seem to be any purpose in my life," I wrote in my diary, "any direction, any date in the future that interests me." I could not accept his death, could not believe that he no longer knew how I felt, that we would never again celebrate another wedding anniversary.

I looked for him everywhere: for hours, I pored over his pictures, his notes, and his poems. I played and replayed tapes of his lectures, and each time Shir would come running to my room, thinking that his father had returned. Three weeks after Kenneth's death, I wrote in my diary, "No! No! No! You are not dead! You are not! How could you slip away from my fingers, from my life?" I kept looking for him. Where could I find him? He came back in my dreams, asking to see the children, telling me that there had been a mistake in the diagnosis, that he was actually healthy and fit as a fiddle. Night after night, dressed in his red shorts and in his "Acting Is Believing" sweatshirt, he would make his eerie visits, and, cheerful and consoling, he'd wipe out, with his magic wand, the grim reality of his death. Once, though, I dreamed that he was lying sick in bed, surrounded by tall doctors with white frocks. I was passing from one doctor to the next, rising on tiptoe to tug at their frocks, pleading with them to save Kenneth. Then I woke up in a welter of tears.

Several times I was compelled to return to Hadassah Hospital, as if I still belonged to it, as if there, among people who knew him, I could revive him. Mostly, I wanted to see Dr. Halperin. He knew Kenneth best, he liked him, cared for him, cared for me, too. One evening, I visited him in the ward, when he was on a shift, and had a long talk with him, on life and death. I was determined to visit him again. The next time I arrived tipsy at the oncology ward at nine in the evening. Dr. Halperin was there, but it was Nagid, the Arab male nurse, who stood between him and me and asked what I wanted. "I am just visiting," I fumbled. Nagid looked at me coldly and said, "Go home, Mrs. Regenbaum. Your husband is not here anymore. There is no one here for you. Don't feel so sorry for yourself," he added with a wry smile, "other people suffer too. And watch out for that alcohol."

That night, I wrote in my diary that Nagid was right. I had become a bitter, confused woman, ridiculously trying to reach her husband through the men who knew him. I resolved not to do that anymore. But time and again, the need to talk about Kenneth would flood my whole being. How could I accept his death without talking about it? And yet I could find nobody to hear me. After the *shiva* and the *shloshim* even friends became silent. They didn't show up; the phone didn't ring; invitations stopped. Nobody wanted to talk about Kenneth. The silence deepened. My next-door neighbor, Simcha, was also a widow who lost her husband to cancer. Surely, I thought, when I befriended her, she'd be willing to talk about death and grief. We talked about children, about work, about men; we even had a good laugh every now and then. But we rarely mentioned loss or widowhood. We had to rise above this shameful state. For a while, I saw a therapist at Hadassah Hospital, but even she cut the therapy short, after a mere two months, to compel me, she said, to find my place in society, in a healthy way, among friends.

But where were my friends? Where was the place of Widow Regenbaum in a society known for its "extreme coupled-ness," in Lesley Hazleton's words, in a country where being single, even by force of circumstances, carries about it an "aura of disaster"?

---

shiva   The week of mourning following the funeral
shloshim   The end of the first month of mourning, often marked by a visit to the grave

And who, in his or her right mind, would want to associate with disaster, especially when new disasters were never really far off? I didn't even have the honorific title of a "war widow"; I was a plain widow, and my husband was an American, rather than an Israeli, and had never fought in any wars. I was not entitled to the hefty payments that war widows received from the Ministry of Defense. For what national purpose did Kenneth's death serve?

Of course, I wrote in my diary, who would want to be my friend? These days I am difficult to get along with—sad, depressed, or angry most of the time. No wonder I am forgotten. But how could I heal without friends? I needed friends, real friends who would allow me to grieve. Of such friends, during the two years I lived in Israel following Kenneth's death, I made only three; all were American Jews. One was Gila Brand, my neighbor downstairs, married to an Israeli; she had several times asked me to join their Friday night meals. The other was Kenneth's friend Paul, who was then living in the States, and who, through my letters, got the brunt of my angry despondency. The third was Norman Fedder, Kenneth's friend from Kansas, who, shocked to learn of Kenneth's death, asked me to write to him in detail about Kenneth's last few months. Who can say where I'd be without these friends? But, I thought, since all my Israeli friends and relatives have scattered, and since the only ones who were willing to share my burden were American, shouldn't I leave Israel for America? In my diary I wrote, "I dream of going to America— but how, when?"

"GO TO YOUR ROOM AND GRIEVE!"

As soon as the seven days of mourning ended, my mother decided to stay in my apartment for three additional weeks, to take care of the children. Quickly and efficiently, she took charge of the place. She shopped, cleaned, fed the children, washed them, and took them out for walks. In addition, she wanted to know who called me, what were my plans, who were my friends, what did I have to wear, how would I get a job, and what would I do with the rest of my life. Crouched on the floor in the study, rummaging through Kenneth's papers and photos, I tried to escape her scrutiny, but whenever I came out of the room, there she was, waiting for me to tell her how, in the world, I was going to manage without Kenneth.

Two weeks after his death, I woke up one morning yearning for the children. Yet when I came out to the living room and saw my mother expertly tending to them, I withdrew. Why should I start a fight with her? After all she took good care of them all those months; how could I now take them away from her? I tried to imagine what Kenneth would say, and I took one step forward. "I want to feed Livi now," I said abruptly.

"Shalom," my mother said, "you've come out? Are you done with the grieving?" She adjusted Livi's bib.

"Not at all," I answered. "I don't know when *that* will happen. But I've got to get on with my life," my heart was beating wildly, "and Livi is my daughter, after all." What a ridiculous statement, I thought. I should at least thank her for all she has done for the children.

"Who said she isn't?" my mother shook the bottle, "of course she is your daughter. You need to tell me that? But I thought you were grieving now and needed my help. So here I am, and when I am here, I do things my own way. You know that."

I felt a hot flush of anger. "But why," I tried again, "can't I hold my own daughter for an hour? Why must you take charge of everything?"

She looked at me. "Listen, Shelly," she said, "if you want to feed Livi, go ahead. But then I am leaving, I tell you. I am tired," her voice became hoarse, "I am tired of everything, tired of my life, tired of funerals, tired of work, tired of the children, what do you want from me? For three and a half months I have taken care of them, and that's the thanks I get from you. You think that I can live here with you telling me what to do, giving me orders when to hand them to you, when to take them back, like a slave, taking orders from you? Who do you think I am? Shelly, no way. It's either me or you!" She put Livi in the crib. "You can't have your cake and eat it too, Shelly. Either you need my help, or you don't. Make up your mind. And after all, aren't you grieving? If you are grieving, go to your room and grieve!"

Shir ran to his *savta* and hid behind her dress, peeping at me with eyes that pleaded for peace. I gave up and went back to my room, but a week later, I asked my mother to leave. It was my first exhilarating and terrifying declaration of independence. As soon as she slammed the door, I went into a tailspin: Who would help me with the children? How would I *schlepp* my babies in their strollers on buses? Where could I get a baby-sitter?

At first, tending to my babies' needs galled me. Chasing Shir's ball in the yard wore me out; taking Livi out for a walk in her stroller drained my spirit. I was an impatient, moody mother. Often I wanted only to be left alone and was tempted, countless times, to pick up the phone and call my mother. But I was determined not to shame Kenneth. "My life," I wrote, "will be a renewed commitment to our values, and to our children." Indeed it was this commitment, which I hated at first, that saved me from despair. I began to see what I couldn't see when my mother was around—that my children needed me. I was touched by Shir's efforts to cheer me up. Whenever I was about to cry, he'd bring me his father's picture album. When I was depressed, he refused to eat. When my mood lifted, he ate. When I yelled at him, or at Livi, he'd look at me with pained indignation, as if to say that I could be a better mother. In time, it was the children who drew me out of death's pit.

Gradually I got used to the hectic routine. "Work! Work! Work!" I wrote in my diary, and work helped. Each day, I'd look forward to the restful evening hour, after the dinner and the bath, when we three sat, talked, played a game, or read from a book. It was in those quiet hours, when our yarn of love was woven, that I began to reflect on the children's future. It took years for the pain to exhaust itself, but during those evening hours, I knew that I would survive Kenneth's death.

My mother found her way back to us; periodically she would pick up the children and take them with her to Tel Aviv for a week. And yet, whenever we met, the tension persisted, and the war, having shifted its ground from Kenneth to the children, raged on. Night after night, as I drifted off to sleep, I dreamed of America, the land of the free—free from Mother Israel.

A TASTE OF HONEY

Shortly after the mourning period, Larry Davies, then chair of the English Department at Haifa University, offered me the opportunity to teach two courses for the coming year, half of Kenneth's schedule. I was excited. What work could be more meaningful? I'd be continuing his life at the same time that I'd be rebuilding my own! True, the arrangements were difficult—once a week, I would have to travel from Jerusalem to Haifa, stay the night in Haifa, and find a baby-sitter for the children. The pay was meager, too, but I longed to teach again and secretly hoped to get a regular position the following year.

Hannah, a young Sephardic woman from a poor family with many children, became my trusted baby-sitter. Having tended to her own younger brothers and sisters, Hannah was experienced in childcare. As soon as I saw her lifting Livi with ease and cradling her securely in the crook of her arm, I knew that I could rely on her. Big, patient, and free from grief and "nerves," Hannah gave the children what they badly needed—laughter and tranquility. There, I thought, I can do it! I can teach and travel and care for two children—without my mother's help. Wasn't Mrs. Silver wrong now!

On Tuesday nights, I stayed in our Haifa villa, which had been uninhabited since Reuven's death. On most nights, I'd invite students to the house to rehearse their skits. I welcomed the hours of extra work because on those cool wintry evenings I feared being alone in the silent villa which, in spite of my mother's caretaking visits, emitted the musty odors of absence. I used to walk from room to room, turning on the lights and the two small electric heaters, in the kitchen and in the living room that overlooked the mountain slope and the ocean, now seen darkly through the shut French windows; but no light or heat could dispel the desolation of the house that once bustled with people, or chase away the shadows that hung in its corners. As I sat huddled by the small heater, which didn't even pretend to be an adequate rival to the chill in the huge living room, and watched my reflection in the glass windows, ghosts of the past clamored for my attention. I imagined Chaim, four years dead, an awkward guest, pacing quickly from the door to the balcony and back, slinking along the walls, uneasy in the house that was all but his, and felt pity for him. Mostly, though, looking at me from the couch, coming out of the kitchen, sitting on his green armchair, laughing, reading the newspaper, caressing my cheek with his stubby fingers, Reuven was everywhere. How I ached for his presence on those long, damp nights when all the springs of my sorrow, it seemed, poured into the burning river of grief for Kenneth.

Even the sunny mornings, when I left the villa and climbed the fifty-one stairs to catch the bus, did not scatter my gloom. Living in Jerusalem, I hadn't expected that the route from the Center to the University, which passed by Ha'prachim Street where we used to live, would shake me up so. As I waited for the bus, the sight of Sifri bookstore, our favorite haunt, seared my eyes. On the bus, I looked at the outdoor café, where we used to lunch, at the deli where the woman with the German accent advised us to have many children, at the old, rickety movie theater that we used to frequent, at our bank, and at the streets we strolled through with Shir and Livi, and none of these familiar sights made any sense to me. "How could it be that those streets and stores, where you walked so often," I wrote in my diary, "still exist after you are gone?"

Apart from my children, only the teaching propped up my spirit. When I faced the students, I felt again the joy in being, as Kenneth used to say. Time passed. I applied for the available position, the one that had belonged to Kenneth but was now being advertised as a regular English position. At the end of the semester, my drama class put on a production of scenes: my all-out pitch for the position. We rehearsed; we worked hard. The show was successful, and the students were elated. My colleagues enjoyed the show, and the chair laughed occasionally, but at the end, he walked away without a word. At the end of the year, I was dismissed. "No budget," I was told.

I remember my last ride down the mountain to the station to get the bus to Jerusalem. One of my students, an American from Idaho, who was also riding the bus, asked me what I'd be teaching the following year. I said that I wouldn't be coming back. "Oh, why?" he asked.

"I've been fired."

"You've been fired? But why? Why? I don't understand."

"They say they don't have money."

"Oh, nonsense," he got excited, "they always say the same thing. But you are an excellent teacher. I've learned so much from you."

"Thank you," I said.

"It's a pity," he continued, "that they don't ask for student evaluations here, as they do in the States, because yours would have been so terrific they would have had to keep you."

"Thank you so much," I said, moved. Soon he got off the bus, waving a broad good-bye.

PAPER AIRPLANES

At first the loss of my position didn't seem a crucial setback. I applied to other universities and was convinced that I would get *something*. But when my applications to universities, in Tel Aviv, Beersheba, and Jerusalem, were rejected or simply ignored, and when my hopes of getting at least a part-time position in an English department vanished, when all the doors to the academic life seemed to be shut, I realized the immensity of my loss. I was outside of academia, and how could I survive in Israel without it? I had to have a corner, at least, in an English department, where I could teach English, converse in English, and associate with American Jews. To me, the English department offered not merely a job but a lifeline, a place where I could think, grow, and hope.

I felt out of that world, with no prospects of returning to it. I understood the audacity of my ambition. In Israel then there were only five "publish or perish" universities and no academic teaching institutions. English was a second language—a luxury; courses were few, English departments and their budgets were usually small, and the competition was rigorous. How could there be

room for a thirty-seven-year-old widow, with two children, who had just finished her dissertation but published no articles? How could she measure up
against younger, male immigrants from the States who had published articles
or books? And yet I railed against my predicament. Here I am, I thought as I
was pounding the Jerusalem pavements, looking for second or third rate teaching jobs, dismissed from my profession. What am I to do? True, I admitted,
squinting in the hot sun, I didn't have publications, but how could I find the
time to publish when my husband was dying?

I was out, and I felt that I'd simply die if I stayed out of the academic
world. I tried to become a doctoral student in Psychology. After all, psycholo-
gists, like English professors, explored the world of feelings. I quickly discovered, however, that under the Israeli system, my English doctorate accrued me
no credits in the psychology department. I would have had to start a bachelor's
degree from scratch, and my schedule would have been heavily loaded with
biology and statistics courses, which I had always dreaded. How could I, at my
age, with two children, start my student life anew?

I gave up this plan and turned to the world of the theater. What I'd
learned from Kenneth could surely be considered as the equivalent of a bachelor's degree in theater. At least. I decided to talk to the director Yossi Izraeli,
who was then directing a play at the Chan Theater. It was a lovely summer
evening. The setting sun splashed the rounded top and the arches of the building with streaks of reddish-gold light. Standing under a tree, smiling distractedly, Izraeli explained to me in long drawn-out sentences the absurdity of
my purpose. The theater world, he intoned, was extremely competitive. My
education, if not irrelevant, amounted to very little. I would have to start from
square one, as a stagehand, working day and night for a pittance. Could I
afford to make such sacrifices with two babies at home? And even if I did, who
could guarantee the outcome in this dog-eat-dog world? "No," his eyes looked
far into the distance, "you'd better find something else to do."

In spite of his warning, I kept showing up in places where theater was
happening. Eventually, I was offered a position, teaching an acting course for
teenagers at the Israel Museum. On the assigned date, I arrived at the museum
with a happy air of anticipation and looked around for the class and the students. I didn't see any. I looked for the woman who interviewed me, but she
was nowhere to be found. Gradually, the realization that there was nobody
around penetrated the thick fog of my excitement. Did I mistake the date? Did
I misunderstand the woman? What happened? I checked my diary. There it
was, Thursday, 2:00 P.M. Where was everybody? Finally the woman showed up.

She looked at me puzzled as if she couldn't remember where she had last seen me. I cleared my throat, "Shelly Regenbaum," I said, "remember? I came to teach the acting class." "Oh, yes, yes," she frowned as if the recollection pained her. "I am sorry to tell you, there weren't enough students." I could barely hide my disappointment. "What does it mean? Would there be a class at a later date perhaps?" The woman shook her head, "No, no class this summer. Sorry." I tried to gather my wits. "So why didn't you call me?" The woman was turning to go. "We don't usually do such things," she said. "You should have called us."

As I walked back from the museum to the bus stop, the sun was shooting down spikes of heat and brilliance. What in the world am I doing here? I thought angrily. The broad museum walk, the Billy Rose Art Garden, the Shrine of the Book with its onion-shaped top, all of which looked so lovely on the way in, had now lost their charm and become glaring slabs of Jerusalem stone. I glared back. You may want to trap me in your whiteness, I addressed the stone, you may conspire to swallow me up, I added as I watched my shadow seemingly shrinking in the sun, but I won't let you. You won't get me. I'll wear you down first.

I finally managed to get three part-time jobs, but they were all ephemeral, dead-end jobs, especially my part-time position with the education department of the Jerusalem municipality *(iriya)*. Officially I was appointed inspector of drama in the high schools, reporting weekly to my boss, Ephraim ("Froyke") Sidon, a famous satirist, who had a regular column in the paper, and who was a playwright of popular children's plays. What was he doing in the municipality? Moonlighting, like many Israeli academics and artists, to make ends meet.

I started work at the municipality with high expectations. I'd be in the theater, again, albeit on its margins. But who knows? Perhaps one job would lead to another. I was proud to be working with the famous Froyke and bragged about it to my family and friends. I got a list of the Jerusalem high schools and visited their scheduled dramatic events. I traveled to the ends of our far-flung city. Sometimes I had to transfer to two or three different buses to reach a remote school. On cold winter evenings, waiting in unfamiliar bus stops could be long and chilling. The hills of Jerusalem rose like dark blotches against the sky, and lonely winds whistled in the ravines.

I did not expect to be a popular visitor at the schools, but I found out that I was quite irrelevant. Upon returning from my trips, I reported to Froyke on what I saw, and he'd say, "Fine, *be'seder,* you did a good job."

"But what exactly is my job?" I asked him once.

"Your job is to find out what is going on in the drama classes in the high schools."

"What does that mean?" I was puzzled.

"It means what it says," he looked at me with innocent blue eyes.

"I don't understand. Suppose I find out that nothing is going on in the drama classes. What then?"

"You tell me about it," he smiled.

"And what do you do about it?"

"Nothing," he shrugged his shoulders.

"Is there some kind of a game going on here?"

"What game are you talking about?" he laughed briefly.

"Suppose I decide not to make any visits in the next two weeks. What would you do?"

"Nothing at all," Froyke said, impatient at having to instruct a simpleton like me. "Didn't I tell you from the beginning? You visit when you visit, when you feel like it."

"And if I don't feel like it?"

"Have I been such a bad boss? If you don't feel like visiting, then don't visit."

"So what exactly am I being paid for?"

"I've never seen anybody like you!" Froyke jumped from his chair. "Are you being paid? Good. Take the money and don't worry about it. What is your problem?"

"My problem is," I said, quite depressed now, "that I want to know what teeth I have, what difference I can make. Nothing seems to be happening here." Froyke smirked. "Should I perhaps write you reports," I ventured, "about my visits, with names, dates, and detailed descriptions?"

Froyke leaned on his knuckles and looked straight at me. "Are you out of your mind? Let me tell you something. I really have no use for your reports. If you write me reports, I'll fold them into paper airplanes for my son."

THE J-1 VISA

Away! Away! The spell of arms and voices . . . their tale of distant nations.

—James Joyce, *A Portrait of the Artist as a Young Man*

One day Livi woke up sick. I called her friendly American pediatrician, who made house calls even when a winter storm was raging (as it did on that day) and who always inquired after my health and mood. He came, examined Livi, and wrote a prescription for antibiotics. "She'll be fine," he smiled, "in a day or two." He looked at me again. "Are you worried about her? No need, Mrs. Regenbaum. . . ." he reassured me.

"It's not that. . . ." I stared out of the window at the driving rain and the huddled trees below.

"Oh?" the doctor's kind eyes looked at me with concern. "Is something the matter?"

"Perhaps it's just a bad day," I blurted. As if by tacit agreement to make as much noise as possible, Livi started howling and Shir burst into the room with his shrieking fire engine. "Quiet!" I yelled at both of them. Then I took Livi in my arms. "You see," I continued, "I can't find my place in this country. Perhaps I am doing something wrong, but I can't find my way here." The doctor put his chin in his hand and listened thoughtfully. "You have no idea," I elaborated, "where I've already been looking for a job, and how many times I've been turned away. Now I have a fragment of a position here, a piece there, and no future prospects. My boss at the *iriya* doesn't give me any responsibilities, keeps me out of meetings, and thinks he's doing me a favor! That's the thing!" I put Livi down. "What am I supposed to do to be taken seriously here? How can I describe to you," I said with something like passion, "the indignity of my life in this country?"

The doctor was quiet for a long moment. Then he said, adjusting his glasses, "Well, perhaps you should leave it."

I was startled. "How can I leave it? It's my country. I was born here, I'm an eighth generation sabra, my family is here. . . ."

"How can you afford to stay here?" the doctor smiled. "If I understand you correctly, you can't even earn enough to support your children."

"That's true," I admitted and stared at the rain whipping the cars on the road. A gust of wind rattled the windows.

"You have a doctorate in English," I heard him speaking again, "perhaps you can teach in America."

"Who needs me in America? They have their own teachers. I wanted to teach here. Besides how am I going to get there?" I asked.

The doctor started to collect his instruments. "If you invested in going to America half of the energy you've used looking for a job here, you'd be there already," he laughed. He was getting ready to go. "Call me if Livi doesn't improve by tomorrow, okay?"

I thanked him for his visit and walked him to the door.

The conversation left me in a feverish state. America! Yes, I often toyed with the fantasy of going to the place Kenneth came from, but as a reality? A possibility? I had never thought of it. Wow! I grabbed Shir and hugged him to death. He started howling. I put him down, laughing. "How would you like to go to America?" I asked. He looked at me as if I had lost my mind and went back to his toys. America, I thought, yes, perhaps, yes. What do I have here? A mother who tells me how to raise my children, a boss who wants me to be invisible, very few friends who care, and a whole society that for a year and a half has been trying to prove to me that I don't exist! Well, then, maybe I don't. But maybe I could exist in America. I am still young. Yes, yes!

But then, at the peak of my ecstasy, darker thoughts brought me down to earth. Where in America? How can I get there? I'm an Israeli. How could I get a visa, or better yet, a work permit? What am I dreaming about? I threw myself on the couch in despair. No, no, how could it ever work? What can I, an Israeli widow with two children, offer to America? And how would I support myself? This is madness! I am a big dreamer, that's all.

But I couldn't get America out of my mind. I made inquiries. I found out that I couldn't switch from one kind of visa to another. If I entered America on a tourist visa, and wanted to stay there, I'd have to come back to Israel to get another kind of visa. After considering my options, I decided to apply for the J-1, a visiting professor's visa, for three years. But in order to get such a visa, I'd have to have a job first. And how could I secure a job, even a part-time job, in America without an interview? But how could I get to America *for* the interview? On a tourist visa? But then, if I got the job, I'd have to come back to Israel to apply for a J-1 visa because one cannot work in the States on a tourist visa! Well, how could I do that? Even if I had the money, it would probably take me three years to get the J-1 visa in Israel. And then it would be time to go back home anyway. Have you ever seen such a catch-22 scheme?

When I joined my American friend Gila on the lawn, for the children's afternoon outing, I heard horror stories from her about people who had been waiting for years for their visas and were still sitting on their suitcases. Her brother-in-law was a case in point, she said. He wanted to emigrate to the States, but each time he went to the American Consulate with the required permits they would hand him a new list of documents! "They've been keeping him dangling for years," Gila's lovely green eyes looked at me unflinchingly, "there is just no end to it. He lost one job here, because he thought his visa was just around the corner. Now he'll probably lose another job before he ever gets to see Lady Liberty!" Gila shook her red curls in the afternoon breeze and laughed. "You think that America is nice, eh?"

That night, I returned home despondent. I wrote to Kenneth's friend, Norman Fedder, in Kansas, that I wished I could come to America but that getting a visa seemed impossible. Could he find out information on his end? Then I tried to forget America. It was too difficult, I cautioned myself, too risky. And yet I could not stop dreaming about it.

For many weeks, Norman tried to get me the papers for the J-1 visa with little success. As late as May 10, 1980, he called to tell me that he couldn't find a way to get the papers. All right, I said to myself, America is over. And yet in my diary, on May 10, 1980, I reported a strange premonition. "Why do I see my future at Kansas State University?"

One day in late May, a perfectly legal loophole materialized. It *was* a miracle. We learned that neither the chair of the Speech Department (where Norman worked), nor the chair of the English Department had to sign the forms for the visa; the signature of the head of the International Students Office was sufficient. In this way, I could come to America for three years and the administration could decide, without constraints, whether to give me a job.

At the end of May the papers arrived. I looked at them in disbelief. There it was, my freedom, my great opportunity, my passage to America! Exhilarated, I put the papers securely on a shelf out of the children's reach. Then I took them down and looked at them again. Unbelievable! I whispered, as I checked and rechecked all the details. Then, I put the papers away, aware of a vague sense of guilt. What would my mother say? How can I take Shir away from her? And how could I tell my friend Gila that I would be going to America when her own brother-in-law was still sitting on his suitcases? Then the pall of my guilt expanded to cover all of Israel. Am I betraying my country? During the 67 war I stayed in Sheffield—and now? Now I am leaving Israel altogether. Am I crazy?

Without fully understanding my action, I took the precious papers, climbed on a tall kitchen chair, and put them on top of a high bookshelf. At least now I won't be able to grab the papers on impulse and rip them apart! By the time I fetch the chair, drag it to the bookcase, and climb it, the impulse will be gone. I looked around in dismay. What is happening? For months I've wanted to go to America, so why am I so upset now? I am not going forever, of course. Just three years. What am I fussing about? I am not

a *yoredet,* am I? I haven't yet left the country, how could I? It's my country.
Always will be. I was born here. As was my mother, and my grandmother,
and my great-grandmother. And my great-great-grandmother, and my
great-great-great-grandmother—born and lived in Safed, Hebron, Jerusalem, and Tiberias. My great-grandmothers—women with dark head coverings, furrowed faces, sun-baked, freckled skin, grim survivors of famine,
disease, poverty, and massacres. Strong women, like my grandmother, who
was stronger than the fickle man she married, my grandfather, who escaped
the Turkish army to Argentina and stayed there, long after the danger of
mobilization was over, for eight years forgetting his wife and daughter, not
even knowing that his daughter had died of meningitis and that his wife
toiled alone, living hand to mouth, a shamed *agunah.* When he came back
much later to my grandmother, she forgave him, and together again they
gave life to my mother, and then to her six brothers and sisters, the uncles
and aunts, to whom I belong—Bracha, Ruth, Nomi, Zipporah, Avram, and
Itzhak—all living here in this country, the country where I grew up with
Imma and Reuven in Yavne'el, where I heard the coyotes howl over the hills
at night, where I jumped from a high post and got an honorable mention,
where I served as a soldier and walked into a glass door. The country where
Reuven and Chaim died. The country where I met, loved, and buried Kenneth on Mount Olives. The country where I became a student, a teacher,
and a mother. This country, and no other, I was now relinquishing.

KANSAS

A week before I left, my friend Gila invited me for a serious talk. "Why
Kansas?" she started. "What would you do in Kansas, Shelly?" she stared at
me. "Do you know what Kansas is?" she bent over her busy stove. "Flat, flat,
flat." She laughed. "There is nothing in Kansas but farms, cornfields, and

---

yoredet   Feminine for a person who emigrates from Israel. The word *yerida* which literally
means "descent" (the opposite of *Alia,* "ascent") is loaded with negative connotations, since
to most Israelis leaving the country for good is reprehensible.

agunah   A woman whose husband has disappeared, and his whereabouts are unknown, is
forbidden by Jewish halakhic law to marry another man. This woman is called Agunah.
When her long-lost husband returned from South America, my grandmother escaped this
terrible fate.

wheat fields. And more farms and cornfields and wheat fields. And the whole state is flat like a *latke*. I swear! No, Aaron," she yelled at her four-year-old, "you can't drive your bicycle in the house. How many times do I have to tell you? Go outside right now. Children!" she sighed, "I don't have to tell you! But Kansas?" looking teasingly at me, "smack in the center of the U.S.A., away from everything—cities, theaters, concerts, *culture*—the Bible Belt! You know? I wonder if there are any Jews in Kansas?" Her rippling laughter made my head spin.

"Of course, there are Jews in Kansas. I already know at least two Jews, Norman Fedder and his wife Deborah, and they're not alone, I'm sure."

"Oh, well, I'm only joking. Of course, there are Jews in Kansas. But still, why Kansas, Shelly? In the middle of nowhere? The great American desert?" she shook her curls and burst out laughing again. "Did you look the place up, find out information about it?"

"No," I admitted, stung. "I know very little about the place, except that it has universities, that I may have a chance to teach, and," I took a deep breath, "that it is in America."

"Yes, of course, Kansas is in America," Gila's face labored to suppress another splash of laughter, "and that's where you want to be, I know," she smiled affectionately. "Forgive my morbid realism. I do hope you are not disappointed. Seriously, I think you'll make a life for yourself, even in Kansas."

"Thanks," I said, convinced more than ever before of the folly of my enterprise.

On July 20, 1980, I flew from Tel Aviv to New York, and from New York, via St. Louis, to Kansas City. My children stayed with my mother in Tel Aviv and were to come to Manhattan, Kansas, with her after I'd "settled down." When I arrived at Kansas City, my ears ringing, my body buzzing with plane drones, my head gyrating with jet lag, and scrutinized, from the airport building, the plane, stationed half a mile away, that was to deliver me from Kansas City to Manhattan, a plane with one propeller and two passenger seats, a plane smaller than most large cars, I felt faint. Is this what I traveled thirty hours for? All the way from Israel, to die on a toy plane just a spitting distance away from my promised land, Manhattan, Kansas? A rush of longing for my children brought tears to my eyes. They just lost their father; do they have to lose their mother too? Who would raise them, my mother? Oh, no! A young man with a friendly smile approached me, introduced himself as the pilot, and offered to carry one of my heavy bags. The pilot? I gulped air. God help me. A mere kid. What have I done? The young man was politely pointing the way to his plane, chatting cheerfully with the other passenger under the broad, blue sky. Why are they so calm? I was thinking furtively as I quickened my step to catch up with them. Where am I? What is this place? I looked around at the huge airfield crowded with planes of every size and shape. Flat, indeed. What if I can't find work here? I groaned as I mounted my heavy bag on my shoulder. What if I hate Kansas, as Gila predicted? What if Kansas hates me? You are mad, I chided myself, to have come here. Mad, mad, mad; I was running after the pilot, my bag swinging on my buttocks from side to side.

Once I sat inside the plane, staring at the confusing array of dials, my panic reached its zenith. No, I heard a mysterious voice; you'll never escape this contraption alive. The pilot cheerfully hopped into his seat and turned the propeller on. In the deafening noise, I uttered a brief yelp. "Don't be concerned," my neighbor said affably, "I make this trip every week. It's perfectly safe." The plane sped down the runway and, after a few seconds, took off. There. I was air-borne, teeth chattering, eyes glued to the dashboard, lips quivering in prayer. A moment later, I noted, I was still alive. The plane reached its altitude. Five minutes passed. The pilot smiled pleasantly and urged me to look down. With an effort, I took my eyes away from the incomprehensible dials and looked around me. Due to its small size, the plane flew low. The land stretched under me, a near, ample, and resplendent plateau. I could clearly see the spacious farmhouses governing a vista of checkered fields, divided by running hedgerows and wooden fences; here and there, clumps of trees, by a creek or a pond, offered shade; on a straight, broad highway, cars traveled calmly, oblivious to the big bird flying above; the Missouri River made its leisurely progress through the land, its placid water sparkling here and there in the sun. Oh, I cried out in surprise, how lovely! Who would have guessed? The sky, which rose high above us, stretching immensely from horizon to invisible horizon, merging imperceptibly with the quiet land, was flushed, as if painted by a Vermeer, with translucent light.

A few minutes later, the inconceivable happened: I relaxed. There, suspended in the Kansas light, high above any kind of help, gazing at our plane's shadow running on the ground ahead of us, or askew to the side of us, a small mercurial speck, making its brave leap across the gleaming distance, I, the anxious mother, the disconsolate widow, the contentious Israeli, who had much to learn, was easing myself into the enveloping peacefulness, thinking that perhaps for the first time (could it be?) I had found the true meaning of my chosen name, Shelly, as in shalom.

LEARNING TWICE OVER

To teach is to learn twice over.

—Joseph Joubert, *Pensées*

Norman and Deborah Fedder waited for me at the tiny Manhattan, Kansas, airport and took me to their home. I was grateful and exhilarated. There I was, in America, safe in the company of friends, moored in a beautiful, ranch style house, surrounded with a green lawn and shaded by massive oaks. The Fedders wined and dined me, took me on tours of Manhattan, and introduced me to the staff of the Speech Department at Kansas State University (K-State) and to the tiny but active Jewish community. The only thing they forbade me to do was to smoke in the house. At first I chafed against the incomprehensible prohibition (who in Israel doesn't smoke?), but I learned to curb my nicotine consumption and, after a futile attempt to smoke secretly in my room (Deborah sniffed the smoke through the vents), I limited my shameful habit to the lawn. It was during one of those smoking breaks, on a long summer evening, the sky opening forever over my head, that I discovered the cicadas. As the sun made its slow exit, distractedly brushing the feathered clouds with pastel pinks, the universe at once filled with the shrill, persistent sound of the cicadas, drowning any other sound, human or insect. I was astounded by this brazen chorus, which I had never heard before, and was somewhat irritated by its interference. But when, after some time, I found myself strangely soothed by the tone-deaf singers and rocked to a peaceful place on the waves of their monotonous melody, I knew that—foolish as it may sound to Gila, or to New Yorkers—I had fallen in love with Kansas.

For days I walked around exuberant, even euphoric. I had arrived. I made it to America. After a week, I rented an apartment, got a driver's license, and bought a used Ford Mustang. I also found out that as Kenneth's widow I was entitled to regular, generous, monthly Social Security payments. I called my mother and instructed her to come with the children at the end of August. "Do you have a job already?" "No," I mumbled, "but I will certainly get one." To this day, I don't know why I was so confident. I must have been drunk on America.

Had I stopped to reflect, though, I would have been less confident. My three-year renewable visa specified that I could teach only in the Speech Department of Kansas State University. How could I, an Israeli with a detectable accent, a doctorate in English, and a smattering of informal experience in theater, how could I, suddenly dropped down in Kansas from outer space, I, who had never seen an American (let alone a midwestern) university, *think, dream, dare* to ask for a teaching position in Speech, to teach Oral Communication to freshmen? I, who had never even heard of the name Oral Communication in my own country, where everybody shouts anyway instead of speaking and would laugh wildly at the notion of a university course that teaches you to organize and deliver speeches? How could I, who was scheduled to present a paper on the Holocaust in Israeli Drama at the American Theater Association Convention in San Diego, in August 1980, and had prepared the reseach and the argument but no written presentation except for some scribbled notes and quotes on a crumpled paper stashed somewhere in my suitcase, how could I teach young students to prepare oral presentations? I must have been stark, raving mad.

It was only during my interview with the chair of the Speech Department, the late Dr. Norma Bunton, that the reality of my absurd position knocked all the euphoria out of me. I found myself, on that early, cool summer morning, shaking and tongue-tied. As Dr. Bunton, Norman, and I were walking from the parking lot to the student union, for a cup of coffee to help the interview along, I forgot all I wanted to say. What could I tell her about my experience in speech? As we sipped our coffee, Norma's calm blue eyes watched me warily through her large, glinting glasses. What could I say? And how could I say it without this damned Israeli accent? Flustered, confused, I clammed up. Fedder, sitting opposite me, shifted in his chair and became visibly uneasy. Laughing nervously and gesticulating, he was pleading with me to speak. "Can you tell us, Dr. Regenbaum about your teaching experience?" he'd start, clearing his throat, making faces to me outside of Bunton's field of vision. Finally, in desperation, I talked about what I knew—my need to leave my country and settle in America, my involvement in the theater, my love of teaching. I must have done fairly well, for Dr. Bunton smiled at me, and Norman looked relieved. I got the job. Did I deserve it? Some of my new colleagues thought not. I was ashamed of benefiting from my connection with Norman. But I was grateful and determined to reward my benefactors by working hard and teaching well.

At the end of August, my mother and the children arrived at Manhattan. I found a day-care center for Shir and Livi near the university. In September, my mother returned to Israel, school started, and my new life in America jumped into high gear.

My duties as a visiting assistant professor comprised of teaching four basic Speech courses a semester. The "visiting" in my title referred to the temporary nature of my position, which had to be renewed each year. If I didn't teach well, I understood, my chair could terminate my contract, which meant, in effect, termination of my visa. I prepared diligently for my new duties; I read my textbook from cover to cover; I consulted my colleagues; I wrote my syllabus; on the first day of the semester, I put on my best face and walked into class. I did not expect to fail.

Indeed, I was usually only one step ahead of my students, but I felt that I was in control of the class. I tried to use my Israeli origin to advantage by drawing parallels between Israeli and American cultures. The fact that many of my midwestern students were not interested in Israeli culture and that I had very little knowledge of American culture, let alone its midwestern variety, didn't faze me. Sometimes, my students must have looked bewildered or frustrated, but I did not see it. I had a syllabus to complete, so I plowed on, like an undaunted icebreaker, through the glossy surface of their hostility. If I had doubts about my teaching, I dispelled them by recalling my knowledge, my hard work, my devotion to the students. Didn't I once receive a bouquet of daisies? Wasn't that a sign that I was a good teacher? And once a good teacher, always a good teacher, no matter what you do, or don't do. Wasn't it true?

Thus, when I received the student evaluations at the end of the first semester, I reeled in pain for weeks, as if my stomach had been hit by an angry fist. In Israel, professors were not required to solicit students' opinions of their teaching. At K-State I found out for the first time what students really thought of me. As I was reading some of the negative comments, I was astounded by the fact that I never saw it coming. I could hardly believe it was *me* the students were describing. Was it I who was unclear and noncommunicative? Could it be I who was lecturing over their heads? Was I the insulting, critical teacher? I, the arrogant instructor who did not listen to her students? Of course, not everybody thought that. Half of the students loved my classes, but the other half—alas—labeled me "unfit to teach." One even suggested that I go back to Israel.

I was wounded. At first I felt betrayed. There I was, working day and night to adjust to the new academic environment only to be told by young, smug students who knew nothing of struggle and suffering, that I was not good enough to teach them, that I could not arouse their interest, that I was too "intellectual," or too foreign! Didn't I care for my students, listen to their problems, help them with the material? How dare they deny or forget all that?

Yet, mixed with my rage, never far-off, was the chilling terror. I had no rights in America. A visiting immigrant, on a restricted visa. Not even a resident. What if I couldn't reach the students? I'd have to go back to Israel. No, I was not going back. I had already made up my mind to stay in America, not only for three years, but forever, no matter the price, except for a fake marriage.

The time came for serious reckoning. "How can I succeed here as an immigrant," I complained to Norman. "How can I teach Speech with an Israeli accent?"

Norman nodded sympathetically. "Yes, it is difficult. But you know what?" his dark eyes darted around the room, "your accent shouldn't matter that much for a basic Speech class. Why should it? You're not teaching them how to speak, how to pronounce words," he burst into a short, thunderous laughter. "You are not *stealing* their American accent from them, are you? Rather, you are teaching them how to present a speech, and in that category, they can still learn from you!"

"Thank you," I muttered. "But some of them obviously don't *trust* my knowledge because of my foreign culture."

Norman scratched his head. His dark beady eyes scrutinized me. "So?" his lips curved in a ruminating half smile. "You're from Israel. True. So what?" his laughter thundered again. "You can't do anything about that. But does that mean you can't teach?" he rubbed his nose. "Does that mean you shouldn't teach? Does that mean you should go back to Israel? I don't think so! Make them trust you. Figure out how to do that. You can, yes, you can," he responded to my vigorous head shaking. "I must go to a meeting," he looked briefly at his watch and started collecting his notes, "but remember what Gide said," he repeated his favorite aphorism. "'The only choice is upward!' Move up, *kadimah,*" he pointed with his index finger, smiling jubilantly, "not down or back. Shalom for now," he stretched out his short, stubby fingers in a benediction.

How could I make the students trust me? I was thinking angrily on my way to my car. Puffy white snowflakes were lightly settling on the ground and on the naked tree branches. My eyes blinked in the vast, bright expanse of the frozen world. If they don't like my accent, I walked gingerly on the slippery surface to my car, there's nothing I can do about it. I reached my car, plopped onto my seat, and turned on the ignition. Grunting, I got out again with my brush to sweep the blanket of snow from the car. How could I change my accent? I was grumpily dumping snow on the ground. How could I get rid of this "slight tremor in the vowels," as one of my colleagues described it? Norman implies it's not the accent, but what else could it be? I got back in the car and rolled it carefully toward Anderson Street, crossed over, and slid down Seventeenth Street to Poyntz to pick up the children from their day-care center on Pierre Street. What else could it be? I wondered. The semester was over. There was barely a car on the road. Why should I pay attention to some disgruntled students who didn't like their grades? The flakes were coming down fast and thick; while removing them, the wipers dragged a slushy blur across the window. True, I admitted, not all my classes in Israel were equally good, but it didn't matter then. I tapped my brakes. Now suddenly it matters, in this democratic American system. A huge Alco truck passed me by and splashed my windows with slush. For a moment I couldn't see a thing. Panic lurched to my throat. The end of me! Haven't I had enough of America? The wipers wheezed *slish, slosh* and after laboring for a while, revealed again the white world. But this is Kenneth's America, too, I peered through the blur. Didn't he used to ask the students to evaluate his teaching, even though he was not required to do so in Israel? He did, every single semester. Why? To learn, to become a better teacher. And if he subjected himself to this ordeal, I winced in the glare, why shouldn't I?

Let's see, I thought, inching closer to the children. What if the students were somewhat right? What if it is not my accent that needed changing but my attitude? I shook my head. Perhaps, I stopped at the light, I had to see myself as the students saw me. Especially those who liked me yet thought I was too harsh. What would Kenneth say about that? Slowly the car continued its jagged progress toward Poyntz. Could it be that I was too arrogant? Could it be that I needed to learn a lesson about humility? My mouth twisted as if I'd swallowed a rotten piece of fruit. Humility!? In my country humility is as rare as snow. Everybody knows everything. Everybody is a doctor, a lawyer, a teacher, a prime minister. Why shouldn't I be Ms. Know-it-all and get away with it? Why can't *I* assert my authority as my mother does? Because you're different from your mother, I could hear Kenneth's voice in the great white stillness, and you don't want *her* kind of authority. I tapped my brakes. Did I have to come all the way to Kansas to learn this lesson from my students?

Gradually, I found ways to reach my students. Every semester of my three years at the Speech Department, my teaching evaluations improved. Instead of being labeled "arrogant," or "insulting," I was described as "understanding," "caring," and "easy to get along with." *(Me?)* One student declared, "Dr. Regenbaum—I came into this class filled with dread and I left it knowing that I had enjoyed it very much. Thank you." How about that? Another student

actually liked my foreign origin and pointed out how "my broadened back-
ground" provided "many excellent insights." When I read this note to Norman, he threw his arms in the air. "You see? You see?" he roared, "what did I
tell you? You made it! *Kadimah!*"

GEORGE WALL

Even before the start of the first semester, I was involved in a secretive relationship with George, a married Speech professor, twenty years my senior,
whom I met at the Fedders' party. A week or two later, fate tossed George and
me together on the same plane to San Diego for the American Theater Association Convention, in August 1980. Our conversation, enlivened by drinks,
soon developed into an exciting intellectual sparring. During the conference,
George became my loyal companion, jealously guarding me from a young
man who pursued me for a while. Intoxicated by my success with interesting
men, I neglected preparations for my talk "The Holocaust in Israeli Drama."
A few hours before the talk, I took my notes out and scanned them with
growing bewilderment. There were far too many marginal notes, arrows leading up and down the page, asterisks pointing to the back of pages. How am I
supposed to make sense of this scrawl? I thought, horrified. I sat down to
work, and an hour before the presentation I had only a sketchy idea how to
get from point A to point B. At the scheduled time, I sat among the panelists,
sick with fear. When my turn came, I got up and approached the podium.
Dear God, I panicked. The podium was too high! I put my notes under the
podium light and stood bolt upright to face my audience. "Can you see me?"
I asked. Everybody laughed. That was the high point of my presentation. My
disorganized lecture dragged on far too long. My panel chair passed me notes
indicating how many minutes I had left, but not knowing how to finish my
paper, I ignored them. Finally the chair asked me point-blank to sit down. I
was crushed.

It was George who then offered me consolation and instruction. He went
over my paper from beginning to end, showing me how I should have presented it. In fact, he became my first Speech teacher. Later, in Manhattan, I
often turned to him with questions about speech and about America. Quickly,
he made himself indispensable. He showed me the stores, the bank, the restaurants; he taught me how to apply for credit cards, write American checks, and
use the university services. He helped me to correct my mistakes in the class-

room. He talked to me passionately about American history, American democracy, and the American love for freedom and fairness. He was my engaging and eloquent mentor.

Yet George was also a persistent suitor. After a month, against my better judgment, I made love to him. I told myself that I was tired of his advances, that I'd do it already, just to shut him up, that of course I'd hate it, and that that would be the end of it. In fact, it was I who was effectively shut up. Instead of hating it, I loved it. Astonished by the intensity of the pleasure, I surrendered myself, in deep hunger, to a year-long clandestine affair. Each morning I'd get up despising my secret life. Why am I having an affair with a married man? I'd ask myself, trying in vain to understand which side of the Oedipal divide I was on. George is not love, I admitted. Kenneth was love. Whatever exists between George and me is not love, although he insists it is, and promises to divorce his wife and marry me. I didn't believe his promises, and yet each day, as I passed by his open office door, struggling to look straight ahead of me but often sneaking a quick glance at his tall frame, his shrewd, all-knowing blue eyes, and his long, graceful fingers, I'd be caught, flying high, my blood racing with desire.

I'd try to justify our affair. Whom am I hurting? He doesn't love his wife, anyway. I've suffered enough. Kenneth is dead. My body has needs. Everybody else has affairs. My mother had them. Why can't I? But my conscience kept pestering me with questions. Have I come to America to be involved in a secret affair? Don't I know it's wrong? How can I tolerate this shame? Am I reliving my sordid London adventures? No, I won't have *that* kind of life again, I resolved. Not in America, not in my new home.

There I was, divided again. My time with George was too interesting, too delicious. I could not let him go. I longed for him. I needed him. Perhaps he really loves me, I used to think; when he talked about marriage, I let him and almost believed we'd marry. Weeks passed. Time and again, George pleaded with me to become pregnant, to ease the task of asking his wife for a divorce. I angrily refused. Finally, he talked to his wife but came back defeated. "I can't ask her," he moaned. "I can't do this to her. She is old. Helpless. Alone. I just can't. . . ." He rubbed his tired cheeks. Suddenly he too looked old, the light in his eyes snuffed out. "I know I have failed you," he said sadly. "What can I do? I can't leave her, but I can't leave you either."

I knew then that I *had* to leave him. But once more I couldn't. Admitting my defeat, I decided to ask for help. Oblivious to George's derisive interjections ("Therapist? Bah! What do *they* know? I would never reveal my secrets to a stranger!"), I found the number for Pawnee Mental Health in the phone book, called, and made an appointment. In a year of many wrong and rash moves, that was my wisest action.

THERAPY

Unlike Mrs. Silver, Edna was a disciplined therapist, a supportive listener, and a skillful healer. As she urged me to examine the source of my attraction to George, a chart of my emotional landscape emerged where, one by one, points of light turned on, illuminating the arteries previously submerged in darkness that connected the planes of my existence. My life was no longer a frozen landscape, splintered off into fragments that did not talk to each other, but rather a growing organism. I found out that I chose George because, as a married man, he was "safe." I also recognized that George was irresistible because the man who stood in his shadow, the charming rogue with the whimsical blue eyes, the seductive father figure—was Chaim. Gradually I freed myself of George and of forbidden attractions.

A year later, I met John, a handsome student in the Construction Science department, thirteen years younger than I, and in all respects the opposite of George. John preferred the physical, rather than the intellectual, world. His indifference to ideas and books ultimately effected our separation, but at the time, it spelled freedom. With John I missed the excitement of debate, but I gained a sense of self. Whereas George tried to control my thoughts and decisions, tolerant, laid-back John accepted me as I was. Unlike George, John also helped with the children and the house chores. And unlike George, John was divorced. I so much enjoyed the freedom from guilt and secrecy that I could not imagine myself ever being involved in an illicit relationship again. A few years later, after John had already moved to Denver, I turned down his surprising, quirky marriage proposal, but I still think of our relationship with pleasure and gratitude, for through it I learned much and reached a healthy plateau in my search for love.

In unraveling my sexual entanglements and in working through my grief over Kenneth, Edna's guidance was vital. But her support was most cogent when I set out on the painful journey to the orphanage.

When I first mentioned Pardes-Hannah to Edna, casually, as if it were a mere historical fact, she raised her eyebrows and wrote "childhood trauma" in her notebook.

I was surprised. "It happened so long ago. Could it affect my life now?"

"Indeed it could," Edna explained. "Such events are never forgotten. They may be suppressed, but they don't disappear."

"My mother," I whispered, as if she were in the room, "wouldn't let me talk about it. Whenever I mentioned the orphanage, she'd rage."

"That's called denial."

"But then I, too, learned to deny it," I admitted.

"Now you'll have to find ways to release the orphan," Edna smiled. For a moment her dark liquid eyes, the circle of light marked by her desk lamp, the huge plant behind her chair, the bookcase along the wall, and the ground under my feet were reeling, taking me inexorably toward the black hole I'd managed to avoid all my life. "Do I have to do it?" I swallowed hard.

"I think so," Edna was firm, "if you want to find peace."

And so I embarked on the most urgent journey of my life, a journey that took years to accomplish, to the eucalyptus trees and the squeaking gate of Pardes-Hannah, behind which the orphan was locked up in the heartland of Israel, surrounded by vast stretches of orchards and red sands. In the thirty-ninth year of my life, I set out to talk to her, to pity her, to reclaim her. While continuing to live my life in all its parts, I began to relive hers, too, to experience her pain, her terrors, her anger. I vowed to visit Pardes-Hannah in person and to take her out of there. Yet, flushed with joy at my progress, I failed to realize the strength of Shelly's resistances. I never mentioned Haya's name to Edna, nor did I tell her that I changed my name to Shelly. And so the guilty secret remained intact, to deepen its hold and to fester.

ABBA

When I came to America, I hadn't spoken to my father in fifteen years. He had drifted out of my life, I thought, for good. For what kind of a father, my mother would say, does not come to his daughter's wedding, does not even send his congratulations, or a little gift? And what kind of a father does not come to the funeral of his daughter's husband, and does not even send his condolences? Not a human father, she'd say. A monster. There he is, her lip would curl up in contempt, sitting in America, with his ugly *dosit* wife, and his ten

---

dosit   A derisive slang expression for an ultra-Orthodox woman

children, not even thinking of you once. And why? You know why? Because you are not keeping kosher, and you don't say *Shema* at night. That's why. He's given up on you, she'd conclude, the monster.

Until I started therapy, I regarded my father as a cardboard figure, painted black. Black for the ultra-Orthodox *dos,* black for his garb, black as night for his heart. It never occurred to me to seek him out. Why should I talk to a monster? Yet as I started my difficult discourse with Haya, in the middle of my second year in America, my father, too, began to take on a human form. He was *her* father and in her name, I had to speak to him. I had to know why he put me in Pardes-Hannah, why he didn't come to visit, why he cut me loose altogether when I reached my twenty-fifth year. I had to know what kind of a man he was and what made him my father. I had to find him, I told Edna. "After all," I said to her, "he lives right here in America." Edna nodded. "I have a father. Can you imagine? Both Reuven and Chaim are dead, but he is still alive. My father. I am his daughter. Who could deny it?" I was thinking and wondering. And it was then that I was struck by a thought.

"How come?" I asked, holding onto the edges of Edna's desk. "How come the idea never occurred to me before?"

"Shelly," Edna laughed. "I know you have a flare for the dramatic, but don't hold me in suspense. What are you talking about?"

"How come I never thought of it before?" I cried out.

"Shelly, what idea?" Edna protested. "Tell me already."

"I'm afraid to speak of it. As soon as I utter it, it will probably evaporate."

"No, it won't." Edna looked at me with a gentle reproach.

"All right," I took a deep breath. "My father is an American citizen."

"Yes. So?"

Still fearful, I whispered the words. "He can petition for me."

"Petition?" Edna looked puzzled.

"Petition for me to become an American citizen."

"I see," Edna took a long drag on her cigarette and stared reflectively at the spirals of smoke.

"You see the beauty of it?" I asked, exhilarated. "He is my father. He can bestow on me the gift of citizenship. I don't have to plead, cheat, or marry someone for it. I can receive it from my father—my honest-to-God right to become an American."

"Very interesting," Edna interjected.

"Moreover," I exulted, "this is his chance to give me his name the second time, to make up for his neglect."

Hours after my astounding discovery, I called my mother, although it was 3:00 A.M. in Israel, and told her of my plan. *"Yoffi, yoffi,"* she cried out, groggy with sleep. "Get everything you can out of that shyster! It's about time he did something for you."

"Can you get me his address?" I urged her.

"I'll call his sister Tova tomorrow. First thing."

A few hours later my mother called me with his address, in Monsey, New York. I sat down to write my momentous letter. My father's response was swift. Florid and effusive, the letter began with a long string of blessings heaped on the head of his eldest daughter Haya ("may she live a long life"). No, he had not forgotten me all those years, but thought of me day and night and fervently prayed for my happiness. He was delighted to find out that I was living in America, and—what a question!—he would be honored to help me become an American citizen! Just tell me, he ends, what you need.

I called him. After fifteen years we were talking again. That night we forgot our old angers; we were buoyed on a tide of goodwill, ready to grant each other life and forgiveness. That night, comforted by my father's rollicking laughter, I defied an old prohibition and addressed him as *Abba.* I still remember the thrill of it. For me, he was no longer Zorah, but *Abba,* my *Abba.*

A few days later, my father sent his American citizenship certificate to my immigration lawyer in Kansas City. The only missing document now was my parents' marriage certificate. Both my father and my mother, in New York and in Tel Aviv, stood their houses on their heads to find the precious proof that they indeed were married before they brought me to the world. But there was no sign, no trace of the document. Without it, I was told, I could never become an American citizen. A frantic search ensued. My mother spent two days at the rabbinical court in Jerusalem, wandering from clerk to scowling clerk, but no marriage certificate of Dina and Zorah Shapira could be found. She pleaded and threatened, but the precious papers had disappeared as if the earth had swallowed them up. Finally, one of the clerks suggested one last place—the archives of *Neturei Karta.* And indeed, that's where the marriage certificate was found. "Can you imagine," my mother called me that night, "how religious I used to be when I married *him? Neturei Karta, tfu, tfu.* Thank God, I had the courage to leave him!"

Neturei Karta   Fanatic ultra-Orthodox Jews who live in *Me'ah She'arim* section in Jerusalem and are suspicious of political Zionism

Two months later, I received from the Naturalization and Immigration authorities the so-called green card, which is really white, a card that enabled me to work in the United States, and to become, in five years' time, an American citizen. Once I received the card, I'd take it out every day and run my fingers on its smooth, laminated surface. I'd gaze at it for a long moment, loving every letter, loving even my own picture on it, in which the photographer captured an immigrant's face illumined with hope and gratitude.

In the summer of 1982, when I was already an American resident, my father invited the children and me to visit him in Monsey and to spend the *Shabbat* with his family. I was determined to talk to him about the orphanage. We landed in New York on a Thursday and waited for my father at Kennedy Airport. Would I recognize him after so many years? Then I saw him approaching on a bridge above us. In spite of his sixty-seven years, he was walking at a fast, sprightly pace, the edges of his black coat lifted in the wind. In a moment, he spotted us, smiled, and came toward us. "Shalom, Haya'le, shalom," he laughed and shook my hand. "You don't look a day older, *Abba,*" I said, impressed by his trim, energetic form and his vital, coal-black eyes. "Oh, yes, Haya'le, I have aged," he laughed and bent down. "And this is Shir?" he patted my son's head. Shir, then six, recoiled from the black hat and the black coat. "And this is Livia," my father intoned. Livi hid her face in my dress and started whining. *"Ma yesh,* Haya'le? What is the matter with her?" I took her in my arms. "Nothing, *Abba,* she is just afraid of strangers." My father laughed, "Strangers, Livia? I am not a stranger. I am your grandfather, you know that?"

"What?" I remembered my mother's warning, as my father's car was confidently whizzing its way north from Kennedy Airport to Monsey. "You are spending the *Shabbat* with him? Are you out of your mind? Remember, you can't turn on the light, can't read, can't smoke, can't watch TV. And his wife Rivka, that fat cow, who knows what kind of reception she'd give you! Do what you like, Shelly, but *I* think you'll regret it." As I was chatting with my father in the car, though, I felt no regrets. No, I had no intention of becoming an Orthodox Jew, I assured my mother. I just wanted to get to know him. "What is there to know?" she shot back at me. "Where I come from," I told her. Now, as I was studying my father's sunny, easygoing disposition, I was proud of him.

When we arrived at his blue house in Monsey, however, I was obliged to credit my mother with superior taste and elegance. My father's house contained several bedrooms. But there was no hint of art. The walls were bare except for a few portraits of grim-looking rabbis. One or two bookcases con-

My father and I after our reconciliation, in New York, 1982.

tained no other books but the Talmud. The kitchen was clean but strictly functional. A soul hungry for beauty would be starved to death in this place. But, on the other hand, my mind was still busy scoring, my mother was definitely wrong about Rivka; my father's wife had given us a warm reception, fussing over Shir and Livi and offering us delicious dishes.

Finally, Friday night arrived. My father went to the synagogue to pray, and Rivka invited me to light the candles with her. I was overcome with shyness. "No," I told her, "I don't know how to pray." She urged me to try and showed me the prayer in the *siddur.* I prayed quickly and lit the candles, watching their flickering flames bring out the sheen in my father's silver cup. The table looked festive with the *Shabbat* dishes, the *challah,* and the wine.

siddur Prayer book

Then my father opened the door and walked in, still wrapped in his white blue *talit*, smiling beatifically as if he'd been touched by an angel. My memory quivered. I had seen him this way before, when, at Shir's age, I visited him and Rivka, for one single time in their one-room apartment in the *Me'ah She'arim* section of Jerusalem. "Should I call him *Abba?*" I asked Rivka then, as I gazed in wonder at my father's radiant face. "*I* don't know what you should call him," she answered, her face concealed in shadows. Now Shir tugged at my dress, telling me that he was hungry and bored and wanted to go home. My father held his face in his warm hand. "Shir?" he laughed. "What's the matter, Shir? You don't like *Shabbat?* Why not, eh? Why not?" Shir buried his face in my dress. My father snapped his fingers and hummed a *Shabbat* song. Then he washed his hands, prayed *Ha'motsi* over the *challah,* tore two pieces off, sprinkled them with salt, bit into one, and gave the other to Shir. "Let's eat," my father said and blessed the wine.

Friday night was followed by a fine *Shabbat* day. I woke up early, to the spirited notes, *per-chick-o-ree, chi-ee,* of the goldfinch. Or was it a house wren? I could not say. On two mattresses on the floor, Shir and Livi were sleeping, their arms and legs thrown about in different directions. I looked out at the shadowy trees and the rising blue sky behind them and savored the morning stillness until I remembered the orphanage. All at once, my stomach curdled. Why do I need to destroy my reunion with my father, our harmonious *Shabbat* with the children, through a futile questioning that might anger him and end up in nothing? What do I expect him to do about it? Why can't I leave well enough alone? I turned in my bed away from the morning glory to the wall. For Haya, I thought, squeezing my eyes shut on her questions.

In the afternoon, while the children and Rivka napped, my father and I took a stroll. The streets and the houses in that religious neighborhood were submerged in a profound *Shabbat* silence, undisturbed by cars or lawn mowers. Arms clasped behind his back, my father was walking leisurely by my side, nodding *Shabbat shalom* to occasional neighbors passing by. The sun stood directly above us, its heat tempered by breezes. "Nu, Haya'le?" my father turned to me, smiling. "What questions did you want to ask me?"

I took a deep breath. "I am really happy to be here with you."

"Of course, Haya'le, of course, and I am also happy you, and the children, are here with me. What a question! Ha-ha-ha."

---

talit   Prayer shawl

"And I am really grateful for your gift of American citizenship. I want you to know. . . ."

"I know, Haya'le. But it was easy to do. So why not?" He laughed. "But is this what you wanted to ask me?"

"No," my eyes followed a squirrel running up a tree. "I wanted to ask you about the orphanage."

"What orphanage, Haya'le?"

"In Pardes-Hannah."

"Oh, *that* orphanage, I see," he patted his beard. "Ask, *meida'le,* ask. I promise to answer if I can."

At least, I thought relieved, he doesn't shut me up. "How long was I in the orphanage before *Imma* and Reuven took me out of there?"

"How long?" he took his black *yarmulke* off, scratched his head, and put it back on. "A year, I always thought. Yes, a year."

"*Imma* said that I was there just a few months, at most six."

He looked at me surprised. "Really? I don't know. Six months? No, I think it was closer to a year. Or perhaps I am also thinking about the time you stayed with your grandmother in Tiberias. That could be." We continued our measured walk. A few yards ahead of us, the road veered into a small shaded park, scattered with benches. Under a big oak tree, a group of young mothers, dressed in long sleeves and head coverings, congregated with their children. Although they were absorbed in a happy conversation, while rocking their babies in prams or strollers, I stared at them with intense pity. What a trap! I thought, noting their thick, black stockings. If my mother hadn't left *him*, I'd be one of them. Fat Haya, a mother of six, in long dresses, thick black stockings, and shaved head. . . .

"Shall we sit on the bench under this tree?" my father asked, bringing my mind up short from its meanderings.

We sat down. "And whose idea was it? To put me in the orphanage?" My heart jumped a beat.

My father took his handkerchief out of his pocket and wiped his forehead. "Your mother put you there, Haya'le, because she had to work nights."

"She says that it was you who put me there, you who insisted that I'd be brought up in a religious institution."

"Me?" my father burst out laughing. "I didn't even know that you were there, Haya'le, until much later."

"So it was all her doing?"

"Yes, of course."

"And once you found out, did you ask her why she put me in an orphanage?"

"No, I didn't."

"Why not?"

"I thought she knew best how to take care of you."

"And why didn't you come to visit me in the orphanage?" my throat felt hot.

"Of course I came, Haya'le." My father took his glasses off and rubbed them carefully on his handkerchief. "Many times."

"Funny. I remember Reuven and *Imma's* visits, but I don't remember yours."

"I promise you that I came, Haya'le."

"And what did you see, when you came?"

"What do you mean?" he laughed. "I saw you."

"Did you see a happy child?"

"Happy?" he caressed his beard. "Yes, I thought you were happy. Why not? You had food, shelter, toys, and good teachers. Your mother came to visit you every week. Yes, I thought you were happy."

"Happy?" anger stirred in my voice. "In spite of the fact that I was suddenly abandoned by my mother and father in a strange place, not knowing when they'd return, or why they'd left?"

"What could we do, Haya'le?" my father's eyes gazed into the distance. "How could we tell you why we were leaving? You were only five years old."

"Did you try to tell me?" My face felt hot.

"No. I didn't."

"Why not?"

"I didn't think you'd understand."

"So you thought it'd be better to leave me in a strange place without saying anything? Did you try to imagine, *Abba,* how terrified, how sad, your little Haya'le must have been?"

My father stared at the oak tree. When he spoke again, there was a faint smile on his face. "I don't know what to tell you, Haya'le. Who knew anything about children in those days? Who knew that children suffered? I must have thought you understood that we had to leave and that we'd come back as soon as we could."

"But I was not a grown-up. . . ."

"I see, Haya'le. I see it now," he sighed. "But then I thought that you'd be all right. You had your mother. She took care of you."

"So you could resign as my father?" I said testily.

"Well, Haya'le, I got married again, had children, emigrated to America. . . ."

"And forgot me."

"No, *chas ve'shalom,* God forbid, Haya'le, I never forgot you. But you had your mother, and you also had your stepfather, Reuven. I didn't think you needed me. In fact, I thought . . . that you didn't want to have anything to do with me."

"Why?"

"You remember our Jerusalem meetings, when you were a student at the Hebrew University?" he pulled on his beard.

"Yes, I do."

"Well, that's it, you see. You used to sulk. Sometimes you were rude. Once you even left the restaurant angry, remember?"

Yes, I remembered, but I pressed on. "Did you ask me why?"

"What was there to ask?"

"Did it ever occur to you that I didn't like those meetings because you always started them with questions about my religious practices? 'Are you keeping kosher?' was your first question. 'Are you observing the *Shabbat?*' was your second. Did it ever occur to you to ask how *I* was doing? Not how God was doing in my world, but how I was doing in His?" Dismayed by my vehemence, I looked away to the edge of the park. Too far, I thought, I have gone too far. I sneaked a look at him. He was studying his hands. "Sorry," I muttered under my breath. "I didn't mean to shout at you."

My father smiled. "It's all right, Haya'le," he spoke calmly. "I told you, I don't mind talking about the past. But you know, God *is* more important. What could be more important than God?" he twirled his fingers in the air as if he were arguing a Talmudic passage. "But it's true, Haya'le, He gave us our life, our breath, and we should be grateful and worship Him. Every day. What could be more precious? What? Of course, Haya'le. And when I asked you about the *Shabbat,* back in Jerusalem, the *Shabbat* that we are now celebrating together, I was asking about *you,* yes, about *your* happiness; you are my daughter, my eldest, and I am fearful for your soul, which is in His keeping. Do you blame me for wanting to save you from eternal punishment?"

I looked at my father astonished. Had he heard what I said? I pictured him shocked, contrite, eager to make amends. I wanted him to beat his fist on his chest as he does on *Yom Kippur* and to ask my forgiveness, or if not mine, at least God's. I imagined him a humbled father, a veritable Jewish

Lear confessing to being a foolish fond old man. But no, my father, on this pleasant summer *Shabbat,* was content with himself, serene, and untouched by tragedy, especially a tragedy that occurred thirty-five years before, a tragedy he would have prevented if he just could. And after all, I summed up as we were returning from the park, what did I have a right to expect? Why couldn't I be content with the father I had? And yet, for weeks afterward, I was stung by disappointment.

In future years, my father and I continued our religious wars. I've been fasting on *Yom Kippur* and celebrating the Passover *Seder,* but for my father that has never been enough. He could not countenance my "pick-and-choose" Jewishness. Our fiercest argument occurred after Shir's *bar mitzvah,* celebrated at our Reform temple in Lawrence, Kansas, on a day different from Shir's Hebrew date of birth. My father declared that Shir was not *bar mitzvahed* at all, for a grandson of his must be *bar mitzvahed* on the exact Hebrew date. Well, I thought then, this is it. Once more, I've lost my father. Surprisingly, however, I haven't yet lost him. After an argument, my father would call me again, and instead of starting off the conversation with an explosive question on religion, he'd begin by asking me about my plans, my teaching, and my children. Although our disagreements have persisted, my father no longer disappears from my life when I refuse to follow his path.

After my visit in Monsey in 1982, my father and I never talked about Haya and the orphanage again. And yet, in some fashion, Haya has won her father back.

FRIENDSHIP IN THE ENGLISH DEPARTMENT

Think where [wo]man's glory most begins and ends,
And say my glory was I had such friends.

—W. B. Yeats, "The Municipal Gallery Revisited"

The green card changed my life. I was no longer a vulnerable immigrant, imagining on sleepless nights the immigration authorities knocking on my door, ordering me to leave America. I was a legitimate resident, free to become a citizen in five years. I felt a thrill of excitement when I thought of voting in the presidential elections of 1988. My heart skipped a beat whenever I saw the American flag flying in the wind. I put a picture of Lady Liberty under my desk's glass and gazed at her often with gratitude. "Give me your tired, your poor, your huddled masses yearning to breathe free. . . ." Yes, that was me, the poor immigrant, yearning for America—the ground of my growth and possibility. When my three years in the Speech department were up, I decided to return to my true home—the English department.

I got a job as a lecturer, teaching required composition courses. Thus started my rigorous and unsentimental education, which gave me the solid basis for becoming an English professor and introduced me to my lifelong friends—Bonnie and Kay.

I always knew that Manhattan, Kansas was only a station on my way, and that I would have to move on. Yet I doubt that I would have had the courage or the ability to face this daunting task without the patience and wisdom of my mentor and friend, Bonnie.

A Jewish New Yorker with a doctorate in English from Penn State University, Bonnie joined our department as a tenure-track professor in the fall of 1984, the beginning of my second year. She soon became the leader of the department's women and spearheaded a successful political action to improve the working conditions of the temporary instructors. I followed the steps in her struggle with great interest and wonder at what was my first encounter with a civilized political action, fueled by a passion for justice and made effective by splendid persuasion, an action initiated and carried out entirely by women.

Our women's group expanded beyond political activity. Every two or three weeks we assembled at a different house, and in between rounds of crackers and cheese, coffee and cookies, we argued about books, beliefs, and questions of right and wrong. We were a feisty, varied group, fired up with ideas, eager to share our stories. Who could have imagined that in Manhattan, the Little Apple in the middle of Kansas, in the center of the United States, far from the urban civilizations on both coasts, surrounded to the south and west by the low, flat-topped, treeless Flint Hills, and to the east by fields of alfalfa and corn, who could have ever guessed that here I'd find my home among friends? They were all excellent, capable women. Each of them made her mark while also struggling valiantly with tough personal problems. They were my great teachers.

We took turns in leading the group activities and discussions, but it was Bonnie who was our real leader. She not only initiated activities and got in touch with everybody but she appealed to our better selves and urged us to take the high road. Her inclusive manner discouraged gossip, anger, and put-downs; instead, it unified and ennobled our group.

It was Bonnie who prepared me for the grueling job search. Whenever I thought of my realistic chances to find a tenure-track position in English, a shudder would run down my spine. It was a field that even the American-born feared to tread, where each available position drew at least two hundred applications. What made me a desirable candidate? Two articles? A few presentations in conferences? A laughable record for a woman with three strikes against her—age, children, and national origin. "Why don't I just give up?" I asked Bonnie. "I can stay a lecturer here in the English department—forever—what's so bad about that?"

Bonnie silenced me with her sweet and earnest look. "I know, Shelly, this is a difficult situation. What can I tell you?" she smiled, showing white, sculpted teeth. "It is a tough market. But you can't give up," she shook her head, as it there were nothing more obvious in the world. "Because here you have no opportunities to advance and to grow. So you must try. Have you written anything about Yezierska yet?"

"No," I muttered despondently. "I was grading papers."

"Why don't you write a page and show it to me?"

And so, countless times, Bonnie's affectionate exhortations pulled me out of my "funk." I developed my idea on Anzia Yezierska and read my paper to the department. Moreover, I published it in *Studies in American Jewish Literature,* in the spring of 1988. Even before it was published, I knew that that was the best paper I'd ever written, better than my master's thesis or doctorate, better than my articles on O'Neill. What was the secret? I identified with Yezierska, the Jewish immigrant in America, who, like me, defied her Orthodox father and resolved to study the English language in a serious and passionate manner, to write in it and shape her feelings, and those of her community, through it. Yet by renouncing her writing, Yezierska lost her way; I was determined to succeed where she failed. I resolved to find my home, and my name, in America.

The paper on Yezierska enabled me to explore my true self. So why be distracted, I asked, by unfamiliar scholarly avenues, which my patriarchal mentors of various ilks and nationalities had hitherto recommended, when my true path, the writings of Yezierska, lay before me in all its shining clarity and promise? Or better still, I thought when I was already an assistant professor (nontenure-track) at the University of Kansas (KU) in Lawrence, Kansas, why not write about . . . myself?

For a few summer months, I worked on a novella, *Anniversary in Jerusalem,* depicting a woman who travels from America to Jerusalem to visit her husband's grave. I read this story, which captured my stations of grief over Kenneth, in my campus interview at Western New England College in Springfield, Massachusetts, where I was hired for a tenure-track position in the fall of 1989.

Bonnie helped me to deal with disappointments, embodied in the one hundred and fifty rejection letters that poured down on me during the four-year job search, and encouraged me to make leaps into the unknown. She was the one who inspired me to be both expressive and disciplined, and, through the example of her own graceful assertiveness, illustrated that the "life higher," in Yezierska's idiomatic pharse, was attainable.

KITTEN CREEK ROAD

I loved being an American. I felt strong, clear, young. I knew what I wanted and where I was going. Even though I was called upon to be mother and father, and often felt stressed by the conflicting demands of children and work, and at times, in fact, quite despondent about the grinding, seemingly endless grading, I was also rewarded by a new sense of an active, burgeoning self that I had never before experienced or thought possible.

Spurred on by the sight of joggers in the streets and aerobics shows on TV, I resolved to exercise. From stretching and toning classes I advanced to running and aerobics, building up endurance by regular workouts and by cutting down my daily consumption of cigarettes from twenty-five to ten, to eight, to six. I could breathe better and run better—first one mile, then two, then three.

Once I became a regular exerciser, armed with spandex and Nikes, I could not understand why in my country, except for professional athletes and soldiers, people so rarely exercised. Their lives are more stressed than anybody's, by far, so why don't they do something about it? I would think as I was pounding the treadmill. Wouldn't running be healthier than blowing up at each other? Through my trusty walkman, U2's "With or Without You" poured mellifluously into my ears. Are Israelis ashamed of their bodies or their sweat? I wondered as I wiped my face. Does exercising remind them of the army? Or is it reluctance, my feet were pounding into the second mile, to cut down on their smoking? Raising the speed on my treadmill board, I charged forward. Look at me, my country. You thought I was good-for-nothing "Turtle" Haya trailing behind in the sand dunes of Hadera, but look at me now, hitting the treadmill belt. You know what? You mocked me, and forgot me, but you were wrong! Two miles wrong! I'll show you yet, my country, how I can run, one day you'll know, and then, 2.10 miles, then you'll say, 2.50 miles., how proud of me you really are!

With each mile I covered on my weekly jogs, my distance from my country grew. Of course, I kept in touch with Israel. Every month I talked to my mother on the phone. Every year she came over to see us and stayed for five or six weeks. Every two or three years, we visited Israel for a month. But even those visits, when Israeli reality surrounded me like a mesh, emphasized my difference. I exulted in that difference. I am better than you, I used to think, you stiff-necked, hot-tempered people! I, by my own efforts, have found out the good life, while you, miserable wretches, are still languishing here in the sultry valley of hate! You haven't changed, but I have. True, sometimes I am still too much like you—prone to angry, nasty explosions—but I am learning new ways. You just wait and see!

For years, I was angry with Israel. For years, I didn't recognize the pain at the root of my anger. Anger felt good, clean, uncomplicated. It was the secret source of my energy, the "juice" driving my progress. It gave me strength, purpose, clarity. It even gave me comfort. For years I thought that I resolved my "Israeli" problem, that I was rid of Israel for good. I was no longer an immigrant, torn between two national identities, but an American. When somebody asked me where my accent was from, I'd say, "I am from Israel, but. . . ." That "but" was everything worthwhile in my life, an introduction to my real self. The rest didn't matter, an accident of birth. My real home was in Kansas. When I met Kay and Charles, who lived on Kitten Creek Road and became my steadfast friends, I seemed to stray as far as I could from my beginnings, and my soul, to quote Emily Dickinson, stood most "ajar" and trembling.

Kay was one of the adjuncts in our English Department. Her husband, Charles, was a doctor at Lafene, the Student Health Center. They were a winning, handsome couple. Charles was (and still is) an attractive, rugged midwesterner, whose broad form and rough-hewn face radiated "cowboy" strength and charm. Yet, for those who knew him, these superficial markers were superseded by a perception of his compassion for human suffering, tempered by a droll and sometimes wicked sense of humor. The target of his humor was human vanity, including his own. "We think we are so high and mighty," he once said, as he opened the door on Christmas morning to a world transformed from dreary grey to shimmering, breathless whiteness. He folded his arms on his chest. "Could you do *that?*" he smiled. "In one night? I get a headache just thinking about it. If I had to dress every branch in snow, measuring two thousand flakes, say, for the big ones and two hundred for each twig, heaping the fluffy stuff here and flattening it there until this whole forest looked like glistening lace against the sky, I'd go mad!" he laughed. "I am so glad I don't have to do it. So glad there is God," he looked up, "who takes care of such things, so I don't have to worry about it. Because if it was left to me," he chortled, "we'd all be in real trouble!"

Not that I could ever imagine the world being in any trouble from Charles. On the contrary. Like laser rays, his compassion sought out his patients' pain, not only in America, but also in Africa that he often visited on missionary assignments. Kay accompanied him, helping him and interviewing Ethiopians for a book on African refugees. I admired their selfless activities. In their presence I have often felt ashamed of my own self-centered pursuits. Of course, I had my reasons: I was the breadwinner in the family, I was too tired, too busy, I had too many papers to grade, too many chores with the children. . . . But the shame remained, scraping against my conscience like a frozen branch against a window.

Once I talked to Kay about this issue. She looked at me with her peaceful grey eyes, and smiled, revealing perfect rows of pearly teeth. "You do what you can do, Shelly. You can't very well drop your children and your livelihood and go to Africa, can you?" Her laughter tinkled. "You are still unsettled, you still need to support yourself. How could you serve others?"

"Still, what you do is beautiful, really."

"We did it because we could," Kay said. "Our three children are grown. But you can do different things, small things in your own immediate environment, for example, you can put these seeds in the bird-feeder outside the kitchen window and watch the birds flock down to eat." She laughed heartily.

I did as I was told. Immediately, sparrows swooped on the seeds, burrowed in them and took off, spraying seeds in all directions. Then the chickadee approached with his husky *chickadee-dee-dee-dee*. "Look at his black cap and black tie," Kay whispered in my ear, "isn't he quite the gentleman?" Word about the food spread quickly. A bright red flashed before our eyes. "Look at this cardinal," Kay pointed, "he loves feeders, and I bet he'll push the chickadee away." The cardinal walked confidently onto the square board, picking grains at his leisure, flicking his proud crest back and forth. The chickadee took a few grains for the road, muttered *dee-dee* under his beak and flew away. More sparrows whirred around, the goldfinch with its black cap descended, and finally the meadowlark, with the bright yellow neck, also joined the chirping company. "Look at the black V on his neck," Kay noted, "quite unusual.

The meadowlark, you know, is the state bird of Kansas, but he doesn't often come to feeders in the valley. Must be in your honor," she smiled.

I've always loved the house on Kitten Creek Road. Situated a mile from the main road, surrounded to its east and south by oaks, cottonwoods, red-buds, hackberries, and undergrowth of prickly ash and Virginia creepers, and to its northwest by hills of grazing land, ensconsed in the silence that enables birds, crickets, and squirrels to make themselves heard, the house is a genuine Lincoln style log cabin built by Charles, Kay, and their sons Jonathan, Tim, and Nat. The logs, shipped from Wisconsin, date from 1860, and into some of them are hammered the square nails typical of the 1800s. Perched on a hill's rib, rising three stories high, the log cabin contains ten spacious rooms, a huge living room, a porch that looks directly at a redbud and behind it at a thick woods; scattered everywhere in the house are cozy, intimate corners. Instead of the usual painted walls, the brown logs, held together by cement chinking, radiate warmth and remind one of country life and of the long vanished pio-neering days. In the front of the living room, there is a fireplace, where wood is blazing on cold winter days, and above it an air-conditioner, humming busily in the summers to alleviate the blistering Kansas heat. The back of the living room, flanked on three sides by large windows overlooking the woods, functions as a dining room, with a large table standing in its middle. On the wall, a statement is inscribed in fine hand on a piece of wood. "The builder of a house has greater honor than the house itself" (Hebrews, 3:3).

"We built such a big house," Kay explained, "so that people could come and stay." Indeed, they have come in droves—family, friends, international students, and all those in need of comfort and advice. The children and I were also among the most regular guests. Charles could hold Shir and Livi's inter-est for hours with stories, walks, and games, while Kay and I plunged into seri-ous conversations about Israel, Ethiopia, English, past and present experiences, the beauty of nature, children, and God. Our friendship deepened. Countless times I'd rush to Kay in turmoil and leave her house with a pacified and enlightened heart. We celebrated holidays and partook in feasts and in nature hikes. We learned from each other. There, I thought, I have found a soul mate, a surrogate mother. Serene, sweet, and high-minded, she is my mother's oppo-site. Perfect in all ways. Except for one thing. She is a devout fundamentalist Christian.

My earthly Eden, my regenerated Tivon was thoroughly Christian. Kay and Charles talked about Christ as if he were an intimate family member or friend, who just happened to be in another town, but phoned every day, and was eagerly anticipated. On Christmas and Easter, certainly, but even on any ordinary day of the week, a visitor could not linger more than an hour in the log cabin without sensing Jesus' presence. Before meals, Kay and Charles prayed to him; in times of stress, they pleaded for his help; on their daily trips to the top of the hill to watch the sunset, they thanked him for giving them not only their daily bread, but also this spectacular performance in the sky, "free of charge," as Kay liked to point out, "and different each day." Mostly they read about him in their heavily marked Bibles, crisscrossed with references to the Old and the New Testaments.

So what is it to me? I used to think. Live and let live. Their sweetness is worth ten, twenty prayers a day, what do I care? But slowly, I began to feel the subtle pressure to join the believers, to "complete" the Jew in me. "Pray to Him," Kay would tell me. "Ask Him to take your burden. Didn't He say 'Come to me, all you who are weary and burdened, and I will give you rest?'" It was as simple as a knock on a door. "All you need to do," Kay's grey eyes filled with liquid light, "is believe in Him. Believe He is who He says He is— the son of God, our divine rescuer!"

How could my dear wise friend, I wondered, present me with such an outrageous proposition? Didn't she know that I was a Jew, that to me the cross signified centuries of persecution? "No, Kay," I'd say politely, "thank you but I'm fine. I've always been Jewish and intend to remain Jewish."

"But so was He," Kay would laugh. "So was He, our Lord, Jewish. A good Jew, who fulfilled the biblical prophecies. The two covenants are interdependent; the old nurtures and prepares for the new that completes the old."

"But why do I have to be completed?" I'd ask. "Why am I not good enough as a Jew?"

"Because it is only through Christ, who sacrificed His life to atone for our sins, that we can be redeemed," Kay would say with sweet seriousness.

"But I can't forget how the church persecuted Jews."

"Must we always be the slaves of history?" Kay would raise her eyebrows. "Can't we rise above it to the truth? Didn't Paul say, in Galatians 3:28, 'There is neither Jew nor Greek, slave nor free, male nor female, for you are all one in Christ Jesus'? He didn't reject the Jews."

And so we went at it, Kay, Charles, and I, as the Jews must have debated the Christians in medieval Europe. Never before did I have to think so hard about my Jewishness, never before at such a disadvantage, facing opponents who knew the Bible by heart, never before with my dearest friends. Whenever I saw them taking their Bibles out on the table, the questions that lay like coiled springs in my mind unwound. If I reject Christ, would they still be my friends? And what if I became convinced that Christ was real? Hadn't I been tempted by Christianity before? In Israel, being a Jew was as natural as breathing. But here, in the land of the free, why do I choose to be a Jew?

THE DAY OF ATONEMENT

When Kay, one year, expressed the wish to celebrate Yom Kippur with me and to fast, I was delighted and touched. My friends at the Reform temple on Wreath Street were surprised by the appearance of my Christian friend, who participated in all of the details of the service. With Kay by my side, asking me questions about the ritual and the prayers, the holiday became more poignant and the fast—more bearable. At the end of Yom Kippur, when the shofar sounded, Kay and I broke bread together and traveled to Kitten Creek Road for dinner with Charles.

Kay's dishes have always been delicious, but after the fast, they were rapturous. The baked chicken, the cranberry sauce, and the seven-layered salad, which Kay had prepared before the fast, tasted like a heavenly repast. "A big day, isn't it, Yom Kippur," Charles said as soon as Kay and I revived our spirits. "What does it mean to you, Shelly?"

"Oh," I swallowed a spoonful of peas, carrots, and cheese, "it's the one day in which I am part of the Jewish community everywhere—in Israel, New York, London, and even Australia. On this day, as I pray and fast, I think of them. On this one day, I belong to all of them, as well as to Jews who are long gone."

"Hmm, that's interesting," Charles stretched his back to a sprawling position on the chair. "Is there anything else you like about this day?" Livi, sensing that we were about to embark on a serious discussion, ran to the chair by the fireplace, where she left her furry rabbit, Edward, and brought it to Charles. "Look who's here, Edward!" Charles made a long, funny face. "I was wondering how he was doing, our friend here, and whether he is still ambulatory, ha-ha . . ." Livi beamed with pleasure. Kay was bringing out the dessert. "Do we have some lettuce for this guy here, Kay?" Charles asked. Livi was giggling. Kay was laughing. Only Shir, disdainful of both furry animals and adult discussions, was looking for something to do. Kay took out the checkers board and set it out for him and for Charles. Livi complained, but Charles was good enough for both kids, and, with his hearing aid, could even respond to their mother.

"No, that's not all," I resumed. "It is the most important day because it is the Day of Atonement." Charles nodded as he was gobbling up a whole row of Shir's checkers. "A day of reckoning," I continued. "That's why it's important." I bit into the strawberry shortcake.

Charles nodded while patting Livi's head. "And God?" he smiled.

"I don't know what to say about him," I laughed nervously, "or her. . . ." I added inaudibly.

"But aren't we fortunate," Kay said, "that Jesus had already offered us forgiveness through His own blood, once and for all, and that we don't have to ask for it every year, on a certain date?"

I stood my ground. "Jews don't believe in vicarious atonement," I said, feeling my throat grow stiff. "Each one of us must atone for his or her own sins."

"Yes, but our efforts couldn't get us anywhere without Christ," Kay laughed and Charles, still with one hand playing checkers with Shir, nodded and smiled. "We are sinners, Shelly, all the way down from Adam." The coffeemaker was gurgling. Kay rose to pour the coffee.

The room felt hot and stuffy. "We are not sinners, Kay, rather we are imperfect," I said. "The enemy is within us, and although it is difficult, we can overcome it. Who's the hero according to Jewish tradition? The one who overcomes the evil inclination. Judaism celebrates moral struggle and growth. That's why I am a Jew." I took a large, hot gulp of coffee.

Kay looked at me with kindness. "But who are we, sinners, to win this struggle without Jesus' help?"

My ears were beginning to burn. "But, Kay, I cannot consider myself a wretched and passive sinner who can do nothing for herself without Christ's intercession! Maimonides said that each one of us is given free will, which means that we have the power to choose between good and evil. We're responsible for our own behavior. God forgives," I ventured; "we don't need Jesus."

Charles began to laugh and soon his whole frame was shaking with good-natured glee. "If I had to stand before God's judgment," he said, "I'd be cre-e-e-mated, in one second. Who am I? A sinner, like the worst of them. I can work on myself day and night, but without Jesus, there is no hope for me."

"You?" I gaped. "No, I don't understand this. You? A sinner? And you, too, Kay? You are a sinner, too?"

"Yes, of course," Kay answered gently. "Just like Adam."

"No," I rose from my chair in excitement. "I don't understand this at all. If you are sinners, then we are all lost forever!" My face was hot. "How can you consider yourselves sinners? Is there no difference between you and a thief, or a murderer?"

"Not really," Kay laughed, while her hands were smoothing the table-cloth. "If we are different in our actions from others, our thoughts are as sinful. The Lord has said that lust in the mind equals adultery."

"Can we go home, Mom?" Shir interjected, fearing that my anger would fly out of control. "I am bored, I am bored," he repeated when he didn't get an answer. "I want to go home!"

"Just a minute, Shir," I said impatiently. "Thoughts are not the same as actions. We can't control our thoughts, but we can control our actions. If we are to be punished for every thought," I added, "we'd be living in KGB land, with Big Brother and Thought Police." I felt spent. How did such a lovely day with Kay, who fasted with me, turn into this hot dispute? "I am sorry I got so worked up," I apologized.

Kay and Charles stretched out their hands. "Let us pray," Kay said. We held hands. "Dear Lord," Kay bowed her head, "thank you for Yom Kippur and for the opportunities You give us to seek You out. Thank you also for Shelly, for her Jewishness, and for the fast we shared in your name. Thank you also for Shir and Livi ['and for Edward,' Charles added] and may your gentle spirit be with us. In the name of Jesus. Amen."

THE WEDDING

I rejected Christ, and yet I could not resist the power of my friends' prayers. Every prayer with Kay and Charles seemed to wrap my soul in silk. It offered a direct channel to God. I no longer needed a siddur, a synagogue, or a rabbi to pray. I could be the author of my own prayers. Under the guidance of Kay, the sky opened up, and there was no end to what I could ask of God.

When Kay asked me whom I was praying to, I said God but declined to define him more precisely. Kay would explain the importance of knowing the nature and the purpose of God, but I resisted that line of inquiry. When the house on Kitten Creek, with its rarefied wholesomeness, became too heady for me, I'd escape to my Jewish or feminists friends, grateful for the familiar, solid ground under my feet. Yet I'd always be drawn back to Kay's spiritual reality. Sometimes I wished I could just forget my Jewish defiance and become a genuine member of the radiant Christian community. My conflict came to a head during the wedding of Kay's son Tim, to Cathy, in November 1987.

That was my second year as an assistant professor (nontenure-track) at the University of Kansas (KU) in Lawrence, Kansas. The three years at KU were my best professional years. My long training period at Kansas State University bore fruit. At KU, my teaching, in all its subjects, was at its most creative and successful, and my student evaluations soared in enthusiasm. Some of them astonished me. "Dr. Regenbaum has been by far *the best* English teacher I have ever had at the university. She was encouraging, enlightening, helped us to strive for new and more profound ideas." How about that? I mumbled to myself, hardly knowing, after so many years of struggle, what to do with such acclaim. Another student recommended "a raise" for me, and another vowed to "encourage anyone" to take a course from me. Still another thankfully pointed out that my criticism "was constructive, so I did not feel stupid when I got a paper back. . . ." But the student I was most grateful for was the one who wrote that "Professor Regenbaum has a vibrant and energetic love for the English language." My boss, Professor Peter Casagrande, awarded me with the generous recognition I'd been seeking for many years. My students, he said in a letter "were not just instructed" by me, they were *"inspired"* by my teaching and my example. "This is," he claimed, "outstanding, exemplary, work." There, I thought, as I was walking in the hall of Wescoe a few inches off the ground. At last, I repeated over and over, after so many years, ah! such sweet recognition.

Yet in spite of my professional success, I was often burdened by dread anticipation of a move out of Kansas. I was also oppressed by the loneliness that followed the end of the affair with my younger lover, John. The intense hours of happiness that his marriage proposal (which I ultimately rejected) effected revealed to me, as lightning illumines a dark landscape, the full expanse of my yearning. I was tired of my solitary life. I didn't want to marry John; I wanted to marry the right man, a Jew who could be both a lover and a soul mate, but I knew that I couldn't find him in Kansas. I could meet Jews on the East or the West Coast, I was told, but how did I know where my new job would take me to? I could end up in a small, midwestern town, like Lawrence. What then? My loneliness would never end. It was at that time, in November 1987, that the preparations for Tim's marriage reached their final stage.

The wound of the separation from John was still fresh, and the more Kay talked about Tim's forthcoming marriage, the sadder I became. I was galled by their happiness and felt the familiar terrible longing to fling myself into their loving, Christian, arms and stay there forever, forgetting who I was and where I came from. If I could just forget that, perhaps I could find a Christian mate and end my loneliness.

With Kay and my children Shir (right) and Livi (left). Lawrence, Kansas, 1986

The wedding was to take place in the Episcopal Church in Lawrence. Kay and Charles planned to come to town in the evening and meet me at the church before the beginning of the ceremony. It was a cold November night. Strong winds were racing through the deserted streets of Lawrence, jostling tops of trees and shaking their limbs. The children and I showered and put on our best clothes. Yet when it was time to go, I couldn't leave the house. I puttered around, doing this and that, having one more coffee, one half cigarette. The children watched TV. The hour was getting late, and then very late, but I still couldn't bring myself to go. I looked outside the window and saw the naked tree branches casting quivering shadows across the street; the whole town, it seemed, was being visited by a troop of jittery ghosts. This is not a night for going out, I thought. Perhaps I can skip the wedding. Just stay home. Who would miss me? Anyway, I'd just be crying my eyes out. . . .

At that moment, the phone rang. Kay was on the line, worried. Had something happened to me? No, I answered coldly. "Please come to the wedding," she pleaded with me. I relented. We put our coats on and left the house.

When we arrived at the church, the ceremony was well on its way. The door was open, and we stood watching. The small church, with its tall graceful arches and stained-glass windows, looked festive. The guests were sitting in rows, listening spellbound to the service, emitting, every now and then, a sob or a sniffle. The bride and the groom stood motionless in the center of the stage, facing the priest. From time to time, the organ chords chimed, and as the air vibrated with their last note, the silence resurged, buoyant with adoration. I have never seen anything as lovely as this, I thought, my heart aching. The bride and the groom were singing the "servant" song, and some of the congregants were humming along with them. I gazed at the bride's long white veil, put my hands on the children's shoulders, took a deep breath, and prepared to walk in.

At that instant, the Eucharist service began. One by one, first the bride and the groom, and then the guests, approached the priest to receive communion. I stopped dead in my tracks. "What's the matter, Mom?" Livi asked, but I could not speak. I was struck by dread, as if an angel with a flaming sword was barring my entrance to the church. No, not the Eucharist. If I step inside now I'd be tempted to take it, with the people I love, and then I'd be lost forever. I stood at the door, listening to the wind howling outside. Soon, the service ended, and the bride and the groom walked out. Through my tears, I could see their beaming faces swimming toward me. They stopped and smiled. "Glad you came, Shelly," but I couldn't even raise my eyes to them. Embarrassed, they walked past me, and I remained standing on the front steps of the church, a forlorn, itinerant Jew.

KAY

As soon as everybody left the church for the wedding reception, I was able to join the celebration. The children and I ate, drank, and wished the newlyweds happiness. When we went home late that night, I thought that the painful part of the event was well behind me. I didn't even know how deeply I had wounded Kay.

Two weeks later, on a visit to Manhattan, Kay invited me for lunch. She'd prepared my favorite dishes, corn chowder and tuna salad, put an end table and two chairs near the fire, and asked me to sit down to eat. It was a cold, sunny December day. A shaft of light from the window landed in a bright square on the table between us. Kay said grace, and we ate, chatting about our lives. When we finished, Kay's kind eyes rested on my face. "Do you mind, Shelly, if we talk about Tim's wedding?" she asked.

"No," I said, unsuspecting. "Go ahead."

"You know, that night you hurt me so," her eyes filled up with tears, "that I didn't rightly know what to do with myself. Had I insulted you in some way?"

I was shocked. "I don't know what you are talking about, Kay," I muttered. "When? How did I do that?"

Kay smiled at me. "You remember when I called you from church, just before the wedding?"

"Yes," I nodded.

"It was such a strange exchange, you know," she sighed. "You talked to me with extreme coldness as if you wanted me dismissed from your life, as if I were your enemy. I was so upset I don't know how I managed to get through the picture-taking session. Since then I have been searching my soul to see if I had done you some wrong."

"No, no," I said with remorse, "you have done me no wrong, Kay. It is I who need to do the soul-searching," I exclaimed, remembering now the conversation and my ugly mood.

"But why were you so angry with me? Why didn't you come into the church?"

I gazed at the motes of dust moving up and down the shaft of light. "Kay," I started, chagrined, "I was overwhelmed by grief. I knew that if I'd walked into the church to witness the joyful ceremony, I'd sob right through it."

"But you know, Shelly, people often shed tears at weddings. Nobody would have minded."

She was right, I knew. But how could I tell her that I was tempted to take the Eucharist and lose myself in her world, the world that two thousand years of Jewish history, and eight generations of Israeli history, forbade me even to contemplate? But there was one thing I could say. "Please, forgive me, Kay. I was so wrapped up in self-pity and so envious of your happiness that I struck out at you, as if it were your fault."

Kay smiled. "Thank you, Shelly. Of course I forgive you. I am so glad we talked," she sighed with relief, gave me a warm hug, and went to the kitchen to make us another cup of coffee.

That evening I drove back to Lawrence uplifted. What would I have done, I thought, if I were unjustly insulted by a friend? Would I have waited patiently for two weeks, then invited my friend for her favorite meal, and then confronted her in an honest and loving manner? Oh, I admitted, I have much to learn.

IMMA

How many mothers does a woman need to save her from her own mother? I had them all, and then some. But they could not protect me from the confrontation with my mother in 1987 that left me anxious for months, prey to nightmares and daily jitters. And yet, it was as vital as it was inevitable, the kind of cathartic confrontation that could pave the way to our modest reconciliation.

When we visited Israel in 1983, I realized that inasmuch as my three years in America might have changed me, they hardly changed my mother. Disregarding my earlier rebellions, my mother took charge of the children. At first, I didn't mind. After all, Israel was now her territory and we were her guests. Besides, I was on vacation. I wanted to rest and see the country. Let her have them! Yet after the first two weeks, I fought to get my children back. But I lost; my resistance was short-lived. My diary for our 1983 and our 1985 visits refers to our squabbles, but it hardly explains my passivity. Mostly, it describes, sometimes with a dose of sentimentality, the good times we shared. What truth was I trying to cover up, even from myself?

It was one thing, though, to let my mother take charge of my children in Israel but quite another to let her control them in America. Kansas was my territory, and she was my guest. Not according to my mother. She was never a guest, and every place was her place. Each of her visits started pleasantly enough, spiraled into bickering and feuds, and ended in a truce that spelled out, "Thank God it's over." Occasionally, when I opposed her, she'd present me with an ultimatum. "If you don't let me do it my way, I am leaving tomorrow morning." In Jerusalem, after Kenneth's death, I let her do that, but in America, I backed down, time after time, and asked her to stay. Why? I didn't really know. There were many reasons, I told myself. The children needed her, and I needed rest from the children. Furthermore, on each of her visits, my mother would buy new clothes for the three of us, which we badly needed. And what's more, the money wasn't just money; as Edna pointed out to me, it was only through her gifts that my mother could show her love. Knowing that, how could I reject them? Still, I rarely admitted the truest reason for my submission—my raw fear of my mother, still alive after all those years.

When I moved to Lawrence, in 1986, tensions between us escalated. My mother didn't like Lawrence. Perhaps she felt lonelier there than in Manhattan, where she had the Fedders. Perhaps she worried about my ability to get a job elsewhere, after my three-year contract with KU expired. Who'd be responsible for the children, she'd ask me, if I don't get a tenure-track position? My career, she'd say, was somewhere in the sky, as far as she could see. Did I ever think of *them?* If I stayed in Israel, none of this would have happened, of course.

It was during her first Lawrence visit that my mother's verbal assaults on Livi started. Livi was growing. She was about ten at the time, with a mind of her own, and with fears galore—of bugs, of the night, and of unfamiliar men. "What normal girl," my mother would complain, "is afraid of so many things?" Once, when we were drinking coffee in the kitchen, my mother, like a conspirator, informed me of my daughter's strange nightly behavior. "Do you know what your daughter does at night?" She stopped for effect and looked at me. I sipped my coffee. "You don't know, do you, because your head is in your books. But *I* know because I've seen her do it."

By now, she got me where she wanted me. "What does she do already?"

"She goes down to Shir's room, with her little blanket and her furry rabbit," her blue eyes turned bluer, "and sleeps on the floor. At dawn she goes back to her bed. Now don't tell me you don't think this is *very* strange behavior."

"Does she wake Shir up?" I asked.

My mother shook her head, "No, she doesn't. She knows Shir would throw her out of his room."

I put my empty cup in the sink, "So what are you making such a fuss about? Let her sleep on the floor."

My mother glowered at me, her face glistening with greasy facial creams. "You just let her do anything she wants, don't you? Anything! No discipline, no rules, she's the queen over here!"

Somehow, I thought, this crazy tirade would just stop on its own one day. Surely, my mother would run out of steam. But she never did. From my room upstairs, I used to hear her castigations coming down, like blows, on Livi's head. "Can you tell me, Livi, why you got only C on your English paper? Your mother is an English professor, and you get Cs in English? Your brother gets As, and you get Cs? Can you tell me why?"

"Leave me alone," Livi hollered. But my mother, continuing her ironing, couldn't stop. "Leave me alone," she mimicked Livi, "that's all you want." Thank God, I thought, secure in my upstairs room, she is leaving *me* alone. "If I left you alone, you'd go to school with egg on your face and spots on your dress. If I left you alone, you wouldn't have a single new pair of shoes to wear. If I left you alone. . . ." the hot iron came down, thud, on Shir's shirt. I put my hands on my ears. "Who would pay attention to you? Who'd want to be your friend?" the steam iron was hissing, sss, tst-tst. "Shir is so popular.

And you? You sit at home all day because nobody wants to be your friend," tst-tst. Livi was weeping. "Crying, are you? Why don't you run to your mother to tell her on me? Go on, tell her what a bad *savta* you have, *savta* that just yesterday took you to the skating rink and bought you three new dresses at K-Mart."

Livi rushed upstairs to my arms. It was then that I fell through the black hole to my childhood terrors.

SHOWDOWN

I had known many anxieties, but the orphanage anxiety was the worst. It settled inside me, like a pale, quaking ghost, after my mother returned to Israel in 1986 and accompanied me everywhere. Simple, familiar things—traffic, shops, classes, the evening hours—made me tremble. I read stories about madness and death. I lived in darkness. Only with a supreme effort of the will did I continue teaching and taking care of my children.

At that time I was visited by a recurrent nightmare. I was standing in front of our Haifa villa, on the slippery stone steps, under a pine tree. Although I could still see the pine-needles throughout the dream, the scenery was suddenly transformed. I was now standing in a military camp, which was surrounded by an electric fence and swept periodically by searchlights. Somewhere in the distance, fierce dogs were barking. I cowered in fear and found my mother squatting next to me. "Where are we?" I asked her. "Where do you think?" she laughed sardonically, "in a concentration camp." I was seized by terror. "Why are we here?" I asked. "I don't know," she shrugged. "But I want to go back to America," I whispered, confident that she would be able to help me. She gazed at me with a far-off, glazed look. "No, you can't get out of here. You'd better get used to it." I would wake up breathless and sit bolt upright. Where am I? Looking around, I would see my desk and computer on it, and the rectangular window visible in the grey dawn light. America, I would realize with a flush of relief, I am in America.

Night after night, with clockwork regularity, the dream stalked my sleep in its chilling details. There was the camp, the pine tree, the fence, the dogs, and the guard in Gestapo boots. There was my mother, indifferent and foreboding. And over all there was the breathless hush of doom. Day and night, I was chased by imaginary frights, which even the loving faces of friends could not erase.

Unable to bear the stress, I sought help. Diane, my therapist in Lawrence, disagreed with Edna's assessment of my mother. Whereas Edna believed that only love could account for my mother's yearly visits to America, Diane focused on my mother's cruelty. Although each of the therapists had a piece of the truth, at the time I came to Diane, I needed her help in freeing my anger. It was no time for makeshift reconciliations, but for war.

Yet keeping the flame of my anger alive and controlled was not easy. As always, I talked to my mother on the phone twice a month; as always we made plans for her next visit and shopping expedition. "My mother," I said to Diane, "doesn't even know about my anger. How can it free me of her tyranny and of my nightmares?"

Diane looked straight at me, as if cutting through my defenses to my innermost dread. "You must protect your daughter," she said, "from her assaults. You can let your mother run the house; you can let her shop, clean, and cook. You can even let her yell at you. But you can't let her steamroll your daughter."

So that's what it was, I thought, as my mother's last attack on Livi swam back to memory. Relieved that she'd left me alone, I let her harangue Livi, time after time, while I stayed disengaged in my safe room. Why didn't I think of it before? Why did I, even as I thought of it then, feel the grip of ice around my heart? As if guessing my thoughts, Diane said, "It's not going to be easy."

The approach of my mother's visit in the fall of 1987 filled me with trepidation. For a few months, I'd been priming myself to shield Livi from my mother's wrath. But once I was driving to the airport to meet her, all evidence to the existence of my resolve vanished. Oh, please, I was pleading, why do I have to do this? It was a fine fall day; the sky was a sparkling blue canvas, touched here and there by light feathery clouds. And out of this benevolent sky, I was thinking, my mother will drop in an hour, knowing nothing, suspecting nothing of my seditious plans. I sighed as I took the 435 North exit. But after all, I am glad she is coming—no cooking, no shopping, no chauffering the children for a month!

This time, though, the celebration was over in a week. My mother could no more tolerate Livi than she could dirt; her strident voice, like an angry broom, tried to sweep Livi away. My orphanage anxiety, which therapy had almost wiped out, returned. In the mornings, it tasted like lead in my mouth. When my mother drove me to KU, and took the car for errands, my throat felt as tight and narrow as a reed, and I wondered how any words could come out of it. My panic reached its apex before the grammar class, my weakest subject then; I imagined my mother sitting in class, among or behind the other students, waiting for me to make my first mistake. At times, my beset mind metamorphosed the whole class into my angry, vengeful mother. Off and on campus, I could find no rest from her.

One day, my mother picked me up from campus. Before I entered the car, I knew that trouble was brewing, for her face was puffed and red with anger. "I tell you, Shelly," she started, "your daughter will be the death of me." Somewhere in the center of my head, the bleakest of all depressions stirred, pouring black ink into my bloodstream. Everything turned black and worthless, my life, my family, my struggles. "I picked her up from school at two today, as usual," my mother's sunglasses pivoted right and left. *"Shulem,* the child is crying. 'What is the matter, Livi'le?' I ask her nicely. 'I can't tell you,' she says. 'Why can't you tell me, Livi'le, I'm your grandmother. Is it a bad grade?' She shakes her head, no. 'Did you dirty your pants?' No. 'So what is it?' Finally, she says that the boy who always plays basketball with her pushed her to the ground. 'So?' I say, 'So? What happened? For this you cry? Get up and push him back.' Am I not right, Shelly? So Livi starts screaming, 'I hate you, *savta,* I hate you.' You have always hated me, and now she hates me. That's the thanks I get."

"She was just angry with you. She'll get over it."

"No," my mother parked the car in our driveway. "She hates me? After all I've done for her? I'll show her."

When we opened the door, we saw Livi's coat, backpack, and shoes strewn all over the living room and the stairs. "Livi?" my mother's voice cracked. "Livi? Come down here right away!"

After a few minutes, Livi's door opened quietly. With tear-stained cheeks, she appeared at the top of the stairs. "What do you want from me, *savta?"* she whimpered.

"Come down here right this minute," my mother said, "and pick up your stuff, you little monster."

It was at that moment that the roaring in my head stopped. I turned to my mother. "Leave her alone," I ordered her.

"What are you saying?" my mother's eyelids fluttered. "What did you just say?"

"I told you," I repeated firmly, "to stop haranguing Livi. I will not let you abuse her anymore."

My mother recovered her posture. "You will not let me? Really? Since when do I have to ask your permission what to do or not to do? *You* will not let me. You will teach me how to talk to my granddaughter! Really!"

"Exactly," I said, astonished at the calm that steadied my speech and my nerves.

"No way!" she spewed, "I will *never* take instructions from you. You will *not* teach me how to behave. Look, Shelly," her finger was stabbing the air, "either you take me as I am, or leave me. I told you that a hundred times. I am too old to change. You don't want me? Fine. I'll leave tomorrow."

"Suit yourself," I said.

"Where will you go, *savta?*" Shir protested. "I don't want you to go. Please stay."

"I don't want to go away from you, Shir," my mother looked in my direction, "but your mother is making me go. Talk to her, not to me. She is throwing me out of the house. Tomorrow I'll stay with a friend in New York, and in a week I'll go back to Israel."

Shir turned to me. "Why are you throwing *savta* out of the house?"

"I am not throwing her out, Shir," I said, feeling the anxiety surging back, "she refuses to be nice to Livi. I have no choice."

"I hate you, Mom, I hate you," Shir heaved a forlorn cry and ran to his room.

"Aren't you ashamed," my mother looked accusingly at me, "of what you are doing to your boy?"

It was a terrible moment. I wanted to take everything back, but instead I heard myself saying, "I am ashamed I didn't do it long ago, *Imma.* "

"Fine, fine," she intoned. "I understand you very well. Tomorrow I'll stay here for Shir. I don't want to break his heart. But the day after tomorrow, I am leaving."

"Very well," I replied.

For a whole year, I refused to talk to my mother. For a whole year, my anger blazed, consuming my terrors and my bondage. My mother was stunned. I had never done anything like this before. At first she responded with sullen silence, but later she began to talk to Shir on the phone. Gradually, he became our mediator, delivering from her to me an olive branch—not an apology, perish the thought, but a request to let her come to prepare Shir's *bar mitzvah*. By then, my anger was well spent, my point well made, and I welcomed her return.

A new phase in our relationship began. Our fights, of course, continued, and Livi was still their chief target. But in my mind, *Imma* could no longer scare me dead and send me back to the orphanage. Several times she threatened to leave, and several times I let her do that. Since she always came back, I realized that I was no longer her victim. I, too, had a say in the relationship and I, too, could make choices.

Gradually, my nightmares subsided and then vanished altogether. Once, in a dream, my mother came to me, serene and peaceful. "I bought you a house in Jerusalem," she said, "and I want you to see it." We traveled to Jerusalem together and climbed one of its highest hills. There stood the house, unfinished. Its foundations were in place, but its walls were only as high as my waist. Winds from the four corners of the earth ruffled my hair. "It's unfinished," I remarked. "You can finish it," my mother smiled and turned away. Then I looked around me, and the view of Jerusalem from my house was of such ineffable sweetness that I woke up weeping.

chapter six

ISRAEL, AGAIN

I n 1989 I moved to Springfield, Massachusetts, to begin my career as a tenure-track assistant professor. My first two years there were miserable. I found its climate cold, its people often unfriendly, its academic and educational standards low. Memories of the golden professional period at the University of Kansas deepened my sense of desolation in the new place, which was marked, I felt, by mediocrity of learning and by the existence of a new concept of students as "customers" who were entitled to purchase not only a good education, but also good grades, regardless, at times, of the level of their achievements. The new academic climate of student coddling, the load of eight courses per year, and the heavy freight of paper grading oppressed my spirit. Is this all there is to it? Is this the tenure-track glory I've pursued for years, the America I left my country for? Lady Liberty gazed at me from under my desk glass cover with a rueful smile. It was during that period that I experienced, for the first time, the pain of being bereft of Israel. When the Israeli writer Amos Oz visited Western New England College in the fall of 1990, the floodgates of longing for my country burst open.

The news of Oz's visit made spirits flutter. I too was excited. He and I were from the same country and spoke the same language. Moreover, I actually knew him. Twenty-seven years before, he and I had taken Shaked's seminar. True, he was the star, but we breathed the same air. I wondered if he would remember me, and as I mused about it, my excitement was checked by worry. What if he remembered me as Haya? Wouldn't he ponder where the name Shelly came from? He would know that such a name couldn't have been mine from birth. How many Hebrew *Shellys* existed when I was born? What would

I say if he asked me embarrassing questions about my name in front of my colleagues? I fretted for days. Yet, to my relief, Oz was gracious, asked no questions, and treated my name as if it were naturally mine, by birthright. I was grateful.

When I heard Oz's address to the college, I felt, for the first time in many years, proud to be an Israeli. This man, who held the audience in rapt attention, was my compatriot. And here he was, talking to us about the struggles of a small, besieged nation facing daily threats to its survival and lifting us from the aimless mediocrity of our daily existence to higher planes of commitment and excellence. All at once, my bitter memories of Israel disappeared, as if by magic, and were replaced by glowing images of Lake Kinneret, Jerusalem, and the desert. What was the value of my life in a small college in Springfield, I wondered, trying to teach "customers" how to construct an English sentence? How did I fit in? Forgetting my painful alienation in my homeland, I felt certain, in a mixture of exhilaration and dread, that only in Israel could my life be meaningful.

After his lecture, my friends and I took Oz for a drink in a bar and listened to his stories. At one point, he declaimed the Hebrew translation of Poe's "The Raven." As he was reciting the poem by rote, to the eager amazement of my friends, I listened to it as to a haunting and forgotten music I had been trying to recall for years. Hebrew! How lovely it sounded in my ears! Coming out of Oz's mouth, Hebrew wasn't harsh or grating, but the racy and noble language I loved in my dreamy adolescence and early student days—the language of my young literary passions. How far I had strayed from it! Where had it been? How did I lose it?

Before our group dispersed, Oz put his arm on my shoulder and asked, "Are you homesick?" For a long moment, I stood motionless. "Yes, I am homesick," I admitted, as if I had just realized it. "Would you like me," he asked, "to find out in Ben-Gurion University if they have a position in English?" I was tossed in the air by a whirlwind. Exhilarated, I saw myself teaching Israeli students hungry for knowledge, living in the desert town, among my people, a life of Zionist passion. There was my opportunity. What? Leave America behind? How could I, after struggling for years to make a place for myself here, suddenly succumb to the strange sweetness of such a vision? How could I think of moving to the desert town of Beersheba with my teenage kids, who would flatly refuse to hear of it? And why? For history?

Long after Oz returned to Israel, my longing for my country persisted. Everyday I played the music of Shlomo Bar, my favorite Israeli singer. I listened to all the news reports, read all the magazine stories on Israel; on the wall of my study, I plastered pictures of our Haifa villa; next to the small American flag growing in a vase on my desk, I planted an Israeli flag; I asked my mother to send me the literary supplements of the Hebrew papers; I joined a Tikkun discussion group in Boston to talk about Israel; and I read and reread Oz's books. But the ache, as I wrote in a long letter to my friend Kirk in Kansas, didn't let up. "As I read Oz," I explained to him, "I am stunned by the energy on the page: words, shimmering and crisp, crowd the white space in ferocious harmony. And more of them congregate on every page, in new formations. I hear the words and the music rising from them. At first, it is a simple song, in colloquial Hebrew, a conversation on a street corner, in a café perhaps. Then I hear other tunes—lyrical, formal, biblical—amplifying each other, gathering to a powerful symphony. Soon I hear all the voices of Israel—the ancient and the new, the intimate and the harsh, the voices of people in the battlefield and in the wheat fields, in the city and in the kibbutz, voices of those tormented by lust, or by hate, voices of those who long to leave and those who long to arrive, voices of husbands and lovers, visionaries, wanderers, and madmen, voices of those who build, those who laugh, and those who kill. And then my longing breaks loose. Everything I lost is in his books—my Israel and my Hebrew! Help! What do I do, Kirk?"

He called me. "Perhaps from a distance, or in his books," he quipped, "Israel looks attractive, but do you remember how upset with it you used to be?"

"Yes, I do," I agreed. "It's madness, I know, and I must overcome it."

I called Richard, my best friend at the college. "What do I do with this crazy, irresponsible longing for Israel?" I asked him.

"Well," Richard chuckled, "why don't you write him a letter?"

"A letter? To Oz? About what?" I asked, startled.

"I don't know," Richard pondered my questions. "You can tell him how much you appreciated his visit, or you might even send him your story 'Anniversary in Jerusalem.' See what he says about it. How about that?"

"Yes," I said in sudden joy, "yes, I will write. What a great idea!"

I sent Oz a letter and enclosed my story. He sent me a friendly letter back with a favorable response to my writing. I sent him another letter in which I inserted one paragraph on the orphanage in Pardes-Hannah—to see what would happen. Oz's response was sympathetic, compassionate. How wonderful, I thought. The first Israeli to greet the orphan. My own parents ran away from her, but Oz, the famous writer whom I barely knew, had prepared a warm reception for her. New feelings awakened in me, an urgent need to tell Oz about Haya and Shelly, how they fought and separated many years before and had only recently begun to talk. The impulse was so strong that I had to force myself to wait a day before I wrote the letter. What was I doing? For years I concealed Haya's identity. Nobody, except my parents and relatives, knew about her. Even my therapists didn't know about her. For years this has been my most protected secret. Just a month ago, I was mortified by the thought that Oz might discover her. And now, of my own free will, I was going to reveal her to him? Why? Because it was time to introduce Haya to the world, I reflected, time to stop hiding her in shame. I can never be called Haya again, but by telling Oz about her, I might be able to redeem her name.

A wondrous correspondence followed. As I needed to tell my story, Oz needed to hear it, for he too was orphaned, as a teenager, by his mother's suicide. Oz never talked about himself, but he drew the orphan's story out of me as if he had a personal stake in it. In each of his letters, he assured me that he was glad that Haya and Shelly had finally met—even if their meeting was a bitter one, because, he said, "I am convinced that they don't cancel each other out. I think," he continued, "that Shelly can now contain Haya . . . because she has a place in the world, and a melody, and a spiritual address. . . ."

Thank you, Amos Oz, I thought, as I began my story about Haya and Shelly, for your bright, bracing words. Several years passed before I could write this book, but it was Oz who first inspired me with the courage and the eagerness to do so.

MARK

The late summer of 1992 was delicious with a sense of accomplishment and promise: I had written a short story and I was making a better adjustment to Massachusetts. Even my mother's visit in August was relatively free of stress, marked here and there by humor and ease.

Sometime in August, my cousin Michal and her husband Uzi, a nephrologist in Ha'sharon Hospital in Israel, came to Providence, Rhode Island, for a medical conference. My mother wanted to spend the day with them and urged me to come with her to Providence. Michal took us on a tour around town. The three of us talked about food and shopping and stopped at the downtown arcade to satisfy both appetites. After lunch, I suggested we visit Brown University.

"Oh," my mother sighed, as we reached the Van Wickle gates. "If you could just teach *here!*" she intoned, "everybody in Israel would die of envy. An Ivy League school. Psss. . . ."

"What big dreams you have, *Imma,*" I said. And then I suddenly remembered. "Wait a minute," I cried out, "stop, stop the car! I have a friend here, Mark Spilka! Do you remember him, *Imma,* the guy with the beard, who looks a bit like Hemingway, my boyfriend for two months in Israel in 1972, just before Reuven died? You don't remember?" I talked excitedly, as I was already getting out of the car, "he's a professor here, in the English department. Park the car somewhere. I must try to find him." My mother was astonished. "A professor *here?* You don't say! Is he married?" but I was already asking a student where the English department was. "Right down the street," she pointed, "the Horace Mann Building, opposite the library; you can't miss it." I walked briskly toward the English department, as memories of our time together flashed vividly before my mind. When I got to the building, the front door was closed for renovations. Men hammered away on scaffoldings, and sounds of drilling machines pierced the air. I followed the signs to the backdoor and walked into a darkened hall. All the doors were closed; the building seemed deserted. I looked for the mailboxes. After awhile, I discovered them, and saw, right in the middle of the middle row, "Mark Spilka." There! He is still here and still alive . . . I searched my pocketbook for a piece of paper but couldn't find any. Outside, my mother was impatiently honking. Well, I thought, ready to walk away, at least I tried. Wait a minute, I stopped; wait just a minute, I'll write him a note on a check! I wrote a friendly note on the back, then turned the check to the front again, and after a short inner debate, scribbled "void" across it. After all, this is an open mailbox—who knows into whose hands it might fall? To this day, Mark loves poking fun at my "void" inscription.

That night Mark called me. Ten days later, he came on the noon bus for a few hours' visit, warning me that he was "older and heavier." But when I saw him at the station, I thought he seemed neither much older nor much heavier than the distinguished-looking gentleman I knew twenty-one years before in Jerusalem. While giving him a welcome hug, I remembered his expressive brown eyes, the kind and whimsical smile that effortlessly spread across his round face, and the beard which, although white now rather than salt-and-pepper was still trim and distinctive.

My mother, who'd returned to Israel, left me instructions for making a marinated chicken sauce. When I brought Mark home from the station, the chicken was baking in the oven and the side dishes were festively laid on the table, which for once, was covered with cloth. The children were out, and the house was wrapped in silence, except for the occasional meowing and scratching of cats' claws on the furniture. As Mark and I sat down to eat, we talked eagerly about our lives since we last met. Is he married? I wondered. As if reading my thoughts, Mark told me that he'd been five years separated from his second wife Ruth. "She was good for me," he admitted with a shy smile, "but apparently I was not good enough for her. She left me for a computer specialist in Boston." How about that, I thought. The "hotshot" from Brown is so unaffected that he does not try to cover up a painful truth, nor does he bad-mouth the woman who left him. Well, I took a juicy bite of the marinated chicken, I really like that. Mark was enjoying his meal, and soon enough his fingers tore at the chicken and swam in the sauce, and before he could wipe them, a few drops fell on his pants. "Delicious meal," he murmured, "thank you. How nice of you to cook for me." I smiled at him, thinking, a messy eater. . . . Then I thought some more, so what? He's oblivious to such trivialities.

After lunch, Mark pulled a picture album out of his bag. "You know what I have here?" he asked. I shook my head. "Pictures of the two us from 1972, when I had the good fortune to spend some lovely time with a cute redhead," his broad smile deepened the creases in his cheeks. "Look at me here," he laughed as he turned the page, "swinging on a high bar on the beach! I couldn't do that today, not after my operations."

"What operations did you have?" I asked, uneasy.

"Oh, a carotid artery reaming in 1985, an aorta aneurysm in 1987, and a quadruple bypass in 1989. I've been paying the wages of my bad eating habits—egg and bacon for breakfast, bagel and lox, you know—but now I am feeling quite good actually for my age."

"Which is?"

"Sixty-seven," he said somewhat proudly.

Sixteen years older than I, I quickly calculated, and with a medical history. Watch out, Shelly. But so what? I brushed the warning aside; Kenneth was young and healthy, and he died anyway. "Look at the two of us here, in the Jerusalem biblical zoo," Mark smiled. "We seemed to be having fun together."

Presently, I suggested that we take a walk down to the nearby pond. It was a mild September day. Mark told me about his life at Brown, and I described to him my tough tenure struggle. By and by, we approached the pond and sat down on a bench to watch the ducks flying on rapid wingbeats before diving into the water.

Not many people visited the pond on that afternoon, but there was one noisy family with kids halfway across the placid water from us. We watched them. The children were running around with the ball, at times disappearing into the woods, and the father was chasing them. They were all giggling and shouting, yet every now and then, the father got angry at the children. We didn't know why, but we clearly saw the punishment he meted out to them. He took his two little girls to the edge of the pond, held each one in turn by the wrists, and plunged them—legs, waists, chests, heads, fully clothed—in the cold, smudgy water. Seeing that, Mark heaved a groan. "What a pissy thing to do," he shook his head. "Those poor kids." For a while, the girls' sobs mingled with the soft quacks of the ducks, but soon the father relented, reached out for a towel, and dried his daughters' hair. The crisis passed, but I was strangely grateful for the glimpse it offered me into Mark's compassionate being.

On the way back, we passed by a run-down house, with a broken window and peeling paint, which carried the sign, Together, A Dating Service. Mark looked at it and laughed. "It doesn't seem to be a very popular place," he said, "glad I don't need their services." We continued our leisurely stroll up the hill. Just before we turned to my house, I dared. "You are not actually divorced from your wife, are you?" I asked.

"No," Mark said, "there was no reason for that hassle, which does not mean," he added, "there won't be one in the future. Who knows?"

"But if you are not divorced," I looked straight at him, "she might come back to you one day."

"No," he said with finality.

It was time to take Mark to the station for his bus to Providence. Before we left the house, I gave him my two stories, and he promised to read them in a week. Yet he did not wait a week. The following night he called. My stories, he said, moved him to tears. *Oi vey,* I thought, the joy, the joy, like a wave sweeping my boat to shore. During the month of October, I was as happy as Shakespeare when he imagined himself a lark at heaven's gate. And even when the trees shed their iridescent red and yellow autumn coats and cold winter winds furrowed the land, and snow lay heavy on the ground and stayed there, frozen, for weeks, even then our love grew into a more perfect bloom. Mark filed for divorce from Ruth and by early summer we were free to marry. And so we did, on the 4th of July, 1993, in Providence's Reform Temple, and invited family, friends, indeed the whole nation to our celebration. Even my father came, with his wife, Rivka, son Shai-Zelig, and daughter Rachel. Not only was this my father's first visit to a Reform temple, it was probably the first time he was treated to a Reform ceremony, where men and women mingled, where poems read by friends replaced many of the traditional prayers, and where the bride and the groom read out loud their personal vows to each other, vows inspired by the biblical story of Noah's renewal after the flood but nowhere to be found in any *siddur* that my father knew. And yet my father bore it all well. Amiable and eager to help, he exhibited true grace under Reform pressure. He was even delighted to speak to my mother (who was much happier with this wedding than with my wedding to Kenneth) and to stand with her briefly under the *huppah*. Before he departed, he attached to the doorpost of our house an authentic *mezuzah,* written by a traditional scribe. No wonder our house has since been blessed with love and happiness.

ONE FOR NOW, ONE FOR LATER

Mark and I often talked about our first meeting in Israel, twenty-one years before, and put our heads together to figure out what happened then to break us apart. At first, each one of us most clearly remembered the tragic flaw of the other. I remembered how conceited Mark was. After all, he was "king of the castle," and I was just a graduate student. It is true that my mind then was unenlightened, but did he try to educate it? No. He was playfully gliding on the edge of our relationship, kind and courteous, but uninvolved.

Mark remembered that he could not understand my admiration for William Golding, especially his novel *The Spire,* and concluded that my literary tastes were sentimental. However most troubling then to Mark had been an event that I had erased from memory. Once I threw an incomprehensibly jealous fit about a woman he parted from long before; Mark became scared. What would I be up to next? he thought. Of course, I was merely imitating my mother's jealous blowups (effective with her men), but how could Mark have known that? In the future I was destined to change, but how could he have guessed that?

Recognizing our shortcomings, we admitted our own share in the blame and reached the wise and humble consensus that we both had to grow up. In 1972 we were simply not ready for each other.

In our pictures from that period I see Mark in the artists' colony in Jaffa, looking guardedly at me, wearing his straw hat. In another picture, he is showing off, doing chin-ups on a high railing by the sea. In yet another one, we are standing together in Haifa, a coquettish smile on my face, an extinguished cigar in his hand. Yes, I said to Mark, it was lovely, but it was not love then. Mark agreed. Thinking about the twenty-one years, I felt a sense of loss, but Mark said that those years were not a waste but a necessity. "It had to be," he noted, "we had to grow, separately rather than together. Besides," he added, and I readily agreed, "you had to marry Kenneth first. When you met me and him in the same year, 1972, it was as if God were saying to you, 'One for now, one for later.'"

ISRAEL

In December 1993, I was awarded tenure. Afterward we traveled to Israel for the wedding party my mother threw for us at the Tel Aviv Sheraton. It was a splendid reception. Friends and relatives came to greet us and sample the elegant display of food and drinks. While New England was heaving under the savage attacks of unprecedented winter storms, we were basking in the sun. As Mark and I were passing from one table of guests to another, glancing occasionally through the large windows at the broad strip of gleaming blue-green ocean scattered with white sails, I felt that the Israeli and the American in me could lay down their weapons and declare peace, or at least a truce. And why not? I was no longer afraid of my past; I was no longer invisible and lost; I no longer needed to prove who Shelly was. I was free to be me—a goodwill emissary, a celebrated guest for two short, sweet weeks in my home country.

After we returned from our sun-filled weeks in Israel to a Providence buried under snow and to a frozen house, whose furnace had shut down during our absence and whose heat could not be restored until 5:00 A.M., we toyed with the idea of returning to Israel for three months, during Mark's retirement and my sabbatical year scheduled for 1996 to 1997. In the summer of 1995, I began to develop my short story on Haya and worked on it during my vacations. My main objective for the sabbatical was to finish the book and to visit Israel. Mark was working on his book, *Eight Lessons in Love: A Domestic Violence Reader,* due for publication in the summer of 1997, and had planned a lecture tour on the book at the Universities of Haifa, Jerusalem, Tel Aviv, and Ben-Gurion. Painstakingly, we worked out the details of our journey.

Before leaving America, Mark and I often discussed our objectives in Israel. His were simple—he was the self-styled "itinerant scholar," as he called himself—mine were more complex. To refresh my memory of details for my book, I made a list of the places I needed to visit: Yavne'el, the moshav that was my first home after my mother and Reuven got married; Tiberias, where my grandparents used to live and where Aunt Zipporah still lives; Tivon, where my mother's affair with Chaim heated up; our villa in Haifa, and Ha'prachim Street on Mount Carmel, where Kenneth and I lived; Bar-Ilan University, where I completed my doctorate; Jerusalem, where I lived after Kenneth died; and most importantly, the orphanage in Pardes-Hannah, whose official records might tell me when I was there and for how long. I knew that Pardes-Hannah would provoke my mother's wrath; she would regard it as a mine-field lying in wait to blow her denials sky-high. That's why I never stopped by the orphanage before, but now I was determined to do it.

At times Mark was apprehensive about our trip. He was afraid, he said, of dying in Israel at the hands of terrorists. Whenever he confessed his anxiety, especially in the hush of the night when we were both restless in bed, I froze with fear. Yet I shook it off and reassured Mark that, although the threat seemed real, it was unlikely. And so, on February 1, 1997, we boarded an El Al plane in a flurry of anticipation.

BOTZ

There was no sun at all when we arrived at Ben-Gurion Airport, after ten hours of an exhausting flight during which we were squashed in the middle of the middle row and forced to execute acrobatic jumps over our sleeping neighbors each time we wanted to stretch our legs or go to the bathroom. Low, fast-moving clouds were riding over Tel Aviv, and fat drops of rain had just begun to fall when we finally clambered into my mother's car and collapsed onto the seats with sighs of relief. "You are exhausted, aren't you?" my mother said from the driver's seat. Meanwhile Elie, who'd single-handedly hoisted our heavy valises into the trunk, was helping my mother navigate the car through the heavy traffic. We talked all the way home as the rain was gathering force.

At my mother's table, I was gulping down the Israeli Sheli yogurt, peerless among the world's yogurts, while Mark was savoring tahini salad. "So what else is new?" I asked my mother. "How is everybody?"

My mother took the herring and the eggplant salad out of the refrigerator. "Well," she reflected a moment, "Aunt Nomi has been deteriorating recently. After her bypass operation in ninety-three, when an aneurysm wiped out her reading and writing abitilities, she still tried to read the paper, but now she has given it up. She can barely finish a sentence," she mimicked Nomi's impaired speech, "but she still looks beautiful. And Itzhak, her loyal husband, takes her everywhere she wants to go."

"That's nice," I said. "She is lucky to have such a devoted husband."

"What kind of coffee would you like Shelly?" Elie asked, "perculated, or *botz?*"

"*Botz,* of course," I said.

"And you, Mark?"

"What is *botz?*" Mark asked puzzled.

Elie smiled. "*Botz* is mud. You want some mud?" Mark shook his head. "But not mud from the street," Elie laughed. "Coffee mud. We put a spoon of Turkish coffee powder in a cup and then pour hot water over it, add milk, and *voila!*"

"Yes," Mark smiled, "I'll have some mud."

"And how is Ruth?" I asked after awhile.

"Your Aunt Ruth," my mother sipped her coffee, "had open heart surgery two months ago."

"Yes, I know. How is she doing?"

"She is getting better slowly, but she's not back to her old self yet. Her vision is impaired and she suffers from panic attacks. Your Aunt Zipporah also had an operation for breast cancer."

"Are they all sick?" I asked with alarm. "Anybody left in good health?"

"Elie and me," my mother smiled. "We have our problems, but we are managing well, thank God."

CYCLAMEN IN THE RAIN

The next day I woke up groggy with jet lag but eager to greet the Israeli morning. I put one foot on the floor, and jumped back under the covers. "Mark," I addressed his sleeping form, "the stone tiles are cold, the stone walls are cold, it's freezing in this house. Take heed!" Grunts and groans told me that he was not contemplating getting up. I lingered in the warmth another minute, then jumped out of bed, grabbed my robe and slippers, and walked resolutely out. Yes, I am glad to be home again, I thought as I crossed the living room to the huge window offering a panoramic view of the sky and tall apartment buildings in the distance. I gazed at the rain coming down the glass in purled rivulets. My mother approached, handing me a cup of coffee and a sesame cookie. Her blue eyes looked uncharacteristically soft and misty. "Eat something," she said. "You see this cyclamen," she pointed to one of her plants on the window ledge, "how beautiful," she shook her head. "In spite of the rain and the winds, it blooms." I looked at her. "Do you remember the song you used to sing to me about the cyclamen growing in the rocks? I loved it. Can you sing it now?" My mother stared at me surprised, the softness gone out of her eyes. "We have no time for nonsense now, Shelly. Hurry up, we must go to your hairdresser, Coco. Did you forget?" She turned around and walked at a fast pace to the kitchen, where Elie was puttering about. "Elie," her strident voice ordered, "get out of the kitchen. What are you doing here? I have to sweep the floor." There she is, I thought, Mother Israel. How am I going to stand her for three months?

DEATH IN THE NORTH

"Seventy-three soldiers are presumed dead near the Lebanon border when two army helicopters collided," Elie announced, as Mark and I returned from our trip to Ben-Yehudah Street, where we bought my mother a silver embroidered vest for her seventy-fifth birthday. "Wait a minute," Elie cried out, "another news edition. Let's hear it." As we gathered around the TV to listen to the declamatory cadences of the grim-faced broadcaster delivering information on the accident, accompanied by stark camera shots of the scene, we felt the electric charge that his words transmitted from house to house to house, throughout Israel. "But how could such a thing happen?" my mother asked. "Sh . . . sh, . . ." Elie hushed her, "be quiet and we'll find out." In the course of the evening, the immensity of the catastophe became evident. No survivors. Officers, soldiers, and rescue workers were interviewed in furtive succession. "The helicopters were too close," one said. "Pilot error," said another. "Traffic controllers' fault," remarked the third. Words like *negligence, irresponsibility,* and *fiasco* whizzed around like darts. Later, some of the victims' families were interviewed, and President Weizmann announced his intention to visit each one of those families. Thursday was declared a national mourning day; as if by a secret command, the whole of Israel—those who yesterday vilified each other—were lifted on the unifying and ennobling tide of grief. I watched them from a distance, with the familiar mixture of longing and aversion.

That day my uncle Avram, who a few months before had returned to Israel from Equador, came for a visit. Having divorced his Israeli wife,

Sharona, he was now married to a young Ecuadorian and was the doting father of a two-year-old daughter. "How wonderful you look," I said to my favorite uncle who, at sixty-four, still looked vigorous and engaging. "And why not?" he said as he gave me a bone-cracking hug. "Of course I look wonderful," he laughed. "I feel wonderful. I have a wonderful wife and a wonderful daughter. All I need is money. And I'll get that too one day. I'll be rich, you'll see." After the greetings, he sat down for a cup of coffee. Soon our conversation, like many others in the country, turned to the helicopters' accident.

"Since Netanyahu became the prime minister of this country," my mother declared, "there are only disasters. Now seventy-three died."

"What does it have to do with Netanyahu?" Avram rolled his eyes.

"Everything!" my mother insisted. "And you, Avram, I can't believe that you were one of the thirty thousand who voted Netanyahu in."

"What?" I turned to Avram, "you voted for Netanyahu?"

"Yes, of course. Didn't you see what Labor did to this country? The terrorists were having a ball when Labor was in."

"Wait a minute," my mother protested, "just wait a minute. You think that Netanyahu is safe from Hamas? We'll see. They'll have a special party for him, too."

"No," Avram adjusted his glasses, "Netanyahu is strong. He'll show the Palestinians who's boss here."

"And then," Elie interjected, "there will never be peace here."

"And seventy-three more soldiers will be killed," my mother added.

"Dina, I am asking you again," Avram got up from his chair, "what do they have to do with Netanyahu?"

"Do you know, Avram, what these soldiers were doing?" Elie asked, his trim Vandyke beard thrust forward.

"Yes," Avram nodded.

"What?"

"Flying back to their base."

"Which base?"

"In South Lebanon."

"That's it," Elie cried out. "What are we doing in Lebanon? Can you tell me? What business do we have in Lebanon? If Peres were prime minister, we'd have left it already."

"I'm not so sure."

"And now seventy-three died in vain." Elie's intense brown eyes bore down on Avram.

"What do you mean, in vain?" Avram waved his hands. "They didn't die in vain. They died for this country, to ensure that you and I are free citizens who can drink their coffee in the morning and take a swim in the ocean. Those soldiers were heroes! Don't you think so, Mark?"

"Didn't they die by accident?" Mark smiled, unhappy to disagree with Avram, whom he had just met.

"But they were fighters," Avram explained.

"But what is heroic about their deaths?" Mark laughed briefly. "They didn't fight in a war. They lost their lives in a tragic accident. Why should we call them heroes?"

"And what is the purpose of this national mourning?" I chimed in, fired up by sudden anger. "It's hypocritical. How can I believe in this sentiment when I see how Israelis hate and despise each other in everyday life?"

"What is this? Are you all ganging up on me?" Avram exclaimed. "But even though you are my favorite niece, Shelly, I must tell you that the national mourning is not hypocritical. How can you say that about the noblest of Israeli sentiments?"

"Noblest, shmoblest," my mother grumbled.

"In how many nations," Avram continued, "would you find this deep empathy for the young who have sacrificed their lives? If seventy-three soldiers died in America, would you find this kind of empathy there, too? No, you wouldn't, and you know it."

My blood rushed to my face. "What sacrifice are you talking about? It was an accident. Why do you? . . ."

"Those were soldiers. In this country, we respect soldiers because without them, we wouldn't be here. And people all over the country are crying for them, as they should."

"Yes, yes," I said. "Israelis show affection and unity in time of catastrophe. But what do they do the rest of the time? They eat each other up."

"Israelis love and hate just as much as people do anywhere else, Shelly. But in addition Israelis feel responsible for each other and for their nation, and this is what you are too blind to see." The tension was palpable. "You don't understand what Israel is about," Avram spoke with deliberation. "Here people help each other; in America they are indifferent. If somebody slips and falls in the street here, instantly ten people would be around to help him. Where do you see it in America, I would like to know?"

"He is right about that, Shelly," my mother conceded.

"Thank you, Dina," Avram said, with a sudden smile. "What are we fighting about, Shelly? Can you tell me? I am your favorite uncle, am I not?" I smiled back at him, and the tension dissolved. But that whole day, as the TV and the radio played songs of grief and lamentation, of struggle and glory, songs of days long past when the country fought for its survival, I was seething with anger at the hypocrisy of it all. As the victims' pictures were shown and as poems were read in subdued pathos, I remembered with disgust how I too, in my childhood, used to cry when my Aunt Ruth sang sad war songs and her green eyes glistened. Oh, how good it is to have grown out of it, to be free of it, to be an American! Yet as soon as I said that to myself, I heard a crackling sound in a hollow chamber of my mind, as if a brittle glass broke. Oh, how I used to love them, love them all, love this country, too!

PARDES-HANNAH

On Saturday, Aunt Nomi threw a surprise party for my mother's seventy-fifth birthday. My uncles and my four aunts arrived, as well as other relatives, all in good cheer. Nomi's dishes simply "melted in the mouth," as my cousin Michal said, and my mother was delighted with the attention and the gifts. In spite of their feuds, I reflected on the five sisters, such deep intimacy, like a dance, binds them together.

On Wednesday, Mark and I decided to visit the orphanage in Pardes-Hannah. My mother gave us the car, but I knew that I couldn't tell her the purpose of our trip. Instead, I said that we were going to see the excavations in Caesarea, and she gave us meticulous instructions how to get there. Finally, we set out on our jouney, not to Herod's port, but through the "first gate," in the words of T. S. Eliot, to my first world.

The day was partly cloudy. We quickly passed by Herzelia, and then Netanya, and in less than an hour arrived at Hadera. It was in the sands of Hadera, a town reputed for dumpiness, that I, as a Gadna recruit, crawled a few decades before. I took the exit. No longer dumpy-looking, Hadera sprouted new, spacious houses along its narrow roads. The traffic grew heavier as we made our way through the densely populated town. The streets were crowded with pedestrians and beyond them orange orchards growing out of red sands stretched for miles around. On the far left, chimney stacks poked the sky, and closer by red-roofed houses jostled for space among cypresses and pines. Along the road, dusty palm trees stood like tired guards. "Look at it, Mark," I said, "every inch of ground is inhabited and planted." Mark nodded. "But where, in this maze, is Pardes-Hannah?" I promised to ask at the gas station.

"Pardes-Hannah?" the amiable young man at the station laughed, as if it were the easiest question in the world. "Go four traffic lights," he said, "and then turn right, and go straight until you get to Pardes-Hannah."

"But where are the signs?" I inquired.

"Here, you know, nobody needs signs; everybody knows the way."

More orchards. First traffic light. My mouth felt dry. Second traffic light. What am I afraid of? Third traffic light. "Look," Mark cried out, "the sign. It says Pardes-Hannah; even I can read it."

"But the man said four lights."

"Well, he made a mistake. Let's turn here."

Orchards, red sands, eucalyptus trees, I noted, just as I remembered it. What will I find here? What am I looking for? "Here's a building that looks like a community center," Mark pointed out, "let's ask for directions."

The place was deserted, but a young, dark-haired girl on a bike told us that we were indeed in Pardes-Hannah.

"Do you know an orphanage called *Beit Ha'yeled?*" I asked her.

She shook her head. "Never heard of it. But why don't you go to the town center on this road here." She made a broad gesture with her arm that pointed in the direction of three or four roads.

"Darn it, she doesn't know, and we are lost," Mark said.

"No, we'll find it," I said as I rolled the car slowly to the broadest of the three roads and just followed my nose. More red sand, houses, and dusty palm trees, but the center of town was nowhere in sight. We tumbled down from street to street, but the town just sprawled out and about, without a discernible downtown, or even a shopping center. None of its houses looked like an orphanage. We stopped and asked. "Over there," the woman said, "beyond that narrow sand road." We crossed the road and saw *Neve Michael,* as it was now called, the only orphanage in Pardes-Hannah.

I parked the car, and we entered the gate. It was no longer the squeaky one I remembered but a new electronic gate. This is a modern place, I thought. What does it have to do with my orphanage? Several people came toward us and greeted us warmly. They were interested in my story. Yes, yes, they said, this is the place that once was called *Beit Ha'yeled,* and yes, it's been around for more than fifty years, and yes, it serves orphans, or children and youth from broken or abusive homes. And please, please, wouldn't we like to eat lunch with them and see the place? After lunch, Mazal, the pretty Yemenite secretary of the school, gave us black coffee and started to look for documents forty-eight to fifty years back. I held my breath. "That's it," I nudged Mark, "now I'll find out if I was really here." In the absence of computers, Mazal perused the documents by hand, but, alas, could find no Haya Shapira anywhere. "How could that be?" I asked her. "Well," she smiled, "we don't usually keep documents of fifty years ago. So sorry." I asked her permission to look through the documents myself. "Sure," she said and left me to it. "What will I do if I don't discover any trace of Haya?" I asked Mark, as the two of us were bent over the heaps of paper. "Wait a minute!" I exclaimed as I came across a group of pictures thrown haphazardly in the pile. "You know who this is?" I pointed excitedly to an august-looking man, leading a group of men dressed in black through the hall of one of the building, "Who?" Mark stared at me. "My uncle, Moshe Chaim Shapira! Imagine that."

"Wow!" Mark hollered, "What a find! What do you suppose he was doing here?"

"Who knows? He was probably one of the trustees of the place, or its overseer." I turned the pictures over but could find no notes or dates on them. Mazal didn't know anything about the pictures, or about my uncle, the first Minister of the Interior of Israel. I was feeling progressively like an old woman in search of ancient history nobody knew anything about. "But this is my uncle," I said, "Now I am sure that I was here."

"And you know what else that means?" Mark's eyes lit up.

"What?"

"It means that it was probably your father, with his brother's help, who sent you into this religious institution. It also means that your mother spoke the truth: it was not her decision, but his."

At that moment, in came Esther Laufer, the public relations director of *Neve Michael.* Tall and noisy, with a deep, raspy voice, a big bust and a small torso, wearing a black hat and thick black glasses, she came toward us with an extended hand and a sweet smile. "There you are!" she said cheerfully and pressed our hands. "I heard about you," she spoke in English, for Mark, "and I think it's just great that you have come to visit. Let me show you the place." Outside the day was warming up. "When were you here?" Esther turned to me.

"Fifty years ago," I said. "And there is hardly any evidence here from my time."

"That's probably true," Esther agreed. "These buildings are new, and the school is new, of course. Nothing goes back that far. . . . Except for this oak tree in the center," she laughed merrily. "This one," she patted the rough, furrowed bark, "has been here for a very long time, before you, Mark, and I were born. And it has survived all the wars, you see."

"Perhaps that's the tree I used to climb on," I ventured.

"Why not?" Esther spoke warmly, "everything is possible. But let me show you the school now. Classes are over for the day."

As we walked through the clean and orderly rooms, Esther told us about the successes of the institution. "We take in orphans, children of abusive mothers or fathers, and children from the *galut,* too, who were rescued from Nazi Germany, in the past, and from Yemen, from Russia, and even from Afghanistan. We take them in," she smiled, "and we offer them a warm shelter and a good school, so that they can grow up as good and happy people." After touring the school, we stopped by the garden surrounding it. "The children planted the flowers by themselves," Esther pointed out proudly, "and also put signs next to each flower." I bent down by one of them.

"Look, Mark, *Ha'yehudi Hanoded.*"

"Which means?" he chuckled.

"The wandering Jew. That's me."

"Me, too," he muttered.

"And me too," Esther smiled. "I am from Egypt, and I do miss my homeland. But Pardes-Hannah is my real home."

Before we set on our journey to Tel Aviv, Esther offered us coffee and cookies. "So tell me, Shelly," she said, "Why did you come here? What do you really want?"

After a short, silent debate, I said, "I have come to take Haya out."

Esther understood. "There she is," she said with a jubilant laugh. "I am giving her to you." She stretched out her arms to me, and we held each other. There was Haya, the angry orphan, released, recognized, returned to me with love, after all those years, her pain transmuted into the pleasure of homecoming. "Thank you, Esther," I murmured, as I turned to Mark. His eyes were moist. "Ah, dearest," he hugged me, "you have found her at last."

"What! What did you do? You took my car, *my* car to Pardes-Hannah? You hate me, I know it, you have always hated me, and you made Livi hate me. Don't I know you? You probably told Mark stories about me, how I tortured you and abused you and left you alone, poor you, in an orphanage, didn't you?

---

galut   The Diaspora

You have always been my enemy and that proves it. Yes, that proves it. Why do you always have to dig up the past, I would like to know? Who does it? Nobody but you. It happened and that's it. Finished. Over. Finito. Can't you leave it alone as everybody else does?"

I expected my mother to blow up, but it seemed that the earth moved. She raged for half an hour. If it weren't for Mark, the whole place would have turned to bedlam. "Look, Dina," he said with quiet intensity, "your daughter is different from you. You leave the past alone, and that works fine for you, but she has to find out everything about it, and that works for her."

"There is nothing to find out," my mother stewed. "And to think that she would deceive me in this way, and take my car without telling me to *that* place!"

"If she told you," Mark asked, "would you have given her the car?"

"NO!" my mother fumed, "of course not!"

"There you are," Mark laughed. "But you know, Dina, although the two of you are so different, you are also similar. I can see where Shelly got her courage and smarts from—from you, yes! Esther Laufer, the woman at Pardes-Hannah, saw your picture and said, 'She is still a beautiful woman.' You are both strong, beautiful women," he spoke with emotion, "please don't fight."

"You think that I am smart?" my mother, much calmer now, asked cautiously, as if unable to believe the compliment.

"Yes, of course you are," Mark said. "And you know what we actually found in Pardes-Hannah? Pictures of Shelly's uncle, Moshe Chaim Shapira, which says to me that it was Shelly's father, not you, who put her in the orphanage, just as you said."

"Ah-ha!" my mother exulted. "So you see I was right, yes, and that I wasn't lying. Finally! All right." She got up from her chair. "Would you like some dinner now?"

And so the storm blew away, and we sat down to eat.

NOSTALGIC TRIPS

Our visit to the orphanage was followed by four good days of family meetings and trips. Winter still reigned supreme with heavy clouds and strong winds, but some of the days sprawled bright and warm across the land. On one such day, we traveled with Nomi and Itzhak to see Aunt Ruth in Afula, about five miles outside of Tel Adashim, where Ruth worked in her *puncheria,* a tire shop, and to visit Safed. We parked the car behind Ruth's store, and as I rushed out to hug her, I was struck by the devastation the operation had wrought in her. She had not only lost weight, she had shrunk. Everything in her, her face, arms, legs, and steps, looked smaller and less definitive. Due to her limited vision, her green eyes, now anxious rather than jolly, were often buried in the ground. "I'm getting better," she reassured me, "but recovery at my age is slow. At night, I still dream that they are taking my heart out," she grinned, "which of course they do during the operation. But why should I feel sorry for myself?" she added with the cheerful toughness I always admired in her. "So what if I can't see so well? Some people are paralyzed after such an operation. What do *I* have to complain about?" she laughed, her green eyes dancing as of old. Before I could answer, Nomi interrupted with a demand for a falafel. "Sure," Ruth said, "it's just around the corner. Let's go."

At the grimy counter, the falafel balls were being fried in old, cloudy oil. Nomi ordered a large pita with everything in it. Itzhak, Mark, and Ruth also ordered large pitas and were busy filling them up with tehini, pickles, olives, and salad. Having eaten our fill, we bade Ruth good-bye and continued our steep climb to Safed.

In Safed, Nomi got off to see her friend, and Itzhak parked the car in a narrow cobblestone alley that seemed to have been preserved intact from earlier centuries. Who knows, I thought, how old these arched stone houses are. In this ancient city of kabbalists the years have passed without notice, blending into each other to create a mystical eternity. The two-room house that Itzhak opened the door to had belonged to my great-grandmother, and before her, to her parents, and thus must have existed at least since the middle of the nineteenth century. Itzhak and Nomi inherited the house, renovated and furnished it, installed electric appliances in it, and turned it into a charming abode, ideal for summer vacations. My mother told me that she used to take me to see her grandmother in this very house, and although I could not recall those visits, I now entered the place as if I too belonged to it.

The house was cold; it hadn't been inhabited in some time, and the stone walls gave off the chill of a tomb. Itzhak made coffee and sandwiches and turned on the heater. He also showed us the bedroom, where we could rest under warm blankets, and then left us to join Nomi. Mark and I were eager to go out to the sun, to wander in the alleys, to visit the synagogues. As we walked down the road, we felt as if we'd been transported to a medieval *shtetl*. We passed by men in black, wearing long earlocks and *shtreimels*, wide hats rimmed with sable furs. The women were covered in black from forehead to toe. Both the men and the women turned their gaze away from us, as if ashamed to look at the epicurean strangers, whose licentious clothing—a woman in slacks, a man without a *yarmulke*—clearly exhibited their hedonistic natures. When their eyes met ours, they looked at us with revulsion and pity, and we looked at them in the very same way.

Coming down cobblestone steps, we stumbled on the synagogue of the kabbalist Isaac Luria, called Ha-Ari. A shabbily dressed beadle let us in for a small sum. A musty odor of old books permeated the round structure of the synagogue, where we were the only guests. A single ray of sunlight slanted across the *bimah,* the high circular platform used for Torah readings and the leading of prayers. Curious, I climbed up the steps to the *bimah,* the one place absolutely forbidden to women who came to the synagogue to pray. From that vantage point, I could clearly see the colorful drawings of harps and fruit trees on the arched ceiling and the ornate chandelier hanging down from it. Closer to heaven, I was above the imagined congregation below. I was free and a stranger in a place where centuries ago, my forefathers immersed themselves in the mystical study of *tikkun,* while their mothers and wives, down the generations to my own great-grandmothers, cleaned their houses, washed their clothes, cooked their meals, worked and earned money for their livelihood, and bore their children. It is you, *savta,* I salute from the *bimah* of learning and privilege, which I, a mere woman, declare for the moment as yours and mine.

When I told my thoughts to Mark he applauded them. Yet after awhile, he got tired and asked to rest in the house. We crawled under the covers, yet for a whole hour Mark couldn't get warm, as if his body had been seized by a chill. At night, on the way to Tel Aviv, he slept most of the time, his head dropping heavily on his chest. The next day, our plans and hopes went up in smoke. Instead of making nostalgic journeys to Yavne'el and Tivon, we were hurled into disaster and into the very heart of frantic Israeli reality.

ICHILOV ER

It started at 1:00 A.M. the following morning. I had just fallen into deep sleep when Mark woke me up, complaining about a sharp pain in his right groin. "What? What?" I mumbled. "I took a sip of ice-cold water," he said, "and the pain started." I sat up in bed. "What pain?" "In here," he pointed, groaning. "It's probably just gas from the falafel you ate," I said, for all I wanted to do was sleep. "Did you go to the bathroom?"

"Yes," he said, "but the pain is getting worse."

I forced myself up. "Perhaps you should take Mylanta," I said.

"I did, I did," he moaned and ran to the bathroom once more. I turned on the light. The familiar room looked eerie. A terrible premonition settled in the pit of my stomach. I listened to him straining and groaning and shot to the living room to wake up my mother. "Yes? What happened?" My mother was up in the blink of an eye. "Mark is not feeling well," I said. "What's the matter?" Her eyes were two blue pools. "Pain in the lower stomach," I muttered breathlessly. "Should we call an ambulance?" she asked. Ambulance. God. I have heard it before. Been there before. "Let's wait a little longer and see," she reconsidered.

Back to the bathroom. "How are you, Mark?" my hands on the door.

"I had a small movement," he spoke softly. "I think I'm feeling a bit better." Soon he came out. "I'll try to sleep again." I breathed in relief. We curled around each other and sank into furtive slumber, Mark's low moans infiltrating my troubled dreams.

At 4:00 A.M. he woke again in such pain that he could neither sit, nor stand, nor lie down. He could only howl. The house jerked into action. My mother called an ambulance and got dressed. Elie got up, dressed, and made coffee. I wrapped Mark in his robe. He was pale and covered with sweat. Please God, please help us now.

At 5:00 A.M., we brought Mark to Ichilov Hospital, on Weizmann Street, mercifully only two miles away from my mother's house. When we arrived, the two young medics took the stretcher out of the ambulance and knocked its wheels against the concrete. Mark groaned. "Please, be careful," I pleaded with them, but they didn't hear. Jockeying the stretcher into the ER, they left it in the middle of a large hall, by the nurse's station. "Can somebody please help us here?" I cried out in no particular direction, for, in spite of the fact that the hour was early and quiet, no nurses or doctors were available. I stopped any man or woman in a white frock. "Can you please help?" I asked, but no, they said, Mark was not their patient. One tall nurse with handsome dark features looked at me with a smile and said, "He is not the only patient, you know. We have all kinds of emergencies here." I glanced around but couldn't see any emergencies. "But look at him," I said, "he is in terrible pain." "Yes, yes, I know," she smiled, "the doctor will soon come."

"Be nice to them," my mother muttered under her breath.

"What?" I whirled to face her. "What are you talking about? Nobody will ever come to see him if I am nice."

"Yes, yes," my mother said, "but don't you know them? If you start arguing with them, they'll deliberately stay away from Mark. This is not America."

"Oh, I can't stand it, *Imma*," I fumed. "Is this a hospital, or a madhouse?"

Finally, a short Russian doctor with a limp came over. "Are you Mark Spilka?" he asked.

"Yes, yes," I said eagerly, "he is in great pain."

"I see," the doctor assented, "and where is he from?"

"From America."

"Does he speak Hebrew?"

"No, but I do."

"So where is pain?" he asked. Mark showed him the place. Slowly, he examined the ailing stomach. "No," he said, "it's not appendicitis, as the medics thought. It's probably," he waved to a nurse passing by, "it's probably hernia. Yes, hernia." Dragging his foot, he walked slowly away from us to the station. "Where is he going now?" I grumbled. "How are you, Mark?" I held his clammy and cold hand. "Where's the doctor?" He spoke with difficulty. "I don't know," I said, looking around in despair, but all I could see was the tall nurse.

At last the doctor came back, holding a pen in his hand, with which he drew a large arrow on Mark's belly. "What are you going to do for him?" I asked.

"We'll operate," the doctor spoke slowly without lifting his eyes. "But we need to take an x-ray of the belly first."

"But look," I pleaded, "he's in pain. Can't you speed things up?"

"I'm doing everything as fast as I can," he reassured me.

It was already 6:00 A.M. The grey morning light filtered in from the windows and from the automatic glass doors. The place became busy as more people poured in. Oh, my God, oh, my God, I was wringing my hands; I can't believe I am here; this is so terrible. Give us help, somebody! The big clock on the wall ticked-tocked the minutes away, and nobody came. "Ouch!" Mark howled. "Stay here," I instructed my mother, as I whirled to the nurse's station, my coat's tails flying in the air. "Where's the doctor?" I demanded of the tall nurse. "*Gveret,*" she said, unflappable, "calm yourself down, please. Why are you getting so excited?"

"No reason, I just tend to get excited on Monday mornings."

"No need to be hysterical," she simpered. "We are waiting for the orderly to take your husband to the x-rays."

"Can't you do it faster?" I protested, "something terrible might happen to him."

"Nothing terrible will happen to him," the nurse picked up the phone, "it's just a hernia."

"And what if it isn't?"

"*Gveret,*" she persisted, "I can't do anything else for you until the orderly comes."

THE FIRST OPERATION

It was eight when Mark was wheeled down to the operating room. I was ordered to stay behind the automatic doors to the OR. Pacing back and forth, I experienced the full force of the event's horror and desolation. "What is he in for?" the volunteer working at the desk behind the doors asked me. "Hernia," I said weakly. "Oh, that's nothing," she reassured me, "he'll be just fine. What's his name?" I told her. "I'll call you as soon as he comes out to the recovery room," she promised. I was not reassured. On the contrary, my sense of dread intensified. This is the second time, the thought pounded inside my head, the second time, my God, I've been in such a place before, waiting for Kenneth behind closed doors. No, no, I put my hands to my face, not again, please, have mercy. A religious woman, in a head covering and thick woolen stockings grabbed my shoulders. "God is merciful," she said and pointed to the small Psalms book she was holding in her hand. She bent down and exhaled oniony breath in my face. "*Hashem* 'will protect him and preserve his life,'" she read to me. "All will be well," she promised as she walked away, her lips moving soundlessly in prayer.

The word got around, and the family began to gather. Nomi and Itzhak came first, then Bracha and Avram. They sat on the benches in the waiting room and motioned to me to join them, but I could not leave my post by the automatic doors. Time passed. The volunteer came out every five minutes to read names, but when she passed by me, she shook her head. "Not yet." My mother walked over. "Any news?" I could see the worry on her face. "No," I said. "Something is wrong, I know it. It's taking too long." My mother sighed and offered me something to eat. "No, no," I protested. "I can't eat." "Would you like some coffee then?" she asked. "Yes."

Time passed. Finally, the name "Spilka" resounded in the hall. "Yes?" I answered. "The surgeon wants to speak to you," the volunteer said. My heart sank. "We opened up his belly," the surgeon explained, his words exploding like shrapnel in my ears, "and there was no hernia. Instead we found a belly cavity full of blood. We called down the vascular surgeons, but they couldn't find the source of the leak. We'll close him up and see what happens."

NIGHT IN THE SURGERY WARD

Sometime on late Monday afternoon, Mark was wheeled up to the surgery ward. A variety of IVs sprouted from his arms; wires from his chest connected to monitors showing his EKG, pulse, and blood pressure; an oxygen mask rested crookedly on his nose. "Hello, partner," I said to him, "how are you doing?"

"Is it over?" he asked.

"The operation is over," I hesitated, "but it wasn't a hernia."

"What was it?" Mark asked with consternation.

"They found blood in your stomach, but they couldn't find the source of the leak."

"I see," Mark said glumly and pulled the oxygen's mask off. A Russian nurse came over and put it back on his nose. Then she checked the blood transfusion and, without a word, released at once the top part of the bed. Mark's head jerked back.

"Are you out of your mind?" I yelled at her savagely. "Why did you do that?"

"*Gveret,*" she said in heavily accented Hebrew, "blood was not coming through IV. I had to straighten him out flat, and now blood is going well again, you see."

"Why didn't you warn us?" I was ready to throttle her slim neck with my bare hands.

"He doesn't speak Hebrew, and I don't speak English."

"But I speak Hebrew," I protested, "you could have told me." She shrugged her shoulders. "And why didn't you take the bed down *gently?*" I insisted.

"I don't have time to be *gentle* here," she smirked and walked away.

What is this strange place, this war zone? I thought despondently. Is it just Ichilov Hospital, or has the whole country gone mad? Amid patients' groans and cries, night finally descended. Mark was sleeping fitfully, his face contorted in pain. I dragged an armchair from the neighboring room and put it, for my night's rest, next to his bed. How did all of this happen? Why did I bring Mark to Israel? Was it a mistake, perhaps a costly mistake? Why couldn't we be right this minute in America? What are they going to do to him here? As I was sinking deeper into depression, I looked up and saw my mother's blond curly head approaching the room. "I'm so glad you came," I said to her with relief. "But of course," she said, "how is Mark doing?"

"He is sleeping but restless. They sedated him."

She looked around the room for a chair. "Sit here," I pointed to the armchair, "my bed for tonight."

"You're not coming home?"

"Of course not! How can I leave him here with the Russian nurse who doesn't speak a word of English and bounces him around?"

"Ichilov is now filled with Russians," my mother asserted. "It seems that half of the educated Russian immigrants settled here in Tel Aviv, and they are all doctors or nurses! Anyway," she searched about in her bag, "I brought you a coffee thermos, sesame cookies, and Sheli yogurt. You must eat something to be strong for him."

"Thank you, *Imma,*" I said and poured myself a cup.

"Elie went to sleep," she said, "but he told me to wake him up if we need him."

"That's very nice of him," I was touched. "Doesn't he hate hospitals?"

"*Hate* is not the word," my mother sipped her coffee, "he loathes them! Every time he has to come here for a checkup, he's in mourning two weeks before." We chuckled softly.

"Avram said that he'll come early tomorrow," my mother continued. "Uzi will come too. As a doctor he may be able to get some information for us."

"Thank you, *Imma,*" I said. An hour later she went home. When I walked back to my post by Mark's bed, I wondered if I had ever been so comforted by my mother's presence.

THE CAT SCAN

It was well past noon when an orderly came to take Mark for a CAT scan. We descended several floors to the basement. The orderly pushed Mark's bed through a maze of halls, his progress impeded by crowds of people milling about. Mark's face was deathly pale, as if all the blood in it was fast pouring out into an invisible hole.

That's how Kenneth looked at the end; a warm wave of panic lurched into my throat, and now, God, oh, help, can't breathe, now Mark too is going away, here, in Israel, a second time, why, tell me why, is it I who is cursed, or is it this country of graves? stop thinking, Shelly, he is *not* dead yet.

"Watch out, watch out," the orderly warned people who walked in the middle of the passageway. "Can't you see that I'm pushing a patient's bed?" We approached a sharp corner so fast that the bed's wheels rattled and the tubes shook, but the orderly skillfully negotiated the corner and parked the bed in front of a door with a sign C.T. SCAN. Above it an angry red light glared. Cold winds penetrated from an area under construction beyond the radiation room. I pulled Mark's blankets up to cover his arms and bent down to kiss him, muttering assurances in his ears. He did not respond. With a start I saw that his eyes were staring petrified into space.

A technician in a white frock and a *yarmulke* came to fetch Mark and wheeled his bed inside the scanning room. I paced the drafty corridor. In spite of my best efforts, my mind reverted back to the radiation rooms in Hadassah, recalling one time when the technician let me watch Kenneth's radiation treatment through the glass. All alone, Kenneth lay under the red light of the radiating machine, his eyes peering into the darkness in wild terror. Now I saw the same look in Mark's eyes. You lay me in the dust of death, I poured my bitterness into the Psalms verse. Why? Why? Fifteen minutes passed, but there was no sign of Mark. An hour later, he was wheeled out.

I rushed to him. "How was it?" I asked. "Terrible," he said, breathing heavily, "terrible." Distraught, he waved his arms so wildly in the air that his IV needles threatened to fly out of his veins. I held his hands. "What happened?" I asked as calmly as I could. "Nobody had the decency to speak English to me," he said, gulping air. "And you know," his hand closed into a tight fist, "they didn't prep me at all. Nobody told me that I'd be lying in that narrow, round tube for forty minutes. All they said was, 'Don't move.' There I was, sick, in the middle of nowhere, away from you, alone among Hebrew speakers, and I thought, what the hell, why don't you kill me already and have done with it!"

"No, Mark," I pleaded, "don't say that, please, I need you. Please, don't despair."

Back at the ward, I asked the nurse about the results of the test. "Ask the doctor," she shrugged. But there was no doctor around to ask. Time passed; it was already close to 5:00 P.M. Finally I saw one of the chief surgeons. "Can I talk to you about my husband?" I asked politely.

"Not now," he said, shuffling through papers. "Go out there to the waiting room, and I'll talk to you when I have time."

"It would only be a minute," I implored him, "my husband had a CAT scan several hours ago. You must have the results by now."

"What did I just tell you?" the surgeon's face was flushed in anger. "Go out there to the waiting room, where other people are waiting for me, and I'll talk to you in your turn." His eyes bore down on me with a hard stony stare.

Resigned, I walked out and joined the company of the waiting families. Ten minutes later, the surgeon came out. He talked to the first group of relatives and then to the second. It was my turn, at last. The surgeon stared at me with concentrated hatred. "When I tell you to wait, you wait," he sputtered, "when I tell you to go out, you go out. Don't argue with me, you understand? The last thing I need here is a stupid, hysterical woman." And then he turned on his heels and walked away.

I called my mother and urged her to call Uzi. "Only a doctor can find out what's going on here," I said to her in a voice choking on sobs and darkness. Yes, she said, she'd call him immediately and come over to spell me. When I returned to the room, Mark was asleep. I watched his monitors bleeping at a steady pace. I must collect myself, I thought, and walked out of the ward to the smoking area. The window was open; a few rain drops, carried on the wind, touched my face. I took a deep breath of the pungent winter air. The horizon was swelling with thick black clouds, gathering like armies to battle, and the sun had sunk in the west, leaving behind a narrow strip of white gleaming light that put up a mighty pitch against the darkness. Underneath, square, concrete apartment buildings lay in the dusk like sluggish blocks of army garrisons, vaguely illumined, here and there, by streetlamps. A sudden gust of wind shook the window. Just as I closed it, heavy rain began to pour.

It must have been six when I returned from my break. An hour and a half later, a tall, elegantly dressed, bearded man entered the room. "Mark Spilka?" he asked and approached the bed in a measured step. "How are you?" he smiled.

"Not so good," Mark said, wetting his lips.

"My name is Dr. Amsterdam, an associate chief surgeon in the hospital. I am going to operate on you now, but first I need your signature."

"What?" Mark groaned. "I haven't yet recovered from yesterday's operation."

"I know," Dr. Amsterdam nodded, "but I must operate on you again, right now."

"Why?" Mark raised himself in the bed, his face puckered with consternation. "What do you mean you are going to operate on me now?" he stared at the doctor. "I have already had an operation, I am telling you. Why couldn't they fix it the first time?" he paused and gazed at the doctor's street clothes, "and *who* are you, anyway? How do I know you are a doctor? I see no white frock, or stethoscope on you, no name tag. What ID can you show me?"

The doctor smiled. "I was called from home, Mr. Spilka, and had no chance to put on my white coat. We just got your CAT scan results: you have a huge aneurysm in your iliac artery. Look," he lifted up the drainer, "you're losing a lot of blood." With horror, I saw that the drainer was full.

"But why can't you operate tomorrow?" Mark insisted.

"If I wait till tomorrow," the doctor answered with measured emphasis, "you'd be dead."

"Please, Mark," I turned to him, "please sign the paper."

"All right," Mark consented, as he picked up the pen with an unsteady hand.

As soon as the doctor walked out, Mark turned to me. "I didn't know who he was. I thought he was some crazy Orthodox rabbi, an impostor who just wandered into the hospital. . . ."

"And decided to kidnap you," I completed his fantastic scenario. In spite of the gravity of the situation, we chuckled.

NIGHT WATCH

An hour later, the night orderly came to take Mark to the OR. Wearing only a thin hospital gown under the blankets, Mark was shivering uncontrollably. We moved quickly through the empty hall. In the window, lightning flashed and low rumbling thunder retorted angrily. Driving rain fell in long slanted strips across the glass. Terror seized me by the throat and twisted my stomach into hard knots. Please, please, ruler of the universe, whoever and wherever you are, please spare him. The elevator door opened. I squeezed myself in between the bed and the wall. "You'll be fine, Mark," I said without conviction. "Now the good doctors are getting into the picture," I held his hand to protect him from the despair that enveloped us both, "and they know what they are doing." Mark looked around in fear. In another minute, we were standing before the automatic doors of the OR. So quickly, I thought, we have arrived so quickly, here we are before those terrible doors, and who knows if I'll ever see him again. The doors opened. "Go out, *gveret,* you can't come in here," the dour-faced orderly hollered. "I love you, Mark," I called out and hugged him. Then the doors closed shut.

It was 10:00 P.M. I turned around and walked to the waiting room. *Imma* and Elie, Uzi and Michal, Nomi and Itzhak were all there, sitting in a row on the black armchairs. In spite of the storm, I thought gratefully, they have come to stay with me. As I approached, my mother held out a cup of coffee in one hand and a sandwich in the other. "Thank you," I said, as we dove into a furtive discussion on Mark's condition. I sat next to Uzi, who had already conferred with one of the doctors and greeted me with an expression of deep worry. "I want you to know, Shelly," he said, "that the situation is very, very serious. You must be prepared for the worst," his kind eyes looked gravely at me. "His aneurysm is very large. Who knows if they'll manage to construct a bypass on time. But even if they do," he explained, "Mark is not a young man. He's had several operations on his arteries, which means that they are pretty lousy, and his kidneys, I understand, are also not in the best shape." He smiled wistfully. "Let's pray he survives the operation." An undertow of terror surged in me, sweeping away all traces of hope.

"Wait and see," my mother intoned, "he is not dead yet, and the doctors are doing their best." I returned the sandwich to her, untouched. "Why don't you eat?" she asked.

"I can't."

"*Oi vey,*" she sighed deeply. "Who could have expected such trouble, suddenly, out of the blue, a man strong and healthy like Mark, wakes up in pain one night, and look what happens."

I could not keep my hands still. They were flying all over the place, rubbing against my black pants, pulling at my coat's buttons, tugging at my cheeks, knotting and unknotting stray threads. My mother observed my jumpiness, but for once did not rebuke me. "What can I say?" she spoke warmly. "You don't deserve this. You really don't deserve this." "Thank you," I murmured, touched by her spirited advocacy, which, I realized, came only in times of crisis, but there it was, sturdy, reliable, big as life, just when I needed it most. I knew that I could trust her.

Two hours passed and still no word from the OR. All the guests left, except my mother. We stretched on the cushiony armchairs, covered ourselves with our coats, and tried to doze off. But I was wide awake; whenever the automatic doors opened, I jumped to my feet. It was already past midnight and still no word from the OR. I paced in front of the doors, looking for signs. Had something terrible happened, they would have come out to tell me. But why is it taking them so long? What if they can't stop the bleeding? Oh, God, I bit my lips, have mercy. "Shelly, *buba'le,* how are you doing?" Avram suddenly materialized, holding his cell phone in his hand. "Any news?" he asked.

"What are you doing here so late at night?" I asked.

"What am I doing here!" he rolled up his eyes. "Don't I know that your husband is being operated on? Am I not your favorite uncle? Why shouldn't I be here? I am worried about you!"

"Thank you," I smiled at him. "No news, we are still waiting here, and *Imma* is asleep on the chairs."

"How long has it been?"

"Almost three hours."

"Listen to me, Shelly," he lifted his index finger, "Mark won't die."

"How do you know?" I looked at him intently.

"I know. I have a feeling. He won't die, you'll see. Now I'm going to talk to your mother."

The three of us sipped the remaining coffee in the thermos and waited. At 2:30 A.M., Avram went home. There was still no news from the OR.

"It's been four and a half hours," I told my mother.

"No news is good news," she said. "It was refreshing to sleep for an hour. Did you get any sleep?" she asked.

"No."

"You'll collapse, Shelly," my mother warned, "that will be the end of it." I smiled at her, "I don't worry. You'll pick me up."

"What nonsense you are talking," my mother frowned. "When Mark comes out, what shall I tell him? That you fell to pieces? And then I'll have to pick both of you up? No, that's too much for me."

I laughed. For a moment, the weight that was oppressing my heart lifted. Perhaps, I thought, life is still possible.

At 3:30 A.M., the doors opened, and a tall, burly Russian doctor called the name "Spilka." "Yes," I jumped to my feet, my heart in my throat. "Is he alive?"

"Yes, he is alive," the doctor said with a glum expression.

"So what's wrong?"

"Well," he was looking for words in his meager Hebrew. "It was a difficult operation. We had complications."

"What complications?"

"Hmm, the bypass operation was fine, but then blood pressure dropped, and kidneys stopped functioning. We don't know if he'll live," his grim gaze rested on my face. "If his kidneys hold out for three days, maybe there is chance. He is in recovery room now."

"Can I see him?"

"Yes, but just for a moment. Put on mask and gown."

In a second I was in, struggling with trembling hands with the mask and the gown. "This way," a nurse pointed, and after all those long hours of waiting, I was finally inside, next to Mark. But when I saw him, I nearly screamed. His face, bloated beyond recognition, looked like a clay mask. His eyes were swollen pockets with two slits that opened up into unknowable depth. I looked in but saw no life there, except for fluid darkness that glistened ominously whenever it caught the light. His mouth was open, and out of it emerged the respirator, rising and falling to the rhythms of automated breathing.

A few hours later, the nurse called me again to see him. His face had shrunk to its normal size, and he was conscious. "You made it," I said excitedly. Mark looked piteously at me, and pointed at the respirator. "I know you can't speak, dear," I said; "this tube makes you choke and gag." He nodded vigorously. "You'll be fine, though." I tried to comfort him. "In a few hours they'll take the tube out." Mark shook his head and looked at me with desperate pleading. With his left hand, he drew four letters on the sheet, T-R-A-P.

TRAPPED

Mark stayed five days in the recovery room. Patients came and went, but he lingered, in deep stupor, his life sustained by tubes. Sometimes I paced the waiting room for twelve hours before I could see him for ten minutes. Whenever I pressed his hand, he turned in my direction, his eyes closed, and his eyebrows contracted in pain. "The problem is," Uzi explained to me, "that they cannot extubate him, namely, take the respirator out. On the good side," he added reluctantly, for he couldn't often see good sides in a bad situation, "his kidneys have been holding out. But don't kid yourself, Shelly," he returned to his natural gloom, "the respirator problem is very serious."

After my visit, I'd walk the two miles home, listening to my walkman and praying. Please, God, I repeated, as in an incantation, let them take the respirator out successfully, please be with them when they try to do it, please, please, give Mark the fighting spirit to pull himself out of the trap. At home, I'd eat something light, take a shower, pour myself a glass of wine, and talk to our children and friends in America. Particularly comforting were Betsy and

Polly, Mark's stepdaughters, both doctors, who pointed out that the situation, although grave, was not necessarily fatal. One night Ruth, Mark's former wife, called, to my surprise, and asserted confidently, "Mark has lousy arteries, but he's as strong as an ox." When I went back to Ichilov Hospital, to face the pessimistic doctors, her echoing words gave me courage.

One night, I was approached by an anaesthesiologist with a *yarmulke,* an immigrant who spoke Hebrew in a French accent. With a gentle smile, he leveled at me more devastating news. "We've tried to extubate him twice but couldn't. Yesterday we discovered that he has pneumonia, so we are sending him tomorrow to the intensive care unit."

That night, sharp needles of rain were falling over the city. I didn't have an umbrella, but what did I care? Mark was dying, what did anything matter? As far as I was concerned, there could be a terrorist kamikaze walking right next to me, and I wouldn't bat an eyelid. Blow me up, if you please, I'm already blown to bits inside, it's only my shell walking here, under the prickly rain. What would Betsy say about the pneumonia? Would she still insist, in her calm doctor's voice, that recovery is possible? Ooh, oooh, I dug my nails in my flesh, why did I bring him here? In America, he would have been saved. Now all is lost, I thought stepping into a puddle, and it's all this country's fault, with its arrogant doctors, who think they know everything. I don't understand it at all, I was shouting in the empty streets, how could I be losing both my husbands in this country where I met them both? How could I be losing both of them after a short period of five years? Not even five in Mark's case. What am I, a professional widow? Is there some logic in it, God? My fist stabbed the darkness. If there is, could you please tell me what it is? I kicked an electricity pole and stubbed my toe. Fine, fine, it hurts, good, I am glad, at least this pain I can tolerate, I hate you, my savage country, I hate you! You are probably punishing me for my indifference to the seventy-three who died in the helicopter crash, aren't you? The rain was coming down fast and thick. Go ahead and soak me, see if I care.

"You are drenched," my mother cried when I opened the door. "Why didn't you take a cab?"

"I don't care," I went straight to my Vermouth bottle.

"What happened, Shelly?" my mother asked quietly.

"He has pneumonia now," I said, gulping the wine, "and they're moving him to the intensive care unit. Why didn't they move him there on the first day? Now he has a multisystem failure, the doctor told me, and he's not going to make it."

"Did he say that?"

"No, but he implied that."

"Shelly, it's not over until it's over," my mother said.

INTENSIVE CARE UNIT

On Monday, Mark was moved to the intensive care unit. Ensconced behind two sets of automatic doors, which opened only with voice identification, the unit was protected from the noise and the frantic pace of the rest of the hospital. In its main large room were eight beds, each equipped with the state-of-the-art monitors and other medical instruments. Close, around-the-clock supervision characterized the place. The nurses were friendly, and the doctors seemed accessible. The unit was brightly lit, spotless, quiet, and well organized. It also had its own special waiting area, with comfortable couches, a public phone, and a coffeepot. Mostly I liked the place for its long and regular visiting hours. Now I was not merely allowed but encouraged to be near Mark for hours at a time. Family and friends were also invited to visit. Thus started the humane chapter in our hospital saga.

Yet the merit of the place offered little protection from the grim reality. I was in the unit but an hour when Dr. Sold, the deputy head, called me to his office. In his courteous and patient manner, so rare in the hospital, he explained to me that Mark's life was in grave danger. What they needed to do was identify, through culture, the exact kind of bacteria that was causing Mark's pneumonia and then match it with the antibiotic that could eliminate it. "But culture," Dr. Sold looked at me with green eyes bordered with deep, dark shadows, "takes time, at least two days. If he survives the two days," he explained, "we could afford to be optimistic." As I looked at him, the familiar hollow drumbeat of terror returned. "I can barely wait one hour; how am I going to wait two days?"

"I know," Dr. Sold smiled. "In the meantime," he added, "your husband seems to be responding well to our special dialysis machine."

"Thank you," for being decent, for letting me hold onto this wisp of hope.

Dr. Barak was the junior doctor on shift most of the time. A medium height, wiry Sephardic with a *yarmulke* and with darting, intelligent eyes that seemed to be everywhere all at once, Barak possessed the kind of commanding energy that called his staff to attention. When he was in the unit, everybody knew it, or felt it, even without seeing him, as if the room had become a magnetic field. He was an exacting, vigilant doctor, and I was glad of it. But, unlike Sold, he was also moody and harsh, and I therefore needed courage to ask him questions about Mark. "Any news about the pneumonia?" I ventured once. He looked at me startled, as if amazed that I had a voice at all. "We sent the culture in," he said, "but it won't be ready for at least two days."

"But he started giving urine," I drew his attention to a positive development.

Barak looked at me askance. "Urine is urine and an infection is an infection," he snapped.

"But isn't it a good sign?" I persisted.

"Look," Barak said with obvious impatience, "your husband is very ill. Why are you so happy about some urine when the pneumonia can kill him any minute?"

"ONLY CONNECT"

I was rarely alone in the waiting room of the ICU. The family came in droves; uncles, aunts, even cousins kept showing up at different hours and days. Avram sat with me for long periods each day, still predicting that Mark would not die, and so did my mother. But she did one better. Every morning, to allow me more sleep, she called at the unit at 6:00 A.M., to check on Mark, and to bring me word of his condition.

Comfort came also from friends. Miriam Mandel showed up almost every day. She wired on the Internet news about Mark to his colleagues and scholars in the Hemingway Society on both sides of the Atlantic. A cascade of responses rushed into her computer; each time she came to the hospital, she brought me reams of paper with printed wishes from all over the world. "Share them with Mark," Miriam said. "He should certainly know how well thought of he is and appreciated by so many people."

On Thursday, Mark's fourth day in the ICU, I sat by his bed and pressed his hand. He pressed my hand back, or was it just a reflex, as Barak used to say? Mark's eyes were closed, his hands and his feet, swollen with edema, jerked and kicked. His arms were connected to IVs and monitors, a feeding tube went into his nose, and the respirator came out of his mouth, making wooshing sounds with every breath. I started reading the messages. From time to time, I was sure, Mark nodded. Yes, he was listening; I knew it.

"What are you doing?" Dr. Barak's strident voice reached me from the nurse's station.

"I'm reading well-wishes from friends and colleagues to my husband, to cheer him up," I said, as I walked toward him.

"Are you out of your mind?" he yelled at me, his square jaw set imperatively. "Don't you know that this can agitate him and raise his blood pressure?"

Shamefaced, I went back to my chair and sat quietly, like a scolded child. In my diary, I wrote that night, "Dr. Barak is wrong, so wrong, about the human heart. And in spite of his grim predictions, I am confident (stupidly as it may seem) that Mark will pull through."

PULLING THROUGH

Every morning, when I woke up, my limbs felt heavy, as if attached to steel chains. Most difficult was seeing Mark's clothes strewn about—his green plaid shirt, his green sweater, his grey pants with the small tear under the back pocket, and his reading glasses in the red case. One morning, I looked at these mute reminders of Mark's healthy days and cried convulsively. I got up, stretched out on my mother's couch in the living room, and sobbed. My mother, Ruth, Bracha, and Zipporah were sitting in the kitchen, whispering. "How can I bear to hear her crying like that?" my mother was saying as she poured me a cup of coffee. "Here," she gave me the coffee, "drink some; you'll feel better. It's all the Valium's fault," she added excitedly. "I told you not to take Valium. I remember how it made me cry after Reuven's death."

"Mark is not dead, Dina," Ruth approached the couch, which by now must have been soaked in salty tears. She sat down and looked at me affectionately. "Wait patiently," she said. "He is still alive." Soon Bracha and Zipporah joined her and sat on chairs around the couch. They didn't say much, but their solid, committed presence gave me strength. Soon I was able to get dressed and return to the hospital.

On Friday, the results of the culture came in and the doctors administered the suitable antibiotic to Mark. On Saturday, I looked for the green lab slip, announcing the test results, "no bacterial growth." Yes, yes, I whispered to myself, one down, two to go. Fight on, Mark. On the second day, the green slip came back saying "no growth." "Look, look," I said to Nomi and Itzhak, who came to visit, "two days in a row. No growth." Nomi smiled and Itzhak said, "He'll make it. It will be all right. It *must* be all right." Dr. Barak passed by. My first impulse was to hide, lest he should somehow prove me wrong. He stopped by Mark's bed and looked at the charts. Then he said, with something that resembled a distant cousin of a smile, "the infection is better, and the breathing is better." "Thank you, Dr. Barak," I said, forgiving him his pessimistic predictions.

The good news was almost as shocking as the bad. I had to check everything over and over again to prove to myself that it was all true. I looked at the monitor—the pulse and the blood pressure were normal, and the heart was beating with magnificent regularity, galloping on at an even clip, like a trusty thoroughbred. Then I looked at the respirator machine. The "spontaneous" light flashed on, but the "assist" light was off. I looked again, still off. "What does this mean?" I asked one of the nurses. "It means," she said, "that he's breathing on his own, and the machine is only helping with the volume." I was ready to jump in joy, but the nurse stopped me. "Too early to be happy," she warned, "they haven't extubated him yet, you know."

It was Wednesday morning. At 11:00 A.M., my mother and I went to the hospital for the mid-day visiting hours. The unit was crowded with visitors and staff. We put our pocketbooks down and put on the mandatory hospital gowns. I looked at the monitors first. Fine, they were just fine. Then it struck me right between the eyes. Mark's bed was raised, and he was sitting up! I looked again. Oh, God in heaven, do I see what I see? Can I truly believe it, or is it a devilish mirage, wrought by an exhausted imagination? *"Imma,"* I called out, "look at Mark." She looked and her mouth fell open. Yes, it was true. They extubated him. The respirator was out. Mark was breathing on his own.

I leaned over to him, laughing and crying, "welcome, love, to the land of the living." He took the oxygen mask off to answer, but all that came out was a hoarse whisper, from which I understood one word, *awful.* I reassured him that tomorrow he'd be able to speak. A nurse came over. "Did you see?" I exclaimed. "Do *you* see?" she laughed, "no respirator." I hugged her, muttering, "thank you." Then, I walked over to my mother and, for the first time in many years, I hugged her, too. *"Oi, oi,"* she said with tears in her eyes, "I want to cry." Soon I was waltzing all over the unit, thanking all the nurses and the doctors, especially Dr. Sold. So many times I rehearsed what I'd say to him if Mark lived, but now I just stood in front of him, repeating "thank you" over and over, as if there were no other words in the language.

REHABILITATION

The doctors were impressed by Mark's survival. For many days, Uzi, who predicted disaster, was thunderstruck. "What can I tell you?" he kept repeating, "it's a miracle." The French anesthesiologist with the *yarmulke* also thought that supernatural forces must have intervened. When I told him about Mark's recovery, he looked at me in disbelief. "The American with the pneumonia and the kidney failure? Impossible!" When he saw Mark resting on a chair, he looked at him as if he were a ghost. Mark, though, was solid flesh and blood, talking and smiling. The doctor pointed his finger up, in the direction of the sky and said, *"Hakadosh Baruch Hu* must have helped." He shook Mark's hand and parted with profuse well-wishes. "What did he say?" Mark asked me later. "That God must have saved you," I explained. Mark nodded hesitatingly. "He, or she, must have had something to do with it."

Although the medical outlook was good, the rehabilitative progress was extremely slow. Mark was in pain most of the time. His aching body, particularly his nasty bedsores, needed continuous relief and treatment. One day the physical therapist lifted the blankets. "Look at him," she said, "he's a noodle." His muscles were atrophied. "With these muscles," she said, "he can't even sit in bed." She gave me ten exercises to administer to Mark every day. Slowly, the muscles began to move again, and after a few days, Mark was able to sit in a chair, at first ten minutes, then twenty, then a whole hour and more.

Avram came every day to carry Mark to the bathroom, give him a shower, and shave him. My mother and I rotated shifts. Bone-weary, I was deeply grateful for her help, but I was also conscious of the fact that for the first time in our lives, we worked together, shoulder to shoulder, both of us active and engaged, neither one dominating the other.

After a few days in the vascular surgery ward, Mark was able to raise himself up to a standing position and later to walk with a walker. "It's like starting your life over again," he used to say, "learning everything from scratch." It was a day of triumph when he walked by himself to the bathroom. Bit by bit, his appetite returned, and so did his sense of humor and his loving gaze. After one week in the vascular surgery ward, he was disconnected from his IVs and could take the walker for a square block around the nurse's station. He'd stop by the narrow window and stare at the clouds and the grimy buildings below. "So lovely to see the sky, even when it's grey," he'd say, with a smile on his pale, deeply furrowed face.

THE SUN HOTEL

In a few days, the doctors sent Mark to a rehabilitation unit, at the Sun, a five-star hotel on the beach, in Bat-Yam. The first thing I noticed at our hotel room were two comfortable beds. "A bed," I exclaimed. "No more sleeping on chairs. Look, Mark," I tried to ignite his enthusiasm, but he was exhausted and morose. I approached the large window. The beach at the foot of the hotel stretched out for miles, all the way to Jaffa and Tel Aviv. The day, Sunday, March 16, was grey, and the ocean was dark blue, but the gentle waves were embroidered with gleaming white froth, like harbingers of peace. "Oh, Mark, you must see this spectacle just outside our own window." He smiled glumly. "Do I have to?" he asked. "Please," I urged him, "I'll help you get there." We walked slowly. "My heavens," Mark's face lit up, "isn't this magnificent? Perhaps one day," he looked at me, "the two of us can walk down to the ocean, and I can dip my feet in the water." I kissed his weary face.

The doctor in charge that week was Yevgeni, a Russian immigrant, whose face was youngish, handsome, and animated by large and expressive brown eyes. His hair was completely white, his body was wiry, and his hands strong. He talked enthusiastically in competent but mistake-ridden Hebrew. English he did not know at all. He measured Mark's blood pressure and pulse, and wrote down his medical history.

After the examination, Yevgeni took Mark to the room and put him gently in bed. Before he left, he looked at his bedsores. *"Mama mia,"* he sighed. "These sores don't look good at all. We'll have to dress them three times a day." Then he washed the wound and dressed it with great care. When he left, Mark dozed off. I stretched on the bed, under the blankets, and fell into a sweet and long sleep.

A few hours later I woke up with a start and didn't know where I was. I saw a pretty young woman sitting on Mark's bed. "I am Marina," she smiled, "the nurse, and I'm giving your husband inhalation," she spoke in a Russian accent. Then I remembered. I sat up. "Is something wrong? How is he doing?" I looked at his face behind the inhaler. "He was feeling a bit stuffed up," Marina said, "but he's all right." Yet when she left, I could see that he was not. "What is it, Mark?"

"I can't find a comfortable position on this bed," his face was drawn, "and no matter how hard I try, I can't raise myself up to a sitting position."

"I'll help you. Look, the walker is right here by your bed."

"But I can't even get to the walker without your help. I want to be able to do things on my own, to go to the bathroom without waking you up. I've been very sick for a month," he moaned. "And it seems to me that I'll never get better. Oh, you should have let me die!"

"No, no," I rearranged his pillows and pulled him up, "don't say that. In a week or two you'll feel quite differently."

Inwardly, though, I was filled with alarm and anger. At nine, having swallowed his medications, Mark fell asleep. I poured myself a glass of wine and gazed at the ocean which was alive with motion, its white surf shimmering in the dark. I opened the window a crack and puffed a half cigarette into the mild air. Then I filled up the tub with hot water, undressed, and abandoned myself to the long-forgotten pleasure. But the loneliness-dread-pain-despair caught up with me. All at once they came—sobs, heaves, unstoppable weeping. Certain that Mark was asleep, I howled like a coyote on a deserted hill. Suddenly, I lifted my eyes and saw Mark standing in front of me in the bathroom, leaning heavily on his walker, his body shaking. "How did you get here on your own?" I asked, astonished.

"I heard you crying," he said. "I crawled on the edge of the bed, and then pulled myself up to the walker. It wasn't easy, but here I am. I couldn't bear the thought of you crying in the bathroom alone."

I got out of the tub to support him. "No, no, I'm fine," he protested. "Get back into the water, or you'll catch a cold. Why were you crying? Please, tell me."

"How can you," I poured my heart out, "after all the scary operations, and the hellish waiting in the intensive care unit for you to pull back from the edge, and after the draining work in the vascular surgery ward, in which at least fifty people participated, how can you now say to me that I should have let you die?"

"What an asshole I am!" Mark exclaimed. "Please forgive me. I'm such a bad patient. Of course I want to live! And it's thanks to your hard work that I *am* alive."

I jumped out of the tub, put my robe on, and hugged him. "You know why I adore you?" I whispered in his ear. "Because you have this gritty courage to correct yourself and to do the right thing even when you're sick. You keep growing all the time, don't you?"

Mark clutched the walker. "Why should I be defensive? I used to be, I admit, but I learned," he smiled. "We'll make it, partner," I said as I eased him into bed, "I promise you."

Yevgeni's thorough and compassionate treatment of the bedsores lifted Mark's spirit, and the regular visits of the physical therapist improved his sense of well-being. During therapy, he was able to sit on his chair by the window and watch the waves. "How is it that they just keep coming?" he wondered. "They never get tired. If I could just borrow some of their energy. . . ." Eventually, the chair by the window, with the view to the sea, became his regular resting and eating place.

In the afternoon, my mother and Elie would come, delivering coffee, cookies, and all kinds of delicacies. They'd bring clean laundry and take the dirty laundry home. In the evening, Avram would come to give Mark a shave. At night, our children, Livi, Shir, Rachel, and Jane, as well as some of our friends, Edwin and Richard, would call from America, delighted to hear of Mark's improvement. At the end of the day, we'd be quite exhausted. "How tiring sickness is," Mark sighed, and I agreed.

TIKKUN

Mark's recovery was slow and fitful. Once we rushed him back to Ichilov Hospital in an ambulance for emergency dialysis. While in the hospital, Dr. Berliner, a slim and intense man with monkish attitude and appearance, was alarmed by the sudden drop in Mark's hemoglobin. "I am sending you to the Ultra-Sound," he said in his serious, unsmiling manner, "to make sure there isn't another artery leaking."

The world went dark. "Does this mean that he'd need another operation?" I asked.

"We don't know yet," Berliner replied. "Let's see what the Ultra-Sound test says."

Berliner himself brought us the test results. "The Ultra-Sound shows blood in the stomach cavity," he said. Mark looked pale, and I felt sick. "But we don't know if this is old blood, or new blood. If new, it's an emergency. But the test is inconclusive, and the technician's description of it is too vague," he flipped the paper in his hand dismissively.

"What does it mean?" I asked.

"We'll have to give him a CAT scan to make sure there is no fresh bleeding. I'll arrange it for tomorrow morning." Having said that, his jaws locked, he turned on his heels and left the room.

The following morning, after dialysis, Berliner announced that Mark's hemoglobin was normal and that he was canceling the CAT scan. We cheered.

It was eight at night when the orderly showed up with a piece of paper in his hand. "Yes?" we asked, confident that he wasn't looking for us.

"Mark Spilka?" he announced. "I am instructed to take you down to the CAT scan."

"There must be a mistake here," Mark remonstrated.

"No, no mistake," the orderly insisted, showing us his paper.

"But Dr. Berliner canceled the test," I yelled. "Go check it in the office."

He checked. "This is correct," he declared. "Dr. Berliner ordered the test."

All our protestations were to no avail. We wrapped Mark in blankets and took him down to the CAT scan in a wheel chair. There was a long line of patients before the radiation room. We stood in the drafty waiting area and shivered. After a while, Nomi and Itzhak, who had just returned from a vacation in Eilat, joined us. "What happened? What happened?" Nomi wanted to know. "We just heard that Mark is back in the hospital. Why?" We explained. *"Oi vey,"* she shook her head. "All the time, only trouble."

"But we shouldn't be here," I said. "There has been a mistake."

Mark motioned to me that he was cold. Itzhak took his coat off and put it on Mark's shoulders. I was seething. "It's outrageous," I spewed, "that we should be waiting in the drafty place, with a sick person, in the middle of the night."

"Calm down," Itzhak urged me, "the main thing is that Mark is alive and doing fairly well from what I see," he smiled.

"I can't bear the thought of another operation. Mark is too weak for it."

"There won't be another operation," Nomi assured me. "I know."

Finally, the nurse called Mark's name. "Did he get his injection?" she asked.

"What injection?"

"For the dye."

"No," Mark said, "I didn't get any injection."

The nurse disappeared. After ten minutes she came back. "There must have been some kind of miscommunication. Anyway, he won't have the CAT scan tonight. Please wait outside for the orderly to pick him up."

"How long will it be?"

"Oh, about half an hour."

"No way," I snapped. "My husband has been waiting her in the cold for forty minutes. He is not going to wait any longer. I am taking him back to the ward."

"He has to wait," the nurse said. "You are not allowed to take a patient yourself. It is absolutely forbidden!"

"Just watch me," I turned around, grabbed the handles of Mark's wheel chair, and started marching towards the elevator.

Mark and I in Paris. July, 1999

"*Gveret, gveret,*" the nurse yelled after me. "You can't do that. Stop! Stop! The hospital will sue you. I am calling the police."

"Call God if you wish. I am not waiting another minute," I shouted back. Mark clapped his hands and laughed. "Yeah, that's my woman." Itzhak came after me, his blue eyes large with alarm. "You can't do that Shelly. Stop. Wait for the orderly."

"Why can't I do that? Why must Mark wait another half an hour in the draft? To get pneumonia?"

"I bet they'll send the guards after you," he admonished me.

"Let them."

"Don't you think that you are being silly?"

"No, I am perfectly capable of taking Mark upstairs. No harm will come to him." As I was wheeling Mark back to the ward without incident, I thought exultantly, we are free, free of the contradictions and the tyrannies of this hospital!

Mark's tests continued to improve, and in ten days he was released from the hospital and sent back to the Sun Hotel. Soon he was able to take his walker everywhere in the hotel, even to the dining room downstairs. One night, I urged him to relinquish the walker and stand on his own two feet. I moved back a few yards and asked him to come to me. He did, joking the while about his second childhood. Soon he was able to walk up and down the hall on his own. One day, he felt that he was strong enough to walk to the ocean.

We stood by the window, studying the short route to the beach. "It's not too long to walk," I cautioned Mark, "but there are three sets of stairs on the way. You think you can make it?" His eyes gazed at the sea with longing. "Yes, I can make it," he said, his voice strong with happy determination, "I *will* make it." He put on his sandals and the grey and blue sports suit Elie loaned him. Then he gave one dismissive look to the walker, rested his arm on my shoulder, and off we went.

It was a lovely, partly sunny April day. My skin tingled with pleasure at the brush of the mild wind that carried the fragrance of summer. "So much light," Mark smiled as his eyes scanned the sky and the distant horizons. We walked slowly on the pavement, step by measured step, until we got to the first set of stairs. "Take it one at a time," I told him. He did, resting one arm on my shoulder and another on the wall, but his muscles were straining. "So many steps," he sighed, "but I'm going to make it." We took a short rest. I looked at the sprawling ocean. A white sail glimmered in the distance, and closer by a white-grey gull, with black wing tips, was scouring the area, flapping its wings vigorously. Mark pressed my hand, and we continued our descent. The three sets of stairs took the better part of half an hour, but when we completed them, Mark laughed with pleasure, "I made it," he exulted. "I haven't gone down any stairs in two months, and now I can do it!"

Soon his sandals traversed the dry, warm sand. "We are almost there," he looked at me. Yet the walk through the dry sand was not easy. No sooner did he lift one foot forward than the other sank in the sand, and, as in nightmares, he seemed to be going backward. "It's all right," I put my arm around his waist and helped him to pull his weight forward. "I must rest," he said, breathing heavily, and we stood for a while. All around us there were sands, the taste of salt in the air, and the hum of the sea. Whoosh, the white foam lapped up the sand, leaving behind, as it retreated, a semicircle of frayed lace. Come, play, the waves murmured. Slowly we reached the stretch of wet, packed sand. "Isn't this beautiful?" Mark exclaimed. "I must dip my feet in the water." He took off his sandals and walked alone, on shaky but determined legs, towards the sea. The waves were flowing in, frothing and full-bodied. Swhoosh, water, foam, and salt swirled around his feet. He threw his head back, lifted his arms up to the sun, the shimmering sky, and the fresh sea breezes, and cried out, with a burst of tears, "Thank God I'm still alive."

EPILOGUE

On April 15 we returned to America. We were escorted by my mother who wanted to make sure we had enough support on the plane. During our first month in America, as tokens of our deep gratitude, we sent gifts to the family, the friends, and the doctors who helped save Mark's life.

Mark has now fully regained his former strength and health, and the doctors have already reduced his time on the dialysis machine. Meanwhile, I've been assisting Mark in his recovery, preparing for the spring semester, and writing my story, which is now approaching its end. Yet before concluding, I must attend to one piece of unfinished business that got lost in the shuffle of tumultuous events: my conversation with Haya after Esther Laufer handed her back to me that cloudy day in February, when Mark and I visited the orphanage in Pardes-Hannah.

Haya wanted to make up her own mind about leaving the orphanage. For that purpose she took me with her to the place where I left her fifty years before. As I was walking by her side, skipping with her over puddles, I noticed that she was wearing a sandal on one foot and a shoe on the other. I wanted to comment on this oddity but ordered myself to be silent. I must be friendly to her, I thought. As we walked, the new school and the garden with the Wandering Jew flower disappeared behind an invisible time screen. Soon Haya and I were standing before the squeaky gate of the old orphanage. "Come," she said, and I followed her down the path shaded with eucalyptus trees, my heart light as a bird and restless with apprehension. Where is she taking me, I wondered. What does she want? As if reading my thoughts, Haya looked up at me and said with a smile that we were almost there. "What is a five-minute walk compared to fifty years?" she asked, and I demurred.

The day was warming up, and the raindrops on the pine needles sparkled like jewels in the sun. Haya lifted up her small face, spotted with the remains of breakfast, and smiled. "There," she said, pointing at a sandbox under the old oak tree, "that's where I've been waiting for you for a long, long time." I took an instant dislike to the place. I sat on the edge of the sandbox, feeling depleted. Haya wandered about in the sand. "Why don't you sit down here?" I asked impatiently. After a few minutes, she sat at some distance from me, her legs in the box.

"Why have you come here?" she finally asked, her eyes scrutinizing me.

"I have come to take you out of here to live with me," I said cautiously.

She picked up a twig and drew shapes in the sand. Suddenly her eyebrows frowned in anger. "You are late."

"What do you mean late?" I said, irritated.

"Where have you been all this time?" she asked, choking on tears.

"I've been trying to come for you," I cleared my throat, "but things got in the way."

"What things?"

"First I was told to forget you, as if you never existed."

"And you did?"

"Yes. What choice did I have? I was small."

"And then?" She was stabbing her twig in the sand.

"Then I was happy for a while, with Kenneth, I had children, and I did forget you. Or rather I thought that you'd join me on your own, that you'd be so attracted to all the light and the space in my life that you'd leave this shabby, lonely," I motioned with my hand, "and depressing corner. But obviously you couldn't."

"Why?" She now seemed absorbed in my story.

"Because there wasn't enough happiness to lift you out of here. Kenneth died after five years, and I moved to America with the children. But then," I said with energy, "I looked for you, discovered you, and have been trying ever since to get to you."

"Tell me how," she rested her face in her hands.

"I talked to my father about you, told Amos Oz about you, wrote this book about you, and, you see, I have come to take you out."

She was silent. A light breeze rustled the leaves of the eucalyptus tree. Flies were buzzing about.

"But you changed my name," she said quietly.

My mind went blank. "Yes," I muttered, "I had to. . . ."

She jumped up on her feet, came over to my perch, and started pounding her small fists on my back and face. "Why did you change my name?" she was crying. "You hated it, didn't you? You hated me, too, all those years you called me a wild animal, and you ran away from people who called you Haya." She stood still, huffing and puffing, her little frame quivering.

A terrible anger seized me. In an effort to control it, I stood up and walked around a few steps.

"Are you going away?" she yelled in consternation. "You coward."

"No, I am not going away," I exploded. "I am going to tell you right now why I hated you all those years. You *were* wild, yes, wild. You always got me into trouble and made me do things I didn't want to do, that's why."

She fell to her knees and started hitting the sandbox. "It's not my fault," she cried, "not my fault."

"But that's exactly what I mean," I said archly, "those temper tantrums of yours that derailed me so many times, and worse, worse. Who was it that led me to the arms of Assai, the heroin addict in London? Who was it that made me betray my friends Sophie and John? Who was it that tempted me to chase a married man in Kansas? Who was it that made me scowling and unloving? You, Haya, it was you."

By now she was stretched full length on the red sands, weeping bitterly. I bent down to her, overwhelmed by remorse. "Please forgive me, Haya," I said as I helped her to get up. "I was acting in the same wild and hurtful way that I reproached you for. It's been so easy to blame you for everything all those years."

Sniffling and coughing, Haya slowly got up, wiped her face with her soiled hands, and sat next to me. "I was only trying to get your attention," she whimpered.

I took a tissue out of my bag. "May I wipe your face?" I asked. She nodded silently. I cleaned off her face gently, recognizing one by one my own features, eyes, nose, and mouth. "I never thought of that," I said after a while. "Of course, that's what you were doing all those years, knocking on the door, and I didn't know how to answer you." She was calmer now, stealing looks at me. "But you know what?" I presently added. "I did not erase your name. No. All those years in England and America, I used it as my middle name. Shelly Haya, I'd say, is my full name."

She considered this new fact for a long while. "Would you come with me?" she asked and jumped into the sandbox. "Yes," I jumped after her. She walked toward a mound in the sand, and pointed at what she had created. "חי" I said, "you have written the two first letters of your name, *chay*, which means 'alive.' That's right, Haya," I smiled at her, "you *are* life."

"Have you thought of that?" she looked at me whimsically.

"Not often," I admitted. "I thought of you as a wild animal, but your name means life, too."

Haya's eyes were shining. "That's what I wanted to tell you all those years, but you wouldn't listen."

"I have much to learn from you," I confessed.

Encouraged by my response, Haya said, "I have one more thing to show you. Would you come with me?"

"Yes, of course," I said, but my heart was beating fast, inexplicably. She walked ahead of me through an open field toward a small woods. We stepped on dry leaves, twigs, and acorns. Where is she taking me? I thought anxiously, as every sound made me jump. Where is she going? Looking around, I could find no clue to her secret progress. Shouldn't I ask her? But, as under a spell, I kept following her in silence. Suddenly she stopped, so unexpectedly that I almost fell all over her. "What is it?" I asked. "Sh-h-h," she put her finger to her mouth. For a long moment, she just stood there, looking intently into the shadows. The trees were brooding. Haya glanced at me. I bent down. She pointed with her finger and whispered in my ear, "Do you see it there?"

"No," I whispered back, "what am I supposed to see?"

"The laughing fox," she said and a tremor slithered down her spine.

"The what?" I asked. "There are no foxes around here."

"Come with me," she said and put her hand in mine. Like lightning, fear traveled from her body to mine. We took a few timid steps forward. "You see?" she asked, her eyes bright with excitement. On the ground, between an oak and an olive tree, lay a thick tree trunk. "Is that what you are afraid of?" I asked and almost burst out laughing but restrained myself.

"It looks like a laughing fox," she grabbed me, "don't you see it?"

I bent down to her level. "You know what?" I said, putting my hand on her shoulder. "You are right. If you look at it from this angle, it looks exactly like a laughing fox. I can see the open mouth, the sharp teeth, the pointed ears. I know why you are scared." I held her close. "But you know, Haya, from here," I got up, "it looks exactly like a tree trunk. Would you like to touch it?"

"No," she shuddered.

"Don't be afraid," I walked forward, but she stayed behind. I sat on the tree trunk and faced her. "I know that you will join me here soon," I said.

"How do you know?" She was hugging herself in fright.

"When I think of the courage a small orphan like you must have had to wait patiently for rescue, all those years, in the dark, all alone, without turning to wickedness and despair, I know that you'll have the strength to jump."

Haya was listening with interest. "You really think so?" she asked. I nodded. "So why do I still feel like an orphan?"

"It is true, Haya," I said, "that your father and your mother abandoned you, and I despised you. But you must remember what happened when Mark was mortally ill."

"What?" she whispered.

"*Imma* was there all the time, by my side, helping me in every breath to bring him back to life. Not only *Imma* but also Avram, Ruth, Uzi, and the whole family. So you see, Haya, you are not alone. You can touch the laughing fox."

For a while she still stared darkly at me when, all at once, she sprinted and ran toward me. I clasped her in my arms. She put her hands on the tree trunk. "It doesn't bite," she laughed and threw her head back, gazing at the top of trees and the patch of blue sky.

On the way back, Haya fell into deep reflection. "A penny for your thoughts," I jested.

"Are you going to take me to America?" she asked.

I stood still. "Yes. Mark and I live in America."

"But I love this place," she said, tears gathering in her eyes. "How could you live without Israel? We were born here. Eighth generation."

How could I? Easily, I wanted to say, remembering the harsh, frantic days in the hospital. But then I saw the waves lapping the soft sand outside the Sun Hotel, the blooming cyclamen on my mother's rainy porch, and Reuven coming down the fifty-one stairs, carrying a box of melons on his shoulders, and above him the bright sun, forever shining, and over all, the ease of summer, the transporting fragrance of orange blossoms, and ah! I wondered, how is it that my heart doesn't break? "Yes, Haya," I murmured, "I shall always, always miss Israel. Terribly. I dream about it every night," I pressed her hand. "But I can't live in it. And I don't know how I can continue being an Israeli without living in Israel. I wish I knew."

"I'll help you to find out," Haya said, as she lifted up a face radiant with promise.

SELECTED BIBLIOGRAPHY

The following list represents books that I cite or mention in my text. Although this is an incomplete list of readings, it contains those that most clearly shaped my thinking and inspired my growth.

Alighieri, Dante. *The Inferno.* In *The Divine Comedy of Dante Alighieri: A Verse Translation.* Trans. Allen Mandelbaum. Berkeley: University of California Press, 1980. 44.

Bacon, Francis. "Of Studies." *The Essays of Francis Bacon.* Ed. Mary Augusta Scott. New York: Charles Scribner's Sons, 1908. 233–235.

Bialik, Hayyhim Nachman. "And If the Angel Should Ask." *Modern Hebrew Poetry: A Bilingual Anthology.* Ed. and Trans. Ruth Finer Mintz. Berkeley: University of California Press, 1968. 24–28.

———. "The Pool." *Modern Hebrew Poetry: A Bilingual Anthology.* 2–18.

Blake, William. "Auguries of Innocence." *Blake: Complete Writings.* Ed. Geoffrey Keynes. London: Oxford University Press, 1966. 431–434.

Clurman, Harold. *On Directing.* New York: Collier Books, 1972.

Defoe, Daniel. *Robinson Crusoe.* New York: A Signet Classic, 1961.

Dickinson, Emily. "Because I could not stop for Death." *The Norton Anthology of Literature by Women.* Eds. Sandra Gilbert and Susan Gubar. New York: Norton, 1985. 858–859.

———. "I dwell in Possibility." *The Norton Anthology of Literature by Women.* 856–857.

———. "I felt a Funeral, in my Brain." *The Norton Anthology of Literature by Women.* 845–846.

———. "The Soul selects her own Society." *The Norton Anthology of Literature by Women.* 846–847.

Donne, John. "The Good Morrow." *The Complete Poetry and Selected Prose of John Donne.* Ed. Charles M. Coffin. New York: The Modern Library, 1952. 8.

Dostoevsky, Fyodor. *The Brothers Karamazov.* Trans. David Magarshack. New York: Penguin Classics, 1969.

———. *The Idiot.* Trans. David Magarshack. New York: Penguin Books, 1967.

Eliot, George. *Middlemarch.* Ed. Gordon S. Haight. Boston: Houghton Mifflin, 1956. 558, 559, 583.

Eliot, T. S. "Burnt Norton." *The Complete Poems and Plays of T. S. Eliot.* London: Faber and Faber, 1969. 171–176.

Elon, Amos. *The Israelis: Founders and Sons.* New York: Penguin, 1981. 236, 288.

Empson, William. *Seven Types of Ambiguity.* Cleveland: Meridian Books, 1964.

———. "Villanelle." *Collected Poems.* London: Chatto and Windus, 1962. 22.

Ezrahi, Yaron. *Rubber Bullets: Power and Conscience in Modern Israel.* New York: Farrar, Straus and Giroux, 1997. 21, 22.

Faulkner, William. *The Bear.* In *The Portable Faulkner.* Ed. Malcolm Cowley. New York: The Viking Press, 1961. 227–363.

Forster, E. M. *Howards End.* New York: Signet, 1992.

Freud, Sigmund. *The Psychopathology of Everyday Life.* In *The Complete Psychological Works of Sigmund Freud.* Trans. James Strachey. Vol. 6. London: Hogarth Press, 1975.

Frost, Robert. "The Road Not Taken." *A Pocket Book of Robert Frost's Poems.* New York: Washington Square Press, 1961. 223.

Goldberg, S. L. *The Classical Temper: A Study of James Joyce's Ulysses.* London: Chatto and Windus, 1963.

Golding, William. *The Spire.* New York: Pocket Books, 1966.

Hazleton, Lesley. *Israeli Women: The Reality Behind the Myths.* New York: Simon & Schuster, 1977. 168, 180, 183.

Joubert, Joseph. *Extracts from the Pensées of Joubert.* Trans. Katherine Littleton. Pittsburgh: The Laboratory Press, 1925.

Joyce, James. *A Portrait of the Artist as a Young Man: Text, Criticism and Notes.* Ed. Chester G. Anderson. New York: Penguin, 1980. 146–147, 169, 203, 207, 253.

———. *Dubliners: Text, Criticism and Notes.* Eds. Robert Scholes and Walton Litz. New York: The Viking Press, 1969.

———. *Ulysses.* New York: The Modern Library, 1961. 5, 45.

Lawrence, D. H. *Lady Chatterley's Lover.* New York: Penguin, 1972. 119, 138, 139, 182.

Lawrence, Jerome and Robert E. Lee. *Inherit the Wind.* New York: Bantam Books, 1960. 38, 59, 89, 100, 102.

Milton, John. *Paradise Lost.* In *The Poetical Works of John Milton.* London: Macmillan, 1954.

Pope, Alexander. "The Universal Prayer." *The Norton Anthology of English Literature.* Eds. M. H. Abrahams, et al., Vol. I. New York: Norton, 1968. 1727–1728.

Potok, Chaim. *My Name Is Asher Lev.* New York: Fawcett Crest, 1972.

Rachel. "Only of Myself I Knew How to Tell." *Modern Hebrew Poetry: A Bilingual Anthology.* Ed. and Trans. Ruth Finer Mintz. Berkeley: University of California Press, 1968. 110.

Regenbaum, Shelly. "Art, Gender, and the Jewish Tradition in Yezierska's *Red Ribbon on a White Horse* and Potok's *My Name Is Asher Lev.*" *Studies in American Jewish Literature.* 7 (Spring 1988): 55–66.

Scholem, Gershom. *Kabbalah.* New York: Dorset Press, 1987. 138.

Shakespeare, William. *As You Like It.* In *The Unabridged William Shakespeare.* Eds. William George Clark and William Aldis Wright. Philadelphia: Running Press, 1989.

———. *King Henry the Fourth, Part Two.* In *The Unabridged William Shakespeare.*

———. *Romeo and Juliet.* In *The Unabridged William Shakespeare.*

———. "Sonnet 29." *Shakespeare: The Sonnets.* New York: The New American Library, 1964. 69.

———. *The Tempest.* In *The Unabridged William Shakespeare.*

———. "Venus and Adonis." In *The Unabridged William Shakespeare.* 1246–1260.

Shelley, Percy Bysshe. "Ode to the West Wind." *Percy Bysshe Shelley: Poems.* Ed. Timothy Webb. London: J. M. Dent & Sons, 1977. 76–78.

Shneour, Zalman. "Poppies." *Modern Hebrew Poetry: A Bilingual Anthology.* Ed. and Trans. Ruth Finer Mintz. Berkeley: University of California Press, 1968. 100.

Singer, I. J. *The Family Moskat.* New York: Bantam Books, 1967.

Spilka, Mark. *Eight Lessons in Love: A Domestic Violence Reader.* Columbia: University of Missouri Press, 1997.

Stanislavski, Constantin. *An Actor's Handbook.* Ed. Elizabeth Reynolds Hapgood. New York: Theatre Arts Books, 1963.

Tennyson, Alfred. *In Memoriam A.H.H.* In *Tennyson: Selected Poetry.* Ed. Douglas Bush. New York: Modern Library, 1951. 147–240.

Thomas, Dylan. "Do Not Go Gentle Into that Good Night." *The Poem: A Critical Anthology.* Ed. Josephine Miles. Englewood Cliffs: Prentice-Hall, 1959. 59–60.

———. "The Force that through the Green Fuse Drives the Flower." *The Poem: A Critical Anthology.* 262–263.

Werblowsky, Zwi. *Lucifer and Prometheus: A Study of Milton's Satan.* London: Routledge and Kegan Paul, 1952.

Wiesel, Elie. *Messengers of God: Biblical Portraits and Legends.* New York: Pocket Book, 1977. 150, 159, 160, 190, 213, 214.

Wordsworth, William. "Lines Composed a Few Miles above Tintern Abbey." *Wordsworth Poetical Works.* Ed. Thomas Hutchinson. London: Oxford University Press, 1969. 163–165.

Yeats, W. B. "The Municipal Gallery Revisited." *W. B. Yeats: Selected Poetry.* London: Macmillan, 1967. 191–193.

Yezierska, Anzia. *Red Ribbon on a White Horse.* New York: Persea Books, 1950.